The Definite Object

THE DEFINITE OBJECT

BY

JEFFERY FARNOL

AUTHOR OF "THE BROAD HIGHWAY"

LONDON

SAMPSON LOW, MARSTON & CO., LTD.

By the same Author
THE BROAD HIGHWAY
THE AMATEUR GENTLEMAN
THE MONEY MOON
THE HON. MR. TAWNISH
THE CHRONICLES OF THE IMP
BELTANE THE SMITH
THE GESTE OF DUKE JOCELYN
OUR ADMIRABLE BETTY
BLACK BARTLEMY'S TREASURE
MARTIN CONISBY'S VENGEANCE
SIR JOHN DERING
PEREGRINE'S PROGRESS
THE LORING MYSTERY
THE HIGH ADVENTURE

TO MY

WIFE

PRINTED IN GREAT BRITAIN BY PURNELL AND SONS
PAULTON, SOMERSET, ENGLAND

THE DEFINITE OBJECT

CHAPTER I

WHICH DESCRIBES, AMONG OTHER THINGS, A PAIR OF WHISKERS

In the writing of books, as all the world knows, two things are above all other things essential—the one is to know exactly when and where to leave off, and the other to be equally certain when and where to begin.

Now this book, naturally enough, begins with Mr. Brimberly's whiskers ; begins at that moment when he coughed and pulled down his waistcoat for the first time. And yet (since action is as necessary to the success of a book as to life itself) it should perhaps begin more properly at the psychological moment when Mr. Brimberly coughed and pulled down the garment aforesaid for the third time, since it is then that the real action of this story commences.

Be that as it may, it is beyond all question that nowhere in this wide world could there possibly be found just such another pair of whiskers as those which adorned the plump cheeks of Mr. Brimberly ; without them he might have been only an ordinary man, but, possessing them, he was the very incarnation of all that a butler could possibly be.

And what whiskers these were ! So soft, so fleecy, so purely white, that at times they almost seemed like the wings of cherubim striving to soar away and bear Mr.

The Definite Object

Brimberly into a higher and purer sphere. Again, what protean whiskers were these! whose fleecy pomposity could over-awe the most superior young footmen and reduce page-boys, tradesmen, and the lower orders generally to a state of perspiring humility; to his equals how calmly aloof, how blandly dignified; and to those a misguided fate had set above him how demurely deferential, how obligingly obsequious! Indeed, Mr. Brimberly's whiskers were all things to all men, and therein lay their potency.

Mr. Brimberly, then, pompous, affable, and most sedate, having motioned his visitor into his master's favourite chair, set down the tray of decanters and glasses upon the piano, coughed, and pulled down his waistcoat; and Mr. Brimberly did it all with that air of portentous dignity and leisurely solemnity which, together with his whiskers, made him the personality he was.

"And you're still valeting for Barberton, are you, Mr. Stevens?" he blandly inquired.

"I've been with his lordship six months now," nodded Mr. Stevens.

"Ah!" said Mr. Brimberly, opening a certain carved cabinet and reaching thence a box of his master's choicest havanas, "six months, indeed! And 'ow is Barberton? I hacted in the capacity of 'is confidential valet a good many years ago, as I told you, and we always got on very well together, very well indeed! 'Ow is Barberton?"

"Oh, 'e'd be right enough if it warn't for 'is gout, which gets 'im in the big toe now and then, and 'is duns and creditors and sich-like low fellers as gets 'im everywhere and constant! 'E'll never be quite 'imself until 'e marries money—and plenty of it!"

"A American hair-ess!" nodded Mr. Brimberly. "Pre-cisely! I very nearly married 'im to a rich widder ten years ago. 'E'd 'ave been settled for life if 'e'd took my advice! But Barberton was always inclined to be a little 'eadstrong. The widder in question 'appened to

2

Which Describes a Pair of Whiskers

be a trifle par-say, I'll admit ; also it was 'inted that one of 'er—lower limbs was cork. But then 'er money, sir ! 'er jools ! " Mr. Brimberly raised eyes and hands and shook his head until his whiskers quivered in a very ecstasy.

" But a wooden leg ! " began Mr. Stevens dubiously.

" I said ' limb,' sir ! " said Mr. Brimberly, his whiskers distinctly agitated—" a cork limb, sir ! And, lord bless me, a cork limb ain't to be sniffed at contemptuous when it brings haffluence with it, sir ! At least, my sentiments leans that way."

" Oh, ditto, certainly, sir ! I'd take haffluence to my 'eart if she came with both le—both of 'em cork, if it meant haffluence like this ! " Mr. Stevens let his pale, prominent eyes wander slowly round the luxuriant splendour of the room. " My eye ! " he exclaimed, " it's easy to see as your governor don't 'ave to bother about marrying money, cork limbs or otherwise ! Very rich, ain't 'e, Mr. Brimberly ? "

Mr. Brimberly set down the decanter he chanced to be holding, and, having caressed each fluffy whisker, smiled. " I think, sir," said he gently, " yes, I think we may answer ' yes ' to your latter question. I think we may tell you and admit 'ole-'earted and frank, sir, that the Ravenslee fortune is fab'lous, sir, stoopendious and himmense ! "

" Oh lord ! " exclaimed Mr. Stevens, and his pale eyes, much wider now, wandered up from the Persian rug beneath his boots to the elaborately carved ceiling above his head. " My aunt ! " he murmured.

" Oh, I think we're fairly comfortable 'ere, sir," nodded Mr. Brimberly, complacently ; " yes, fairly comfortable, I think."

" Comfortable ! " ejaculated the awe-struck Mr. Stevens, " I should say so ! My word ! "

" Yes," pursued Mr. Brimberly, " comfortable, and I ventur' to think, tasteful, sir, for I'll admit young Ravenslee—though a millionaire and young—'as taste.

3

The Definite Object

Observe this costly bricky-brack! Oh yes, Young Har is a man of taste indoobitably I think you must admit?"

"Very much so indeed, sir!" answered Mr. Stevens, with his pallid glance on the array of bottles. "'Three Star' I think, Mr. Brimberly?"

"Sir," sighed Mr. Brimberly in gentle reproach, "you 'ere be'old cognac brandy as couldn't be acquired for twenty-five dollars the bottle! Then 'ere we 'ave Jubilee port, a rare old sherry, and whisky. Now, what shall we make it? You being, like myself, a Englishman, in this 'ere land of eagles, spread and otherwise, suppose we make it a B and a Hess?"

"By all means!" nodded Mr. Stevens.

"I was meditating," said Mr. Brimberly, busied with the bottles and glasses, "I was cogitating calling hup Mr. Jenkins, the Stanways' butler across the way. The Stanways is common people, parvynoo, Mr. Stevens—parvynoo, but Mr. Jenkins is very superior, and plays the banjer very affecting. Our 'ousekeeper and the maids is gone to bed, and I've give our footmen leave of habsence—I thought we might 'ave a nice quiet musical hour or so? You perform on the piano-forty, I believe, sir?"

"Only very occasional!" Mr. Stevens admitted. "But," and here his pale eyes glanced towards the door, "do I understand as 'e is out for the night?"

"Sir," said Mr. Brimberly ponderously, "what 'e might you be pleased to mean?"

"I was merely allooding to—to your governor, sir."

Mr. Brimberly glanced at his guest, set down the glass he was in the act of filling, and—pulled down his waistcoat for the second time. "Sir," said he, and his cherubic whiskers seemed positively to quiver, "I presoom—I say I presoom—you are referring to Young Har?"

"I meant Mr. Ravenslee."

"Then may I beg that you'll allood to 'im 'enceforth as Young Har? This is Young Har's own room, sir.

4

Which Describes a Pair of Whiskers

These is Young Har's own picters, sir. When Young Har is absent I generally sit 'ere with me cigar and observe said picters. I'm fond of hart, sir; I find hart soothing and restful. The picters surrounding of you are all painted by Young Har's very own 'and—subjeks various. Number one—a windmill very much out o' repair, but that's hart, sir. Number two—a lady dressed in what I might term dish-a-bell, sir, and there isn't much of it, but that's hart again. Number three—a sunset. Number four—moonlight; 'e didn't get the moon in the picter, but the light's there, and that's the great thing—effect, sir—effect! Of course, being only studies, they don't look finished—which is the most hartistikest part about 'em! But, lord! Young Har never finishes anything—too tired. 'Ang me, sir, if I don't think 'e were born tired! But then 'oo ever knew a haristocrat as wasn't?"

"But," demurred Mr. Stevens, staring down into his empty glass, "I thought 'e was a American—your—Young Har?"

"Why, 'e is and 'e ain't, sir. 'Is father was only a American I'll confess, but 'is mother was blue blood, every drop guaranteed, sir, and as truly English as—as I am."

"And is 'e the Mr. Ravenslee as is the sportsman? Goes in for boxing, don't 'e? Very much fancied as a 'eavy-weight, ain't 'e? My governor's seen him box, and says 'e's a perfect snorter, by Jove!"

Mr. Brimberly sighed, and soothed a slightly agitated whisker. "Why, yes," he admitted, "I'm afraid 'e does box, but only as a amitoor, Mr. Stevens, strickly as a amitoor, understand."

"And 'e's out making a night of it, is 'e?" inquired Mr. Stevens, leaning back luxuriously and stretching his legs. "Bit of a rip, ain't 'e?"

"A—wot, sir?" inquired Mr. Brimberly with raised brows.

The Definite Object

" Well, very wild, ain't 'e—drinks, gambles, and hetceteras, don't 'e ? "

" Why, as to that, sir," answered Mr. Brimberly, dexterously performing on the siphon, " I should answer you, drink 'e may, gamble 'e do, hetceteras I won't answer for, 'im being the very hacme of respectability, though 'e is a millionaire and young."

" And when might you expect 'im back ? "

" Why, there's no telling, Mr. Stevens."

" Eh ! " exclaimed Mr. Stevens, and sat up very suddenly.

" 'Is movements, sir, is quite—ah—quite metehoric ! "

" My eye ! " exclaimed Mr. Stevens, gulping his brandy-and-soda rather hastily.

" Metehoric is the only word for it, sir," pursued Mr. Brimberly with a slow nod. " 'E may drop in on us at any moment, sir."

" Why then," said his guest, rising, " p'r'aps I'd better be moving ? "

" On the other 'and," pursued Mr. Brimberly, smiling and caressing his left whisker, " 'e may be on 'is way to Hafghanistan or Hasia Minor at this pre-cise moment—'e is that metehoric, lord ! These millionaires is much of a muchness, sir, 'ere to-day, gone to-morrer. Noo York this week, London or Paris the next. Young Har is always upsetting my plans, 'e is, and that's a fact, sir. Me, being a nat'rally quiet, reasonable, and law-abiding character, I objects to youthful millionaires on principle, Mr. Stevens—on principle."

" Ditto," nodded Mr. Stevens, his glance wandering uneasily to the door again, " ditto with all my 'eart, sir. If it's all the same to you, I think p'r'aps I'd better be 'opping—you know."

" Oh, don't you worry about Young Har, 'e won't bother us to-night, 'e's off Long Island way to try his nooest 'igh-power racing-car 'e's driving in the Vanderbilt Cup Race next month. To-night 'e expects to do

Which Describes a Pair of Whiskers

eighty miles or so, and 'opes to sleep at one of 'is clubs. I say 'e 'opes an' expects so to do."

"Yes," nodded Mr. Stevens, "certainly, but what do you mean ? "

" Sir," sighed Mr. Brimberly, " if you'd been forced by stern dooty to sit be'ind Young Har in a fast automobile, as I 'ave, you'd know what I mean. Reckless ! Speed ! Well, there ! " and Mr. Brimberly lifted hands and eyes, and shook his head until his whiskers vibrated with horror.

" Then you're pretty sure," said Mr. Stevens, settling luxurious boots upon a cushioned chair, " you're pretty sure 'e won't come bobbing up when least expected ? "

" Pretty sure," nodded Mr. Brimberly. " You see, this nooest car is the very latest thing in racing-cars— cost a fortune, consequently it's bound to break down— these here expensive cars always do, believe me."

" Why then," said Mr. Stevens, helping himself to one of Mr. Brimberly's master's cigars, " I say let joy and 'armony be unconfined ! 'Ow about Jenkins and 'is banjer ? "

" I'll call 'im up immediate," nodded Mr. Brimberly, rising. " Mr. Jenkins is a true hartist, equally facetious and soulful, sir."

So saying, Mr. Brimberly arose and crossed towards the telephone. But scarcely had he taken three steps when he paused suddenly and stood rigid and motionless, his staring gaze fixed upon the nearest window; for, from the shadowy world beyond came a sound, faint as yet and far away, but a sound there was no mistaking— the dismal tooting of an automobile horn.

" 'Eavens an' earth ! " exclaimed Mr. Brimberly, and crossing to the window, he peered out. Once again the horn was heard, but very much nearer now, and louder, whereupon Mr. Brimberly turned almost hastily, and his visitor rose hurriedly.

" It's very annoying, Mr. Stevens," said he, " but can

The Definite Object

I trouble you to—to step—er—downstairs—*with* the glasses? It's 'ighly mortifying, but may I ask you to —er—step a little lively, Mr. Stevens?"

Without a word Mr. Stevens caught up the tray from the piano and glided away on his toe-points; whereupon Mr. Brimberly, being alone, became astonishingly agile and nimble all at once, diving down to straighten a rug here and there, rearranging chairs and tables, he even opened the window and hurled two half-smoked cigars far out into the night; and his eye was as calm, his brow as placid, his cheeks as rosy as ever, only his whiskers—those snowy, tell-tale whiskers—quivered spasmodically, very much as though endeavouring to do the manifestly impossible, and flutter away with Mr. Brimberly altogether. Yes, it was all in his whiskers.

Thus did Mr. Brimberly bustle softly to and fro until he paused, all at once, arrested by the sound of a slow, firm step near by. Then Mr. Brimberly coughed, smoothed his wing-like whiskers, and—pulled down his waistcoat for the third time. And lo! even as he did so, the door opened and the hero of this history stood upon the threshold.

8

CHAPTER II

GEOFFREY RAVENSLEE was tall and pale and very languid, so languid, indeed, that the automobile coat he bore across his arm slipped to the floor ere Mr. Brimberly could take it; after which he shed his cap and goggles and dropped them, drew off his gauntlets and dropped them, and, crossing to his favourite lounge-chair, dropped himself into it and lay there staring into the fire.

" Ah, Brimberly ! " he sighed gently, " making a night of it ? "

" Why, sir," bowed his butler—" indeed, sir—to tell the truth, sir——"

" You needn't, Brimberly. Excellent cigars you smoke, judging from the smell. May I have one ? "

" Sir ! " said Brimberly, his whiskers slightly agitated. " Cigars, sir ? "

" In the cabinet, I think," and Mr. Ravenslee motioned feebly with one white hand toward the tall carved cabinet in an adjacent corner.

Mr. Brimberly coughed softly behind plump fingers. " The—the key, sir ? " he suggested.

" Oh, not at all necessary, Brimberly, the lock is faulty, you know."

" Sir ! " said Brimberly, soothing a twitching whisker.

" If you are familiar with the life of the Fourteenth Louis, Brimberly, you will remember that the Grand Monarch hated to be kept waiting, so do I. A cigar— in the cabinet yonder."

With his whiskers in a high stage of agitation, Mr.

9

The Definite Object

Brimberly laid by the garments he held clutched in one arm, and, coming to the cabinet, opened it, and taking thence a box of cigars very much at random, came back carrying it rather as though it were a box of highly dangerous explosives, and, setting it at his master's elbow, struck a match.

Now, as he watched his master select and light his cigar, it chanced that Young R. raised his eyes and looked at Mr. Brimberly, and to be sure those eyes were surprisingly piercing and quick for one so very languid ; indeed, Mr. Brimberly seemed to think so, for he coughed again, faint and discreetly, behind his hand.

" You're 'ome quite—quite unexpected, sir ! "

" Brimberly, I'm afraid I am, but I hope I don't intrude ? ''

" Intrude, sir ! " repeated Mr. Brimberly. " Oh, very facetious, sir—very facetious indeed ! " and he laughed deferentially and soft.

" I blew the horn, but I see he left his hat behind him ! " sighed Young R., nodding languidly toward the headgear of Mr. Stevens, which had fallen beneath a chair, and thus escaped notice.

" Why, I—indeed, sir," said Mr. Brimberly, stooping to make a fierce clutch at it, " I took the liberty of showing a friend of mine your—your picters, sir. No offence, I 'ope, sir ? "

" Friend ! " murmured his master.

" Name of Stevens, sir, valet to Lord Barberton— most sooperior person indeed, sir ! "

" Barberton ! I don't agree with you, Brimberly."

" Stevens, sir ! "

" Ah ! And you showed him my—pictures, did you ? "

" Yes, sir, I did take that liberty. No offence, sir, I——"

" H'm ! Did he like 'em ? "

" Like 'em, sir ! 'E were fair overpowered, sir ! Brandy-and-soda, sir ? "

Of a Mournful Millionaire

"Thanks! Did he like that too?"

"Why, sir—I—indeed——"

"Oh, never mind—to-night is an occasion, anyway—just a splash of soda! Yes, Brimberly, when the clocks strike midnight I shall be thirty-five years old."

"Indeed, sir!" exclaimed Brimberly, clapping his plump hands softly and bowing. "Then allow me to wish you many, many 'appy returns, sir, with continued 'ealth, wealth, and all 'appiness, sir!"

"Happiness!" repeated Young R, and smiled quite bitterly, as only the truly young can smile. "Happiness!" said he again. "Thank you, Brimberly. Now take your friend his hat, and have the extreme goodness to make up the fire. I love a fire, as you know, but especially when I am mournful. And pray hurry, Brimberly!"

Forthwith Mr. Brimberly bowed and bustled out, but very soon bustled in again; and now, as he stooped, menial-like, to ply the coal-tongs—though his dome-like brow preserved all its wonted serenity—no words could possibly express all the mute rebellion of those eloquent whiskers. "Hanything more, sir?" he inquired as he rose from his knee.

"Why, yes," said Young R., glancing up at him; and beneath the quizzical look in those sleepy grey eyes Mr. Brimberley's whiskers wilted slightly. "You're getting a trifle too—er—portly to hop round on your knees, aren't you, Brimberly? Pray sit down and talk to me."

Mr. Brimberly bowed and took a chair, sitting very upright and attentive while his master frowned into the fire.

"Thirty-five is a ripe age, Brimberly," said he at last. "A man should have made something of his life at thirty-five."

"Certingly, sir."

"And I'm getting quite into the sere and yellow leaf, am I not, Brimberly?"

The Definite Object

Mr. Brimberly raised a plump, protesting hand. " 'Ardly that, sir—'ardly that ! " said he. " We are hall of us getting on, of course."

" Where to, Brimberly ? On where, Brimberly ? On what ? "

" Why, sir, since you ask me, I should answer—begging your parding—'eaven knows, sir ! "

" Precisely ! Anyway, I'm going there fast."

" Where, sir ? "

" Heaven knows, Brimberly."

" Ah—er—certingly, sir ! "

" Now, Brimberly, as a hard-headed, matter-of-fact, common-sense being, what would you suggest for a poor devil who is sick and tired of everything, and, most of all, of himself ? "

" Why, sir, I should prescribe for that man change of hair, sir—travel, sir. I should suggest to that man Hafghanistan, or Hasia Minor, or both, sir. There's your noo yacht a-laying in the river, sir."

His master leant his square chin upon his square fist, and, still frowning at the fire, gently shook his head. " My good Brimberly," he sighed, " haven't I travelled in most parts of the world ? "

" Why, yes, sir, you've travelled, sir ; very much so indeed, sir. You've shot lions and tigers and a helephant or so, and exchanged sentiments with raging 'eathen—as rage in nothing but a string o' beads—but what about your noomerous possessions in Europe, sir ? "

" Ah, yes," nodded Young R., " I do possess some shanties and things over there, don't I, Brimberly ? "

" Shanties, sir ! " Mr. Brimberly blinked, and his whiskers bristled in horrified reproof. " Shanties ! Oh dear me, sir ! " he murmured. " Shanties ! Your magnificent town mansion situate in Saint James's Square, London, as your respected father hacquired from a royal dook, sir ! Shanties ! Your costly and helegant res-eye-dence in Park Lane, sir ! "

Of a Mournful Millionaire

"H'm!" said Young R., moodily.

"Then in Scotland, sir, we 'ave your castle of Drumlochie, sir—rocks, turrets, battlements, 'ighly grim and romantic, sir!"

"Ha!" sighed his young master, frowning at his cigar.

"Next, sir, in Italy we find your ancient Roman villa, sir—halabaster pillows and columns, sir—very historical, though a trifle wore with wars and centuries of centoorians, sir, wherefore I would humbly suggest a coat or two of paint, sir, applied beneath your very own eye, sir."

"No, Brimberly," murmured Young R., "paint might have attractions, Italy none."

"Certingly not, sir, cer-tingly not. Which brings us to your *Schloss* in Germany, sir."

"Nor Germany. Lord, Brimberly, are there many more?"

"Ho yes, sir, plenty," nodded Mr. Brimberly. "Your late honoured and respected father, sir, were a rare 'and at buying palaces, sir. 'E collected 'em, as you might say, like some folks collects postage stamps, sir."

"And a collection of the one is about as useless as a collection of the other, Brimberly."

"Why, true, sir, one man can't live in a dozen places all at once. But why not work round 'em in turn, beginning, say, at your imposing Venetian *palazzo*—canals, sir, gondoleers—picturesque, though dampish? Or your *shally* in the Tyro-leen Halps, sir, or——"

"Brimberly, have the goodness to—er—shut up!"

"Certingly, sir."

"To-day is my birthday, Brimberly, and to-night I've reached a kind of 'jumping off' place in my life, and—between you and me—I'm seriously thinking of—er—jumping off!"

"I crave parding, sir?"

"I'm thirty-five years old," continued Young R., his frown growing blacker, "and I've never done anything

13

The Definite Object

really worth while in all my useless life! Have the goodness to look at me, will you?"

"With pleasure, sir!"

"Well, what do I look like?"

"The very hacme of a gentleman, sir!"

"Kind of you, Brimberly, but I know myself for an absolutely useless thing—a purposeless, ambitionless wretch, drifting on to God knows what. I'm a hopeless wreck, a moral derelict, and it has only occurred to me to-night—— But"—and here the speaker paused to flick the ash from his cigar—"I fear I'm boring you?"

"No, sir—ho no, not at all, indeed, sir!"

"You're very kind, Brimberly. Light a cigarette! Ah no, pardon me, you prefer my cigars, I know."

"Why—why, sir," stammered Mr. Brimberly, laying a soothing hand upon his twitching whisker, "indeed, I—I——"

"Oh, help yourself, pray!"

Hereupon Mr. Brimberly took a cigar very much at random, and, while Young R. watched with lazy interest, proceeded to cut it—though with singularly clumsy fingers.

"A light, Mr. Brimberly—allow me!"

So Ravenslee held the light while Mr. Brimberly puffed his cigar to a glow, though to be sure he coughed once and choked as he met Young R.'s calm, grey eye.

"Now," pursued his master, "if you're quite comfortable, Mr. Brimberly, perhaps you'll be good enough to —er—hearken further to my tale of woe?"

Mr. Brimberly choked again, and, recovering, smoothed his writhing whiskers and murmured, "It would be a honour!"

"First, then, Brimberly, have you ever hated yourself —I mean, despised yourself so thoroughly that the bare idea of your existence makes you angry and indignant?"

"Why, no, sir," answered Mr. Brimberly, staring, "I can't say as I 'ave, sir."

14

Of a Mournful Millionaire

"No," said his master with another keen glance, "and I don't suppose you ever will!"

Now here again, perhaps because of the look or something in Young R.'s tone, Mr. Brimberly took occasion to emit a small, apologetic cough.

"You have never felt yourself to be a—a cumberer of the earth, Brimberly?"

Mr. Brimberly, having thought the matter over, decided that he had not.

"You are not given to introspection, Brimberly?"

"Intro—ahem! No, sir, not precisely—'ardly that, sir, and then only very occasional, sir."

"Then you've never got on to yourself—got wise to yourself—seen yourself as you really are?"

Mr. Brimberly goggled and groped for his whisker.

"I mean," pursued his master, "you have never seen all your secret weaknesses and petty meannesses stripped stark naked, have you?"

"N-naked, sir!" faltered Mr. Brimberly, "very distressing indeed, sir—oh dear me!"

"It's a devilish unpleasant thing," continued Young R., scowling at the fire again, "yes, it's a devilish unpleasant thing to go serenely on our flowery way pitying and condemning the sins and follies of others and sublimely unconscious of our own until one day—ah yes, one day—we meet ourselves face to face, and see beneath all our pitiful shams and hypocrisies, and know ourselves at last for what we really are—behold the decay of faculties, the degeneration of intellect bred of sloth and inanition, and know ourselves at last—for exactly what we are!"

Mr. Brimberly stared at the preoccupation of his master's scowling brow and grim-set mouth, and, clutching a soft handful of whisker, murmured, "Certingly, sir!"

"When I was a boy," continued Ravenslee absently, "I used to dream of the wonderful things I would do

The Definite Object

when I was a man. By the way, you're quite sure I'm not boring you ? ''

'' No, sir—certingly not, sir, indeed, sir ! ''

'' Take another cigar, Brimberly. Oh, put it in your pocket, it will do to—er—to add to your collection ! But, as I was saying, as a boy I was full of a godlike ambition, but, as I grew up, ambition and all the noble things it leads to sickened and died—died of a surfeit of dollars. And to-day I am thirty-five, and feel that I can't—that I never shall—do anything worth while.''

'' But, sir,'' exclaimed Mr. Brimberly with a bland and reassuring smile, '' you are one as don't have to do nothing. You're rich ! ''

Mr. Ravenslee started. '' Rich ! '' he cried, and, turning, he glanced at Mr. Brimberly, and his square chin looked so very square and his grey eyes so very piercing that Mr. Brimberly, loosing his whisker, coughed again and shifted his gaze to the Persian rug beneath his feet ; yet when Young R. spoke again his voice was very soft and sleepy. '' Rich ! '' he repeated. '' Yes, that's just the unspeakable hell of it—it's money that has crippled all endeavours and made me what I am ! Rich ! I'm so rich that my friends are all acquaintances ; so rich that I might buy anything in the world except what I most desire ; so rich that I am tired of life, the world, and everything in the world, and have been seriously considering a—er—a radical change. It is a comfort to know that we may all of us find oblivion when we so desire.''

'' Ohblivion ! '' nodded Mr. Brimberly, mouthing the word sonorously ; '' ohblivion, sir, certingly—my own sentiments exactly, sir, for, though not being a marrying man myself, I regard it with a truly reverent heye, and 'umbly suggest that for you such a ohblivious change would be——''

'' Brimberly,'' said Young R., turning to stare in lazy wonder, '' where in the world are you getting to now ? ''

16

Of a Mournful Millionaire

Mr. Brimberly coughed and touched a whisker with dubious finger. "Wasn't you allooding to—hem—to matrimony, sir?"

"Matrimony! Lord, no! Hardly so desperate a course as that, Brimberly. I was considering the advisability of—er—this!" And, opening a drawer in the escritoire, Young R. held up a revolver, whereat Mr. Brimberly's whiskers showed immediate signs of extreme agitation, and he started to his feet.

"Mr. Ravenslee, sir, for the love o' Gawd!" he exclaimed, "if it's a choice between the two, try matrimony first, it's so much—so much wholesomer, sir!"

"Is it, Brimberly? Let me see. There are about five hundred highly dignified matrons in this—er—great city wholly eager and anxious to wed their daughters to my dollars (and incidentally myself) even if I were the vilest knave or most pitiful piece of doddering antiquity. Faugh! let's hear no more of matrimony."

"Certingly not, sir!" bowed Mr. Brimberly.

"And I'm neither mad, Brimberly, nor drunk, only—speaking colloquially—I'm 'on to' myself at last. If my father had only left me a few fewer millions I might have been quite a hard-working, useful member of society, for there's good in me, Brimberly, I am occasionally aware of quite noble impulses, but they need some object to bring 'em out. An object—h'm!" Here Mr. Ravenslee put away the revolver. "An object to work for, live for, be worthy of!" Here he fell to frowning into the fire again, and stared thus so long that at last Mr. Brimberly felt impelled to say:

"A hobject, of course, sir! A hobject—certingly, sir!" But here he started and turned to stare toward the windows, as from the darkness beyond two voices were uplifted in song; two voices, these, which sang the same tune and words, but in two different keys; uncertain voices, now shooting up into heights, now dropping unto unplumbable deeps; two shaky voices whose inconsequent quaverings suggested four legs in much the same condition.

"Brimberly," sighed his master, "what doleful wretches have we here?"

"Why, sir, I—I rather fancy it's William and James —the footmen, sir," answered Mr. Brimberly between bristling whiskers. "Hexcuse me, sir—I'll go and speak to 'em, sir."

"Oh, pray don't trouble yourself, Mr. Brimberly, sit down and hearken. These sad sounds are inspired by deep—er— potations—beer, I fancy. Be seated, Mr. Brimberly."

Mr. Brimberly obeyed, and, being much agitated, dropped his cigar and grovelled for it, and it was to be noted thereafter that as the singers drew nearer he shuffled on his chair with whiskers violently a-twitch, while his eyes goggled more and his dome-like brow grew ever moister. But on came the singing footmen, and passed, full-tongued, wailing out each word with due effect, thus:

> "My—sweet'eart's—me mother,
> The best—the dearest—of—'em all."

"H'm!" murmured Young R., "I admire the sentiment, Brimberly, but the execution leaves something to be desired, perhaps."

"If you'll only let me go out to 'em, sir!" groaned Mr. Brimberly, mopping himself with a very large, exceeding white handkerchief, "if you honly will, sir."

"No, Brimberly, no—it would only distress you. Besides, hark! their song is ended, and rather abruptly. I rather fancy they have fallen down the terrace steps."

"And I 'opes," murmured Mr. Brimberly fervently, "I do 'ope as they've broke their necks!"

"Of course, I ought to have gone out and switched on the lights for them," sighed Young R.; "but then, you see, I thought they were safe in bed, Brimberly!"

"Why, sir," said Mr. Brimberly, mopping furiously,

Of a Mournful Millionaire

"I—I ventured to give 'em a hour's leave of habsence, sir. I ventured so to do, sir, because, sir——"

"Because you are of rather a venturesome nature, aren't you, Brimberly?"

"No offence, sir, I 'ope?"

"None at all, Mr. Brimberly. Pray calm yourself, and—er—take a little brandy."

"Sir!"

"Your glass is under the chair yonder, or is it your friend's?"

Mr. Brimberly goggled toward Mr. Stevens's betraying glass, picked it up, and sat staring at it in vague and dreamy fashion until, rousing at his master's second bidding, he proceeded to mix brandy and soda, his gaze still profoundly abstracted and his whiskers drooping with an abnormal meekness.

At this juncture a knock sounded at the door, and a chauffeur appeared, looking very smart in his elegant livery; a thick-set man, mightily deep of chest, whose wide shoulders seemed to fill the doorway, and whose long, gorilla-like arms ended in two powerful hands; his jaw was squarely huge, his nose broad and thick, but beneath his beetling brows blinked two of the mildest blue eyes in the world.

"What is it, Joe?"

"And what time will ye be wantin' the car in the mornin', sir?" he inquired.

"The morning, Joe? Who can say what may happen between now and then?"

"Shall I have her round at eleven, sir, or——"

"Eleven will do as well as any other time; let it go at that."

"You was to see your broker, Mr. Anderson, in the mornin' over them steamship shares, sir."

"Shares, Joe, are a vanity, they weary me. Mr. Brimberly yawns and you look sleepy. Good-night, Joe; pleasant dreams."

The Definite Object

" Good-night, sir ! " and, touching his right eyebrow, Joe went out, closing the door behind him.

" And now," said Mr. Ravenslee, puffing languidly at his cigar, " referring to the necessary object, there is a chance that it may be found even yet, Mr. Brimberly ! "

" Hobject, sir," murmured Mr. Brimberly ; " found, sir—to be sure, sir."

" Yes, I intend you shall find it for me, Brimberly."

Mr. Brimberly's abstraction gave place to sudden amaze. " Find it ! Wot ! me, sir—hexcuse me, sir— but did you say me ? " Mr. Brimberly actually gaped.

" You, Brimberly, of course."

" But—but wot kind of a hobject—and where, sir ? "

" Really," sighed Young R., " these are quite fool questions for one of your hard-headed common-sense ! If I knew exactly ' what ' and ' where ' I'd go and find it myself, at least, I might."

" But 'ow in the world, sir—beggin' your parding I'm sure—but 'ow am I to go a-finding hobjex as I've never seen nor 'eard of ? "

" Brimberly, I pass ! But if you manage it in, say, a week I'll double your wages, and give you a—er—a bonus into the bargain. Think it over."

" I—I will, sir, indeed, sir ! "

" Very well, you may go."

" Certingly, sir." Mr. Brimberly bowed and crossed to the door, but, being there, paused. " Double me wages I think it were, sir, *and* a bonus ? Very 'andsome, very 'andsome, indeed, sir, thank you, sir." Saying which Mr. Brimberly bowed himself out, but immediately bowed himself in again. " Sir," said he, " if you could give me some hidea, sir."

" Some what ? "

" A few 'ints, sir, as to the nature of said hobject— whether animal, mineral, or nooter, sir ? "

" Well, perhaps ' animal ' might be the more interesting."

20

Of a Mournful Millionaire

"Now, as to gender, sir. Masculine shall we say, or shall we make it feminine?"

"Oh, either will do! And yet, since you offer so wide a selection, perhaps—er—feminine."

"Very good, sir!"

"And you'd better make it singular number, Brimberly."

"Certingly, sir; much obliged, sir! Will you be wanting me again, sir?"

"Not again, Brimberly."

"Then good-night, sir! Thank you, sir!" And Mr. Brimberly went softly forth, and closed the door noiselessly behind him.

Being alone, Mr. Ravenslee switched off the lights and sat in the fire-glow. "Feminine gender, singular number, objective case, governed by the verb to love—I wonder!" And he laughed a little bitterly (and very youthfully) as he stared down into the dying fire.

CHAPTER III

A CLOCK in the hall without struck midnight, but Mr.
Ravenslee sat there long after the silvery chime had
died away, his chin sunk upon his broad chest, his sombre
eyes staring blindly at the fading embers, lost in profound
and gloomy meditation.   But all at once he started and
glanced swiftly round toward a certain window, the
curtains of which were partially drawn, and his lounging
attitude changed instantly to one of watchful alertness.

Now, as he sat thus, broad shoulders stooped, feet
drawn up—poised for swift action—he beheld a light
that flashed here and there, that vanished and came
again, hovering up and down and to and fro outside the
window ; wherefore he reached out a long arm in the
gloom, and silently opened a certain drawer in the
escritoire.

Came a soft click, a faint creak, and a breath of cool,
fragrant air as the window was cautiously opened, and a
shapeless Something climbed through, while Mr. Ravenslee
sat motionless—waiting.

The flashing light winked again, a small, bright disc that
hovered uncertainly and finally steadied upon the carved
cabinet in the corner, and the Something crept stealthily
thither   A long-dr wn, breathless minute, and then the
room was flooded with brilliant light, and a figure, kneeling before the cabinet, uttered a strangled cry and leapt
up, only to recoil before Mr. Ravenslee's levelled revolver.

A pallid-faced, willowy lad this, of perhaps seventeen,

who, sinking to his knees, threw up an arm across his face, then raised both hands above his head.

"Ah, don't shoot, mister!" he gasped "oh, don't shoot—I got me hands up!"

"Stand up!" said Ravenslee grimly. "Up with you, and shutter that window. You may have friends outside, and I'm taking no chances! Quick, shutter that window!"

The lad struggled to his feet, and, crossing to the window, fumbled the shutter into place, his ghastly face turning and turning toward the revolver that glittered in such deadly fashion in Mr. Ravenslee's steady hand. At length, the shutters barred, the boy turned, and. moistening dry lips, spoke hoarsely and with apparent effort. "Oh mister, don't go for to croak a guy as—as ain't done nothin'."

"You broke into my house."

"But I haven't took nothin'."

"Because I happened to catch you."

"But—but—— Oh, sir," stammered the boy, taking off his cap and fumbling with it while he stared wide-eyed at the threatening revolver, "I—I ain't a real thief —'cross me heart and hope to die I ain't! Don't croak me, sir!"

"But why in the world not?" inquired Mr. Ravenslee. "Alone and unaided I have captured a desperate criminal, a bloodthirsty villain—caught him in the very act of burgling a cabinet where I keep my cigars of price—and Mr. Brimberly's, of course! Consequently to—er—croak you is my privilege as a citizen, it's all quite just and proper, really, I ought to croak you, you know."

"I ain't desprit, mister," the boy pleaded. "I ain't a reg'lar crook, dis is me first try-out, honest it is!"

"But then I prefer to regard you as a deep-dyed desperado. You must be quite—er—sixteen! Consequently, it is my duty to croak you on the spot, or hand you over to the police."

The Definite Object

"No, no!" cried the boy, his tremulous hands reached out in a passion of supplication, "not de cops! Don't let th' p'lice get me. Oh, I never took nothin' from nobody. Lemme go! Be a sport, and let me beat it, sir!"

All Mr. Ravenslee's chronic languor seemed to have returned, as, leaning back in the deep cushioned chair, he regarded this youthful malefactor with sleepy eyes, yet eyes that missed nothing of the boy's quivering earnestness as he continued, breathlessly, "Oh, I ain't a real crook. I never done nothin' like this before, an' I never will again if—if you'll only let me chase meself."

"And now," sighed Mr. Ravenslee, "I'll trouble you for the 'phone yonder."

"Are ye goin' to call in de cops?"

"That is my intention. Give me the 'phone."

"No!" cried the boy, and, springing before the telephone, he stood there, trembling but defiant.

"Give me that telephone!"

"Not much I won't!"

"Then, of course, I must shoot you!"

The boy stood with head up-flung and fists tight-clenched. Mr. Ravenslee lounged in his chair with levelled pistol. So they fronted each other, but, all at once, with a sound between a choke and groan, the lad covered his face. "Go on!" he whispered hoarsely, "go on—what's keepin' you? If it's th' cops or croaking, I—I'd rather croak."

"Why?"

"'Cause if I was ever sent to prison it 'u'd break her heart, I guess."

"Her heart?" said Mr. Ravenslee, and lowered the pistol.

"Me sister's."

"Ah, so you have a sister?" and Mr. Ravenslee sat up suddenly.

"Lots o' guys has, but there ain't a sister like mine in all N'York, nor nowheres else."

Ravenslee Seeks an Object

"Who are you? What's your name?"

"Spike. Me real name's Arthur, but Arthur sounds kinder soft an' sissy, nobody don't call me Arthur 'cept her, an' I don't mind her."

"And what's her name?"

"Hermy—Hermione, sir."

"Hermione! Why, that's Greek! It's a very beautiful name."

"Kind o' fits her too!" nodded the boy. "Hermy's ace-high on the face and figure question. Why, there ain't a swell dame on Fift' Av'ner, nor nowheres else, got anythin' on Hermy as a looker!"

"And what of your father and mother?"

"Ain't got none, don't remember havin' none, don't want none. Hermy's good 'nuff for me."

"Good to you, is she?" inquired Mr. Ravenslee.

"Good t' me!" cried the lad. "Good? Well, say, when I think about it I—I gets watery in me lamps, kinder sloppy in me talk, an' all mushy inside. Good t' me? Well, you can just bet on that!"

"And," inquired Mr. Ravenslee sleepily, "are you as good to her?"

Hereupon Spike turned his cap inside out, and looked at it thoughtfully. "I—I dunno, mister."

"Ah! perhaps you make her cry sometimes?"

Hereupon Spike began to pick at the lining of his cap, and finally answered: "Sometimes, I guess."

"Would she cry if she could see you now, I wonder?"

Hereupon Spike began to wring and twist his cap in nervous hands ere he answered, "I—I guess she might."

"She must love you a good deal?"

At this Spike twisted his cap into a ball, but spoke nothing. Seeing which, Mr. Ravenslee proceeded: "You are luckier than I, there isn't a soul in the world to do as much for me."

Spike gulped audibly, and thereafter sniffed.

"Now, suppose," said Mr. Ravenslee, "let us suppose

25

she found out that the brother she loved so much was a
--thief ? "

Hereupon Spike unrolled his cap and proceeded to
rub his eyes with it, and when at last he spoke it was in
a voice broken by great sobs :

" Say, cut it out ! cut it out ! I never meant to—to
do it. They got me soused, doped me, I think, else I'd
never have done it. I ain't good, but I ain't so rotten
bad as—what I seem, I ain't no real crook, but if you
wanter croak me for what I done, go ahead ! Only don't
—don't let de cops get me, 'cause o' Hermy. If you
croak me she'll think I got it in a scrap maybe, so if you
wanter plug me, go ahead ! "

" But what are you shivering for ? "

" I—I'm just waitin', sir," answered Spike, closing his
eyes. " I—I seen a guy shot once."

Mr. Ravenslee sighed and nodded. " After all," said
he, " I don't think I'll croak you," and he slipped the
revolver into his pocket, while Spike watched him in
sudden tense eagerness.

" Whatcher mean to do wi' me ? " he asked.

" That's the question, what shall I do with you ?
Let me think."

" Say," cried the boy eagerly, " you don't have to do
no thinkin', leave it all to me ! It's de winder for mine,
I'll chase meself so quick——"

" No, you don't ! Sit down—sit down, I say ! "

Spike sighed and seated himself on the extreme edge
of the chair his captor indicated. " Won'tcher lemme
beat it, sir ? " he pleaded.

" No ! Some one else might catch you next time, and
have the pleasure of—er—croaking you, or handing you
over to the police."

" There won't be no next time, sir ! " cried Spike eagerly.
" I'll never do it no more. I'll cut de whole gang. I'll
give Bud M'Ginnis de throw-down—on de dead level, I
will, if you'll only let me——"

Ravenslee Seeks an Object

" Who's Bud M'Ginnis ? "

" Say ! " cried the boy, staring, " don'tcher know that ? Why, Bud's de main-squeeze wi' de gang, de whole cheese he is—an' he kind o' thinks I'm de candy-kid 'cause he's stuck on me sister."

" Ah ! " nodded Mr. Ravenslee, frowning a little, " and is she—er—stuck on him ? "

" Not so as you could notice it, she ain't. No, she can't see Bud with a pair of opry-glasses, an' he's a dead-game sport too. Oh, there ain't no flies on Bud, an' nobody can lick him either, but Hermy don't cotton none, she hasn't got no use for him, see ? But, say——" Spike rose tentatively and looked on his captor with eyes big and supplicating.

" Well, what now ? "

" Why, I thought if you was tired of me chewin' de rag, and wanted to hit the feathers, I'd just cop a sneak. Say, if you'll only lemme go I'll do de square thing, and get a steady job like Hermy wants me to—honest, I will, sir ! Ye see, me sister's away to-night—she does needle-work for swell folks, an' stops with 'em sometimes, so if you'll only let me beat it, I can skin back an' she'll never know. Ah, lemme go, sir ! "

" Well then," sighed Mr. Ravenslee, " for her sake I will let you go. Wait ! I'll let you go, and never speak of your —er—little escapade here, if you will take me with you."

Now at this Spike gaped and fell back a step in sheer amazement. " Go wi' me—wi' me ? " he stammered. " You—go wi' me to Hell's Kitchen —to Mulligan's Dump —you ! Say, what kind o' song and dance are you givin' me, anyway ? Aw, quit yer kiddin,' sir ! "

" But I mean it."

" On—on de level ? "

" On the level."

" Holy Gee ! " and Spike relapsed into wide-eyed, voiceless wonder.

" Is it a go ? " inquired Mr. Ravenslee.

The Definite Object

" But—but, say," stammered the boy, glancing from the elegant figure in the chair round the luxurious room and back again—" but you're a—a——"

" Just a poor, disconsolate, lonely—er—guy."

" What ! " cried Spike, staring round him again, "with all this ?   Oh yes, you're homeless and starvin', you are—I don't think ! "

" Is it a go ? "

" But say, whatcher want to go wi' me for ?   What's yer game ?   Put me wise."

" I am filled with desire to breathe awhile the salubrious air of Hell's Kitchen. Will you take me ? " Now, as he spoke, beholding the boy's staring amaze, Mr. Ravenslee's frowning brows relaxed, his firm, clean-shaven lips quivered, and all at once curved up into a smile of singular sweetness, a smile before which the hopelessness and fear died out of the boy's long-lashed eyes, his whole strained attitude vanished, and he smiled also—though perhaps a little tremulously.

" Will you take me, Spike ? "

" You bet I will ! " exclaimed the boy, his blue eyes shining, " and I'll do my best to show you I—I ain't so bad as I—as I seem—an' we'll shake on it if you like." And Spike advanced with his hand outstretched, then paused, suddenly abashed, and drooping his head, turned away. " I—I forgot," he muttered, " I—I'm—you said I was—a thief."

" You meant to be," said Mr. Ravenslee, and, rising, he stretched himself and glanced at his watch.

" Are you comin' wi' me, sir ? " inquired Spike, regarding Mr. Ravenslee's length and breadth with quick, appraising eyes.

" I surely am."

" But—but not in them glad rags ? " and Spike pointed to Mr. Ravenslee's exquisitely tailored garments.

" Ah, to be sure," nodded their wearer, " we'll soon fix that," and he touched the electric bell.

28

Ravenslee Seeks an Object

" Say," cried Spike, starting forward in sudden terror, " you—you ain't goin' to give me away ? "

" No."

" 'Cross your heart—hope to die, you ain't ? "

" Across my heart and hope to die I'm not, and there's my hand on it, Spike."

" What ! " exclaimed the boy, his eyes suspiciously bright, " d'you mean you will shake—after—after what I——"

" There's my hand, Spike."

So their hands met and gripped, the boy's hot and eagerly tremulous, the man's cool and steady and strong ; then of a sudden Spike choked, and, turning his back, brushed away his tears with his cap ; also at this moment, with a soft and discreet knock, Mr. Brimberly opened the door and bowed himself into the room. His attitude was deferential as always, his smile as respectful, but, beholding Spike, his round eyes grew rounder and his whiskers slightly bristly.

" Ah, Brimberly," nodded his master, " you are not in bed yet—good ! "

" No, sir," answered Mr. Brimberly, " I'm not in bed yet, sir, but when you rang I was in the very hact, sir."

" First of all," said Young R., selecting a cigar, " let me introduce you to—er—my friend Spike."

Hereupon Mr. Brimberly rolled his eyes in Spike's direction, glanced him over, touched either whisker, and bowed, and, lo ! these fleecy whiskers were now eloquent of pompous dignity, beholding which, Spike shuffled his feet, averted his eyes, and twisted his cap into a very tight ball indeed.

But now Brimberly turned his eyes (and his whiskers) on his master, who had taken out his watch.

" Brimberly," said he, " it is now very nearly two o'clock."

" Very late, sir—ho, very late, sir. Indeed, I was in the very hact of goin' to bed, sir—I'd even unbuttoned

29

The Definite Object

my waistcoat, sir, when you rang—two o'clock, sir—dear me! a most un'oly hour, sir——"

"Consequently, Brimberly, I am thinking of taking a little outing——"

"Certingly, sir. Oh, certingly!"

"And I want some other clothes—— "

"Clothes, sir—yessir. There's the noo 'Arris tweed sir——"

"With holes in them, if possible, Brimberly."

"'Oles, sir! Beg parding, sir, but did you say 'oles, sir?"

"Also patches, Brimberly—the bigger the better."

"Patches!—hexcuse me, sir, but—patches! I beg parding, but——" Mr. Brimberly laid a feeble hand upon a twitching whisker.

"In a word, Brimberly," pursued his master, seating himself upon the escritoire and swinging his leg, "I want some old clothes, shabby clothes—moth-eaten, stained, tattered, and torn. Also, a muffler and an old hat. Can you find me some?"

"No, sir, I can't—that is, yessir, I can. Hexcuse me, sir—'arf a moment, sir." Saying which, Mr. Brimberly bowed and went from the room with one hand still clutching his whisker very much as though he had taken himself into custody and were leading himself out.

"Say," exclaimed Spike in a hoarse whisper and edging nearer to Mr. Ravenslee, "who's His Whiskers—de swell guy with de face trimmings?"

"Why, since you ask, Spike, he is a very worthy person who devotes his life to—er—looking after my welfare, and—other things."

"Holy Gee!" exclaimed Spike, staring. "I should have thought you was big 'nuff to do that for yourself, unless——" and here he broke off suddenly and gazed on Mr. Ravenslee's long figure with a new and more particular interest.

"Unless what?"

30

Ravenslee Seeks an Object

"Say, you ain't got bats in your belfry, have you? You ain't weak in the think-box, or soft in the nut, are ye?"

"No, at least not more than the average, I believe."

"I mean His Whiskers don't have to lead you around on a string, or watch out you don't set fire to yourself, does he?"

"Well, strictly speaking, I can't say that his duties are quite so far-reaching."

"Who are you, anyway?"

"Well, my names are Geoffrey, Guy, Eustace, Hughson, and—er—a few others, but these will do to go on with perhaps?"

"Well, I guess yes!"

"You can take your choice."

"Well, Guy won't do—no, siree—ye see, every mutt's a guy down our way—so I guess we'll make it Geoff. But, say, if you ain't weak on the think-machinery, why d'ye keep a guy like His Whiskers hangin' around?"

"Because he has become a habit, Spike—and habits cling—and speaking of habits, here it is."

Sure enough, at that moment Brimberly's knuckles made themselves discreetly heard, and Brimberly himself appeared with divers garments across his arm, at sight of whom Spike stood immediately dumb in staring, awestruck wonder.

"Ah, you've got them, Brimberly?"

"Yessir! These is the best I can do, sir."

"Say rather the worst!"

"'Ere's a nice big 'ole in the coat, sir," said Mr. Brimberly, unfolding the garments in question, "and the weskitt, sir, the pocket is tore, you'll notice, sir."

"Excellent, Brimberly!"

"As for these trousis, sir——"

"They seem rather superior garments, I'm afraid," said Mr. Ravenslee, shaking his head.

"But you'll notice as they're very much wore round the 'eels, sir."

The Definite Object

"They'll do. Now the hat and muffler."

"All 'ere, sir; the 'at's got its brim broke, sir."

"Couldn't be better, Brimberly." So saying, Mr. Ravenslee took up the clothes and turned toward the door. "Now I'll trouble you to keep an eye on—er— young America here while I get into these."

"Sir," said Mr. Brimberly, turning his whiskers full upon Spike, who immediately fell to shuffling and wringing at his cap, "sir, I will, certingly, sir."

Now, when the door had shut after his master, Mr. Brimberly raised eyes and hands to the ceiling and shook his head until his whiskers quivered. Quoth he, 'Hall I arsks is, wot next?" Thereafter he lowered his eyes and regarded Spike as if he had been that basest of base minions—a boy in buttons. At last he deigned speech:

"And w'en did *you* come in, pray?"

"'Bout a hour ago, sir," answered Spike, dropping his cap in his embarrassment.

"Ah!" nodded Mr. Brimberly, "about a hour ago. Ho! By appointment, I pre-zoom?"

"No, sir, by a winder."

"A wot?"

"A winder, sir."

"A—winder? 'Eavens and earth—a winder! 'Ow? Where? Wot for?"

"Say, mister," said Spike, breaking in upon Mr. Brimberly's astounded questioning, "is 'e nutty?" and he jerked his thumb toward the door through which Mr. Ravenslee had gone.

"Nutty!" said Mr. Brimberly, staring.

"Yes. I mean, is 'e batty? Has he got wheels?"

"W'eels?" said Mr. Brimberly, his eyes rounder than usual.

"Well then, is he daffy—off his trolley?"

"Off 'is wot?" said Mr. Brimberly, fumbling for his whisker.

"Holy Gee!" exclaimed Spike, "can't you under-

stand English? Say, is your brother as smart as
you ? "

" The honly brother as ever I 'ad was a infant as died,
and—— But wot was you saying about a winder ? "

" Nothin'."

" Come, speak up, you young vagabone," began Mr.
Brimberly, his whiskers suddenly fierce and threatening;
but just then, fortunately for Spike, the door swung open,
and Mr. Ravenslee entered.

And, lo, what a change was here ! The battered hat,
the faded muffler, and shabby clothes seemed only to
show off all the hitherto hidden strength and vigour of
the powerful limbs below ; indeed, it almost seemed that
with his elegant garments he had laid aside his lassitude
also, and taken on a new air of resolution, for his eyes
were sleepy no longer, and his every gesture lithe and
quick. So great was the change that Spike stared
speechless, and Mr. Brimberly gaped with whiskers
a-droop.

" Well, shall I do ? " inquired Mr. Ravenslee, tightening
his faded neckerchief.

" Do ? " repeated Spike. " Say—you look all to de
mustard, Geoff ! You—you look as if you could do
things now ! "

" Strangely enough, Spike, I rather feel that way too."
So saying, Mr. Ravenslee took a pipe from the rack, filled
it with quick, energetic fingers, and proceeded to light
it, watched in dumb amaze by the gaping Brimberly.

" Brimberly," said he, " I shall probably return to-
morrow."

" Yes, sir," said Mr. Brimberly faintly.

" Or the day after."

" Yes, sir."

" Or the day after."

" Yes, sir."

" Or the day after that. Anyhow, I shall probably
return. Should any one call—business or otherwise—

tell 'em to call again. Say I'm out of town ; you understand ? "

" Out of town ? Certingly, sir."

" Referring to—to the matter we talked of to-night, Brimberly——"

" Meanin' the hobject, sir ? "

" Precisely. Don't trouble yourself about it."

" No, sir."

" No, Brimberly. I'm going to try to find one for myself."

" Ho, very good, sir ! "

" And now," said the new Mr. Ravenslee, laying one white, ringless hand on Spike's shoulder, and pointing toward the open door with the other, " lead on, young Destiny ! "

CHAPTER IV

IT was past three o'clock and dawn was at hand as, by
devious ways, Spike piloted his companion through that
section of New York City which is known to the initiated
as Hell's Kitchen. By dismal streets they went, past
silent, squalid houses and tall tenements looming grim
and ghostly in the faint light; crossing broad avenues
very silent and deserted at this hour; on and on until,
dark and vague and mysterious, the great river flowed
before them, only to be lost again as they plunged into a
gloomy court where tall buildings rose on every hand,
huge and very silent, teeming with life, but life just now
wrapped in that profound quietude of sleep which is so
much akin to death. Into one of these tall tenement
buildings—its ugliness rendered more ugly by the net-
work of iron fire-escape ladders that writhed up the face
of it—Spike led the way, first into a dark hallway, and
thence up many stairs that echoed to their light-treading
feet. On and up they went, past dim-lit landings where
were doors each of which shut in its own little world, a
world distinct and separate, wherein youth and age, good
and evil, joy and misery, lived and moved and had their
being. Behind these dingy panels were smiling hope
and black despair, blooming health and pallid sickness,
and all those sins and virtues that go to make up the
sum-total of humanity.

Something of all this was in Geoffrey Ravenslee's mind

35

The Definite Object

as he climbed the dingy, interminable stair behind Spike, who presently halted to get his wind and whisper, " It ain't much farther now, Geoff, only another two flights and—— " He stopped suddenly to listen, and from the landing above a sound reached them, a sound soft but unmistakable—a woman's muffled sobbing.

Slowly, cautiously, they mounted the stair, until in the dim light of a certain landing they beheld a slim figure bowed upon its knees in an agony of abasement before a scarred and dingy door. Even as they stared, the slender, girlish figure sobbed again, and, with a sudden, yearning gesture, lifted a face, pale in the half-light, and kissed that battered door ; then, weeping still, she rose to her feet and turned, but, seeing Spike, stood very still all at once and with hands clasped tight together.

" Holy Gee ! " exclaimed Spike beneath his breath ; then, in a hoarse whisper, " Is that Maggie—Maggie Finlay ? "

" Oh ! is that you, Arthur ? " she whispered back. " Arthur—oh, Arthur !—I—I'm going away. But I couldn't go without coming to—to kiss dear mother good-bye, and now I'm here I daren't knock for fear of—father. I've been up to your door and knocked, but Hermy's away, I guess. Anyway, you—you'll say I came to thank her and kiss her for the last time, won't you, Arthur ? "

" Sure I will ! But where ye goin', Maggie ? "

" A long way, Arthur. I don't s'pose I shall ever see this place any more—or you. So, Arthur, will you—kiss me good-bye—just once ? "

Spike hesitated ; but she, quick and light-treading, came down to him and caught his hand and would have kissed that, but he snatched it away, and, leaning forward, kissed her tear-stained cheek, and blushed thereafter despite the dark.

" Good-bye, Arthur," she whispered, " and thank you —and dear Hermy. Oh, good-bye ! "

36

How he came to Hell's Kitchen

So saying, she hurried on past Ravenslee, down the dark stairway, while Spike leaned over the balustrade to whisper, " Good-bye, Maggie ; an' good luck, kid ! " At this she paused to look up at him with great, sad eyes, a long, wistful look, then, speaking no more, hurried on down the stair—down, down into the shadows, and was gone.

"We used to go to school together, Geoff," the boy explained a little self-consciously. "She never kissed me before, she ain't the kissin' sort. I wonder why she did it to-night ! I wonder——"

Spike turned and led the way on again until they reached the landing above, across which two doors, dark and unlovely, seemed to scowl upon each other. One of these Spike proceeded to open with a latchkey, and so led Ravenslee into the dark void beyond.

Spike struck a match and lighted the gas ; and, looking about him, Ravenslee stared.

A little, cramped room, sparsely furnished, yet dainty and home-like, for the small deal table hid its bare naked- ness beneath a dainty cloth, the two rickety arm-chairs veiled their faded tapestry under chintz covers cunningly contrived and delicately tinted to match the cheap but soft-toned drugget on the floor and the self-coloured paper on the walls, where hung two or three inexpensive repro- ductions of famous paintings, and in all things there breathed an air of refinement wholly unexpected in Hell's Kitchen. Wherefore Mr. Ravenslee, observing all this with his quick glance, felt an ever-growing wonder. But now Spike, who had been clattering plates and dishes in the kitchen hard by, thrust his head round the door to say :

"Oh Geoff ! I don't feel like doin' the shut-eye business, d'you ? How about a cup of coffee ? An' I dare say I might dig out some eats. What d'ye say ? "

"Is this your sister ? " inquired Mr. Ravenslee, taking up a photograph from the little sideboard.

37

The Definite Object

" Yep, that's Hermy all right, taken las' year. Does
her hair different now. How about some coffee, Geoff ? "

" Coffee ! " said Mr. Ravenslee, staring at the photo,
" coffee—certainly—er—thanks ! She has light hair,
Spike ?"

" Gold," said Spike, and vanished, whereupon Mr.
Ravenslee laid the photo on the table, and, sitting down,
fell to viewing it intently.

A wonderful face, low-browed, deep-eyed, full-lipped.
Here was none of smiling prettiness, for these eyes were
grave and thoughtful; these lips, despite their soft,
voluptuous curves, were firmly modelled, like the rounded
chin below, and in all the face, despite its vivid youth,
was a vague and wistful sadness.

" Oh Geoff ! " called Spike, " d'ye mind havin' yer
coffee *à la* milko condenso ? "

" Milk ! " exclaimed Mr. Ravenslee, starting. " Oh—
yes—anything will do ! "

" Why, hallo ! " exclaimed Spike, reappearing with a
cup and saucer, " still piping off Hermy's photo, Geoff ? "

" I'm wondering why she looks so—sad ! "

" Sad ! " repeated Spike, setting down the crockery
with a rattle. " Hermy ain't sad, she always looks like
that. Ye see, she ain't much on the giggle, Geoff, but
she's most always singing, 'cept when her kids is sick or
Mulligan calls."

" What do you mean ? "

" Oh, Hermy mothers all the kids around here when
they're sick, an' lots o' kids is always gettin' sick. An'
when Mulligan comes it's rent day, an' sometimes Hermy's
a bit shy on the mazuma."

" Is she ? " said Mr. Ravenslee, frowning.

" You bet she is, Geoff ! An' Mulligan's an Irishman,
an' mean. Say, he's the meanest mutt you ever see.
A Jew's mean, so's a Chink, but a mean Harp's got 'em
both skinned 'way to Frisco an' back again ! Why,
Mulligan's that mean he wouldn't cough up a nickel to

38

see the Statue o' Liberty do a Salomy dance in de bay. So when the mazuma's shy Hermy worries some."

" Don't you help her ? " demanded Mr. Ravenslee.

" Help her ? Why, ye see Geoff, I—I ain't in a steady job yet. But I do my best, an'—— Why, there's de kettle boilin' at last ! " saying which, Spike turned and vanished again, leaving Mr. Ravenslee still staring down at the photo.

Presently Ravenslee sank back in his chair, and, lolling thus, looked sleepily at the opposite wall, but saw it not, nor heard the clatter of cups and saucers from the kitchen accompanied by Spike's windy whistling ; and, as he lounged thus, he spoke softly and to himself. " An object ! " he murmured.

" Hey, Geoff," Spike called, " this ain't goin' to be no *à la carte* hock an' claret feedin' match, nor yet no table-de-hoty eat-fest, but if you can do in some bacon an' eggs you're on."

" Why, then," said Mr. Ravenslee, rising and yawning, " count me decidedly ' on.' "

" D'you mind givin' me a hand wid de coffee ? "

" Delighted ! " and forthwith Mr. Ravenslee stepped out into the kitchen ; and there, in a while, upon a rickety table covered with a greasy newspaper, they ate and drank with great relish and gusto, insomuch that Mr. Ravenslee marvelled at his own appetite.

" Say, Geoff," inquired Spike, " how long are you stoppin' at Mulligan's ? A week ? "

" A week—a month—six months," replied his guest sleepily—" it's all according——"

" Accordin' to what ? "

" Well—er—circumstances."

" What circumstances ? "

" Circumstances over which I have no control—yet ! "

" You don't mean—me ? " queried Spike anxiously.

" Lord, no ! "

" And you'll never tell nobody that I——"

The Definite Object

"Meant to be—a thief?" drawled Mr. Ravenslee. "Not a word!"

Spike flushed, took a gulp of coffee, choked, and fell to sulky silence, while Mr. Ravenslee filled his pipe and yawned.

"Say," demanded Spike at last, "where'll you live while you're here?"

"Oh, somewhere, I suppose. I haven't bothered about where yet."

"Well, I been thinkin' I know where I can fix you up —perhaps."

"Very kind of you, Spike."

"There's Mrs. Trapes 'cross de landin', she lost her lodger last week—she might take you."

"Across the landing? She'll do," nodded Mr. Ravenslee.

"But I'm wonderin' if *you'll* do, she's a holy terror when she likes, Geoff."

"Across the landing! I'll put up with her," murmured Mr. Ravenslee.

"But say, you don't know Mrs. Trapes."

"Not yet, Spike."

"Well, she ain't no easy mark, Geoff! Most everybody in Mulligan's is scared of her when she cuts loose, she can talk ye deaf, dumb, an' paralysed, she can so. She sure is aces up on de chin-music, Geoff."

"But then she lives just opposite, and that circumstance, methinks, doth cover a multitude of——" Mr. Ravenslee yawned again.

"Anyway, it's a sure thing she won't take you if she don't like ye, Geoff."

"Why, then, she must like me!" said Mr. Ravenslee, and proceeded to light his pipe.

Whereupon Spike produced a box of cigarettes, but in the act of lighting one paused, and, sighing, put it away again.

"I promised de Spider I wouldn't, Geoff," he explained. "Ye see, I'm sort of in trainin,' and Spider says smoke's bad for de wind, and de Spider knows."

"Spider!" said Mr. Ravenslee, glancing up. "Do you mean Spider Conolly the light-weight?"

"That's de guy!" nodded Spike.

"Is he a friend of yours?"

"Sure! Him an' Bud M'Ginnis is goin' to get me some good matches soon."

"Boxing matches?"

"That's what they call 'em, Geoff. But there ain't much boxin' to it, real boxin' don't go down wid de sports, it's de punch they wanter see—good stiff wallops as jars a guy an' makes his knees get wobbly, swings an' jolts as makes a guy blind an' deaf an' sick. Oh, I been like that, an' I know, an' it ain't all candy t' hear everybody yellin' to the other guy to go in an' finish ye!"

"Does your sister know you fight?"

"Not much, she don't! I guess she'd like me to be a mommer's pet in lace collars an' a velvet suit, an' soft an' pretty in me talk. She's made me promise t' cut out de tough-spiel, an' so I'm tryin' to."

"Are you really, Spike?"

"Well, when she's around I do, Geoff."

"And she doesn't like you to fight, eh?"

"Nope! But, ye see, she's only a girl, Geoff."

"And that's the wonder of it," nodded Mr. Ravenslee.

"Wonder! What d'ye mean?"

"I mean that all these years she has managed to feed you, and clothe you, and keep a comfortable home for you, and she's—only a girl!"

"Well, an' ain't I tryin' to make good?" cried the boy eagerly.

"Are you really, Spike?"

"Sure! There's lots o' money in de fightin' game, an' I'm fightin' all for Hermy. If ever I get a champ I'll have money to burn, an' then she'll never be shy on de dollar question no more, you bet. There'll be no

The Definite Object

more needlework or Mulligan's for Hermy, no siree. It'll be a farm in de country, wid roses climbin' around, an' chickens, an'—an' automobiles, an' servants to come when she pushes de button—you bet!"

"Is she so fond of the country?"

"Well, I guess, yes! An' flowers—gee, she nearly eats 'em!"

"On the other hand," said Mr. Ravenslee, watching the smoke from his pipe with a dreamy eye, "on the other hand, I gather she does not like Mr. M'Ginnis. I wonder why?"

"You can search me!" answered Spike, "but it's a sure thing she ain't got no use for Bud."

"And yet you go around with him, Spike."

"But don't I tell ye he's been good t' me! He's goin' t' match me with some top-liners, he says if I can stick it I'll be a champion sure."

"Yes," nodded Mr. Ravenslee, "but when?"

"Oh, Bud's got it all doped out. But say——"

"And in the meantime your sister will go on feeding you, and clothing you, and——"

"Cheese it, Geoff," cried the boy, flushing, "you make a guy feel like a two-spot in the discard! I told you I'd try to get a steady job, an' so I will, but I ain't goin' to quit the fightin' game for nobody! 'N' say, I'm sleepy. How about it? You can have my bed, or the couch here, or you can get in Hermy's."

"Thanks, the couch will do, Spike."

"Then I guess it's me for the feathers!" said Spike, rising and stretching. "So long, Geoff!"

And in a while, having finished his pipe and knocked out the ashes, Mr. Ravenslee stretched his long limbs upon the chintz-covered sofa, and, *mirabile dictu*, immediately fell asleep.

CHAPTER V

HE awoke suddenly, and sat up to find the room full
of sunshine, and Spike standing beside him, a bright-
faced, merry-eyed Spike, very spruce and neat as to
person.

"Say, Geoff," said he, "I've seen Mrs. Trapes, an'
she wants you to go over so's she can pipe you off. 'N'
say, you're sure up against a catty proposition in her,
if you don't hit it off on the spot as soon as she gets her
lamps on to you it'll be nix for you, Geoff, an' nothin'
doin'."

"Lucid!" said Ravenslee, yawning, "and sounds
promising."

"Why, ye see, Geoff, she's got a grouch on because I
was out last night, so, if she gives you the gimlet eye at
first, just josh her along a bit. Now, slick yourself up
an' come on."

Obediently Mr. Ravenslee arose, and, having tightened
his neckerchief and smoothed his curly hair, crossed the
landing and followed Spike into the opposite flat, a place
of startling cleanliness as to floors and walls, and everything therein ; uncomfortably trim of aspect, and ornate
as to rugs and carpet and sofa cushions.

Mrs. Trapes herself was elderly ; she was also a
woman of points, being bony and sharp-featured, particularly at the elbows, which were generally bare—
indeed, they might be said to be her most salient and
obtrusive features, but her shrewd, sharp eyes held an

43

The Definite Object

elusive kindliness at times, and when she smiled, which was rarely, her elbows and her general sharpness were forgotten. She was awaiting them in her parlour, enthroned in her best easy-chair, a chair of green velvet where purple flowers bloomed riotously, her feet firmplanted upon a hearthrug cunningly enwrought with salmon-pink sunflowers. Bolt-upright and stiff of back she sat, making the very utmost of her elbows, for her sleeves being rolled high (as was their wont) and her arms being folded within her apron, they projected themselves to left and right in highly threatening fashion. Sphinx-like she sat, very silent and very still, while her sharp eyes roved over Mr. Ravenslee's person from the toes of his boots to the dark hair that curled short and crisp above his brow. Thus she looked him up and down, viewing each garment in turn ; lastly, she lifted her gaze to his face and stared at him eye to eye.

And eye to eye Mr. Ravenslee, serene and calm as ever, met her look, while Spike, observing her granite-like expression and the fierce jut of her elbows, shuffled and glanced toward the door. But still Mrs. Trapes glared up at Mr. Ravenslee, and still Mr. Ravenslee glanced down at Mrs. Trapes wholly unabashed, nay, he actually smiled, and, bowing his dark head, spoke in his easy, pleasant voice :

"A beautiful afternoon, Mrs. Trapes."

Mrs. Trapes snorted.

"This room will suit me—er—admirably."

Mrs. Trapes started slightly, opened her grim lips, shut them again, and—wriggled her elbows.

"Yes, indeed," continued Mr. Ravenslee pleasantly, "I like this room—so nice and bright, like the rug and wall-paper—especially the rug. Yes, I like the rug and the—er—stuffed owl in the corner !" and he nodded to a shapeless, moth-eaten something under a glass case.

Mrs. Trapes wriggled her elbows again, and spake harsh-voiced :

Mrs. Trapes acquires a New Lodger

" Young feller, that owl's a parrot ! "

" A parrot—of course," assented Mr. Ravenslee gently,
" and a very fine parrot, too. Then the wax flowers
and the antimacassars ! What would a home be without them ? " said he dreamy-eyed and grave. " I
think I shall be very bright and cheerful here, my dear
Mrs. Trapes."

Mrs. Trapes swallowed audibly, stared at Spike until
he writhed, and finally bored her sharp eyes into Mr.
Ravenslee again.

" Young man," said she, " what name ? "

" I think our friend Spike has informed you that I am
sometimes called Geoffrey. Mrs. Trapes, our friend
Spike told the truth."

" Young feller," she demanded, " 'oo are you, and—
what ? "

" Mrs. Trapes," he sighed, " I am a lonely wight, a
wanderer in wild places, a waif, a stray puffed hither and
thither by a fate perverse——"

" Talking o' verses, you ain't a poet, are you ? " inquired Mrs. Trapes. " Last poet as lodged wi' me useter
go to bed in 'is boots reg'lar. Consequently I ain't nowise drawed to poets."

Mr. Ravenslee laughed and shook his head. " Have
no fear," he answered, " I'm no poet, nor ever shall be.
I'm quite an ordinary human being, I assure you."

" Young feller—references ? "

" Mrs. Trapes, I have none—except my face. But
you have very sharp eyes ; look at me well. Do I strike
you as a rogue or a thief ? "

Here Spike, chancing to catch his eye, blushed painfully, while Mr. Ravenslee continued, " Come, Mrs.
Trapes, you have a motherly heart, I know, and I am
a very lonely being who needs one like you to—to cook
and care for his bodily needs, and to look after the good
of his solitary soul. Were I to search New York I couldn't
find another motherly heart so suited to my crying needs

45

The Definite Object

as yours. You won't turn me away, will you?" Saying which, Mr. Ravenslee smiled his slow, sleepy smile, and, wonder of wonders, Mrs. Trapes smiled too.

"When d'ye wanter come?"

"Now!"

"Land sakes!" she exclaimed.

"If it won't trouble you too much," he added.

"There's sheets to be aired——" she began, but checked suddenly to stare at him again. "Look a here, Mr. Geoffrey," she went on, "my terms is two-fifty a week, ten dollars *with* board, and a week in advance."

"Good!" nodded Mr. Ravenslee; "but since I'm coming in at such short notice I'll pay three weeks ahead just to—er—bind the bargain. See, that will be thirty dollars, won't it?" And, speaking, he drew a handful of crumpled bills from his pocket and proceeded to count out thirty dollars upon the green-and-yellow tablecloth.

"Sakes alive!" murmured Mrs. Trapes.

"And now," said he, "I'll just step round the corner with Spike to buy—er—a toothbrush."

"Toothbrush!" echoed Mrs. Trapes faintly.

"And a few other things. I shall be in early to supper."

"Would a nice English mutton-chop wiv tomatoes——"

"Excellent! And thank you, Mrs. Trapes, for sheltering a homeless wretch." So saying, her new boarder smiled and nodded, and, following Spike out into the hallway, was gone.

But Mrs. Trapes stood awhile to stare after him, lost in speculation.

"A toothbrush!" said she. "My! my!" Then she turned to stare down at the pile of bills. "Now I wonder," said she, right hand caressing left elbowjoint, "I jest wonder who he's been a-choking of to get all that money? But I like his eyes! And his smile! And he looks a man, and honest! Well, well!"

46

CHAPTER VI

HOW SPIKE INITIATED MR. RAVENSLEE INTO THE GENTLE ART OF SHOPPING

" Gee ! " exclaimed Spike as they descended the many stairs, " she sure give you the frosty face, Geoff, but it didn't seem to joggle you any."

" No, it didn't joggle me, Spike, because, you see, I like her."

" Like Mrs. Trapes ! You 'n Hermy are about the only ones, then, most every one in Mulligan's hates her an' gets scared stiff when she cuts loose ! But say, you do keep on rubbin' it in, I mean about—about thievin'."

" Probably it's your conscience, Spike."

" You won't ever go tellin' any one or blowin' de game on me ? "

" Spike, when I make a promise I generally keep it."

" Ye see, Geoff, it ain't as though I was a—a real crook."

" You meant to be."

" But I never stole nothin' in me life, Geoff."

" Suppose I hadn't caught you ? "

" Oh well, cheese it, Geoff—cheese it. Let's talk about somethin' else."

" With pleasure. When does your sister return ? "

" This evenin', I guess. But, Geoff, say now, do I look like a real crook—do I ? "

" No, you don't, Spike, that's sure. And yet, only last night——"

47

The Definite Object

"Ah yes, I know—I know," groaned the lad, "but I was crazy ; I think it was the whisky, Geoff, an' they doped me too, I guess. I don't remember much, after we left, till I found myself in your swell joint. God ! if I was only sure they doped me——"

" Who ? "

" Who ? Why—gee ! you nearly had me talkin' that time. Nix on the questions, Geoff. I ain't goin' to give 'em away, it ain't playin' square. Only, if two or three guys dopes a guy till a guy's think-box is like a cheese an' his mind as clear as mud, that poor guy ain't to be blamed for it, now, is he ? "

" Why, certainly," nodded Ravenslee.

" How d'ye make that out ? "

" For being such a fool of a guy as to let other guys fool him, of course. Sounds a little cryptic, but I guess you understand."

" Oh, I get you," sighed Spike drearily. " But say, didn't you come out to buy a toothbrush ? "

" And other things, yes."

" Well, say, s'pose we quit chewin' th' rag an' start in an' get 'em. There's a Sheeny store on Ninth Av. where you can get dandy shirts for fifty cents a throw."

" Sounds fairly reasonable," nodded Mr. Ravenslee as they turned up Thirty-ninth Street.

" Then you want a new lid, Geoff."

Mr. Ravenslee took off the battered hat and looked at it. " What's the matter with this ? " he inquired.

" Nothin', Geoff, only it wants burnin'," sighed Spike. " An' then, them boots—oh, gee ! "

" Are they so bad as that ? "

" Geoff, they sure are the punkest pavement-pounders in little old New York. Why, a Dago hod-carrier wouldn't be seen dead in 'em, look at th' patches. Gee-whiz ! Where did His Whiskers dig 'em up from ? "

" I fancy they were his own once," answered Mr.

48

The Gentle Art of Shopping

Ravenslee, surveying his bulbous, bepatched footgear a little ruefully.

"Well, I'll gamble a stack of blue chips there ain't such a phoney pair in Manhattan village."

"They're not exactly things of beauty, I'll admit," sighed Mr. Ravenslee, "but still——"

"They're rotten, Geoff. They're all to th' garbage-can. They are th' cheesiest proposition in side-walk slappers I ever piped off."

"H'm! You're inclined to be a trifle discouraging, Spike."

"Why, ye see, Geoff, I wancher t' meet th' push, an' I don't want 'em to think I'm floatin' around with a down-an'-out from Battyville. You must have some real shoes, Geoff."

"Enough, it shall be done," nodded Mr. Ravenslee.

"Well, tan Oxfords are all to th' grapes just now, Geoff. I don't mean those giddy-lookin' pumps with flossy bows onto 'em, but somethin' sporty, good an' yellow that'll flash an' let folks know you're comin'. An' here's Eckstein's."

With which abrupt remark Spike plunged into a shop, very dark and narrow by reason of a heterogeneous collection of garments, of ribbons and laces, of collars and ties of many shapes and hues, together with a thousand and one other things, that displayed themselves from floor to ceiling, amidst which Mr. Ravenslee observed a stir, a slight confusion, and from a screen of vivid-bosomed shirts a head protruded itself, round as to face and sleek as to hair.

"Greetin's, Ikey," said Spike, nodding to the head. "How's pork to-day?"

"Aw, vat you vant now, hey!" inquired the head, "vat's the vord? Now shpit it out."

"It ain't me, Moses, it's me friend wants a sporty fit-out, an' discount for spot cash, see? Show us your half-dollar shirts for a start, an' sporty ones, mind."

49

The Definite Object

Immediately out came drawers and down came boxes, and very soon the small counter was littered with piles of raiment variously gaudy, which Spike viewed and disparaged with such knowing judgment that the salesman's respect proportionately grew, and Mr. Ravenslee, lounging in the background, was forgotten quite, the while they chaffered after this manner :

Salesman—" Here vos a shirt as can't be beat for de money, négligée boosom an' turn-over cuffs, warranted shrunk, an' all for vun dollar."

Spike—" Come off, Aaron, come off ! Fifty cents is th' bid."

Salesman—" Fifty cents ! Vy, on Broadvay dey'd sharge you——"

Spike—" Wake up, Ike ! this ain't Broadway. An' fifty's the limit."

Salesman—" But shust look at dem pink shtripes, so vide as an inch. Dere's fifty cents' vorth of dye in dem shtripes, an' I'll give it you for seventy-five cents. On Broadvay——"

Spike—" We're gettin' there, Ikey, we're gettin' there, keep on, fifty's the call."

Salesman—" Fifty cents, oi ! oi ! I vould be ruined. A négligée boosom an' turn-over cuffs ! Vell, vell, I'll wrap it up, so, an' I make you a present of it for—sixty. An' on Broadvay——"

Spike—" Come on, Geoff, Aaron's talkin' in his sleep. Come on, we'll go on to Mendelbaum's, see, we want shirts, an' ties, an' socks, an' collars, an——"

Salesman—" Vait, vait ! Mendelbaum's a grafter—vait ! I got th' best selection of socks an' ties on Ninth Av'noo, an' here's a négligée shirt with turn-over cuffs, an' only fifty cents. But at Mendelbaum's or on Broadvay——"

In this way Mr. Ravenslee became possessed of sundry shirts whose bosoms blushed in striped and spotted splendour, of vivid-hued ties, and of handkerchiefs with

50

The Gentle Art of Shopping

flaming borders. From shop to shop Spike led him, and, having a free hand, bought right royally, commanding that their purchases be sent round hot-foot to Mulligan's. Thus Spike ordered and Mr. Ravenslee dutifully paid, marvelling that so much might be bought for so little.

"I guess that's about all the fixin's you'll need, Geoff!" said Spike, as they elbowed their way along the busy avenue.

"Well," answered Mr. Ravenslee as he filled his pipe, "it will certainly take me some time to wear 'em out, especially those shirts!"

"They sure are dandies, Geoff! Yes, those shirts are all to the lollipops! But say, you made a miscue gettin' them black shoes." And here Spike turned to stare down at his companion's newly acquired footwear. "Why not buy the yellow boys I rustled up for you? They sure were some shoes!"

"They were indeed, Spike."

"Gee, but it must feel good t' be able t' buy whatever you want!" sighed Spike dreamily. "Some day I mean to have a wad big enough t' choke a cow, but I wish I had it right now!"

"What would you do with it?"

"Do with it—well, say, first off I'd—I'd buy Hermy them roses—th' whole lot," and he pointed where, among the push-carts drawn up against the curb was one where roses bloomed, filling the air with their sweetness. "An' next she should——"

"Then go and buy 'em, Spike!" and, speaking, Mr. Ravenslee thrust a bill into Spike's hand.

"Gee—a twenty-spot! Can I, Geoff?" he cried, his blue eyes shining. "Th' whole lot—on de level?"

"On the level."

Spike started joyfully away, paused, turned, and came back with head adroop. "I guess it can't be done, Geoff," he sighed.

The Definite Object

" Why not ? "

" Well, ye see, it ain't as if it was my own money, really."

" But it is ! "

" No, it ain't ! I haven't earned it, Geoff, an' I ain't a guy as sponges on his pals—not much I ain't. Take your money, Geoff. When I buy Hermy anythin', it's goin' to be bought with money as I've earned."

So Mr. Ravenslee thrust the bill back into his pocket, and thereafter walked on, frowning and very silent, as one lost in perplexed thought.

Wherefore, after more than one furtive glance at him, Spike addressed him with a note of diffidence in his voice.

" You ain't sore with me, are you, Geoff ? "

" Sore with you ? "

" I mean, because I—I didn't take your money ? "

Here Mr. Ravenslee turned to glance down at Spike and clap a hand upon his shoulder. " No," he answered, " I'm not sore with you. And I think—yes, I think your sister is going to be proud of you one day."

And now it was Spike's turn to grow thoughtful, while his companion, noting the flushed brow and the firm set of the boyish lips, frowned no longer.

" Hello, there's Tony ! " exclaimed Spike, as they turned into Forty-second Street, " over there, behind th' push-cart—th' guy with th' pea-nuts ! " and he pointed where, from amid a throng of vehicles, a gaily painted barrow emerged, a barrow whereon were pea-nuts unbaked, baked, and baking, as the shrill small whistle above its stove proclaimed to all and sundry. It was propelled by a slender, graceful, olive-skinned man, who, beholding Spike, flashed two rows of brilliant teeth and halted his barrow beside the curb.

" How goes it, Tony ? " questioned Spike.

Whereat the young Italian smiled, and thereafter sighed and shook his head.

52

The Gentle Art of Shopping

"Da beezeneez-a ver' good," he sighed; "da pea-nut-a sell-a all-a da time! But my lil' Pietro he sick, he no da same since his moder die-a, me no da same—have-a none of da luck—noding—nix!"

"Hard cheese, Tony!" quoth Spike. "But say, have you seen th' Spider kickin' around?"

"No, I ain't! But you tell-a da signorina——"

"Sure I will."

"My lil' Pietro he love-a da signorina, me, I love-a her—she so good, so generosa, ah yes!" and taking off his hat in one hand, Tony kissed the other and waved it gracefully in the air.

"Right-oh, Tony!" nodded Spike. "You can let it go at that. An' say, this is me friend Geoff."

Tony gripped Mr. Ravenslee's hand and shook it. "You one o' da bunch—one o' da boys, hey? Good-a luck."

So saying, Tony nodded, flashed his white teeth again, and, seizing the handles of his barrow, trundled off, his pea-nut oven whistling soft and shrill.

"Tony's only a guinney," Spike explained as they walked on again, "but he's white, Geoff, 'n' say, he's a holy terror in a mix-up! Totes one o' them stiletto-knives. I've seen him stab down into a glass full of water an' never spill a drop, which sure wants some doin'."

Evening was falling, and dismal Tenth Avenue was wrapping itself in shadow, a shadow made more manifest by small lights that burned dismally in small and dingy shops, a shadow, this, wherein moving shadows jostled with lounging shoulder or elbow. Now, as they passed a certain dark entry where divers of these vague shadows lounged, a long arm was stretched thence, and a large hand gripped Spike's shoulder.

"Why, hello, Spider!" said he, halting, "what's doin'?"

"Nawthin' much, kid—only little M—— Say, who's wid you?"

53

The Definite Object

" Oh, this is a friend o' mine—Geoff, dis is de Spider ! "

Visualised in the Spider, Ravenslee saw a tall, slender youth, very wide in the shoulder and prodigiously long of arm and leg, who looked at him keen-eyed from beneath a wide cap-brim, while his square jaws worked with untiring industry upon a wad of chewing-gum.

" Good-evening," said Ravenslee, and held out his hand.

The Spider ceased chewing for a moment, nodded, and, turning to Spike, chewed fiercer than ever.

" Where you'se goin', kid ? " he inquired, masticating the while.

" What was you goin' to tell me, Spider ? " demanded Spike, a note of sudden anxiety in his voice.

" Nawthin', kid."

" Aw, come off, Spider. What was it ? "

The Spider glanced up at the gloomy sky, glanced down at the dingy pavement, and finally beckoned Spike aside with a quick back-jerk of the head, and, stooping close, whispered something in his ear—something that caused the boy to start away with clenched hands and face of horror—something that seemed to trouble him beyond speech, for he stood a while dumb and staring, then found utterance in a sudden, hoarse cry :

" No, no ! It ain't true. Oh, my God ! "

And with the cry Spike turned sharp about, and, springing to a run, vanished into the shadows.

" What's the matter ? " demanded Ravenslee, turning on the Spider.

" Matter ! " repeated that youth, staring at him under his cap-brim again, " well, say, I guess you'd better ask de kid."

" Where's he gone ? "

" How do I know ? "

" It isn't his sister, is it ? "

" Miss Hermione ? Well, 1 guess not." So saying,

the Spider, chewing ferociously, turned and vanished down the dark entry with divers other shadows.

For a moment Mr. Ravenslee stood where he was, staring uncertainly after him. Presently, however, he went on toward Mulligan's, though very slowly, and with black brows creased in frowning perplexity.

CHAPTER VII

IT was in no very pleasant humour that Geoffrey Ravenslee began to climb the many stairs (that much-trodden highway) that led up to his new abode. He climbed them slowly, frowning in a dark perplexity, and wholly unconscious of the folk that jostled him or paused to stare after him as he went.

But presently, and all at once, he became aware of one who climbed half a flight above him, and, glancing up, he saw a foot in a somewhat worn shoe, a shapely foot nevertheless, joined to a slender ankle, which peeped and vanished alternately beneath a neat, well-brushed skirt that swayed to the vigorous action of the shapely limbs it covered. He was yet observing the soft, rounded curves of this most feminine back when he became aware of two facts : one, that she bore a heavy suit-case in her neatly gloved hand ; two, that the tress of hair peeping rebellious beneath the neat hat-brim was of a wondrous yellow gold.

Instantly he hastened his steps, and, reaching out his hand, almost instinctively, sought to relieve her of her burden.

"Allow me," said he.

She stopped, and, turning on the stair above, looked down on him with a pair of wondering blue eyes ; her cheeks glowed and she was panting a little. For a long moment they fronted each other thus silently upon that grimy, narrow stair, she above with gracious head

56

Ankles, Stairs, and Neighbourliness

stooped, her dark eyes questioning and wistful. And, looking up into the flushed loveliness of her face, those eyes deep and soft beneath their long black lashes, the tender droop of those vivid lips—beholding all this, he knew her to be a thousand times more beautiful than any photograph could possibly portray, wherefore he bared his head, and, striving to speak, could find no words to utter. For a moment longer she hesitated, while her clear eyes searched his face, then the red lips curved in a little wistful smile.

" Thank you," she said, and, yielding him her burden, led the way upstairs. " I'm afraid it's rather heavy," she said over her shoulder after they had climbed another flight.

" It's quite too heavy for you," he answered.

" Oh, but I've carried it often before now."

" Then you shouldn't."

" But I have to."

" No," said Ravenslee, shaking his head, " you should let your brother bring it up for you."

" My brother ! " she exclaimed, pausing to look her amazement.

And again, as she stood thus poised above him, he took note of the warmth of her rich colouring, the soft, round column of her white throat, the gracious breadth of hip and shoulder.

" You know I have a brother ? "

" Oh yes, Spike—er—that is, Arthur and I are quite —er—ancient cronies—pals, you know—friends, I mean." Mr. Ravenslee was actually stammering.

" Oh, really ? " she said softly ; but, all at once becoming aware of the fixity of his regard, the colour deepened in her cheek, the long lashes drooped, and, turning away, she went on up the stair.

" It's a long way up yet. Hadn't you better let me take it ? "

" Not for worlds," he answered.

The Definite Object

"Isn't it getting heavier?" she inquired, as they climbed the next flight.

"Decidedly heavier."

"Then, please," said she, slackening her pace—"please let me take it."

"On the contrary," he answered, his gaze on her slender foot and ankle, "I should like to carry it for you all my—er—ah, that is, I mean——"

Mr. Ravenslee was stammering again.

"Yes?"

He was aware that the shapely foot had faltered in its going. "As often as I may, Miss Hermione."

Hereupon the shapely foot halted altogether, and once again she turned to look at him in wide-eyed surprise.

"You know my name?"

"I learned it from Arthur, and I shall never forget it."

"Why not?"

"Well, because it is rather uncommon, and very beautiful."

"Oh!" said Hermione, and went on up the stair again, yet not before he had seen the flush was back in her cheek. "Are you getting tired yet?" she inquired, without looking round.

"Not appreciably," he answered, "but if you think I need a rest——"

"No, no!" she laughed, "we should never get off these frightful stairs."

"Even that might have its compensations," he murmured.

"And we've been much longer than if you'd let me carry it up myself."

"But then we've no cause for panting haste, have we?" he suggested.

"And we have four more flights to climb," she answered.

"So few!" he sighed.

Ankles, Stairs, and Neighbourliness

"You see, I live at the very tip-top."

"Good!" said he.

At this she glanced down at him over the sweep of her shoulder. "Why 'good'?" she demanded.

"Because I also live at the tip-top."

"Do you—oh!"

"With the excellent Mrs. Trapes."

"But I thought she had lost her lodger?"

"She had the—er—extreme good fortune to find a new one to-day."

"Meaning you?"

"Meaning me."

By this time they had reached the topmost landing, where Mr. Ravenslee set down the suit-case almost reluctantly.

"Thank you!" said Hermione, looking at him with her frank gaze.

"Heaven send I may earn your thanks again, and very soon!" he answered, lifting the battered hat.

"You didn't tell me your name," said she, fumbling in a well-worn little hand-bag for her latchkey.

"I am called Geoffrey."

Hermione opened the door, and, taking up the suit-case, held out her hand. "Good-bye, Mr. Geoffrey."

"For the present," said he; and though his tone was light, there was a very real humility in his attitude as he stood bareheaded before her. "For the present," he repeated.

"Well, we are very near neighbours," said she, dark lashes adroop.

"And neighbourliness is next to godliness—er—isn't it?"

"Is it?"

"Well, I think so, anyway. So, Miss Hermione, not 'good-bye.'"

Now at this she glanced swiftly up at him, flushed, and turning about, was gone. But even so, before her door closed quite, she spoke soft-voiced, "Good-evening, Mr. Geoffrey."

Thereafter, for a space, Mr. Ravenslee stood precisely where he was, staring hard at the battered hat. Yet it is not to be supposed it was the sight of this that could possibly have brought the smile to his lips and into his eyes a look that surely none had ever seen there before—such a preposterously shabby, disreputable old hat! Of course not.

CHAPTER VIII

OF CANDIES AND CONFIDENCES

"Oh!" said Mrs. Trapes, "so you've come? Good land! Mr. Geoffrey, there's parcels an' packages been a-coming for you constant ever since you went out. Whatever have you been a-buying of?" and, opening the door of his small bedroom, she indicated divers packages with a saucepan-lid she happened to be holding.

"Well," said her lodger, seating himself upon the bed, "if I remember rightly, there are shirts, and socks, and pyjamas, and a few other oddments of the sort. And here, when I can get it out of my pocket, is a box of candies. I don't know if you are fond of such things, most of the sex feminine are, I believe. Pray take them as a mark of my—er—humble respect."

"Candy!" exclaimed Mrs. Trapes, turning the gaily bedecked box over and over, and glaring at it fierce-eyed. "Fer me?"

"If you will deign acceptance."

"Candy!" she repeated, elbows a-twitch, "Fer me? Land sakes, Mr. Geoffrey, I—I——" Here, very abruptly, she turned about and vanished into the kitchen.

Mr. Ravenslee, lounging upon his white bed, was taking languid stock of his purchases when Mrs. Trapes suddenly reappeared, clutching a toasting-fork. "Mr. Geoffrey," she said, glaring still, "them candies must ha' cost you a sight o' money?"

"True, certain monies were expended, Mrs. Trapes."

"They must ha' cost you well-nigh a dollar-fifty, I reckon?"

The Definite Object

"They did," nodded Mr. Ravenslee, smiling.

"My land!" exclaimed Mrs. Trapes, and vanished again.

Mr. Ravenslee was sighing over a hideously striped shirt when Mrs. Trapes was back again, flourishing a very large tablespoon.

"Mr. Geoffrey," said she, "it's nigh forty years since any one bought me a box o' chocolates. An' now they look so 'cute, all done up in them gold an' silver wrappin's, as I don't wanter eat 'em, seems a sin, it do. But, Mr. Geoffrey, I—I'd like to thank ye." And lo! she was gone again.

Mr. Ravenslee had just pitched the striped shirt out of the window, when, behold, Mrs. Trapes was back yet once more, this time grasping a much-battered but much be-polished dish-cover.

"Mr. Geoffrey," said she, "I ain't good at thankin' folks, no, I ain't much on gratitood, never having had much to gratify over, but them candies is goin' to be consoomed slow an' reverent, and in a proper sperrit o' gratitood. And now, if you're ready to eat your supper, your supper's a-waitin' to be ate."

So saying, she led the way into the parlour, where, upon a snowy cloth, in a dish tastefully garnished with fried tomatoes, the English mutton-chop reposed, making the very most of itself, the which Mr. Ravenslee forthwith proceeded to attack with surprising appetite and gusto.

"Is it tender?" inquired Mrs. Trapes anxiously. "Heaven pity that butcher if it ain't! Is it tasty, kind of?"

"It's delicious," nodded her lodger. "Really, Hell's Kitchen seems to suit me. I eat and sleep like a new man."

"So you ain't lived here long, Mr. Geoffrey?" queried Mrs. Trapes, eagle-eyed.

"Not long enough to—er—sigh for pastures new.

Candies and Confidences

Don't go, Mrs. Trapes, I love to hear folks talk. Sit down and tell me tales of dead kings, and—er—I mean, converse of our neighbours, will you?"

"I will so, an' thank ye kindly, Mr. Geoffrey, if you don't mind me sucking a occasional candy."

"Pray do, Mrs. Trapes," he said heartily. Whereupon, having fetched her chocolates, Mrs. Trapes ensconced herself in the easy-chair, and, opening the box, viewed its contents with glistening eyes.

"You're an Englishman, ain't you?" she inquired after a while, munching luxuriously.

"No; but my mother was born in England."

"You don't say!" exclaimed Mrs. Trapes. "So was I—born in the Old Kent Road, Mr. Geoffrey. I came over to N' York thirty long years ago as cook-general to Hermy Chesterton's ma. When she went and married again I left her an' got married myself to Trapes, a fireman, Mr. Geoffrey, with a noble 'eart, as 'ad wooed me long." Here Mrs. Trapes opened the candy-box again, and, after long and careful deliberation, selected a chocolate with gentle, toil-worn fingers, and, putting it in her mouth, sighed her approbation. "They sure are good," she murmured. "But talkin' of Hermy Chesterton's ma," she went on after a blissful interval, "I been wondering where you came to meet that b'y Arthur."

"Ah, Mrs. Trapes!" sighed Ravenslee, leaning back in his chair and shaking a rueful head, "you touch on gloomy matters. As the story-books say, 'thereby hangs a tale,' the dismal tale of a miserable wretch whose appetite was bad, whose sleep was worse, and whose temper was worst of all—oh, a very wretched wretch indeed!"

"My land!" exclaimed Mrs. Trapes, stopping abruptly in the act of masticating a large chocolate walnut, "so bad as that, Mr. Geoffrey?"

"Worse!" he nodded gloomily. "It is, indeed, a gloomy tale, a tale dark and dismal that I love not the

The Definite Object

telling of, for, Mrs. Trapes, that more than hopeless wretch stands, or rather sits, before you."

" Save us ! " ejaculated Mrs. Trapes. " Meanin' yourself ? "

" My unworthy self."

" Lord ! " she whispered, " what you been a-doin' of ? "

" Wasting a promising life, Mrs. Trapes."

" You mean," she questioned in a harsh whisper —" you mean as you've killed some one accidental ? "

" Oh no, the life was mine own, Mrs. Trapes."

" Land sakes, Mr. Geoffrey, you give me quite a turn ! Ye see, sometimes folks gets theirselves killed around here, an' it's always accidental, sure ! " and Mrs. Trapes nodded meaningly, and went on chewing. " But say," she demanded, suddenly sharp of eye, " where does Arthur come in ? "

" Arthur comes in right here, Mrs. Trapes. In fact, Arthur broke into my—er—life just when things were at their darkest generally. Arthur found me very depressed and gloomy. Arthur taught me that life might yet have its uses. Arthur lifted me out of the Slough of Despond. Arthur brought me to you ! And, behold, life is good, and perchance shall be even better, if—ah yes, if ! So you see, my dear Mrs. Trapes, Arthur has done much for me, consequently I have much to thank Arthur for. Indeed, I look upon Arthur——"

" Shucks ! " exclaimed Mrs. Trapes, " that'll be about enough about Arthur—Arthur, indeed ! You oughter know his sister."

Now at this her lodger started and glanced at her so suddenly, and with eyes so unexpectedly keen, that once again she suspended mastication.

" Now, in the name of all that's wonderful, Mrs. Trapes, why mention her ? "

" Why, because she's worth knowin'. Because she's the best, the bravest, the sweetest thing that ever went

in petticoats. She's beautiful inside and out, mind!
I've nursed her in these arms years ago, an' I know
she's—oh, well, you ought t' meet Hermy."

"Mrs. Trapes, I have."

"Eh? You have? My lan——!" Mrs. Trapes bolted
a caramel in her astonishment, and thereafter stared at
Ravenslee with watering eyes. "An' you to sit there
an' never tell me!" quoth she; "an' Hermy never
told me. Well, well! When did ye meet her? Whereabouts? How?"

"About half-an-hour ago. Coming up the stairs. I
carried her grip."

"Well!" exclaimed Mrs. Trapes, staring, "well,
well!" and she continued to munch candy and to
stare and say "well" at intervals until arrested by a
new thought. "That b'y!" she exclaimed. "Was
Arthur with her?"

"No," answered Ravenslee, wrinkling his brows, "I
lost him on my way home."

Mrs. Trapes sighed and shook her head. "The sun
sure rises and sets for her in that b'y, an' him only her
step-brother at that."

"Her step-brother?"

"Yes," nodded Mrs. Trapes emphatically. "Hermy's
ma were a lady, same as Hermy is, so were her pa—I
mean a gentleman, of course. But Hermy's father died,
an' then her ma, poor soul, goes an' marries a good-
lookin' loafer way beneath her, a man as weren't fit
to black her shoes, let alone take 'em off! An' Arthur's
his father's child. Oh, a good enough b'y as b'ys go,
but wild now an' then, an' rough, like his dad."

"I see," nodded her hearer thoughtfully.

"Now, me, though married ten long year, never 'ad
no children so, ever since Hermy's mother died, I've
tried to watch over her an' help her as much as I could.
Ah! she's had a mighty hard struggle, one thing an'
another, Mr. Geoffrey, an' now I've known her an'

The Definite Object

loved her so long it kind o' seems as if she belonged to me almost."

"She looks very good and brave," said Mr. Ravenslee.

"Good!" cried Mrs. Trapes, and snorted. "I tell you she's jest a angel o' light, Mr. Geoffrey. If you'd seen her, like I have, goin' from one poor little sick child to another, kissing their little hot faces, tellin' 'em stories, payin' for doctor's stuff out of her bit o' savings, mendin' their clo'es—ah, yes! an' prayin' over 'em when they died, why, I guess you'd think she was a angel too. One sure thing," said Mrs. Trapes rising, "there ain't a breathin' man in all this whole round earth as is fit to go down on 'is knees an' kiss 'er little foot—not a one! No, sir!"

"No, I don't think there is," said Mr. Ravenslee slowly.

"As for that Bud M'Ginnis," cried Mrs. Trapes, seizing on the coffee-pot much as if it had been that gentleman's throat, "I'd—I'd like to bat him one as would quiet him for keeps. I would so!" and she jerked the coffee-pot fiercely, much to the detriment of her snowy tablecloth. "There, now, see what I've done! But I do get all worked up over that loafer."

"Pray, why?"

"Why?" snorted Mrs. Trapes indignantly. "Hasn't he made eyes at her ever since they was kids together? Hasn't he worried an' worried at her, an' because she won't look at him if she can help it, don't he try to get back at 'her through that b'y?"

"How does he?"

"How? By puttin' him up to fightin' an' all sorts o' devilment, by teachin' him to be tough, by gettin' him drunk."

"Oh, does he?"

"Oh, bless ye, Bud M'Ginnis can do anything with him."

"How so?"

Candies and Confidences

"Because Arthur jest worships M'Ginnis for his strength an' toughness."

"Ah, I see."

"Yes, Arthur thinks there's nobody in the world could lick Bud M'Ginnis."

"H'm! May I smoke, Mrs. Trapes?"

"Sure ye may," she nodded, and began to collect the supper things. "I tell you what," she exclaimed suddenly, flourishing the fork she had just taken up, "if somebody would only come along an' thrash M'Ginnis —thrash him good—it would be a sight better for every one round here—it would so! M'Ginnis is always makin' trouble for some one or other, an' there ain't a man big enough or got heart enough to stand up to him, not even Spider Conolly. Wish I was a man, that's all, just for an hour! Ah!" Here Mrs. Trapes snorted fiercer than usual, and the jut of her elbows was deadly.

"And he gets Arthur drunk, does he?" said Ravenslee, puffing dreamily at his pipe.

"Yes," sighed Mrs. Trapes as she loaded a tray with the supper things. "Hermy's seen him drunk twice to my knowing, an' I thought it would break her heart, poor dear. Ye see, Mr. Geoffrey, his father died o' the drink, an' she's frightened for fear Arthur should go the same road. Oh, Hermy's life ain't all ice-cream-sodas an' lollipops—not much it ain't, poor, brave, beautiful thing!"

Saying which, Mrs. Trapes, sighing again, took up her tray. Mr. Ravenslee, having opened the door for her, closed it, lighted his pipe, and, sinking into the easy-chair, fell into frowning thought.

The windows were open, and from the crowded court below rose the shrill babel of many children's voices, elfin shrieks and cries, accompanied by the jingle of a barrel-organ, very wiry and very much out of tune, but Ravenslee, deep-plunged in thought, heard nought of it, nor heeded the fact that the pipe, tight-clenched between his strong white teeth, was out. For Geoffrey Ravenslee had set himself a problem.

The barrel-organ ceased its jangle; the children's voices were gradually hushed as, one by one, they were called in by shrill-voiced mothers, and led away to bed, and the gloomy court grew ever gloomier as evening deepened into night. But still Mr. Ravenslee lounged in the easy-chair, so motionless that he might have been asleep except for the grim set of his jaw and the bright, wide-open eyes of him.

At last, and suddenly, he sat erect, for he had heard a voice whose soft murmur he recognised even through the closed door.

"I don't know, Hermy dear," came in Mrs. Trapes's harsh tones. "I'm afraid he's gone to bed. Anyway, I'll see." Ensued a knocking of bony knuckles, and, opening the door, Ravenslee beheld Mrs. Trapes, and behind her Hermione, in whose eyes he saw again that look of wistful, anxious fear he had wondered over at the first.

"Oh, Mr. Geoffrey," said Mrs. Trapes, "it's eleven o'clock, an' that b'y ain't in yet. Here's Hermy been out hunting the streets for him, an' ain't found him. Consequently she's worriting herself sick over him—drat 'im!"

"Out on the streets!" repeated Ravenslee, "Alone?"

"Yes," answered Hermione, "I had to—try and find him."

"But alone. And at this hour, Miss Hermione, that was surely very—er—unwise of you?"

"Yes, you see I didn't know where to look," she sighed. "I've been to the saloon, but he wasn't there."

"The saloon! Good Lord!" exclaimed Ravenslee, his placidity quite forgotten, his face set and stern, "that is no place for you, or any girl."

"I must go to find Arthur," she said softly.

Candies and Confidences

"No, not there, even for that. Think of the—the risks you run. No girl should take such chances."

"Oh, you mean that!" said Hermione, meeting his eyes with her frank glance. "But no one would try to insult me hereabouts, this isn't Broadway or Fifth Avenue, Mr. Geoffrey!" and she smiled a very sad, weary little smile. "But I came to ask if you happened to know where Arthur is, or whom he was with?"

"Wasn't wid that Bud M'Ginnis, was he?" questioned Mrs. Trapes sharply.

"No, he wasn't with M'Ginnis," answered Mr. Ravenslee in frowning perplexity, "but that's about all I can tell you."

"Thank you," sighed the girl. "I must go and try again. I know I shall find him soon." But, though she tried to speak in a tone of cheerful confidence, her shapely head drooped rather hopelessly.

"You mean you are going out on to the—to look for him again?"

"Why, of course," she answered, "I must find Arthur."

"Don't, Hermy, don't—so pale an' tired as you are, don't go again," pleaded Mrs. Trapes, her usual sharpness transfigured into a deep and yearning tenderness, even her voice seemed to lose something of its harshness, "don't worry, my sweet, the b'y 'll find his way home right enough, like he did last time."

"Like last time!" cried Hermione, and, shivering, she leaned against the wall as if she were faint. "Ah, no, no!" she whispered, "not like last time!" and, bowing her head, she hid her face in her hands.

Close, close about that quivering form came two motherly arms, and Mrs. Trapes fell to passionate invective and tender soothing thus:

"There, there, my love, my pretty, don't remember that last time! Oh, drat my fool's tongue for remindin' you, drat it, my dear, my honey! Ah, don't go breakin'

69

The Definite Object

your angel's heart along of Arthur, my precious—and drat him too! That b'y 'll come back all right, ne will —he will, I know he will, oh, if I was only behind 'im with a toasting-fork! There, there, Hermy dear, don't fret, Arthur 'll come home all right. My honey, you're all tuckered out, an' here it's gettin' on to midnight, an' you go to Englewood by the early car. Go to bed, dear, an' I'll sit up for Arthur. Only don't cry, Hermy."

"Oh, I'm not crying, dear," said Hermione, lifting her head. "See, I haven't shed a tear. But I must find Arthur. I couldn't rest or sleep, I should lie listening for his step. So, you see, dear, I must go out and find him."

Hereupon, with swift, dexterous fingers, Hermione straightened the very neat hat which the embrace of Mrs. Trapes had rendered somewhat askew, and, turning to the door, came face to face with Mr. Ravenslee, and in his hand she beheld his battered head-gear, but she did not notice how fiercely his powerful fingers gripped it.

"Miss Hermione," said he, in his soft, indolent voice, and regarding her beneath languid, drooping lids, "pray accept the hospitality of my—er—apartment. You will find the easy-chair is very easy, and while you sit here with Mrs. Trapes I'll find your brother and bring him here to you."

"Thank you," she answered, a little shortly because of his lazy tone or his sleepy eyes, or his general languid air, or all of them together, "thank you, but I'm going myself, I must go, I—I couldn't wait."

"Oh, but really you must, you know."

"Must?" she repeated, looking her surprise.

"Ab-solutely must," he answered softly, nodding so sleepily that she almost expected him to yawn. "You really can't go out again to-night, you know," he added.

Hermione's blue eyes flashed, her delicate brows knit

themselves, and Mr. Ravenslee saw that she was taller than he had thought.

" You mean you will try to stop me ? " she demanded.

" No, I mean that I will stop you."

" But you'd never dare."

" I would dare even your anger in so good a cause. Ah, please don't be angry with me, Miss Hermione, because "—and here his sleepy voice grew positively slumberous—" you shall not go out into the streets again to-night."

" Ah, an' that's right too, Mr. Geoffrey ! " cried Mrs. Trapes. " Hermy needs some one strong enough to master her now an' then, she is that wilful, she is so ! "

But now all at once, as he watched, Hermione's eyes filled with great, slow-gathering tears, her firm-set lips grew soft and quivered pitifully, and she sank down in the easy-chair, her golden head bowed upon the green-and-yellow tablecloth. The battered hat tumbled to the floor, and, striding forward, he had bent and caught one of her listless hands all in a moment, and there-after, though it struggled feebly once, he held it close prisoned in his own.

" Ah, don't ! " he pleaded, his words coming quick and eager, " don't do that ! Oh, do you think I can't see that you're all overwrought ? How can I let you go tramping out there in the streets again ? You couldn't go—you mustn't go ! Stay here with good Mrs. Trapes, I beg of you, and I swear I'll bring Arthur to you. Only you must promise me to wait here and be patient how-ever long I am. You must promise, Hermione."

Now at this she lifted her heavy head and looked at him through her tears. And surely, surely in the face that bent above her was none of indolence or languor ? These lips were firm now and close-set, these lazy eyes were wide and bright, and in them that which brought the warm colour to her cheeks ; but reverence was there also, wherefore she met his look, and her fingers were not withdrawn from his until she had answered, "I promise."

"That's my wise dearie!" nodded Mrs. Trapes, "An' good luck to you, Mr. Geoffrey, an' when you find that b'y say as I wish—ah, how I wish! I was back of him with a toasting-fork, that's all!"

Then Mr. Ravenslee caught up the shabby hat, opened the door, and, going out, closed it softly behind him.

"Hermy," said Mrs. Trapes, clasping the girl's slender waist in her long arm, and leading her into the brightest of bright little kitchens, "I like that young feller. Who he is I don't know, what he does I don't know, but what he is I do know, an' that's a man, my dear. An' he called you Hermione. Sounds kind o' pretty the way he says it, don't you think?"

But Hermione didn't answer.

Meanwhile Mr. Ravenslee, descending the monotonous stairs, paused suddenly to smile and clap hand to thigh.

"A toasting-fork!" said he, "a toasting-fork is an instrument possessing three or more sharp points. Ha! Mrs. Trapes is a woman of singularly apposite ideas." And he smiled a little grimly as he went on down the stairs.

CHAPTER IX

WHICH RECOUNTS THE END OF AN EPISODE

MIDWAY down he beheld two burly policemen, who mounted one behind the other, their grey helmets, blue coats, and silver buttons seeming to fill the narrow stairway.

"Anything wrong?" he inquired as they drew level.

"Not wid you dis time, bo," answered one, blandly contemptuous, and strode on up the stair, twirling his club in practised hand, his fellow-officer at his heels.

Thus rebuked, Mr. Ravenslee looked after them with quick-drawn brows, until, remembering his broken hat-brim and shabby clothes, he smiled and went upon his way. Reaching the dingy lower hall, he beheld the solitary gas-jet aflare, whose feeble light showed five lounging forms, rough fellows, who talked together in hoarse murmurs and with heads close together.

He was passing by, when, in one of these deep-throated talkers, he recognised the long limbs and wide, sloping shoulders of the Spider. Mr. Ravenslee paused, and nodded. "Good-evening," said he, but this time kept his hands in his pockets.

The Spider eyed him somewhat askance, shifted his wad of chewing-gum from one cheek to the other, and spoke.

"'Lo!" said he.

"Do you know where Spike is?"

"S'pose I do—then what?" demanded the Spider, with a truculent lurch of his wide shoulders.

73

The Definite Object

"Then I shall ask you to tell me where I can find him—or, better still, you might show me."

"Oh, might I?"

"You might."

Now here, the feelings of the Spider waxing beyond mere words, he looked at the speaker, viewed him up and down with a glance of contemptuous hostility, whereat Ravenslee's whole expression melted into one of lamb-like meekness.

"Say," quoth the Spider at last, "there's only one thing as I can't stand about you, an' that's—everything!"

"Sorry for that," murmured Ravenslee, "because I rather like you, Spider. I think you could be quite a decent fellow if you tried very hard. Come, shake your grouch and let's be friends."

"Say," growled the Spider, "what you're sufferin' from 's a hard neck. You ain't no friend o' mine, not much you ain't—savvy? So crank up an' get on yer way like a good little feller."

"But, you see, I'm anxious to find Spike, because——"

"Well, say, you keep on bein' anxious, only do it somewhere else, I don't want youse around where I am —see? So beat it while de goin' 's good."

"Why—er—no," said Ravenslee in his laziest tones— "no, I don't think I'll beat it. I guess I'll stay right here and wait until you are so kind, so—er—very kind and obliging as to show me where I can find Spike." And he sighed plaintively as he lounged against the wall behind, but his eyes were surprisingly bright and quick beneath the shadow of the battered hat.

"Hully chee!" exclaimed the Spider, expectorating contemptuously, "hark to the flossy-boy, fellers!—Aw, run away now," said he, scowling suddenly, "run away before ye get slapped on th' wrist." And, while divers of his companions laughed hoarsely, he turned a contemptuous back on Mr. Ravenslee, but, even then, he

74

Which Recounts the End of an Episode

was seized in iron fingers that clutched his shoulder, and in that painful grip was jerked suddenly round again, to behold a face vicious-eyed, thin-lipped, square-jawed, fiercely out-thrust; and, recognising the "fighting-face," the Spider, being a fighter of a large and varied experience, immediately "covered up," and fell into that famous crouch of his that had proved the undoing of so many doughty fighters ere now. Then, like a flash, his long arm shot out; but, in that same instant, Ravenslee, timing the blow to a fraction, moved slightly, and the Spider's knuckles bruised themselves against the wall at the precise moment that Ravenslee's open hand flipped lightly on the side of the Spider's square, lean jaw.

The Spider drew back, staring from Ravenslee's tall, alert figure to his broken knuckles and back again, while his companions stood by in mute and wide-eyed wonder.

"Spider," said Ravenslee, shaking his head in grave reproof, "you were rather slow that time! Very foolish to leave your point uncovered, and offer me your jaw like that, you know."

Five pairs of eyes stared at the speaker with a new and sudden awakened interest, and, beholding in him that lithe assurance of poise, that indefinable air that bespeaks the trained pugilist, and which cannot be mistaken, elbows were nudged and heads wagged knowingly.

Ravenslee's grey eyes were shining and his pale cheeks tinged with colour.

"Ah, Spider," said he, "life is rather worth while after all—isn't it? Spider, I like you better and better. Come, don't be a surly Spider, shake hands!"

"T' hell wid youse!" growled the Spider, covering up again and, though his face was sulky, yet was no trace of contempt there now.

"I suppose," mused Ravenslee, looking him over with knowledgeful eye, "yes, I judge, as you are now, you would fight about seven or eight pounds over your ring-

The Definite Object

side weight. Spider, you'd have to give me thirty pounds! Spider, I could eat you! Come, shake hands and let's go and fetch Spike."

Now, speaking, Ravenslee smiled with eyes as well as lips, beholding which, the Spider grew slowly upright, his knotted fists unclenched and, staring Ravenslee in the eyes, he reached out slowly and by degrees and grasped the proffered hand.

"Say," said he, falling to violent mastication of his eternal chewing-gum, "who'd you have de mitts on with last, an' when?"

"Oh, it seems ages ago!" sighed Ravenslee, "but where's Spike?"

"Say, bo, who wants him, an' whaffor? Spike's me pal, see—so I jest shore wants ter savvy who wants him, an' why."

"His sister."

"Hully chee! why didn't youse say so at first? When Miss Hermione wants anything she's gotta have it, I guess!—Ain't that right, fellers?"

"You bet," chimed the four.

"So if she wants de kid, I guess I'll jest have to fetch him for her. Come on, bo! S' long, fellers."

Hereupon, having acknowledged the friendly salutes of the four, Ravenslee followed the Spider out into the court, empty now and silent.

"Say, bo, where'd you meet up wid Spike anyway?" inquired the Spider, as they strode along Tenth Avenue. "You don't belong around here, do you?"

"No. Do you know where he was last night?"

"You can search me, bo. All I savvy is he was off on some frame-up or other."

"Who with?"

"Well, not wid me."

"Did you see any one with him beside M'Ginnis at O'Rourke's?"

"No, there was only them two."

76

Which Recounts the End of an Episode

"Ah, I guessed as much," said Ravenslee, nodding, "he went away with M'Ginnis—good!"

"Say, bo," questioned the Spider when they had gone some way in silence, "I ain't seen you fight anywheres, have I?"

"No, but I've seen you, Spider. I saw you beat Larry M'Kinnon at 'Frisco."

"Which sure was some fight!" nodded the Spider. "Them half-arm jolts of his sure shook me some. He'd have got me in the third if I hadn't clinched."

"He was a terror at in-fighting."

"He sure was, bo."

"It was your jabbing and foot-work won you that fight, Spider, one of the best I've ever seen—very little clinching and clean breakaways."

"Larry sure was game all through, yes—right up to the knock-out. A good, clean fighter. 'N' say, bo, I was real sorry to see him counted out."

"It meant a big purse for you, I remember."

"Oh, sure, I had money to burn. I ain't got much left now, though," said the Spider ruefully.

"You came pretty near being a world's champion, Spider."

"Aw—jest near enough t' miss it, I guess. Talkin' o' champeens, the greatest of 'em, th' best fightin' man as ever swung a mitt, I reckon, was Joe Madden, as retired years ago. Nobody could ever lick Joe Madden."

"Did you know him?"

"Not me, bo, I wasn't in his class. But I seen him fight years ago."

"Do you think Spike will ever make a champion?" inquired Ravenslee suddenly, "I mean if he were given every chance?"

"Well," answered the Spider slowly, "he sure has the grit, there ain't nothin' on two legs he's afraid of except—himself, bo. He's too high-strung—nerves is his trouble, I reckon. Why, chee! when he's in de ring

77

The Definite Object

he can't be still a minute, can't let himself rest between rounds, see ? He kinder beats himself, I guess."

" I know what you mean," nodded Ravenslee, " and I'm sure you're right. By the way, have you ever seen M'Ginnis fight ? "

" I seen him scrap once or twice—he's sure ugly in a rough-house, but in th' ring—well, I dunno."

" Has he a punch ? "

" Bo, he's got a sleep-pill in each mitt if—if he can land his wallop right. Yes, siree, if Bud can hit a guy where it'll do most good, that guy's sure goin' to forget his cares an' troubles for a bit. But he's slow an' heavy, Bud is, though I ain't never seen him mix it in th' ring, mind."

" H'm," said Ravenslee thoughtfully. " Ha ! M'Ginnis seems to have it all his own way around here—why ? "

" Well, because Bud's Bud, an' because Bud's old man is a Tammany boss—which gives Bud a big pull wid de police—'nuff said, I guess ? "

" Quite ! " nodded Ravenslee, and walked thereafter deeper in thought than ever. " Where are you taking me ? " he inquired as they turned a sudden corner.

" To de river."

" This is Eleventh Avenue, then ? "

" Yep ! Watch out you don't trip on de railroad tracks." And now the Spider seemed to have become thoughtful also, and somewhat gloomy, judging by his face as seen by an occasional feeble light as they traversed the unlovely thoroughfare.

" Bo," said he suddenly, " I'm thinkin' there's some guys in this world as would be better out of it. I'm thinkin' of some guy as got a little girl into trouble—an' left her to it. Her kid died, an' her folks turned her out, an' she'd have died too, I guess, if it hadn't been for Miss Hermione an' old Mother Trapes—ye see, she was all alone, poor little kid. Now a man as would treat a girl that ways ain't got no right t' live, I reckon.

Which Recounts the End of an Episode

I should like t' know who that guy was! I should like t' meet that guy—once." After this the Spider became more gloomy than ever, and spoke only in surly monosyllables. Suddenly he turned off along a narrow, ill-lighted alleyway that led them between divers small, mean houses, and tall, dark warehouses, and brought them suddenly out upon the misty foreshore, beyond which the dim and mighty river flowed. On they went, the Spider's depression growing perceptibly, until at last their feet trod the rough planking of a narrow causeway which ended in a dark, raft-like structure moored out in the river. Here was a small and dismal shack, from whose solitary window a feeble ray of light beamed.

What was it?

Ravenslee shivered suddenly and stopped to stare about him, while his listless hands changed to tight-clenched fists.

What was it?

What was there about this dismal, silent place that seemed to leap at him all at once from the dimness, he knew not whence? Was it the shack, with its solitary light, or the broad river lapping with soft sighings and low weeping sounds among the piles below, or was it something in the altered aspect of the guiding figure that led him forward, slow and ever slower, as if with dragging feet, and yet with feet that trod so softly?

"Spider," said he at last, speaking in a hushed and breathless manner, "Spider, where are we?" and, speaking, he shivered again even while his clenched hand wiped the sweat from his brow. The Spider made no answer, for the feeble light was blotted out by a very solid something which, approaching softly, resolved itself into a burly, blue-clad form whose silver buttons and shield showed conspicuous.

"What's doin'?" demanded a voice, "who is it?" The voice was hoarse and authoritative, but the gruff tones were schooled, it seemed, to an almost unnatural softness.

The Definite Object

" 'S all right, Micky," answered the Spider in the same subdued tone, " it's only me come for de kid."

" Who you got wid you there, Spider ? "

" A pal o' mine an' de kid's—he's all right, Mick."— Then to Ravenslee, " Come on, bo ! " Slowly they approached the shack, but, reaching the door, the Spider hesitated a long moment ere, lifting the latch, he led the way in.

A fairly large room lighted by a lamp that stood upon a rickety table, where sat a young-faced, white-haired man, very industriously writing within a small account book ; upon the table before him were a number of articles very neatly arranged, among which Ravenslee noticed a cheap wrist-watch, a hair-comb, a brooch, and a small chain purse. He was yet gazing at these and at the white-haired man, who, having nodded once to the Spider continued to write so busily, when he was startled to hear a long-drawn, shuddering sigh. Turning suddenly sharp about, he stared toward a certain dark corner where, among a litter of oars, misshapen bundles, boxes, and odds and ends, was a small stove, and, crouched above it, his head between his hands, he beheld Spike.

With the same instinctive feeling that he must be silent, Ravenslee approached the boy and touched him on the shoulder. Spike started and glanced up, though without lifting his head.

" Your sister is anxious about you. Why are you here ? "

" Don't you know, Geoff ? Ain't no one told ye ? "

" What do you mean ? "

" I'll show ye ! "

The boy took a hurricane lamp from the floor beside him, and, having lighted it, brought Ravenslee farther into that littered corner, where, among the boxes and bundles and other oddments, lay what seemed to be two or three oars covered with a worn tarpaulin.

Which Recounts the End of an Episode

"Look, Geoff—you remember—only this morning!"
Very gently he raised a corner of the tarpaulin, and,
looking down, Ravenslee's breath caught suddenly.

A woman's face, very young and very placid-seeming.
The long dark hair framing the waxen features yet oozed
drops of water like great, slow-falling tears; then, beholding this pale, still face, Ravenslee knew why he had
shivered and hushed voice and step, and instinctively
he bowed his uncovered head.

"You remember Maggie Finlay, Geoff—this morning
on the stairs? She—she kissed me good-bye, said she
was goin' away; this is what she meant—the river,
Geoff! She's drowned herself, Geoff! Oh, my God!"
and letting fall the tarpaulin, Spike was shaken suddenly
by fierce, hysterical sobbing.

Whereat the man, looking up from his writing spoke
harsh-voiced:

"Aw, quit it, kid, quit it! Here I've just wrote down
three rings, and she's only got one, an' that a cheap
fake. Shut up, kid, you'll make me drop blots next.
Cut it out—it ain't as if she was your sister."

Hereupon Spike started and lifted a twitching face.

"My sister!" he repeated, "my sister—whatcher
mean? My God, Chip, Hermy could never—come to—
that;" and, shivering violently, Spike turned and
stumbled out of the shack.

Once outside, Ravenslee set his long arm about him
and felt the lad still trembling violently.

"Why, Spike," said he, "buck up, old fellow."

"Oh Geoff, Hermy could never——"

"No, no, of course not." So, very silently, together
and side by side, they crossed the narrow causeway.

"Gee, but I'm cold," said the boy between chattering
teeth as they turned along the wide avenue. "I—I
guess it's shook me some, Geoff. Ye see, I used to go
to school with Maggie once—an' now, my God!"

Reaching Mulligan's at last, they beheld numerous

The Definite Object

groups of whispering folk who thronged the little court, the doorway, and the hall beyond; they whispered together upon the stairs and murmured on dim landings. But as Ravenslee and Spike, making their way through these groups, mounted upward, they found one landing very silent and deserted, a landing where was a certain battered door whose dingy panels had been wetted with the tears of a woman's agony, had felt the yearning, heart-broken passion of a woman's quivering lips such a very few hours ago. Remembering which, Geoffrey Ravenslee, turning to look at this grimy door, beheld it vague and blurred and indistinct as he climbed that much-trodden stair.

Upon the top landing they found Mrs. Trapes, who leaned over the rails to greet them.

"So you found that b'y, Mr. Geoffrey. Hermy 'll be glad. You'll have heard of poor little Maggie Finlay? Poor lass! poor lonesome lass! 'Twas her father drove her to it, an' now he's had a fit—a stroke, the doctor's with him now, an' Hermy of course. She's always around where trouble is. I guess there won't be much rest for her to-night, long past midnight now. I'm glad you found that b'y, I said you would. I'll just go down and tell Hermy, she'll be glad."

Spike stood a while, after Mrs. Trapes had gone downstairs, very silent and with head a-droop, then slowly and heavily turned and opened his door, but paused to speak over his shoulder in a hoarse whisper.

"Geoff, if ever any man made my sister go through what Maggie Finlay went through I'd shoot him dead, by God in heaven I would!"

CHAPTER X

IT was a week later, and Mr. Ravenslee leaned from the window of his room observing the view, which chiefly consisted of dingy brick walls and dingier windows, and swaying vistas of clothes in various stages of dampness, clothes that fluttered from many lines stretched across the court from window to window, at different altitudes ; for to-day it had been washing-day in Mulligan's, also the evening was warm. So Mr. Ravenslee lounged and smoked and gazed upon the many garments, viewing them with eyes of reverie. Garments these, of every size and hue and shape and of either sex, garments that writhed and contorted themselves in fantastic dances when the soft wind gently stirred them—a small, cool wind which, wafting across the river from the green New Jersey shore, breathed faintly of pine-woods. He was yet in absorbed contemplation of the aerial gambols of these many garments when to him came Mrs. Trapes, clutching a hot iron.

" Mr. Geoffrey, what'll you eat for supper ! " she demanded.

" Mrs. Trapes, what do you suppose I'm worthy of ? "

" How about a lovely piece o' liver ? "

" Liver ! " he repeated, rubbing a square, smooth-shaven chin. " H'm ! liver sounds a trifle clammy, doesn't it ? Clammy and cold, Mrs. Trapes ? "

" Cold," said she, staring, " cold—of course not. It would be nice an' hot, with thick gravy an' a tater or so. An' as for clammy, whoever heard o' liver as wasn't ? Calves' liver, mind ! They can't put me off with sheep's, no, siree ! Skudder's young man tried to once, he did so."

" Foolish, foolhardy young man ! " murmured Ravenslee.

" Mr. Geoffrey," sighed Mrs. Trapes, and her elbows were particularly needle-like, " I jest took that piece o' sheep's liver an' wrapped it round that young man's face."

" Unhappy young man ! " murmured Mr. Ravenslee.

" Ye see, Mr. Geoffrey, though a widder, an' therefore lorn, I ain't to be trod on in the matter of livers or anything else."

" I'm sure of it, Mrs. Trapes."

" But if you don't kind of fancy liver, how about sassiges? Sassiges is tasty an' filling, an' cheap. What d' ye say to sassiges ? "

" Sausages ! " answered Mr. Ravenslee, shaking grave head, " sausages demand such unbounded faith in the —er—sausagee, or should it be sausageor ? "

" Oh, well, a chop cut thick an' with a kidney in it, what d' ye say to a chop now ? "

" No, a chop in an hour, Mrs. Trapes, or say two hours, will be most welcome. Are you very busy ? "

" Washing's all done, but there's a lot o' your shirts waiting to be ironed, an' me here lettin' me iron get cold."

" Oh, never mind the shirts, Mrs. Trapes. Pray sit down, I need your counsel and advice."

" But me iron ? "

" Give it to me. There ! " and Mr. Ravenslee deposited it outside on the fire-escape.

" Now, Mrs. Trapes," said he, " first of all I must find work. " 'Man is born to labour as the sparks fly upward,' you know."

" Born to sorrer, you mean," she corrected.

84

How Mr. Ravenslee went into Trade

"Precisely," he nodded, "work is sorrow and sorrow is work, at least I know a good many people who think so."

"More fools them," quoth Mrs. Trapes, folding her arms.

"My own idea exactly," he answered, lazily tapping out his pipe on the window-sill.

"I ain't noticed you sweating none lately," quoth Mrs. Trapes sarcastically.

"Alas, no, Mrs. Trapes, there being no wherefore to call forth the aforesaid—er—moisture. Still, 'man is as grass that withereth' unless he 'goeth forth unto his labour.'"

"An' quite right too," nodded Mrs. Trapes. "If I had my way I'd make 'em all work."

"That would be rather hard on our legislators and Fifth Avenue parsons, wouldn't it? Anyway, I want work, that's sure."

"Ye mean as your money's all gone?"

"Very nearly," sighed Mr. Ravenslee with a suitable air of dejection. And he did it so well that Mrs. Trapes, viewing him askance, frowned, bit her lip, wriggled her elbows, and finally spoke. "Are ye up against it good, Mr. Geoffrey?"

"I am."

"Well," said she, frowning down at the vivid-coloured hearthrug, "I got twenty-five dollars put away as I've pinched and scrinched to save, but, if you want the loan of 'em, you can have 'em and welcome."

Her lodger was silent, indeed he was so long in answering that at last Mrs. Trapes looked up, to find him regarding her with a very strange expression. "And you will lend me your savings?" he asked softly.

"Sure I will," and she would have risen then and there but that he stayed her.

"God bless you for a generous soul!" said he, and laughed rather queerly, also his grey eyes were a little

85

The Definite Object

brighter than usual. " Why should you trust me so far ? "

" Well, you look honest, I guess. An' then we all help each other in Mulligan's now an' then, one way or another, we jest have to. There's Mrs. Bowker, third floor, the tea an' sugar as I've loaned that woman, an' last week a lovely beef-bone! Well, there! but if you want the loan of that twenty-five——"

" Mrs. Trapes, I don't. Things aren't so desperate as that yet. All I need is a job of some sort."

" What kind o' job ? "

" I'm not particular."

" Well, what have you been used to ? "

" Alas ! Mrs. Trapes, hitherto I have lived a life of— er—riotous ease."

" That means as you ain't worked at all, I guess. H'm ! " said Mrs. Trapes viewing him with her sharp hawk's eye, " and yet you ain't got the look of a confidence man nor yet a swell crook, consequently I take it you was the only son of your father, an' lost all he left you, eh ? "

" Mrs. Trapes, you are a truly wonderful woman ! "

" T' be born the only son of a rich father is a pretty bad disease, I reckon," she continued. " Yes, siree, it's bad for the child an' worse for the man, it's bound to be his ruination in the end—like drink. An' talkin' o' drink, I'm glad to see that b'y Arthur's so fond o' you."

" Oh ! why ? "

" Because you don't drink."

" Well, I don't go to bed in my boots, do I, Mrs. Trapes ? But then I promised you I wouldn't, and, for another thing, I'm not a poet, you see," said he, and yawned lazily.

" Hermy says she's glad too."

Mr. Ravenslee cut short his yawn in the middle.

" Hermione ! Did she say so ? When ? "

How Mr. Ravenslee went into Trade

"Ah, I guessed that would wake ye up a bit!" said Mrs. Trapes, noting his suddenly eager look. "It's a pity you're so poor, ain't it?"

"Why? What do you mean?"

"I mean if you had been in a good situation an' makin' good money—twenty-five per, say—you might have asked her."

"Asked her?" repeated Ravenslee, staring, "asked her what?"

"Why, t' marry you o' course," nodded Mrs. Trapes. "You love her about as much as any man can love—which is sometimes a thimbleful an' sometimes a bit more! But you sure love her as much as a man knows how, I guess. An' don't try for ter deny it, Mr. Geoffrey. I ain't blind, leastways I can see a bit out o' one eye sometimes, specially where Hermy's concerned, I can so! O' course you ain't worthy of her, but then no man is."

"No, I'm not worthy of her, God knows!" said Ravenslee quite humbly.

"An' Hermy's goin' to marry a man with money. Her heart's set on it firm."

"Money!" said Ravenslee, scowling, "she seems anything but mercenary!"

"Mercenary!" cried Mrs. Trapes. "I should say not. I tell ye she could be a-rollin' around in a six-thousand-dollar automobile at this very hour if she was that kind. With her face an' figure, she could so."

"What do you mean?"

"I mean as there's men—rich men—ah, an' married too—as is mad after her."

"Ah!" said Ravenslee, frowning again.

"You may well say 'ah!'" nodded Mrs. Trapes. "Men is all beasts more or less. Why, I could tell you things—well there! Hermy ain't no innocent babe, but there's some things better than innocence, and that's a chin—will-power, Mr. Geoffrey. If a woman's sweet

an' strong an' healthy like Hermy, an' got a chin, nothin'
can harm her. But beauty like hers is a curse to any
good woman if she's poor, beauty being a quick-seller,
ye see."

"Yes, I see—I know!" said Ravenslee, clenching his
hands and frowning blacker than ever.

"But," continued Mrs. Trapes, and here she leaned
forward to touch him with an impressive, toil-worn
hand, "Hermy Chesterton's jest an angel o' light an'
purity, she always has been an' always will be, but she
knows about as much as a good girl can know. She's
seen the worst o' poverty, an' she's made up her mind,
when she marries, to marry a man as is a man an' can
give her all the money she wants. So ye see it ain't no
good you wastin' your time danglin' around after her,
an' sighin'—now, is it?"

"Why, no, Mrs. Trapes? I think I'll speak to her
to-night——"

"My land! Ain't I jest been tryin' to show you as
you ain't a fit or worthy party to speak, an' as you won't
have a chance if you do speak, her heart bein' set on
wealth? But you can't speak—you won't speak—I
know you won't?"

"Why not?"

"First, because t'night she's away at Englewood
makin' a dress for Mrs. Crawley as is very fond of her.
An', second, because you ain't the man to ask a girl to
marry him when he ain't got nothin' t' keep her on—you
know you ain't!"

"Which brings us back to the undoubted fact that
I must get a job—at once."

"H'm!" said Mrs. Trapes, viewing his clean-cut
features and powerful figure with approval, "What could
ye do?"

"Anything, so long as I can make good, Mrs. Trapes.
What would you suggest?"

"Well," said Mrs. Trapes, caressing an elbow thoughtfully, "grocers' assistants makes good money, an' I know Mr. Smith wants a butter-man."

"Good!" nodded Ravenslee, "should like to batter butter about——"

"Are ye used to butter?"

"Oh, I've a decided taste for it!"

"Know much about it?"

"Certainly. It is a yellowish fatty substance concocted by human agency, supposedly from the lacteous secretion of the graminivorous quadruped familiarly known as the common (or garden) cow."

"Landsakes!" said Mrs. Trapes, drawing a deep breath, "you sure do know something about it. Ever worked in it before?"

"Only with my teeth."

"Ah, quit your jollying, Mr. Geoffrey, if you want me t' help you."

"Solemn as an owl, Mrs. Trapes."

"Well, then, there's Jacob Pfeffenfifer wants a young man in his delicatessen store."

"Mrs. Trapes, I can slice ham and beef with any one on earth."

"D' ye understand picklin' an' seasonin'?"

"Ah, there you have me again. I fear I don't."

"Then you ain't no good to Jacob Pfeffenfifer!"

"On second thoughts I'm not wholly sorry," answered Ravenslee gravely, "you see, a name like that would worry me, it would shake my nerve. I might cut beef instead of ham, or ham instead of——"

"Mr. Geoffrey!" quoth Mrs. Trapes, squaring her elbows.

"Sober as a judge, Mrs. Trapes, and—— By Jupiter!"

"My land! What is it?"

"An idea—look!" and Ravenslee pointed down into the yard.

"Why, it's only Tony!" said Mrs. Trapes, glancing down a vista of riotous garments.

The Definite Object

" Precisely," answered Ravenslee, rising and stretching his long arms. " Tony has solved my difficulty, I'll go into the pea-nut trade."

" What ! Sell pea-nuts ? You ! "

" Why not ? 'Man is born '——you know."

" But—my land ! Only dagos an' guinneys sells pea-nuts ! "

" Splendid ! I shall be the exception, Mrs. Trapes. Anyway, a pea-nut man I'll be ! " And, catching up his disreputable hat, Ravenslee nodded and left his landlady staring after him and murmuring " Well ! " at intervals. But presently she reached for her iron, stone-cold long since, and stood a while clutching it in bony fingers, and staring at nothing in particular.

" He's sure a man, Hermy, my dear ! " she said at last, nodding at the stuffed parrot in the corner. " I've watched him careful, an' I know. An' there's some things better than money, my dear—ah, much better ! So, if I should help to bring you into his arms—man' an wife, my dear—why, I guess it would be the best thing Ann Angelina Trapes ever done—yes, ma'am." Saying which, she went back to her ironing.

On the stairs Ravenslee met Spike, who hailed him joyously. " Say, Geoff, I'm all alone to-night, come an' eat supper with me—how about it ? "

" Suppose you have supper at Mrs. Trapes's with me ? "

" No, she gets on me nerves, so come on over, will you ? "

" With pleasure."

" 'N' say, I'm a few chips shy on butter, Geoff—bring in ten cents' worth, will you ? "

" Right-oh, comrade, I'll be with you anon. Make boil the kettle against my coming," and Ravenslee hasted down the stairs. Reaching the court, he met the Italian trundling his barrow toward a certain shed, its usual nocturnal biding-place.

How Mr. Ravenslee went into Trade

"How goes it, Tony?" he inquired, shaking hands. The Italian nodded and flashed his teeth.

"Ver-a good, pal!" he answered.

"Tony, where can I get a pea-nut outfit like yours?"

"Ha! You go-a in-a da pea-nut-a beezneez, hey? You want-a push-a-de-cart, hey?"

"That's it, Tony."

"Ver-a good!" nodded the good-natured Italian. "You come-a long-a me, pal. I take-a you get-a push-a-de-cart, up-a de street—yes."

Having very soon locked away his barrow, the loquacious Tony forthwith led Ravenslee along certain streets and into a certain yard, where presently appeared a stout man with rings in his ears, who smiled and nodded and greeted them with up-flung finger and the word *altro*. Presently Ravenslee found himself examining a highly ornate barrow fitted with stove, etc., complete unto the whistle, and mounted upon a pair of the rosiest wheels he had ever seen. Thereafter were more smiles and nods, accompanied by the ever-recurrent *altro*, the transfer of certain bills into the stout man's pocket, and Geoffrey Ravenslee sallied forth into the street, bound for Mulligan's, with the chattering Tony beside him and the gaily-painted barrow before him, receiving many friendly hints as to the pitfalls and intricacies of the pea-nut trade, and hearkening with unflagging interest to the story of "lil Pietro," and the unbounded goodness of "da Signorina Hermione."

CHAPTER XI

ANTAGONISM IS BORN, AND WAR DECLARED

"Why, hello, Hermy!" exclaimed Spike, pausing in the doorway. "Gee, I thought you was—were in Englewood."

Hermione lifted her golden head, stayed her humming sewing-machine, and smiled at him. "And I thought I'd come home and surprise you. Aren't you glad to see me, boy dear?"

"Why, sure I am!" he answered, and, stooping, kissed a certain golden curl that wantoned at her white temple; which done, he sprawled in the easy-chair, and, taking a newspaper from his pocket, fell to studying the latest base-ball scores, while Hermione, head bent above her work again, glanced at him now and then rather wistfully.

"Gee-whizz!" he exclaimed suddenly, "the Giants put it all over Cincinnati to-day, Hermy. Ye see, Matty was in th' box, an' he sure pitched some game!"

Hermione stopped her machine and looked at him under wrinkling brows. "I thought you were hunting through the 'wanted' columns, Arthur?"

"Why, ye see I ain't—haven't got to the ads. yet, Hermy."

Hermione sighed softly, and, resting her round chin in her hands, viewed him silently a while, until, becoming aware of the steadfast gaze of those sweet and gentle eyes, Spike shuffled uneasily and changed colour.

"Arthur," she said softly, "when you promised me to try and find a situation you meant it, didn't you?"

Antagonism is Born, and War Declared

"Sure I did."

"That was a week ago, dear."

"But, Hermy, I went after that office-boy's job. You know I did."

"Yes, dear, though you got there too late."

"No, I wasn't late, Hermy, only another guy happened t' get there first, an' got the job. A kid I could have licked with one hand too, one of these mommer's pets in a nobby sack-suit, all dolled up in a clean collar an' a bow-tie an' grey kid gloves. I guess his outfit helped him a whole lot, an' ye see I'm a few chips shy on clothes, I guess."

Hermione looked at her brother's worn garments, shiny at elbow and knee, and as she looked her eyes were suddenly suffused.

"Yes, dear, I—I'm afraid they are—rather shabby," she admitted humbly. "Your clothes always did seem to wear out so very quickly. And—and it costs so much to live. And—sometimes I grow—afraid."

The smooth, low voice faltered and ended upon a sob. Spike stared in wide-eyed amaze, for seldom had he seen his sister thus; but now, beholding the droop of that brave head, seeing how her strong white hands gripped each other, he tossed the paper aside, and, flinging himself on his knees, clasped her in his arms.

"Don't cry, Hermy!" he pleaded. "Oh, don't cry! I—I can't bear it. You know I love you best in the world. Ah, don't cry, dear! I—I'll hunt up a job first thing—honest, I will."

"But your clothes are so very shabby!" she sobbed. "And oh, boy dear, I have only just enough to—to pay our rent this month, so I can't get you any more—yet, dear!"

"Hermy," said he brokenly, "oh, Hermy, you make me feel so mean, I—I—— One sure thing, you're never goin' t' spend your money on clothes for me any more—the money you work so hard for!—never any more,

The Definite Object

Hermy dear. You've done enough for me I guess, an'
now it's up t' me to help you, and—and—oh gee!" Here
Spike's voice broke altogether; whereupon Hermione,
quite forgetting her own sorrows and worries, fell to
soothing and comforting him as she had done many and
many a time during his motherless childhood.

"Say, Hermy," said he at last, his tear-stained cheek
pillowed on her soft, round bosom, "you won't think me
a—an awful kid for—for cryin', will you?"

"I think I love you all the better, boy dear, and—
I'm sure it has done us both good." And, smiling down
at him through her tears, she kissed him.

"I'll start in an' rustle up a job right away, Hermy,"
said he, rising and nodding grimly.

"Oh boy," said she, looking up at him fondly, "I
shall be so proud of you! It wouldn't matter what it
was, or how little you got at first, so long as it was decent
and honourable. And I'm sure you'll get on. Mr.
Geoffrey thinks so too."

"Does he? I'm glad o' that. Say, how d'ye like
Geoff?"

"Oh, well, I've only seen him two or three times,"
said Hermione, folding away her work preparatory to
cooking supper.

"Is that all?" said Spike, smoothing out the paper
and scowling at the long columns headed "youths
wanted."

"Ye-es, I think so."

"But you an' him's always meetin' on the stair, ain't
—aren't you?"

"You should say 'you and he,' dear."

"Well; but aren't you?"

"We have met—once or twice."

"D'ye like him?"

"Well, he's so very—different! And rather lazy!
And awfully sleepy! And yet I don't think he's sleepy
really, somehow."

94

Antagonism is Born, and War Declared

"Sleepy!" exclaimed Spike, "well, I guess not! Lazy I dunno, but he sure is all to the wide-awake-o. When he looks sleepiest I guess he's widest awakest. And he ain't a—isn't a bad looker, is he?"

"He has nice eyes," Hermione admitted.

"Oh, I don't mean his eyes!" quoth Spike disgustedly. "I mean his arms an' legs an' shoulders."

"They are nice and wide," nodded Hermione.

"I should like t' see Geoff in th' ring. He'd strip big."

"Oh, really," said Hermione, taking a very large apron from the table-drawer. "Boy dear, I do wish you weren't always thinking of fighting."

"All right, Hermy dear. But there ain't no flies on Geoff. 'N' say, I wantcher to like him, 'cause I kinder think he's all to the cream-puffs an'——"

"Boy!" cried Hermione, lifting an admonishing finger.

"I'm sorry, my tongue kinder slipped, Hermy. But I have been tryin' t' keep tabs on me talk—honest, I have."

"Yes, dear. You haven't been quite so frightful lately."

"Ye see, Hermy, you're different. You went to a swell school, an'——"

"And you never did, I know, dear. But oh, Arthur, I did the best I could!"

"And a lot better than I deserved," said he, reaching out to pat her hand caressingly. "When I get a good job I'll stay in nights and study hard like you want me to. I sure will."

"Yes, dear, and you'll soon be heaps cleverer than I am," said she, stooping to kiss his curly head as she tied the apron about her shapely hips, and thereafter, giving him a smiling nod, vanished into the kitchen, while Spike laboured through the long columns headed "youths wanted."

The Definite Object

And presently, as she moved lightfooted to and fro in the kitchen, he heard her singing softly to herself an old, old song of other days that had often been his lullaby when he was a small, motherless armful of sleepiness hushed in her young, protecting clasp.

" Arthur ! " she called.

" Hello ! " he answered.

" Are you hungry ? "

" You bet I am ! "

A long pause, whereafter ensued the following conversation between kitchen and parlour :

Hermione—" Boy dear ! "

Spike—" Hello ! "

Hermione—" Be a dear and lay the cloth for me."

Spike—" Right-oh ! "

A longer pause, during which Spike rises and takes cloth from sideboard drawer.

Hermione—" Arthur ! "

Spike—" Yes ? "

Hermione—" Where did you meet him ? "

Spike (starting)—" Who ? "

Hermione—" Mr. Geoffrey. How did you happen to meet each other ? "

Another pause, while Spike stands frowning in perplexed thought.

Spike—" Where did you say the cloth was ? "

Hermione—" In the sideboard drawer. How long have you known him ? "

Spike (beginning to lay the cloth feverishly)—" Oh, a goodish time. Say, Hermy, he sure likes your name a whole lot ! "

Hermione—" Oh ! " (a very small pause) " Likes my name, does he ? "

Antagonism is Born, and War Declared

Spike—"He sure does. He told me so."

Hermione—"Oh!" (another small pause) "Just what did he say, boy dear?"

Spike—"He said it was Greek an' very beautiful, an' then I said it kind of fitted you, because you were aces up on the face an' figure question."

A rush of petticoats, and enter Hermione, flushed and laughing.

"You dear boy!" she cried, "for that you shall be kissed!" which he was forthwith; after which she turned to the mirror to smooth back a shining tress of hair—that same rebellious curl that glistened above her fine, black eyebrow. "Where did you say you first met him—Mr. Geoffrey?" she inquired suddenly, still busied with the rebellious curl.

Spike started, and glanced uneasily at her shapely back.

"Say, Hermy," said he, a little huskily, "have you got anything for supper?"

"Not much, dear, I'm afraid."

"That's a pity!"

"Why?"

"Oh, because I asked him in to supper."

"You asked Mr. Geoffrey—here?" she gasped.

"Surest thing you know. Ye see, I thought you was staying over at Englewood."

"Oh Arthur," she sighed, "and there are only two wretched little chops! And not a bit of butter! And the rent's due to-morrow—I can't spare a cent—and me in this shabby old gown! And you broke the best tea-pot!"

"Sounds kind of gay an' festive!" sighed Spike ruefully. "But don't worry about the eats, dear. Geoff won't mind, an' he'll never notice your old gown."

97

The Definite Object

"He seems to notice a great deal," said Hermione doubtfully, as she hastily untied the big apron, "and, besides—oh, gracious goodness!" she cried as a knock sounded at the front door, "You must let him in, Arthur, and don't let him know I'm changing my gown." Saying which she vanished into her bedroom, while Spike hastened to the door.

"Why, hello, Tony!" he exclaimed, "what's wrong now?"

"My lil Pietro," cried the Italian excitedly, "he no sleep, he burn-a burn-a all-a da time—all-a da time cry! You tell you sis—she come-a like-a da las' time, den he no cry-a——" But here Tony broke off to flourish his hat and bow gracefully as he caught sight of Hermione herself. "Ah, signorina!" he cried, "my lil Pietro he seeck. You please-a come see my lil Pietro? He flush-a, he cry, he all-a da fire! he burn-a, burn-a like-a da fire! You so good, so generosa—you come see my lil Pietro?"

"Why, of course I will," said Hermione in her calm, soft voice, "poor little mite—is he feverish?"

"Si, si, signorina," answered the anxious young father, "he burn-a, burn-a all-a da time."

"Reach me the aconite, boy dear, yes, that's it."

"But what about supper, Hermy?" queried Spike wistfully.

"Oh, well—finish laying the table. I'll be back as soon as ever I can, dear."

"Oh gee!" sighed Spike, as their footsteps died away down the stairs, "she sure is keen on knowing how I met Geoff. And if she ever finds out——" Spike cowered down into a chair, and, clasping his head between his hands, sat thus a long while, staring moodily at the floor, striving for a way out of the difficulty. He was yet wrestling with this knotty problem when he started, to hear muffled knocks at the front door, which, being opened disclosed the object of his thoughts. "Why, Geoff," he

Antagonism is Born, and War Declared

cried gladly, " I thought you weren't comin'. Say, what you got there ? " he inquired, for Ravenslee's arms were filled with sundry packages and parcels.

" Come and see," said Ravenslee mysteriously. " Catch this one before I drop it."

" Why—hello ! " said Spike, sniffing at the package in question as he led the way into the parlour, " it smells good. It sniffs like—holy gee, it's a roast turkey ! And —oh, say, Geoff—she's a beaut' ! "

" Precisely what Mr. Pffeffenfifer assured me," said Ravenslee, depositing his other burdens on the table. " Mr. Pffeffenfifer is a man educated in eats, a food fancier, an artist of the appetite. Mr. Pffeffenfifer is fat and soulful. Mr. Pffeffenfifer nearly wept tears over the virtues of that bird—pledged his immortal soul for its tenderness, vowed by all the gods it had breast enough for twins. Mr. Pffeffenfifer seemed so passionately attached to that bird that I feared he meant to keep it to gloat over in selfish secrecy. But no, base coin seduced him, did the trick, and —here it is. Also, we have a loaf ! " and from beneath one arm Ravenslee dropped a package that resolved itself into a Vienna roll. " Also, ham——"

" Hey, Geoff ! " said Spike in awestruck tones, " are all these eats ? "

" Certainly. I should have brought more if I could have carried 'em."

" More ? "

" Most decidedly. When I buy eats, my lad, I buy everything in sight that looks worth while—if Mr. Pffeffenfifer sells. Mr. Pffeffenfifer sells in such a soulfully seductive way that eats acquire virtues above and beyond their own base selves—Mr. Pffeffenfifer can infuse soul into a sausage. Behold now, eats the most alluring. See, what's this ! Ah yes, here we have—item : Salmi, redolent of garlic ; here again a head cheese, succulent and savoury ; here's ham, most ravishingly pink ; and a Camembert cheese."

The Definite Object

"But, Jiminy Christmas! you bought such a lot of each. Who's goin' t'eat all these?"

"We, of course!"

"But we can't eat 'em all," sighed Spike.

"Can't we?" said Ravenslee, beginning to view the quantity of the numerous viands with dubious eyes. "They do seem rather a lot now I see 'em all together. But I'm ravenous, and if we can't manage 'em we'll find some one who can."

"Ye see, Geoff, I sha'n't be able t'eat any o' the rest when I'm through with the turk'!" sighed Spike a little reproachfully. "My, but I'm hungry! Strange, how hungry cold turkey makes a guy!"

"Why then," said Ravenslee, pitching his hat into a corner, "sit down, comrade, and 'let mirth with unconfined wing '—— " Ravenslee yawned.

"I guess we'd better wait a bit, Geoff."

"What for?"

"Hermy."

"Is she—d'you mean she's back?" inquired Ravenslee, sitting up.

"Yes, she didn't stay at Englewood, she's downstairs, doctoring Tony's kid."

"But what will she think of all these confounded messes?"

"Messes!" cried Spike indignantly. "Cheese it, Geoff—look at that turk'!"

"But—do you think she'll mind?" inquired Ravenslee uneasily.

"Mind?" said Spike, staring, "not on your life. Why should she? Besides, it's kind o' lucky you happened to blow in with this free lunch, she's a bit shy on the dollar question this month—an' Mulligan comes t'-morrow. An', oh, say, Geoff—she's dead set on findin' out how I met you an'—an' where."

"Very naturally," murmured Ravenslee.

"An' we must tell her something, but what?"

Antagonism is Born, and War Declared

"Spike, you've forgotten the mustard. And as for—er—lying to your sister, let our motto be 'sufficient unto the day.' Our present need is mustard, Spike."

"Say, this sure is goin' t' be some supper, Geoff!" said Spike, setting on the mustard and gazing at the array of edibles with shining eyes. "Gee, I could eat cold turkey all night!"

"Have we everything ready, Spike?"

"Except butter, Geoff."

"Ha! the one thing I forgot, of course. Cut off and get some like the good fellow you are," and Ravenslee flicked a bill into Spike's hand, who, seizing his cap, promptly vanished. Being alone, Ravenslee crossed to the sideboard, and, taking thence a certain photo, seated himself in the easy-chair and fell to studying it with deep and grave attention. And sitting thus, he let fancy run riot—and fancy was singularly pleasing, to judge by the glow in his eyes and the tender smile that curved his lip.

He was lost deep within his dreams when he was aware of a loud knock upon the outer door, which Spike had left unlatched, and, setting by the photo, he rose.

"Come!" said he.

A heavy step sounded in the little hall, the door was pushed open, and a man entered. He was a young man, big and broad-shouldered, and Ravenslee's keen eyes were quick to heed the length and ponderous carriage of the arms, the girth of chest, and firm, heavy poise of the face; lastly, he looked at the face, aggressively handsome, with its dominating nose and chin, and blue eyes shaded by thick lashes, that looked out beneath heavy brows—a comely-seeming face from the dark, close-cropped hair to the deep cleft in the strong, fleshy chin.

But now, beneath Ravenslee's persistent regard, the full-curved, shapely lips grew slowly into a cruel, down-trending line, the nostrils expanded, while the blue eyes narrowed to shining slits beneath quick-scowling, black brows. For a long moment the two men stared at each other eye to eye, then, in a hoarse, assertive tone, the new-comer spoke.

" What ye doin' here ? Who are ye ? "

Mr. Ravenslee sat down and began to fill his pipe.

" Where's de kid ? "

Mr. Ravenslee brushed stray grains of tobacco from his knee with elaborate care.

" Hey, you—where's Spike—'n' what you doin' here anyway ? "

Mr. Ravenslee glanced up casually.

" And pray, who the devil may you be pleased to be ? " he inquired.

" Me name's M'Ginnis."

" Oh, indeed ! "

" Yes—indeed ! Bud M'Ginnis—is that good 'nuff for ye ? "

" Well, since you ask," said Ravenslee, shaking languid head, " I should scarcely class you as a ' bud ' myself. No, I should say you were perhaps just a trifle—er—overblown. But have it your own way ! " and Mr. Ravenslee smiled engagingly.

" Where's Spike ? " demanded M'Ginnis, his tone a little gruffer, " An' say—you can cut out the comedy, see ? Nix on the funny business——"

" You are a pessimist, I presume, Mr. Flowers ? "

" Where's de kid ? Speak up now—where is he ? "

" Also, your conversation grows a little montonous, Mr. Flowers."

M'Ginnis stared, then shot out his big chin viciously.

" What you doin' in Hermy's flat, eh ? "

Mr. Ravenslee's brows wrinkled slightly, but his soft voice grew softer, as, pausing in the act of lighting his pipe, he answered :

" On the whole, I think you are a rather—er—unpleasant young man, so suppose you—er—go."

" What ! Go ? Are ye tryin' t' tell me t' go ? "

Antagonism is Born, and War Declared

" I'm suggesting that you—er—crank up the machine, Mr. Flowers, and beat it while the going's good ! "

M'Ginnis clenched his fist and took a threatening step toward Ravenslee, then checked and stood breathing heavily.

" May I further suggest," said Ravenslee in his pleasantest voice, " that you look in again—say next Thursday fortnight, Mr. Flowers ? "

" T' hell with you—me name's M'Ginnis."

" Of course you might leave a message, Mr. Flowers."

" Now, see here, you," said M'Ginnis, his words coming thick with passion, " I wanter know, first, where Spike is. An' then I wanter know who you are. An' then I wanter know what you're after in Hermy Chesterton's flat—an' you're sure goin' t' tell me ! "

" Am I ? "

" You sure are ! "

Mr. Ravenslee opened the match-box.

" Seems a pity to shake a confidence so sublime," he sighed, " and yet——"

" An' see here again ! I've known Hermy since we was kids, an' I don't allow no man t' come monkeyin' around here—see ? So you're goin' t' quit, an' you're goin' t' quit right now ! "

" Do I look like a quitter, Mr. Flowers ? "

Now beholding the speaker's lazy assurance of pose, the contemptuous indifference of his general air, M'Ginnis stood speechless a moment, his clenched fists quivering, while, above the loosely-tied scarf, his powerful neck seemed to swell and show knotted cords that writhed and twisted, and when at last he spoke his words came in a panting rush.

" This is Hermy's flat, an' I guess—you think you're safe here, but you ain't ! I'm thinkin' out which 'll do th' least harm to her furniture—to lick ye here, or drag you out on to the landin' first ! "

Mr. Ravenslee lounged lower in the armchair, and

The Definite Object

yawned behind the box of matches. And in that moment, like a maddened animal, M'Ginnis leapt upon him, and, striking no blow, seized and shook Ravenslee in powerful, frantic hands, while from between his lips, curled back from big, white teeth, came a continuous vicious hissing sound.

"I'll wake ye up," he panted. "Come out—come out, I say! Oh, I'll wake ye up when I get ye outside, I guess. Come out! What you doin' in Hermy's flat? By God! I'll choke ye till ye tell me!" and his hands came upon Ravenslee's throat—came to be met there by two other hands that, closing upon his wrist, wrenched and twisted viciously in opposite directions, and, loosing his hold, M'Ginnis fell back, staring down at bruised and lacerated skin where oozed a few, slow drops of blood.

"And now," said Ravenslee rising, "after you, Mr. Flowers, let us by all means step outside, where we will each earnestly endeavour to pitch the other downstairs, personally, I shall do my very damnedest, for really I don't —no, I do not—like you, Mr. Flowers, you need some one to tread on you a little. Step outside, and let *me* try."

But now, while M'Ginnis stared from his swelling, bloody wrist to Ravenslee's face—a face quite as fierce and determined as his own—steps were heard, and Spike's voice called:

"Hermy come in yet, Geoff?"

"Not yet, but our friend Mr. Flowers has dropped in —socially, I fancy."

"Mr. who?" inquired Spike at the door, but, beholding M'Ginnis, he paused there, staring aghast. "Why, hello, Bud," said he nervously, "what's wrong?"

"Nothin' much yet, kid, only it's kinder lucky for this guy as you happened in. Who is he? What's he doin' here?"

"He's only a friend o' mine, Bud, an' he's all right, 'n'say——"

Antagonism is Born, and War Declared

"Tell him t' beat it."

"But ye see, Bud——"

"Tell him as we don't want his kind around here, or——"

"Spike, did you bring in the butter?" inquired Ravenslee, serenely unconscious of M'Ginnis.

"Yes, here it is, Geoff, but say——"

"It doesn't feel much," said Ravenslee, weighing the package in his hand.

"It's half a pound. But say, here's Bud, he says you're to——"

"My Spike, I'll trouble you for the butter-dish—thanks!" and, turning away, Ravenslee busied himself at the table, whistling softly the while.

"But, Geoff, this is Bud!" cried the lad, glancing from one to the other in an agony of suspense. "Oh, don't ye know—dis is Bud M'Ginnis?"

"Ah, still here, is he?" said Ravenslee without looking round.

"See here, kid," growled M'Ginnis, "you tell your friend t' clear out, an' t' do it real quick, see. You tell him if he ain't out in two minutes I'll run him out meself."

"Spike, this butter is nearly oil."

"Oh Geoff," groaned the boy, "you've got to go, here's Bud——"

"Why then, Spike, tell him to—er—chase himself, I'm busy."

Came the sound of a chair set roughly aside, and a shrill cry from Spike:

"My God, Bud, don't! Look out, Geoff!"

But, as M'Ginnis came, Ravenslee turned swiftly, ducked the expected blow, and swinging his fist up beneath his assailant's extended arm, smote him hard and true upon the elbow; and Spike, staring pale and wide of eye, saw that arm fall and dangle helplessly at M'Ginnis's side, while his face was contorted with sharp agony.

The Definite Object

" My God, Geoff ! what you done to him ? "

" Pins and needles, Spike, that's all. A hoary old trick, but useful now and then. Mr. Flowers isn't so very wideawake as folk seem to think. You see it wouldn't have done to knock him out here, he might have upset the table."

" Knock out Bud ! " cried Spike aghast, " but there ain't nobody can lick Bud M'Ginnis."

" Oh, I don't know, Spike. Anyway we'll see what can be done outside. After you, Mr. Flowers. Pray go first, Mr. Flowers. A fellow who would attack a man sitting down isn't to be trusted behind one, so, after you, Mr. Flowers. Oh, we'll wait until you can use your arm, but we'll wait outside. Miss Chesterton's flat is no place for your sort, so, out with you, and quick, d'ye hear ? "

M'Ginnis opened his lips to retort, but passion choked him, and, snarling unintelligibly, he turned and strode out upon the landing.

Now, as they stood fronting each other very silent and grim and menacing, running feet were heard ascending the stairs, and a slender boy appeared, who, perceiving M'Ginnis, panted out :

" Say, Bud, O'Rourke's been pinched by de cops ! He wants ye t' skin over an' fix it up."

" O'Rourke pinched ! " growled M'Ginnis, " Say you, Larry. Whatcher givin' me ? "

" S' right, Bud, dere's a noo captain on de precinct, an' he's pinched O'Rourke. 'N'say, Bud, de game 's all balled up, de push is all up in de air. 'N'say, O'Rourke's crazy, an' can't do nothin', so he sent me t' fetch ye. You're de only one as can fix de police, so come on right now before de whole show's busted up."

During this breathless speech the narrowed eyes of M'Ginnis never left Ravenslee's pale, placid face, and in the persistence of this ferocious glare was something animal-like.

106

Antagonism is Born, and War Declared

"Say you, Mr. Butt-in," said he, "I ain't through wid you, not by a whole lot, I ain't. Oh, I'll get ye yet, an' I'll get ye good. There won't be nothin' left for nobody else when I'm through wid you. Savvy this, there ain't nobody ever goin' t' queer me with Hermy Chesterton. Oh, I'll get ye good, an' I'll get ye soon!" So saying, Bud M'Ginnis turned and went slowly and unwillingly down the stair.

"Gee, but I'm glad he's gone," said Spike as he closed the door. "Gee, but I'm glad!" and he drew a deep breath.

"So am I," said Ravenslee, sinking into the armchair, "there's always to-morrow, isn't there?"

But instead of replying, Spike stood to stare on Ravenslee with eyes of admiring awe.

"I guess you know how t' handle y'self, Geoff," said he.

"I used to think I could, once upon a time," answered Ravenslee, stooping to recover his pipe.

"That, sure, was some wallop you handed him."

"'Twas fair, I thank you, comrade."

"I shall be awful sorry to have you leave me, Geoff."

"Leave you?"

"Well, you heard what he said?"

"Yes, I heard."

"An' you know what he meant?"

"I can guess."

"You'd best skin out o' Mulligan's first thing to-morrow."

"What for?"

"Bud says you must, an' he'll make you, I guess!"

"Oh, how?"

"Well," said Spike in low, troubled tones, "he'll sick de gang on to you if you don't make your getaway while you can."

"My God!" exclaimed Ravenslee, his eyes suddenly very bright, "I never thought of that."

107

The Definite Object

"Yes, so I'm thinkin' you'd best skin off t'-night, Geoff," sighed the lad gloomily.

Whereupon Ravenslee pocketed his pipe and clapped him joyously upon the shoulder.

"Banish that dejection, my comrade," said he, "for now, my Arthur—Spike, " 'now is the winter of our discontent made glorious summer in this brutal Bud,' and——"

"Whatcher mean, Geoff?"

"I mean that life's erstwhile dull monotony is like to be forgotten quite in the vigorous, exhilarating air of Hell's Kitchen. Hell's Kitchen suits me admirably, consequently in Hell's Kitchen I'll stay."

"Stay! Geoff, are ye crazy? What about Bud M'Ginnis?"

"M'Ginnis, my Arthur? Oh, Bud M'Ginnis may be— Hush! Straighten the cloth yonder, Spike, she's coming at last, by heaven!"

CHAPTER XII

CONTAINING SOME DESCRIPTION OF A SUPPER-PARTY

" OH ! " said Hermione, as she caught sight of Ravenslee's tall figure, " You've come then, Mr. Geoffrey ? I've been hoping and praying you wouldn't. I mean," she added hastily, in answer to his look, " I mean I have only two miserable little chops for supper."

" S' all right, Hermy," cried Spike. " I told you not to worry about the eats, look what's here! Stand out o' the light, Geoff, so 's she can see the table."

" Why, what—whatever's all this ? " she exclaimed, staring at the numerous well-filled dishes with blue eyes very wide. " Oh goodness, gracious me ! " and she turned to look at Mr. Ravenslee, who, meeting that wondering glance, actually found himself stammering again.

" The fact is, Miss Hermione—er—I say the fact is we —Arthur and I—are giving a little supper to-night in honour of—of—er—my birthday."

" You bet we are, Hermy," added Spike. " Will you pipe the turk' ? "

" We have been waiting for you," continued Ravenslee, placing a chair for her. " You see—er—you are to be our guest of honour—if you will ? "

" Sure you are," nodded Spike, " and I am head-waiter, eater-in-chief t' the turk' while she lasts, an' chief mourner when she's gone ! So now I'll go an' make th' tea, only don't begin without me, a fair start an' all together— see ? " and, speaking, he vanished into the kitchen.

The Definite Object

"But a whole turkey!" said Hermione, viewing it with feminine, knowledgeful eyes, "and then all this ham and tongue, and—Mr. Geoffrey, how extravagant of you!" and she shook her shapely head at him reprovingly, but with a smile curving her red lips; and lo! there was the shining curl above her eyebrow again more wantonly alluring than usual. "Whatever made you buy so much?"

"Mr. Pffeffenfifer," answered Ravenslee, staring at the radiant curl, whereupon she, becoming aware of it, would have sent it into immediate retirement among its many fellows, but that he stayed her humbly. "Please don't," he said.

"But it—tickles."

"Well, let it!"

"But why should I?"

"For m—Arthur's sake."

"Arthur's!" she laughed. "Mr. Geoffrey, as if he would ever notice!"

"Well then, for the—er—turkey's sake!"

"The turkey!" she laughed. "I'm afraid I'm dreadfully untidy to sit down at such a luxurious feast."

"Are you?"

"Well, aren't I? Look at this poor old gown."

"I'm afraid I didn't notice your—er—gown."

"What did I tell you, Hermy?" said Spike, entering with the teapot. "Geoff ain't—I mean, isn't—that kind o' guy—I mean mutt—no, I mean feller. Ye see, Geoff, a girl always thinks a feller's got his lamps—I mean eyes —on her rags—clo'es, I mean. 'S' funny, ain't it? Gee but I'm hungry!"

"So am I," said Hermione.

"So am I," said Ravenslee.

"Why then," quoth Spike, "I'll tell you what. Let's all sit down an' eat. I guess I'm full o' brilliant ideas to-night, but this ain't no time to talk—not with that turkey starin' us in the face, it ain't—isn't I mean. So quit chewin' de rag an' let's chew d' turk' instead—an', gee, but that's some brilliant too, I guess."

So down they sat forthwith ; and, while Hermione presided over the cups and saucers, Ravenslee carved.

" Light or dark meat, Miss Hermione ? " he inquired.

" Hermy likes th' light, but a drumstick for mine, an' please don't forget th' stuffin', Geoff."

" Tea, Mr. Geoffrey ? "

" Thanks ! " he answered, pausing to watch the curve of her shapely neck as she bent to pour the tea, and to note how her white hand grasped the battered teapot, little finger delicately poised.

" Say, Geoff, get busy ! " said Spike wistfully. " I know the teapot's a bit off on looks, but I broke the best one, an'——"

" I didn't even notice the teapot, Spike," said Ravenslee, meeting Hermione's quick, upward glance.

" Oh, cheese it, Geoff, here you've sat with your fork in th' turk' an' your knife in th' air starin' at that teapot a whole minute."

" No, Spike, no. I was only thinking that tea never tastes quite right unless poured out by a woman's hand, and the fairer the hand the better the tea."

" Which means—just what, Mr. Geoffrey ? " laughed Hermione.

" Why, that Spike and I are about to drink the most delicious tea in the world, of course."

" I'd rather be eatin' that turk' when you've sawed me off a leg," sighed Spike. " I say, *when* you have."

" Ah, to be sure," said Ravenslee, turning his attention to his carving again, while Hermione bowed her golden head above the tea-cups.

" Gee, but she cuts tender," quoth Spike ; " that bird sure has the Indian sign on me ! "

" Sugar, Mr. Geoffrey ? "

" Two lumps, please."

" Milk, Mr. Geoffrey ? "

The Definite Object

" Thank you."

" Geoff," said Spike wearily, " I cracked that milk-jug last night, but you don't have to sit starin' at it that way, an' me dyin' of hunger by inches."

" My humble apologies," said Ravenslee, wresting his gaze from a certain curl and fixing it upon the turkey again. " I'm a little—er—distracted to-night, it seems."

" Oh gee ! " said Spike in a hopeless tone, " now Hermy's gone an' filled my cup with milk."

" Why, boy dear, so I have ! " she confessed with a rueful laugh, and her cheeks were very pink as she rectified her mistake.

" Are you distracted too, then ? " demanded Spike.

" No, I—I don't think so, no, no, of course I'm not. I—I was just thinking, that's all."

" Not about tea, I reckon. Say, what's getting you two anyway ? "

" Arthur," said she serenely as she passed his tea, " please fetch some more hot water."

Spike sighed, rose, and, taking the jug, went upon his mission.

" And how do you like Mulligan's, Mr. Geoffrey ? " inquired Hermione, regarding him with her calm, level eyes.

" Very much," he answered, " I like it better and better. I think—no, I'm sure—I would rather be in Mulligan's than anywhere else in the world."

" Oh ! Why ? "

Down went carving knife and fork, and leaning toward her he answered, " Because in Mulligan's, among many other wonders, I have found something more beautiful and far more wonderful than I ever dreamed of finding."

" In Mulligan's ? " she asked, looking her amazement

" In Mulligan's," he answered gravely.

Now here, all at once, her glance wavered and sank before his.

" What do you mean ? " she inquired, staring into her cup.

Some Description of a Supper-party

" Shall I tell you ? "

" Yes—no ! " she murmured hastily and a little breathlessly, as Spike re-entered, who paused, jug in hand, to stare.

" What—haven't you served Hermy yet ? " he inquired in an injured tone.

" Certainly I have," answered Ravenslee, " here it is, you see—all ready."

" Only you forgot t' hand it t' her, and she forgot t' take it. Well, say, for hungry folks you two are the limit."

" ' Man doth not live by bread alone,' boy ! We were talking," said Ravenslee, handing Hermione her plate.

" You said you liked milk and sugar, didn't you, Mr. Geoffrey ? "

" Holy gee ! " murmured Spike.

" Milk and sugar, thank you," said Ravenslee, heedful of her deepened colour.

" Geoff," inquired Spike gently, " if I was to hang on to that drumstick d'ye suppose you might be able to hack it off for me—some day ? "

" My Arthur," said Ravenslee, plying knife and fork energetically, " 'tis done—behold it ! "

" But surely," said Hermione, glancing up suddenly, " surely you don't like Mulligan's, Mr. Geoffrey ? "

" Like it, Miss Hermione ? I—abominate it."

" Oh ! "

" Say, Geoff." mourned Spike, " don't I get any stuffin' after all ? "

" Mr. Geoffrey, I've been wondering how you and Arthur met—and where, and——"

" Gee, Hermy ! " Spike exclaimed, " you sure do talk. If you go on asking poor old Geoff s' many questions he'll forget t' serve himself this week. Look at his plate."

" Why, Mr. Geoffrey, do serve yourself, please. And— oh, my gracious ! I've forgotten to give you your tea, I'm so sorry."

Here Spike, having once again staved off the inevitable

explanation, grew hilarious, and they laughed and talked the while they ate and drank with youthful, healthy appetite.

And what a supper that was! What tongue could tell the gaiety and utter content that possessed them all three? What pen describe all Hermione's glowing beauty, or how her blue eyes, meeting eyes of grey, would, for no perceptible reason, grow sweetly troubled, waver in their glance, and veil themselves beneath sudden, down-dropping lashes? What mere words could ever describe all the subtle, elusive witchery of her?

And Spike ate, of course, in blissful silence for the most part, and whole-heartedly, his attention centred exclusively upon his plate, thus, how should he know or care how often, across that diminished turkey, grey eyes looked into blue? As for Ravenslee, he ate and drank he knew and cared not what, content to sit and watch her when he might—the delicious curves of white neck and full round throat, the easy grace of movement that spoke her vigorous youth; joying in the soft murmurs of her voice, the low, sweet ring of her laughter, and thrilling responsive to her warm young womanhood.

" But Mr. Geoffrey," she inquired suddenly, "if you hate Mulligan's as much as I do, whatever made you choose to live here? "

" A thrice blessed fate," he answered. " I came because—er——"

" You were a poor, lonely guy," added Spike hastily.

" Precisely, Spike. Compared to my sordid poverty, Lazarus was rich, and as for the loneliness of my existence the—er—abomination of desolation was a flowery garden."

" And how did you happen to meet Ar——"

A plate crashed to pieces on the floor, and, turning, she beheld Spike very red and rueful of visage.

" 'Fraid I've bent a plate, Hermy," he explained, and, winking desperately at Ravenslee, he stooped to gather up the fragments.

Some Description of a Supper-party

"Oh Arthur! and we have so few."

"Yes, I know, but it's only the old cracked one, Hermy."

"You've broken an awful lot of things lately, boy dear," she sighed. "Never mind, get on with your supper, dear."

"Oh, I'm all right, but what about you? Gee, Hermy, you sure do talk!"

"Do I, dear?"

"Well, I guess. You keep on at poor old Geoff so he don't get a chance for a real proper chew."

"But then, you see," said Ravenslee, "I would much rather talk than eat—sometimes."

"But say, Geoff——"

"Miss Hermione, you were asking how I met——"

"Hey, Geoff!" said Spike hoarsely.

"How I met your brother," continued Ravenslee, silencing the boy with a look. "Miss Hermione, I'll tell you full and free." Here Spike took a gulp of tea and choked, also his brow grew clammy, and he stared with dilating eyes at Ravenslee, who began forthwith: "Once upon a time, Miss Hermione, that is to say upon a certain dark night, a man sat alone, physically and mentally alone, and very wretched because his life was empty of all achievement; because, having been blessed with many opportunities, he had never done anything worth while. And as he sat there, looking back through the wasted years, this miserable fool was considering, in his wretched folly, the cowardly sin of self-destruction because he was sick of the world and all things in it—especially of his own useless self. But I hope I don't—er—bore you, do I?"

"No," she answered a little breathlessly, and gazing at him with eyes deep and tender, "go on—please go on."

"Well," continued Ravenslee gravely, "Destiny, or Heaven, or the Almighty, taking pity on this sorry fool, sent to him an angel in the shape of—your brother."

The Definite Object

" Of—Arthur ? " she exclaimed, while Spike's rigid attitude relaxed and he drew a sudden, deep breath.

" Of Arthur," nodded Ravenslee. " And Arthur lifted him out of the Slough of Despond, and taught him that life might be a useful thing after all, if he could but find some object to help him ; one who might inspire him to nobler things. And so he came here, hoping to find this object."

" An object ? " she inquired softly.

" The Definite Object ! " he answered, " with capital letters. One who might make life truly worth while. One who, teaching him to forget himself, should lift him to better things. An object to live for, work for, and if necessary to—die for."

Here Spike, finding himself utterly forgotten again, sighed in deep and audible relief, and, taking up knife and fork, fell to with renewed appetite, while Hermione, chin rested on folded hands, gazed into Ravenslee's grave face.

" Do you think he will ever—find his Object ? "

" Oh yes."

" You seem very confident."

" I am. You see, she's found."

" She ! " exclaimed Hermione, her eyes beginning to waver.

" With a capital S," said he, leaning nearer—" The Woman ! And it's right here that his difficulties begin, because, in the first place, he is so humble and she is so proud and——"

" Proud ? " said she, glancing up swiftly.

" And so very beautiful," he continued.

" Oh ! " said she, and this time she did not look at him.

" Say," quoth Spike, " I think I could go another drumstick, Geoff."

" And in the second place, he is so unworthy, and she so——"

" An' a bit more stuffin', Geoff," sighed Spike.

116

Some Description of a Supper-party

" Can she help him ? " inquired Hermione, stirring her tea absently.

" She is the only one who can help me."

" Oh ! " said Hermione again, very softly this time, and stirring a little faster, and, conscious of his glance, flushed deliciously and was silent a while. As for Spike, he glanced from one rapt face to the other, and unostentatiously helped himself to more turkey.

" But," said Hermione at last, " how can she help ? "

" By constant association," answered Ravenslee. " By affording me the daily example of her sweet self-forgetfulness and blameless life."

" Are you sure she is so very good ? "

" I am sure she is braver and nobler than any woman I have ever known."

Once more Spike glanced from the flushed beauty of his sister's half-averted face to Ravenslee's shining eyes, and boldly helped himself to more seasoning.

" Have you known her very long, Mr. Geoffrey ? "

" Long enough to know she is the only woman."

" Say, Geoff," sighed Spike, " I guess old Pffeff. was right about this bird, she kind o' melts—'n', say, she's meltin' fast. If you two don't stop chewin' de rag an' get busy you'll be too late for this bird, because this bird is sure a bird of passage an'—holy gee ! " he broke off as a knock sounded on the outer door, "Who's this, I wonder ? "

Before he could rise, Hermione had vanished into the passage.

" Say, Geoff," he whispered, " how if it's Bud ? "

Ravenslee frowned and pushed back his chiar.

But in that moment they heard Hermione's glad welcome :

" Why, Ann, you dear thing, you're just in time for the turkey. Come right in."

" Turkey, my dear," spoke the harsh voice of Mrs. Trapes. " Turkey, land sakes ! But I only jest stepped

The Definite Object

over t' ask if you'd happened to find that lodger o' mine anywheres. Why, Lord bless me ! " she broke off, halting in the doorway as she beheld Ravenslee, "Lordy-lord, if he ain't a-settin' there, cool as ever was ! If he ain't a-eatin' an' drinkin', an' me cookin' him at this moment the loveliest mutton-chop you ever see. A mutton-chop wiv a kidney as he ordered most express, Lord ! Mr. Geoffrey ! "

" Why, to be sure," said Ravenslee, rising. " I forgot all about that chop, Mrs. Trapes."

" Didn't you order it most express—cut thick, an' wiv a kidney ? "

" I did," said Ravenslee penitently.

" Well, there it is, cooked to a turn an' nobody t' eat it. An' kidneys is rose again, kidneys is always risin', Lord, Mr. Geoffrey ! "

" Why you see, Mrs. Trapes, we—that is, I—had a birthday not long ago, and we're celebrating."

" And so shall you, Ann," said Hermione. " Sit down, dear."

" An' me in me oldest apron ? " said Mrs. Trapes, squaring her elbows. " My dear, I couldn't an' I wouldn't. But oh ! Mr. Geoffrey, what about that beautiful chop ? I might warm it over for your breakfast ? "

" Heaven forbid ! "

" Then I must eat it myself, I suppose, though it do seem a shame to waste such a lovely chop on Ann Angelina Trapes ! But, Hermy dear, I just been down to see Mrs. Bowker, an' her little Hazel's very bad—her poor little hip again, an' she's coughin', too, somethin' dreadful ! "

" Poor little Hazel ! Did she ask for me, Ann ? "

" Well, my dear, she did, an' Mrs. Bowker did ask if you'd go an' look at her, but I do hate t' disturb ye, that I do."

" Oh, it's all right, Ann. Tell Mrs. Bowker I'll be right down."

Some Description of a Supper-party

" I will so ! But it's a dratted shame as you should shoulder everybody's troubles, that it is."

" Oh Ann ! as though I do.   And then, how about yourself, dear ?   What of the Baxters and the Ryders, and Mrs. Tipping's baby, and——"

" My land ! " cried Mrs. Trapes, " that chop'll be a cinder ! " and, speaking, she hurried away.

" Poor little Hazel ! " said Hermione, coming to a small corner cupboard.   " She's such a dear, quaint little person.   You must have seen her on the stairs, Mr. Geoffrey."

" I see so many on the stairs, Miss Hermione, and they are always small and generally quaint."

" Hazel's got a game leg, Geoff," said Spike ; " an' she hops around on a little crutch.   She told me yesterday she thought you was—I mean were—a fairy prince because you always bow an' tip your lid to her when she says ' good-morning.'   So now she waits for you every morning, Geoff, says it makes her feel like she was a real fairy princess in a story-book.   Sounds kind o' batty to me, though."

Hermione was standing on tiptoe endeavouring to reach a certain bottle upon the top shelf, where were ranged many others of various shapes and sizes, when Ravenslee's big hand did it for her ; but when she would have taken it he shook his head.

" I should like to go with you, if I may," he said, " to be—er—formally introduced to the princess."

" But——" began Hermione hesitating.

" Also I could carry the bottle for you."

" Why, if you will do all that——" she smiled.

" Thanks ! " he answered, and, putting the bottle in his pocket, he opened the door.

" Hey, Geoff," Spike called after him, " you've forgot to kiss the turkey good-bye."

" Why, then, you can do it for me, Spike ! " he answered, and followed Hermione out upon the stair.

The Definite Object

Side by side they descended the stair, in the doing of which her soft shoulder met his once, and once he thrilled to feel her hand touch his in the shadow, but this hand was hastily withdrawn. Also, though the light was dim, he saw that she was frowning and biting her red underlip.

"These stairs are rather narrow, aren't they?" said she, drawing to the wall.

"Delightfully!" he answered, drawing to the rail; and so they went down very silently, with the width of the stairs between them.

CHAPTER XIII

MRS. BOWKER was a small woman, worn and faded like her carpets and curtains and the dress she wore, but, like them, she was very clean and neat.

"'Tis real good of you to come, Miss Hermy," said this small, faded woman, and Ravenslee thought her very voice sounded faded, so repressed and dismally soft was it. "I wouldn't have had the face t' send for you, Miss Hermy, only Hazel calls an' calls like she's doin' now—listen !"

And sure enough from somewhere near by a small voice reached them, pitifully faint and thin :
"Hermy dear, come t' me ; oh Hermy dear !"

"She allus lays an' calls like that lately when her poor hip's worse 'n usual," sighed Mrs. Bowker. "An' your gentleman friend, would he like t' see her too ?"

"Thank you, I should," answered Ravenslee in his soft, pleasant voice.

"Oh, Mrs. Bowker, this is Mr. Geoffrey," said Hermione a trifle hurriedly ; "he came with me to—to——"

"Be presented to the Princess if she will honour me," he added.

"Ah !" said Mrs. Bowker, looking up at him with a faded smile. "Hazel told me you had a pretty voice, sir, an' I guess I know what she meant. She sets out on the stairs when she's well enough, an' has often seen ye."

"Hermy dear, come t' me ! oh Hermy dear !" called the little voice.

121

The Definite Object

"Yes, go in, my dear, you know yer way I guess," sighed Mrs. Bowker, passing a small, worn hand across her faded eyes. "There's five dozen more collar-bands I must stitch an' buttonhole t'-night, so go your ways, my dear." So saying, Mrs. Bowker went back to her labour, which was very hard labour indeed, while Hermione led the way into a tiny room, where, on a small, neat truckle-bed, covered by a faded quilt, a small, pale child lay fading fast. But at sight of her visitors two big brown eyes grew bigger yet, and her pale, thin little cheeks flushed eagerly.

"Oh Hermy dear!" she cried, clasping frail hands. "Oh Hermy, you've brought him! You've brought me our fairy Prince at last!"

Now what was there in these childish words to cause Hermione's eyes to droop so suddenly as she took the bottle from Ravenslee's hand, or her rounded cheek to flush so painfully as she stooped to meet the child's eager kiss, or when she turned away to measure a dose of the medicine to be such an unconscionable time over it? Observing all of which, Ravenslee forthwith saluted the small invalid with a grave bow, his battered hat gracefully flourished.

"It is truly an honour to meet you, Princess!" said he, and, lifting the child's frail little hand, he touched it to his lips. Thereafter, obeying the mute appeal of that hand, he seated himself upon the narrow bed, while Hermione, soft-voiced and tender, bent above the invalid, who having obediently swallowed her medicine, leaned back on her pillow and smiled from one to the other.

"And now," said she, drawing Hermione on her other side and snuggling between, "now please let's all tell some more fairy tale, an' please you begin, Hermy, just where you had t' leave off last time."

"Why I—I'm afraid I've forgotten, dear," said Hermione, bending to smooth the child's pillow.

"Forgotten, oh Hermy! But I 'member quite well

Of the Beautiful City of Perhaps

you got where poor Princess Nobody was climbing the mountain very tired an' sad, an' carryin' her heavy pack, an' all at once along came the Prince an' took her heavy bundle an' said he'd love to carry it for her always if she'd let him. An' poor Nobody knew he was the real Prince at last, the Prince she'd dreamed of an' waited for all her life, 'cos he'd got grey eyes so brave an' true, an' he was so big an' strong an' noble. So he helped her to the top of the mountain, an' then she thought at last she could see the beautiful City of Perhaps. That's where you got to, don't you 'member, Hermy dear ? "

Now why should Hermione's shapely head have drooped and drooped until at last her face was hidden on the pillow ? And why should Geoffrey Ravenslee reach to touch the child's soft, dark hair with hands so light and tender ?

" The beautiful City of Perhaps ! " said he gently. " Why, Princess, where did you learn about that ? "

" From dear Princess Nobody ! "

" And who is she ? "

" Why, she's Hermy, Prince—and I'm Princess Somebody. Oh, Hermy dear, you do 'member where you left off now—don't you ? "

" Yes, I remember, but I—don't feel like fairy stories, now, dear."

" Oh, are ye sick ? " cried the child anxiously, touching Hermione's golden hair with loving fingers, " is it a headache like mumsey gets ? "

" N-no, dear, only I—I don't feel like telling any more of our story—to-night—somehow, dear."

" Princess," said Ravenslee, " do you know much about the wonderful City of Perhaps ? "

" Oh yes—an' I dream about it sometimes, Prince—such beautiful dreams ! "

" Why, of course," nodded Ravenslee, " because it is the most beautiful city that ever happened, I guess ! "

" Oh, it is ! " cried the child. " Shall I tell you ? "

The Definite Object

" Please do, Princess."

" Well, it's all made of crystal an' gold, an' every one's happy there an' never sick—oh, never ! An' all the children can have ices an' cream sodas whenever they want, an' lovely doll-carriages with rubber on the wheels, an'—an' everything's just lovely. 'Course every one's daddy's got lots an' heaps an' piles of money, so they never get behind with the rent an' never have to sit up all night stitchin' an' stitchin' like mumsey an' Hermy have to sometimes. An' I'm Princess Somebody, an' Hermy's Princess Nobody, an' we're on our ways through the valley of gloom, trying to find the beautiful City of Perhaps—but oh, it's awful hard to find ! " she ended, with a weary little sigh.

" And yet, Princess, I'm sure we shall find it."

" We ? Oh, are you comin' too, Prince ? " cried the child joyfully.

" To be sure I am ! " nodded Ravenslee.

" Oh, goody, I'm glad—so glad, 'cause I know we shall find it now ! "

" Why ? "

" W l," answered the child, looking at him with her big, wistful eyes, " 'cause you look like you could find it, somehow. You see, Prince, you've got grey eyes so brave an' true—an' you're big an' strong an' could carry me an' Hermy over the thorny places—when we get very, very tired—couldn't you ? "

" I could," answered Ravenslee almost grimly, " and I—surely will ! "

" When we get there, Prince, I want first—a doll-carriage an' a doll with lovely blue eyes that wink at you, an' a big box of candy, an' a new dress for my mumsey, an' no more work, an' I want lots an' lots of flowers for my daddy, 'cause he loves flowers—oh, an' I want my leg t' be made well. What d' you want, Hermy ? "

" Well, dear, I want to—say good-bye to my sewing-machine for ever and ever and ever ! "

Of the Beautiful City of Perhaps

"Why, Hermy," exclaimed the child, "last time you said you wanted some one who could give you your heart's desire."

"Perhaps that is my heart's desire, little Hazel," said Hermione, rising and taking up the medicine bottle.

"An' what do you want, oh Prince?"

"I want a great deal," answered Ravenslee, smiling down into the big, soft eyes. "I want some one who is my heart's desire now and for ever and ever. Good-night, dear little Princess!"

"You'll come again, Prince?" she pleaded, holding up her face to be kissed. "You'll come again soon?"

"As soon as—Princess Nobody will bring me."

"Good-night, Hermy dear—you'll bring our Prince again soon?"

"If you wish, dear," said Hermione, stooping to kiss her in turn.

"Why, Hermy—what makes your cheeks so hot to-night?"

"Are they?" said Hermione, making pretence to test them with the back of her hand.

"Why, yes," nodded the child, "an' they look so red an'——"

"Of course you believe in fairies, don't you, Princess?" inquired Ravenslee rather hurriedly.

"Oh yes, Prince, I often see them in my dreams. They just wait till I'm asleep, an' then they come an' show themselves. Do you ever see any?"

"Well, your Highness, I fancy I have lately, and when fairies are around things are sure to happen—wishes get the habit of coming true. So, little Princess, just go on wishing and dreaming, and—watch out!"

Then Ravenslee turned and followed Hermione out upon the dingy landing; but as he climbed the stair there went with him the memory of a little face, very thin and pale, but radiant and all aglow with rapturous hope. Silently as they had come they mounted, until,

The Definite Object

reaching the topmost landing, they paused as by mutual consent.

"Poor little Hazel!" said Hermione very gently. "If only there were real fairies to spirit her away to where the air is sweet and pure, and flowers grew for little hands to gather—the doctor told me it was her only chance."

"Why, then, of course she must have her chance!" said Ravenslee with a sleepy nod.

"But, Mr. Geoffrey, how?"

"Well—er—the fairies, you said something about fairies spiriting——"

"The fairies!" said Hermione a little bitterly. "I guess they are too busy over their own affairs to trouble about a poor little sick child! Besides, what fairy could possibly live five minutes in—Mulligan's?"

"Which leaves us," said Ravenslee thoughtfully, "which leaves us the beautiful City of Perhaps. It is a wonderful thought that!"

"But only a thought!" she sighed.

"Is it? Are you quite sure?"

"Well, isn't it?" she questioned wistfully.

"No," he answered gravely, "the City of Perhaps is very, very real."

"What do you mean?"

Now once again their hands touched in the shadow, but this time his fingers closed upon her hand, the hand that held the medicine bottle, drawing her nearer in the dimness of that dingy landing.

"I mean," he answered, "that for every one of us there is a City of Perhaps waiting to open its gates to our coming, and I am sure we shall reach it sooner or later, all three of us—the Princess and you and I—yes, even I when I have done something worth while. And then, Hermione, then—nothing shall keep me from—my heart's delight—nothing, Hermione!" As he ended she felt an arm about her in the dimness, an arm fierce and strong that gripped and swept her close, then as suddenly loosed

126

Of the Beautiful City of Perhaps

her; for a breathless moment he stood with head bowed in seeming humility, then, stooping, he crushed her hand, medicine-bottle and all, to lips that burned with anything but humility.

"Good-night, dear Princess Nobody!" he said, and watched her turn away, nor moved until the door had closed upon her.

That night he smoked many pipes, weaving him fancies of the beautiful City of Perhaps, and dreamed dreams of what might be, and his eyes glowed bright and wide, and his mouth grew alternate grim and tender; and, that night, long after he lay asleep, Hermione's golden head was bowed above her work, but more than once she stayed her humming sewing-machine to look at one white hand with eyes shy and wistful—the hand that had held the medicine-bottle, of course.

CHAPTER XIV

OF A TEXT, A LETTER, AND A SONG

RAVENSLEE opened his eyes to find his small chamber full of a glory of sun which poured a flood of radiance across his narrow bed, it brought out the apoplectic roses on the wall-paper, and lent a new lustre to the dim and faded gold frame that contained a fly-blown card, whereon was the legend :

LOVE ONE ANOTHER

And with his gaze upon this time-honoured text Ravenslee smiled, and, leaping out of bed, proceeded to wash and shave and dress, pausing often to glance glad-eyed from his open window upon the glory of the new day. And indeed it was a morning of all-pervading beauty, insomuch that even Mulligan's, its dingy brick and mortar mellowed by the sun, seemed less unlovely than its wont, and its many windows, catching a sunbeam here and there, winked and twinkled waggishly.

So Ravenslee washed and shaved and dressed, glancing now and then from this transfigured Mulligan's to the fly-blown text upon the wall, and once he laughed, though not very loudly to be sure, and once he hummed a song, and so fell to soft whistling, all of which was very strange in Geoffrey Ravenslee.

The sun, it is true, radiates life and joy. Before his beneficence, gloom and depression flee away, and youth and health grow strong to achieve the impossible ; even age and sickness, bathed in his splendour, may forget

Of a Text, a Letter, and a Song

awhile their burdens and dream of other days. Truly sunshine is a thrice blessed thing. And yet—as Ravenslee tied the neckerchief about his brawny throat, was it by reason of the sun alone that his grey eyes were so bright and joyous, and that he whistled so soft and merrily ?

Having brushed his hair and settled his vivid-hued neckerchief to his liking, he turned, and, stooping over his humble bed, slipped a hand beneath the tumbled pillow and drew thence a letter ; a somewhat crumpled missive this, that he had borne about with him all the preceding day, and read and re-read at intervals even as he proceeded to do now, as, standing in the radiant sunbeams he unfolded a sheet of very ordinary note-paper, and slowly scanned these lines written in a bold, flowing hand :

"DEAR MR. GEOFFREY,
    "I find I must be away from home all this week ; will you please watch over my dear boy for me, then I shall work with a glad heart. Am I wrong in asking this of you, I wonder ? Anyway, I am, your grateful
                                    "HERMIONE C.
    "P.S.—I hear you are a pea-nut man. You ! "

Truly the sun is a thrice blessed thing—and yet——
Having read this over with the greatest attention, taking preposterous heed to every dot and comma, having carefully refolded it, slipped it into the envelope, and hidden it upon his person, he raised his eyes to the spotted text upon the wall.

"You're right," quoth he, nodding, "an altogether wise precept, and one I have had by heart ever since she blessed my sight. I must introduce you to her at the earliest—the very earliest—opportunity."

Having said which he fell to whistling softly again, and, opening the door, stepped out into the bright little sitting-room. Early though it was, Mrs. Trapes was

The Definite Object

already astir in her kitchen ; and since sunshine is indubitably a worker of wonders, Mrs. Trapes was singing, rather harshly to be sure, yet singing nevertheless, and this was her song :

> Said the young Obadiah to the old Obadiah,
> Obadiah, Obadiah, I am dry.
> Said the old Obadiah to the young Obadiah,
> Obadiah, Obadiah, so am I.
>
> Said the young——

The song ended abruptly as, opening the door, she beheld her lodger.

" Lordy-lord, Mr. Geoffrey ! " she exclaimed a little reproachfully, " whatever are you a-doin' of, up an' dressed an' not half-past five yet ? "

" Enjoying the morning, Mrs. Trapes, and yearning for my breakfast."

" Ah, that's just like a man. They're almighty good yearners till they get what they yearns for—then they yearns for somethin' else—immediate ! "

" Well, but I suppose women yearn too, sometimes, don't they ? "

" Not they. Women can only hope an' sigh an' languish an' break their 'earts in silence, poor dears ! "

" What for ? "

" Would a couple o' fresh eggs an' a lovely ham-rasher suit ye ? " inquired Mrs. Trapes.

" They will suit."

" Then I'll go an' fry 'em."

" And I'll come and look on, if I may," said he, and followed her into her neat kitchen.

" An' how," said Mrs. Trapes, as she prepared to make the coffee, " how's the pea-nut trade, Mr. Geoffrey ? "

" Flourishing, thanks."

" The idea of you a-sellin' pea-nuts ! "

" Well, I've only been guilty of it four days so far, Mrs. Trapes."

Of a Text, a Letter, and a Song

"Anyway, you've disgusted Hermy."

"Ah! so you told her, did you?"

"O' course I did."

"And what did she say?"

"Laughed at first."

"She has a beautiful laugh," said Ravenslee musingly.

"An' then she got thoughtful."

"She's loveliest when she's thoughtful, I think," said Ravenslee.

"An' then she got mad at you an' frowned."

"She's very handsome when she frowns," said Ravenslee.

"Oh, shucks!" said his landlady, slapping the ham-rasher into the pan.

"And she was very angry, was she?"

"I should say so," snorted Mrs. Trapes, "stamped her foot an' got red in the face."

"I love to see her flush," said Ravenslee musingly again.

"Said she wondered at you, she did. Said you was a man without any pride or ambition, an' that's what I say too. Pea-nuts!"

"They're very wholesome," he murmured.

"Sellin' pea-nuts ain't a man's job no more than grindin' a organ is."

"There's money in pea-nuts."

"Money!" said Mrs. Trapes, wriggling her elbow-joints. "How much did you make yesterday—come?"

"Fifty cents."

"Fifty cents!" she almost screamed, "is that all?"

"No—pardon me. There were three pimply youths on Forty-second Street, they brought it up to seventy-five."

"Only seventy-five cents! But you sold out your stock. Tony told me you did."

"Oh yes, trade was very brisk yesterday."

"And you sold everything for—seventy-five cents?"

"Not exactly, Mrs. Trapes. You see, the majority of

The Definite Object

customers on my beat are very—er—small, and their pecuniary capabilities necessarily somewhat—shall we say restricted. Consequently I have adopted the—er—deferred payment system."

" Land sakes ! " said Mrs. Trapes, staring, " d'ye mean ter say——"

" That my method of business is strictly—credit."

" Now, look-a-here, Mr. Geoffrey, I'm talkin' serious an' don't want none o' your jokes or jollyin'."

" Solemn as an owl, Mrs. Trapes."

" Well then, how d'you suppose you can keep a wife, an' children maybe, by selling pea-nuts that way or any way ! "

" Oh, when I marry I shall probably turn my—attention to—er—other things, Mrs. Trapes."

" What things ? "

" Well, to my wife, in the first place."

" Oh, Mr. Geoffrey, you make me tired ! "

" Alas, Mrs. Trapes, I frequently grow tired of myself."

Mrs. Trapes turned away to give her attention to the ham.

" Did ye see that b'y Arthur yesterday ? " she inquired presently over her shoulder.

" Yes."

" How's he like his noo job ? "

" Well, I can't say that he seems—er—fired with a passion for it."

" Office work, ain't it ? "

" I believe it is."

" Well, you mark my words, that b'y won't keep it a week."

" Oh, I don't know," said Ravenslee, " he seemed quite content."

" You took him to the theayter las' night, didn't you ? Wastin' your good money, eh ? "

" Not very much, Mrs. Trapes," said her lodger humbly.

Mrs. Trapes sniffed.

Of a Text, a Letter, and a Song

"Anyway, it's a good thing you had him safe out o' the way, as it happens."

"Why?"

"Because that loafer M'Ginnis was hangin' around for him all the evenin'. Even had the dratted imperence to come in here an' ask me where he was."

"And what did you tell him?"

"Tell him!" she repeated. "What did I not tell him?" Her voice was gentle, but what words could convey all the quivering ferocity of her elbows? "Mr. Geoffrey, I told Bud M'Ginnis just exactly what kind o' beast Bud M'Ginnis is. I told Bud M'Ginnis where Bud M'Ginnis come from an' where Bud M'Ginnis would go to. I told Bud M'Ginnis the character o' his mother an' father very plain an' p'inted."

"And what did he say?"

"He say! Mr. Geoffrey, I didn't give him a chance to utter a single word, o' course. An' when I'd said all there was to say I picked up my heaviest flat-iron as happened to be handy, an' ordered him out, an', Mr. Geoffrey, Bud M'Ginnis—went."

"Under the circumstances," said Ravenslee, "I'm not surprised that he did."

"Ah! but he'll come back again, Mr. Geoffrey. He'll find Arthur alone next time, an' Arthur 'll go along wi' him, an' then—good-night! The b'y 'll get drunk an' lose his job like he did last time."

"Why, then, he mustn't find Arthur alone."

"An' who's to stop him?"

"I."

"Mr. Geoffrey, you're big an' strong, but M'Ginnis is stronger—an' yet——" Mrs. Trapes ran a speculative eye over Ravenslee's lounging form. "H'm!" said she musingly, "but even if you did happen to lick him, what about th' gang?"

"Echo, Mrs. Trapes, promptly answers, 'what?'"

"Well, Mr. Geoffrey, I can tell ye there's been more 'n

133

one poor feller killed around here to my knowin'—yes, sir ! ''

" But the police ? "

" Perlice ! " snorted Mrs. Trapes. " M'Ginnis an' his father have a big pull wi' Tammany, an' Tammany is the perlice. Anyways, Mr. Geoffrey, don't you go havin' no trouble wi' Bud M'Ginnis. Leave him to some one as is as much a brute-beast as he is."

" But then, what of Spike ? "

" Oh, drat him ! If Arthur ain't got the horse-sense to know who's his worst enemy he ain't worth a clean man riskin' his life over, for it would be your life you'd risk, Mr. Geoffrey—mark my words."

" Mrs. Trapes, your anxiety on my account flatters me, also I'm glad to know you think me a clean man. But all men must take risks—some for money, some for honour, and some for the pure love of it. Personally, I rather like a little risk, just a suspicion, if it's for something worth while."

" Mr. Geoffrey, what are you gettin' at ? "

" Well, I would remind you that Spike has—a sister."

" Ah ! " said Mrs. Trapes, and her lined face took on a sudden anxious expression.

" Therefore I've been contemplating—er—tackling Mr. M'Ginnis—at a proper and auspicious time, of course."

" An' what o' the gang ? "

" Oh, drat the gang, Mrs. Trapes."

" But you don't mean as you'd—fight M'Ginnis ? "

" Well—er—the thought has occurred to me, Mrs. Trapes, though I'm quite undecided on the matter, and —er—I believe my breakfast is burning."

" My land ! " ejaculated Mrs. Trapes, turning to snatch the pan from the stove, " I'm afraid the fire's ketched it a bit, Mr. Geoffrey."

" No matter."

" An' now there's the coffee b'ilin' over."

" Let me help you," said Ravenslee, rising.

Of a Text, a Letter, and a Song

"Anyway, your breakfast's ready, so come an' eat it while it's good an' hot."

"On condition that you eat with me."

"What, eat wi' you, Mr. Geoffrey—in my best parlour—an' me in me workin' clo'es?"

"Ah, to be sure—not to be thought of, Mrs. Trapes.; then we'll breakfast here in the kitchen."

"Would ye mind?"

"Should love it."

So down they sat together, and Ravenslee vowed the ham was all ham should be, and the eggs beyond praise. And when his hunger was somewhat appeased, Mrs. Trapes leaned her bony elbows on the table and questioned him.

"You ain't ever spoke to Hermy, have you, Mr. Geoffrey?"

"Very often lately."

"I mean—you ain't opened your heart to her—matrimonially, have you?"

"No."

"Why, then, I'll tell you what. There's been times when I've been afraid that for the sake o' that b'y she'd sacrifice herself to Bud M'Ginnis."

"No, she would never do that, Mrs. Trapes."

"Oh, but she would."

"But, you see, she couldn't."

"An' why not?"

"Oh, well, because—er—I should kill him first."

"Land sakes, Mr. Geoffrey!" and Mrs. Trapes actually blenched before the glare in his eyes that was so strangely at odds with his soft, lazy tones.

"And that ends it," he nodded. "Mrs. Trapes, I've made up my mind."

"What about?"

"Mr. M'Ginnis. I'll begin to-day."

"Begin what?"

"To prepare myself to bestow on him the thrashing of

E2 135

The Definite Object

his life." So saying, Ravenslee stretched lazily and finally got up. "Good-morning, Mrs. Trapes!" said he.

"But where are ye goin'?" she demanded.

"To my pea-nuts," he answered gravely. "'Man is born to labour,' you know."

"But it's early yet."

"But I have much to do. And she laughed at me for being a pea-nut man, did she, Mrs. Trapes? She frowned and flushed, and stamped her pretty foot at me, did she?"

"She did so, Mr. Geoffrey."

"I'm glad," he answered, "yes, I'm very glad she frowned and stamped her foot at me. By the way, I like that text in my bedroom."

"Text?" said Mrs. Trapes, staring.

"'Love one another,'" he nodded. "It is a very—very beautiful sentiment—sometimes. Anyway, I'm glad she frowned and stamped at me, Mrs. Trapes. You can tell her I said so if you happen to think of it when she comes home." And Ravenslee smiled, and, turning away, was gone.

"Well," said Mrs. Trapes, staring at the closed door, "of all the—well, well!" Then she sighed, shook her head, and fell to washing up the breakfast things.

CHAPTER XV

THE clocks were striking nine as, according to his custom of late, Geoffrey Ravenslee trundled his barrow blithely along Thirty-eighth Street, halting now and then at the shrill, imperious summons of some small customer, or by reason of the congestion of early traffic, or to swear whole-heartedly and be sworn at by some indignant Jehu. At length he came to Eleventh Avenue, and to a certain quarter where the whistle of a pea-nut barrow was seldom heard and pea-nuts were a luxury.

And here, in a dismal, small street hard by the river, behold Ravenslee halt his gaily-painted push-cart, whereat a shrill clamour arises that swells upon the air, a joyous babel; and forth from small and dismal homes, from narrow courts and the purlieus adjacent, his customers appear. They race, they gambol, they run and toddle, for these customers are very small and tender and grimy, but each small face is alight with joyous welcome, and they hail him with rapturous acclaim ; even the few tired-looking mothers, peeping from windows, or glancing from doorways, smile and nod and forget a while their weariness in the children's delight, as Ravenslee, the battered hat cocked at a knowing angle, proceeds to " business." Shrill voices supplicate him, little feet patter close around him, small hands, eagerly outstretched, appeal to him. Anon rise shrieks and infantile crowings of delight as each small hand is drawn back grasping a plump paper-bag—shrieks and crowings that languish and die away,

The Definite Object

one by one, since no human child may shriek properly and chew pea-nuts at one and the same time. And in a while, his stock greatly diminished, Ravenslee trundles off and leaves behind him women who smile still, and small boys and girls who munch in a rapturous silence.

On he went, his oven whistling soft and shrill, his long legs striding between the shafts, until reaching a certain bleak corner he halted again, though to be sure there were few people hereabouts, and no children ; but, upon the opposite corner was a saloon, with a large annexe and many outbuildings behind, backing upon the river, and Ravenslee, lounging on the handles of his barrow, examined this unlovely building keen-eyed beneath his hat-brim, for above the swing-doors appeared the words :

O'ROURKE'S SALOON

He was in the act of lighting his pipe when the doors of the saloon were swung open and three men came out, in one of whom he recognised the tall, powerful figure and broad shoulders of Bud M'Ginnis ; his companions were remarkable but in very opposite ways, the one being slender and youthful, and very smartly dressed, with a face which, despite its seeming youth, was strangely haggard and of an unhealthy pallor, while the other was plethoric, red-faced, and middle-aged, a man hoarse of voice and roughly clad, and Ravenslee noticed that this fellow lacked the upper half of one ear.

"Saturday night, mind !" said M'Ginnis, loud and authoritative.

"But say, Bud," demanded the smartly dressed youth, "what's comin' to us on that last deal ? "

"Nix, that's what you get, Soapy ! "

The youth's pale cheek grew livid. "So you've got the deck stacked against us—eh, Bud ? " said he.

"I got a close mouth, Soapy. I guess you don't want me t'open it very wide, now or any other old time. Saturday night, mind !" and, nodding, M'Ginnis turned away.

Which Introduces Joe and the Old 'un

The youth looked after him with venomous eyes, and his right hand made a sinister movement towards his hip pocket.

"Aw, quit it, are ye crazy?" grunted his companion. "Bud's got us cinched."

"Got us—hell!" snarled the youth. "Bud's askin' for it, an' some day he's goin' to' get it—good."

Towards mid-day Ravenslee was trundling light-heartedly eastward, his barrow emptied to the last pea-nut. Having reached Fifth Avenue he paused to mop his perspiring brow, when a long, low automobile, power-fully engined, that was creeping along behind, pulled up with a sudden jerk, and its driver, whose immense shoulders were clad in a very smart livery, pushed up the peak of his smart cap to run his fingers through his close cropped hair, while his mild blue eyes grew very wide and round.

"Crikey!" said he at last. "Is that you, sir, or ain't it?"

"How much?" demanded Ravenslee gruffly.

"Crumbs!" said the chauffeur. "Sir, if you—ain't you, all I say is—I ain't me."

"Aw, what's bitin' ye, bo?" growled Ravenslee.

"Well, if this ain't the rummest go, I'm a perisher!"

"Say now, crank up de machine an' beat it while de goin's good. How's that, Joe?"

"Lord, Mr. Ravenslee, so you are my guv'nor, an', blow me tight, shoving a barrer. I knowed it was you, sir, leastways, I knowed your legs an' the set o' them shoulders, but—with a barrer! Excuse me, sir, but the idea o' you pushing a perishing pea-nut barrer so gay an' 'appy-'earted—well, all I can say is, love-a-duck!"

"Well now, cut along, Joe, and get ready. I mean to put in some real hard work with you this afternoon."

"Right-o, sir," nodded Joe eagerly. "Lord, but we've missed you terrible—the Old 'un an' me."

"Glad of it, Joe! Tell Patterson to have my bath

The Definite Object

ready when we've finished. Off with you, drive in the Fifth Avenue entrance."

Joe nodded, and the big car turned and crept silently away, while Ravenslee, trundling onward, turned off to the left, and so into a very large, exceedingly neat place, where stood five or six automobiles of various patterns, in one of which, a luxurious limousine, an old, old man snored blissfully. At the rumble of the barrow, however, this ancient being choked upon a snore, coughed, swore plaintively, and finally sat up. Perceiving Ravenslee, he blinked, rubbed his eyes, and, stepping from the car very nimbly despite his years, faced the intruder with a ferocious scowl.

He was, indeed, a very ancient man, though very nattily dressed, from spotless collar to shiny patent-leather shoes ; a small, dandified, bright-eyed man, whose broken nose and battered features bore eloquent testimony to long and hard usage.

" 'Ook it ! " he croaked, with square, bony jaw fiercely out-thrust, " we don't want no pea-nuts 'ere, d'j'ear ? 'Op off, 'ook it, before I break every blessed bone in yer bloomin' body."

" What, Old 'un, don't you know me either ? "

" Lumme ! " exclaimed the little old man, blinking beneath hoary brows. " Ho lor' lumme, it's 'im ! Blimy, it's the guv'nor. 'Ow do, guv ! " and shooting immaculate cuffs over bony wrists, he extended a claw-like hand.

" How are you, Old 'un ? "

" Well, sir, what with the rheumatix an' a stift j'int or two, an' a touch o' lumbager, not to mention all my other ailments, I ain't quite s' spry as I was."

" But you look very well."

" That's where your heyes deceives you, guv. A great sufferer I be, though patient under haffliction, ho yus, except for a swear now an' then, which do do me a power o' good—yus. If I was to tell you all the woes as my poor old carkiss is hair to you could write a book on 'em, a big

140

Which Introduces Joe and the Old 'un

'un. I got everything the matter wi' me, I 'ave, from a thick ear an' broke nose as I took in Brummagem sixty an' five years ago, to a hactive liver."

"A what ? " inquired Ravenslee.

" A hactive liver. Lord, guv, my liver gets that hactive lately as I can't set still. Joe knows, ax Joe! All as I ain't got o' human woes is toothache, not 'avin' no teeth to ache, ye see, an' them s' rotten as it 'ud make yer 'eart bleed. An' then I get took that short o' breath, look at me now, dang it ! "

" Why then, sit down, Old 'un," said Ravenslee, drawing up a somewhat worn armchair. " Joe and I are going at it hard and fast this afternoon, and I want you to time the rounds." And he proceeded to remove his garments.

" Oh j'y ! " cried the Old 'un, hugging himself in bony arms. " Oh, j'yful words ! Ah, but you peels like a good 'un, sir," he croaked, viewing white flesh and bulging muscle with knowing old eyes, " good an' long in the arm an' wide slope o' shoulder. You might ha' done well in the ring if you'd been blessed wi' poverty, an' I'd 'ad the 'andling of ye ; a world's unbeat champion, like Joe. A good fighter were I an' a wonnerful trainer. Ho yus, I might ha' made a top-notcher o' ye if you 'adn't been cursed wi' money."

" I suppose," said Ravenslee thoughtfully, " I suppose Joe was one of the best all-round fighting men that ever climbed into a ring ? "

" Ah, that 'e were. Joe were better 'n the best, only don't let 'im 'ear me say so, 'e'd be that puffed up—Lord ! But nobody could beat Joe—black, yaller, or white ; they all tried danged 'ard, but Joe were a world-beater. Ye see, I trained Joe, an' to-day 'e's as good as ever 'e was. Ye see, Joe's allus lived clean, sir, consequent Joe's sound, wind an' limb. Joe could go back an' beat all these fancy bruisers an' stringy young champs to-day, if 'e only would, but don't let 'im 'ear me say so."

The Definite Object

" You're fond of Joe, Old 'un ? "

" An' why for not, sir, s'long as 'e don't know it ? Didn't 'e look arter poor old me when 'e 'ad money, an' when 'e lost everything didn't 'e look arter me still ? An' now 'e's your shuvver don't he keep a roof over me poor old 'ead like a son ; don't he give me the run o' your garridge, an' let me watch 'im spar wi' you an' your gentleman friends ? Ain't 'e the best an' truest-'earted man as ever drawed breath ? Ah, a king o' men is Joe, in the ring an' out, sir, only never let 'im 'ear me say so, 'e'd be that proud. Lord ! there'd be no livin' wi' 'im. Sh ! 'ere 'e be, sir."

Joe had laid by his chauffeur's garb, and looked bigger and grimmer than ever in flannels and sweater.

" Ho you, Joe," cried the old man, scowling, " did ye bring me that 'bacca ? "

" S'posin' I didn't ? " demanded Joe.

" Then dang ye—twice."

" An' s'posin' I did ? "

" Then give it 'ere ! "

" An' that's his gratitood, sir ! " growled Joe, shaking his head, and giving the packet into the old man's clutching fingers. " A unnat'ral old bag-o'-bones, that's what 'e is, sir."

" Bones ! " croaked the Old 'un viciously, " Bag-o'-bones, am I ? Yah, look at ye'self—pork, that's what you are, all run to pork an' blubber an' fat, Joe, me pore lad."

" Fat ! " growled Joe. " Ye know I ain't fat ; ye know I'm as good a man as ever I was. Look at that, you old sarpent ? " and he smote himself with mighty fist, a blow to fell an ox. " Fat, am I ? "

" As—lard ! " nodded the old man, filling half an inch of blackened clay pipe with trembling fingers, " As a 'og."

" Now, by crumbs ! " began Joe fiercely.

" You're flabby and soft, me pore lad," grinned the old man. " Flabby as a babby, an' soft as a woman, and fat as a——"

Which Introduces Joe and the Old 'un

But hereupon Joe reached out very suddenly, and, picking up the old man, armchair and all, shook him to and fro until he croaked for mercy.

"Lorgorramighty!" he panted, as Joe set him down again.

"Fat, am I?" demanded Joe, scowling.

"Fat as a 'og—fat as forty bloomin' 'ogs!" cried the old man vindictively, "An', what's more, your wind's all gone. You couldn't go five rounds wi' a good 'un."

"Couldn't I?"

"No!" shrieked the Old 'un, "you'd be 'angin' on an' blowing like a grampus!"

"Should I?"

"Ah—like a grampus!"

"Right-oh!" nodded Joe, turning away, "no jam for *your* tea to-night."

"Eh, what—what, would ye rob a pore old man of 'is jam, Joe—a pore, afflicted old cove as is dependent on ye 'and an' fut, Joe—a pore old gaffer as you've just shook up to that degree as 'is pore old liver is a-bobbin' about in 'is innards like a jelly? Joe, ye couldn't be so ' artless!"

"Ah, but I can!" nodded Joe. "An' if ye give me any more lip it'll be no sugar in yer tea."

"No sugar!" wailed the Old 'un; then clenching a trembling old fist he shook it in Joe's scowling face. "Then dang ye—three times!" he cried. "What's the old song say?"

> Dang the man with three times three
> Who in 'is 'eathen rage
> Can 'arm a 'armless man like me,
> Whose 'ead is bowed wi' age!

An' there's for ye. Now listen again:

> Some men is this an' some is that,
> But 'ere's a truth I know:
> A fightin' cove who's run to fat
> Is bound t' puff an' blow!

143

The Definite Object

And there's for ye again!" saying which the Old 'un nodded ferociously and proceeded to light his fragmentary pipe. During this colloquy Ravenslee had laid by his shabby clothes and now appeared clad and shod for the ring.

"Sir," said Joe, taking a set of gloves from a locker, "if you are ready to box a round or so——"

"Why, no," answered Ravenslee, "I don't want to box to-day, Joe."

"Eh!" said Joe, staring. "Not?"

"I want to fight, Joe."

"To—fight, sir?" repeated Joe.

"Fight?" cried the Old 'un rapturously. "Oh music —sweet music t' me old ears! Fight? Oh, j'yful words! What's the old song say?—

> 'Appy is the fist as goes
> To black a eye or punch a nose!

Get the mufflers on, Joe; get 'em on, an' don't stand staring like a fool."

"But, sir," said Joe, his mild eyes kindling, "d'ye mean as you want—the real thing?"

"To-day," said Ravenslee, "instead of boxing a round or two with Joe Madden, my chauffeur and mechanic, I want to see how long I can stand up to Joe Madden, undefeated champion of the world."

Joe's lean cheek flushed, and he looked Ravenslee over with eyes of yearning; noted the thin flanks and slender legs that showed speed, the breadth of shoulder and long arms that spoke strength, and the deep, arched chest that showed endurance. Joe looked and sighed and shook his head:

"Sir," said he, "I honour and respect you to that degree as it would be a joy to fight such a man as you, and a rare privilege t' knock you down; but, sir, if I was to knock ye down——"

"You'd earn a five-dollar bill."

144

Which Introduces Joe and the Old 'un

" Five dollars—for knockin' you down, sir ? "

" Every time ! " nodded Ravenslee.

" But lord, sir——"

" Shut up, Joe, shut up," snarled the Old 'un, hopping out of the armchair, " don't gape like a perishin' fish! Come on upstairs an' knock the guv'nor down like 'e tells ye, an' 'arves on the money, mind. It was me as taught ye all ye know or ever will, so 'arves on the money, Joe, 'arves on the money. Come on, Joe, d'j' 'ear ? "

" Crumbs ! " said Joe.

" Look at 'im, guv'—look at 'im ! " shrieked the old man, dancing to and fro in his impatience. " 'Ere's a chance for 'im to earn a pore old cove a bit o' 'bacca money, an', what's better still, t' show a pore old fightin' man a bit o' real sport, an' there 'e stands, starin' like a perishin' pork pig ! Blimy, guv, get behind an' 'elp me to shove 'im upstairs ! "

" But, crikey, sir ! " said Joe, " five dollars every time I——"

" Yus, yus, you bloomin' hadjective, two dollars fifty for each of us ! 'Urry up, oh 'urry up afore 'e changes 'is mind an' begins to 'edge."

Thus presently Joe follows his guv'nor and the Old 'un up a flight of stairs and into a large chamber fitted as a gymnasium, where are four roped and padded posts socketed into the floor ; close by is a high-backed armchair in which the Old 'un seats himself with an air of heavy portent.

But now, when Joe would have ducked under the ropes, the Old 'un stayed him with an imperious gesture, and, clambering into the ring, advanced to the centre and bowed gravely as if to a countless multitude.

" Gentlemen," he piped in his shrill old voice, " I take pleasure to introduce Joe Madden, undefeated 'eavy-weight champion o' the world, an' The Guv, both members of this club, an' both trained by me, Jack Bowser, once light-weight champion of England and 'all

The Definite Object

the Americas. Gentlemen, it will be a fight to a finish—
Markis o' Queensberry rules. Gentlemen, I thank ye."

Having said which the Old 'un bowed again and gravely
stepped from the ring, and, ensconcing himself in the
armchair, drew out a large and highly ornate watch,
while Ravenslee and Joe vaulted over the ropes.

And now behold them facing each other, the brown-
skinned fighting man wise in ring-craft and champion of
a hundred fights, and the white-fleshed athlete, each alike
clean and bright of eye, light-poised of foot, quivering
for swift action, while the Old 'un looks heedfully from
one to the other, watch in one bony hand, the other
upraised.

" Get ready ! " he croaked. " Go ! "

Comes immediately a quick, light tread of rubber-
soled feet and the flash of white arms as they circle about
and about, feinting watchful and wary. Twice Ravenslee's
fist shoots out and twice is blocked by Joe's open glove,
and once he ducks a vicious swing and lands a half-arm
jolt that makes Joe grin and stagger, whereat the Old 'un,
standing upon his chair, hugs himself in an ecstasy, and,
forgetful of such small matters as five-dollar bills, urges,
prays, beseeches and implores the guv to " wallop the
blighter on the p'int, to stab 'im on the mark, an' to jolt
'im in the kidney-pit." " Go it, guv ! " he shrieked, " go
it ! In an' out again, that's it. Gorramighty, I never
see sich speed. Oh, keep at 'im, guv—make 'im cover
up—sock it into 'im, guv ! Ho, lumme, what foot-work !
You're as quick as light-weights. Oh 'appy, 'appy day !
Go to it, both on ye ! "

And " to it " they went, with jabs and jolts, hooks and
swings, with cunning feints and lightning counters, until
the place echoed and re-echoed to the swift tramp of feet
and dull thudding of blows, while the Old 'un, hugging
himself in long, bony arms, chuckled and choked and
rocked himself to and fro in an ecstasy. Moreover, when
Joe, uttering a grunt, reeled back against the ropes, the

Which Introduces Joe and the Old 'un

Old 'un must needs shriek and dance and crow with delight, until, bethinking him of his duty, he checked his excitement, seated himself in the armchair again, and announced :

" Time ! End o' round one."

And now it is to be noticed that as they sit to take their two minutes' rest, neither Ravenslee nor Joe, for all their exertions, seem unduly distressed in their breathing.

" Sir," says Joe, looking his pupil over, " you're uncommon quick on your pins. Never knowed a quicker ; did you, Old 'un ? "

" No, me lad, never in all me days."

" An' you've surely got a punch, sir; ain't 'e, Old 'un ? "

" Like a perishin' trip-hammer ! " nodded the Old 'un.

" Likewise, sir, you've a wonderful judgment o' distance ; but, sir, you need experience."

" That's what I'm after, Joe."

" And you take too many chances ; you ain't larned caution yet."

" That you must teach me, Joe."

" Which I surely will, sir. In the next round, subject to no objection, I propose to knock ye down, sir."

" Which means two dollars fifty for each on us, Joe, mind that," added the Old 'Un.

" So fight more cautious, sir, do," pleaded Joe, " and— look out."

" I will," nodded Ravenslee.

" Time ! " croaked the Old 'un. " Round two ! "

Once again they faced each other, but this time it was Joe who circled quick and cat-like, massive shoulders bowed, knees bent, craggy chin grim and firm-set, but blue eyes serene and mild as ever. A moment's silent sparring, a quick tread of feet, and Joe feints Ravenslee into an opening, swings for his chin, misses by an inch, ducks a vicious counter, drives home a smashing body-

147

blow, and, staggering weakly, Ravenslee goes down full-length.

"Shook ye up a bit, sir?" inquired Joe, running up with hands outstretched. "Take a rest, now do, sir."

"No, no," answered Ravenslee, springing to his feet, "the Old 'un hasn't called 'Time' yet."

"Not me," piped the old man, "not bloomin' likely! Go to it both on ye; mind, that's two-fifty for me, Joe!"

What need is there to tell the numerous feints, the lightning shifts, the different tricks of in-fighting, and all the cunning strategy and ring-craft that Joe brought to bear and carefully explained between rounds? Suffice it that at the end of a certain fierce "mix up," as Ravenslee sat outstretched and panting, the white flesh of arms and broad chest discovered many livid marks and patches that told their tale, also one elbow was grazed and bleeding, and one knee showed signs of recent contact with the floor.

"Joe," said he, when his wind was somewhat recovered, "that makes it thirty dollars I owe you, I think?"

"Why, sir," said Joe, who also showed some slight signs of wear, but whose breathing was soft and regular, "why, sir, you couldn't call that last one a real knock-down."

"You 'm a liar, Joe, a liar!" cried the Old 'un. "Blimy, guv, Joe's a-tellin' you crackers, s' help me. Your 'ands touched the floor, didn't they?"

"And my knees too," nodded Ravenslee, "also my elbow—no, that was last time or the time before."

"Well then, tell this lying Joe-lad o' mine as 'e surely did knock ye down. Lord, Joe!" cried the Old 'un, waxing pathetic, "'ow can ye go takin' money from a pore old cove like I be. Joe, I blushes for ye an'—Time, Time there, both on ye!"

"But we don't want any more, do us, sir?" inquired Joe.

"Why, yes, I think I can go another round or so."

Which Introduces Joe and the Old 'un

"There y' are, Joe, the guv's surely a game cove. So get at it, me lad, an' try an' knock it up to fifty dollars. 'Arves, Joe, mind."

"But, sir," began Joe, eyeing the livid blotches on Ravenslee's white skin, "don't ye think——"

"Time—oh, Time, Time!" shrieked the Old 'un. Whereupon Ravenslee sprang to the centre of the ring and once again the air resounded with tramp of feet and pant of breath. Twice Ravenslee staggers beneath Joe's mighty left; but watchful ever, and having learned much, he keeps away, biding his time—ducks a swing, side-steps a drive, and, blocking a vicious hook, smacks home his long left to Joe's ribs, rocks him with a swinging upper-cut, drives in a lightning left and right, and Joe goes down with a crash.

Even while the Old 'un stared in wide-eyed, gaping amaze, Joe was on his feet again serene and calm as ever, only his great chest laboured somewhat; but Ravenslee shook his head.

"I guess that'll be about enough, Joe," said he.

"Guv," cried the Old 'un, seizing Ravenslee's right hand, boxing-glove and all, and shaking it to and fro, "you're a credit to us, you do us bloomin' proud—strike me pink ye do. 'Ere's Joe 'ammered you an' 'ammered you—look at your bloomin' chest—lumme! 'Ere's Joe been knockin' ye down an' knockin' ye down, an' you comin' up smilin' for more an' gettin' it—'ere's Joe been a-poundin' of ye all over the ring, yet you can finish strong an' speedy enough to put Joe down—blimy, guv, you're a wonder, an' no error."

"I don't think Joe fought his hardest, Old 'un."

"If 'e didn't," cried the old man, "I'll punch 'im on the nose so 'e won't never smell nothink no more."

"Sir," said Joe, "in the first round p'r'aps I did go a bit easy-like, but arter that I came at you as 'ard an' 'eavy as I could. I 'it you where an' 'ow I could, barrin' your face."

The Definite Object

" I hope I shall soon be good enough for you to go for my face as well, Joe."

" But, sir—if I give you a black eye ? "

" How will, say, ten dollars do ? "

" Ten dollars ! For blacking your eye, sir ? "

" Lumme, Joe ! " cried the Old 'un, " get back into the ring and black 'em both."

" Shut up," said Joe, scowling down into the Old 'un's eager face, " you 'eartless old bloodsucker, you."

" Bloodsucker," screamed the old man, " w'ot, me ? I'll punch you on the ear'ole, Joe, so 's you never 'ear nothin' no more."

" Are you on, Joe ? " asked Ravenslee, while the Old 'un, swearing softly, unlaced his gloves.

" But, crumbs, sir—axin' your pardon, things 'll come a bit expensive, won't they—y' see——"

" So much the better, ye blighted perisher," snarled the Old 'un, " an' don't forget as the guv owes you thirty dollars a'ready—an' 'arves, mind."

" Stow it, you old bag o' wickedness."

" Bag o'——" The Old 'un let fall the boxing gloves, and turning on Joe reached up and shook a feeble old fist under the champion's massive chin, " look at this, me lad —look at this ! " he croaked, " some day I shall ketch you sich a perishin' punch as 'll double ye up till kingdom come, me lad, and—Lord, the guv's countin' out our money."

" Thirty of 'em, Joe," said Ravenslee, holding out a wad of bills.

" Why, sir," said Joe, backing away, " axing yer pardon, but I'd rayther not—you give me such uncommon good wages, sir, an' a bonus every race we run, win or lose—so, sir, I—I'd rayther not."

" Not ? " cried the Old 'un, " not take money as is 'arf mine ! Oh, kick 'im, somebody—kick 'im. Pound 'im for a pigeon-'earted perishin' pork pig."

" That'll be no sugar in your tea to-night, old viciousness. But, sir, I'd rayther not."

Which Introduces Joe and the Old 'un

" Don't 'eed 'im, guv—don't 'eed the flappin' flounder.
If 'e won't obleege ye in a little matter like thirty dollars,
I will—I'll always obleege you."

" That's enough from you, old tombstones."

" Tombstones ! " hissed the Old 'un, scowling darkly
and squaring his fists, " all right, me lad. 'Ere's where
I ketch ye one as 'll flatten ye out till the day o'
doom."

But hereupon Joe caught him above the elbows, and,
lifting him in mighty hands that yet were gentle, seated
the snarling old fellow in the armchair.

" Old 'un," said he, shaking his finger, " if ye give me
any more of it—off t' bed I take ye without any tea at
all." The Old 'un, cowering beneath that portentous
finger, swore plaintively and promptly subsided.

" And now," said Ravenslee, thrusting the money into
Joe's reluctant hand, " when I make a bargain I generally
keep it. I wish all my money had been spent to such
good purpose."

" What about me ? " whined the old man humbly,
" don't I get none, Joe-lad ? "

" Not a cent, you old rasper."

" Blimy, guv, you won't forget a old cove as 'u'd shed
'is best blood for ye ? "

" The guv'nor don't want yer blood, old skin-and-bones.
And now, come on, sir."

" Stay a minute, Joe, the Old 'un generally keeps time
for us when we spar rounds."

" That I do, guv," cried the old man, " an' give ye
advice worth its weight in solid gold. You owe me a lot,
s' 'elp me."

" About how much ? "

" Well, guv, I ain't got me ledger-book 'andy, but
roughly speakin' I should say about five or six 'undred
dollars. But seein' you's you an' I'm me—a old man
true-'earted as never crossed nobody—let's say—fifteen
dollars."

The Definite Object

" Why you old—thievin'—vagabone," gasped Joe as Ravenslee gravely handed over the money.

" Vagabone yourself! " said the Old 'un, counting the bills over in trembling fingers, " The guv wants a bath—take 'im away—'ook it, d'j' 'ear ? "

" Has Patterson got everything ready, Joe ? " inquired Ravenslee, taking up his clothes.

" No, sir," mumbled Joe, " but I'll have yer bath ready in a jiffy, sir."

" But where's Patterson ? "

" Well 'e—'e's out, sir."

" And the footmen ? "

" They're out, sir."

" Oh ! And the housekeeper—er—what's her name—Mrs. Smythe ? "

" Gone to call on her relations, sir."

" Ah ! And the maids ? "

" Mrs. Smythe give 'em leave of habsence, sir. Ye see, sir," said Joe apologetically, " you're 'ere so seldom, sir."

" My servants are not exactly—er—worked to death, Joe ? "

" No, sir."

" Manage to look after themselves quite well ? "

" Yes, sir."

" It seems I need some one to look after them—and me."

" Yes, sir."

" A woman, Joe—one I can trust and honour and—er —what d'ye think ? "

" I think—er—yes, sir."

" Well, what do you suggest ? "

" Marry her, sir."

" Joe, that's a great idea! Shake hands! I surely will marry her—at once—if she'll have me."

" She'll have you, sir."

" Do you really think she will, Joe ? "

Which Introduces Joe and the Old 'un

" I'm dead certain, sir."

" Joe, shake again.   I'll speak to her when she comes home. To-morrow's Saturday, isn't it ? "

" As ever was, sir."

" Then, Joe, wish me luck.   I'll ask her—to-morrow."

CHAPTER XVI

OF THE FIRST AND SECOND PERSONS SINGULAR NUMBER

IT was Saturday morning, and Hermione was making a pie and looking uncommonly handsome about it and altogether feminine and adorable ; at least, so Ravenslee thought as he watched her bending above the pastry-board, her round, white arms bared to each dimpled elbow, and with the rebellious curl wantoning at her temple as usual.

"But why kidneys, my dear ? " demanded Mrs. Trapes, glancing up from the potatoes she was peeling ; " Kidneys is rose again, kidneys is always risin' it seems to me. If you must have pie, why not good plain beef-steak, it's jest as fillin' an' cheaper, my dear—so why an' wherefore kidneys ? "

" Arthur likes them, and he'll be hungry when he comes in."

" Hungry ! " snorted Mrs. Trapes, " that b'y's been hungry ever since he drawed the breath o' life. How's he gettin' on with his noo job ? "

" Oh, splendidly," cried Hermione, flushing with sisterly pride, " they've promised him a rise next month."

" What, already ? " exclaimed Mrs. Trapes, cutting viciously into a potato, " if he don't watch out they'll be makin' him a partner next."

" Oh, Ann, I wish you were not quite so—so hard on him," sighed Hermione ; " remember, he's only a boy."

" You were a woman at his age, earnin' enough t' keep ye both. But there, I don't mean t' be hard, Hermy ; anyway, a man's never much good till he's growed up,

154

an' then only because some woman teaches him how t' be."

"What do you say to that, Mr. Geoffrey?" inquired Hermione, pausing, flour-dredger in hand, to glance at him slyly under her brows.

"I think Mrs. Trapes is a wonderful woman," he answered.

"Ah now, Mr. Geoffrey, quit yer jollyin'," said Mrs. Trapes, smiling at the potato.

"Mrs. Trapes has taught me much wisdom already, and, among other things, that I shall never be or do anything worth while without the aid of a woman."

"Lord, Mr. Geoffrey, I never remember sayin' no sich thing."

"Not in so many words perhaps, but you implied it, Mrs. Trapes."

"H'm!" said Mrs. Trapes, dubiously.

"Consequently, I mean to ask that woman—on the very first opportunity, Miss Hermione."

Seeing that Hermione was silent, all her attention being centred in the dough her white fists were kneading, Mrs. Trapes spoke instead:

"D'ye mean as you want some one t' look after you —to sew an' cook an' wash an' sew buttons on for ye?"

"I certainly do, and——"

"Ah, it's a slave you want, Mr. Geoffrey, an' pea-nut men don't have slaves—not unless they marries 'em, an' a woman as would marry a pea-nut man has only herself t' blame—pea-nuts!"

Hermione laughed, reached for the rolling-pin, and immediately fell to work with it, her head stooped rather lower than was necessary. As for Ravenslee, he lounged in his chair, watching the play of those round, white arms.

"But why the kidneys, Hermy? You've got to cut out luxuries now, my dear—we all have, I guess. It'll be dry bread next, I reckon."

"Why so?" inquired Ravenslee, lazily.

The Definite Object

" Why ? " cried Mrs. Trapes, bitterly, " I'll tell you why, because me an' Hermy an' every one else is bein' squeezed dry t' fill the pockets of a thing as calls itself a man—a thievin' beast on two legs as is suckin' our blood, gnawin' our flesh, grindin' the life out of us—a great, fat man as is treadin' us down under his great boots, down an' down to slavery—death—an' worse—it's such men as him as keeps the flames o' hell goin'—fat frizzles well, an' so will Mulligan, I hope."

" Mulligan ? " inquired Ravenslee.

" He's raised the rents on us, Mr. Geoffrey," sighed Hermione.

" Raised the rents ? " said Ravenslee, forgetting to lounge.

" Sure ! " nodded Mrs. Trapes grimly. " I guess he thinks we live too easy an' luxoorious, so he's boosted it up a dollar per. A dollar a week don't sound a whole lot p'r'aps, but it sure takes some gettin'; folks expect a deal o' scrubbin' an' sewin' an' slavin' for a dollar—yes, sir."

" We shall have to work a little harder, that's all, Ann dear."

" Harder ? I guess you work hard enough for two; an' who gets the benefit ? Why, Mulligan does. Oh, it's a great comfort t' remember the flames o' hell sometimes. Lord, when I think how we have to slave t' make enough t' live ! "

" There are others worse than us, Ann."

" Why, yes, there's poor Mrs. Finlay, she's got to go, an' her husband paralysed ! There's little Mrs. Bowker sewed herself pretty well blind t' keep her home together —she's got to go. There's Mrs. Sims with all those children, and the—— But there, who cares for the likes o' them—who cares—eh, Mr. Geoffrey ? An' what might you be dreamin' over this time ? " she inquired, eyeing Ravenslee's long figure a little contemptuously, for he had fallen to lounging again, sleepy eyes half-closed.

Of First and Second Persons

"I was thinking what a lot of interest we might find in this busy world—if we only would take the trouble to look for it!" he answered. "The fool who complains that his life is empty, is blind and deaf and—damnably thick—er—pardon me, I—er—nearly got excited."

"Excited!" snorted Mrs. Trapes. "I'd pay good money t' see you like that!"

"You see, I had an idea—a rather original idea."

"Then take care of it, Mr. Geoffrey, nurse it careful, an' we'll have ye doin' bigger things than push a pea-nut barrer—pea-nuts!"

"Mrs. Trapes, I've got a stranglehold on that idea, for it is rather brilliant."

"There's that kettle b'ilin' at last, thank goodness!" sighed Mrs. Trapes, crossing to the stove. "Tea's a luxury, I suppose, but—oh, drat Mulligan, anyway!"

So Mrs. Trapes brewed the tea while Ravenslee gazed at Hermione again, at her shapely arms, her dimpled elbows, her preoccupied face—a face so serenely, so utterly unaware of his regard, of course, until he chanced to look away, and then Hermione stole a glance at him.

"There, my dear," said Mrs. Trapes, after a while, "there's a cup o' tea as *is* a cup o' tea, brewed jest on the b'ile, in a hot pot, an' drawed to perfection. Set right down an' drink it, slow an' deliberate. Tea ain't meant to be swallowed down careless like a man does his beer! An' why," demanded Mrs. Trapes, as they sipped the fragrant beverage, all three, "why ain't you out with your precious—pea-nuts, Mr. Geoffrey?"

Ravenslee set down his cup and turned to Hermione.

"Mrs. Trapes has told you, I think, that I am become—er—an itinerant vendor of the ubiquitous pea-nut."

"Mr. Geoffrey!" gasped Mrs. Trapes, gulping a mouthful of hot tea and blinking, "I never did! Never in all my days would I allow myself such expressions. Mr.

The Definite Object

Geoffrey, I'm ashamed at you ! An' that reminds me—it was chicken fricassee, wasn't it ? For your supper, I mean ? "

"I believe it was."

"Then," said Mrs. Trapes, rising, "I'll go an' buy it. Was you wantin' anything fetched, Hermy ? "

"If you wouldn't mind, bring a bunch of asparagus."

"Sparrergrass !" exclaimed Mrs. Trapes in horror-struck tones, "Why it's anywhere from thirty to sixty cents."

"But Arthur loves it, dear, and now that he's working so hard——"

"Arthur !" cried Mrs. Trapes indignantly. "Mr. Geoffrey, it's been Arthur ever since he was born, an' her scrinchin' an' pinchin' herself for the sake o' that b'y. O' course he likes sparrergrass—so do I ; but I make shift with pertatoes or cabbidge or carrots—an' so should he. Come now, Hermy, you take a bunch o' carrots instead, carrots is healthy an' cheap ! Come now, is that sparrer-grass to be carrots or not ? "

"Ann, that asparagus is to be—asparagus ! "

"Such wicked extravagance, an' all for that b'y ! Hermy, I'm surprised at ye ! "

For a long moment after Mrs. Trapes had departed there was silence, while Ravenslee sat gazing where Her-mione stood busy at her pastry again.

"Mr. Geoffrey," said she at last, "I want to thank you for watching over my boy. Arthur told me how good you were to him while I was away. I want you to know how grateful I am."

"What beautiful hands you have, Hermione ; and I shall dream of your arms."

"My arms ? " she repeated, staring.

"They're so—smooth and white."

"Oh, that's flour !" said she, bending over the table again.

"And so—round."

158

Of First and Second Persons

" Oh, Mr. Geoffrey ! Can't you find something else to talk about ? "

" Why, of course," he answered, " there are your feet, so slender and shapely."

" In these frightful old shoes ! " she added.

" Worn out mostly in other people's service," he nodded. " God bless them ! "

" They let the wet in horribly when it rains ! " she sighed.

" So heaven send us dry weather ! Then there is your wonderful hair," he continued, " so long and soft and——"

" And all bunched up anyhow ! " said she, giving the heavy, shining braids a tentative shake. " Please don't say any more, Mr. Geoffrey, because I just know I look a sight—I feel it ! And in this old gown, too—it's the one I keep to scrub the floors in."

" Scrub the floors ? " he repeated.

" Why, of course, floors must be scrubbed, and I've had plenty—oh, plenty of experience. Now what are you thinking ? "

" That a great many women might envy you that gown for the beauty that goes with it. You are very beautiful, you know, Hermione."

" And beauty in a woman is—everything, isn't it ? " she said a little bitterly and with head suddenly averted.

" Have I offended you ? "

" No," she answered without looking round, " only sometimes you are so very—personal."

" Because the First and Second Persons Singular Number are the most interesting persons in the world, and, Hermione, in all this big world there is only one person I want. Could you ever learn to love a pea-nut man ? "

" That would all depend—on the pea-nut man," she answered softly, " and you—you don't talk or act a little bit like a real pea-nut man."

" Well, could you stoop to love this pea-nut man just

The Definite Object

as he is, with all his faults and failures, love him enough to trust yourself to his keeping, to follow him into the unknown, to help him find that Beautiful City of Perhaps—could you, Hermione?" As he ended he rose to his feet, but swiftly, dexterously, she eluded him.

"Wait!" she pleaded, facing him across the table, "I—I want to talk to you—to ask you some questions, and I want you to be serious, please."

"Solemn as sixty judges!" he nodded.

"Well, first, Mr. Geoffrey—why do you pretend to sell pea-nuts?"

"Pretend!" he repeated, trying to sound aggrieved.

"Oh, I'm not blind, Mr. Geoffrey."

"No, indeed—I think your eyes are the most beau——"

"Oh please, please be serious!"

"As a dozen owls!"

"I—I know," she went on quickly, "I'm sure you haven't always had to live in such—such places as Mulligan's; I know you don't belong here as I do. Is it necessity has driven you to live here, or only—curiosity?"

"Well—er—perhaps a little of both," he admitted.

"Then you're not obliged to sell pea-nuts for a living?"

"'Obliged' is scarcely the word perhaps, let us call it a pea-nut *penchant*, a hobby, a——"

"You are not quite so—poverty-stricken as you pretend?" Her voice was very soft and gentle, but she kept her head averted, also her foot was tapping nervously in its worn shoe.

"Oh, as to money," he answered, "I have enough for my simple needs, but in every other sense I am a miserable pauper. You see, there are some things no money can buy, and they are generally the best things of life."

"And so," she said, interrupting him gently, "you come here to Mulligan's, you deceive every one into thinking you are very poor, you make a pretence of selling pea-nuts, and push a barrow through the streets—why?"

Of First and Second Persons

" First, because pushing a barrow is—er—very healthy exercise."

" Yes, Mr. Geoffrey ? " she said in the same soft voice.

" And second," he continued, wishing he could see her face—" second, because I find it—er, well—highly amusing."

" Amusing ! " she cried, turning suddenly, her eyes very bright and her cheeks hot and anger-flushed. " Amusing ! " she repeated, " ah, yes—that's just it— it's all only a joke to you, to be done with when it grows tiresome ; but my life here—our life—is very real—ah, terribly real, and has been sordid sometimes. What is only sport to you for a little while is deadly earnest to me. You are only playing at poverty, but I must live it."

" And, thirdly," he continued gently, " because I love you, Hermione ! "

" Love me ! " she repeated, shaking her head. " Ah, no, no—your world is not my world, nor ever could be."

" Why then, your world shall be mine."

" Yes, but for how long ? " she demanded feverishly. " I wonder how long you could endure this world of mine ? I have had to work and slave all my life ; but you—look at your hands, so white and well-cared for— yours are not the hands of a worker ! "

" No, I'm afraid they're not ! " he admitted, a little ruefully.

" Now look at mine—see, my fingers all roughened by my needle."

" Such busy, capable hands ! " said he, drawing a pace nearer, " hands always working for others, so strong to help the distressed. I love and honour them more just because of those work-roughened fingers." As he spoke he reached out very suddenly, and, clasping these slender hands, stooped and kissed them reverently. Now glancing up he beheld her red lips all a-quiver, while her eyes were suffused all at once, as, drooping her head, she strove to loose his hold.

The Definite Object

"Let me go!" she whispered. "I—I—ah, let me go!"

"Hermione," he breathed, "oh, Hermione, how beautiful you are!" But at this she cried out almost as if he had struck her, and, wrenching her hands free, covered her face.

"Oh God! are all men the same?"

"Hermione," he stammered, "Hermione—what do you mean?"

"I mean," she answered, proud head upflung, "there were always plenty of men to tell me that—when I was an office scrub-woman. Well," she demanded fiercely, stung by something in his look, "what did you think I'd been? When a girl is left alone with a baby brother to care for she can't wait and pick and choose work that is nice and ladylike, she must take what comes along, or starve—so I worked. I used to scrub floors and stairs in an office building—I was very young then, and Arthur hardly more than a baby, and it was either that or starvation, or——" she flushed painfully, but her blue eyes met his regard unflinchingly. "Anyway, I preferred to be a scrub-woman. So now you know what I mean by your world not being my world, and I—I guess you see how impossible it all is?"

For a long moment was a silence, wherein she stood turned from him, her trembling fingers busily folding and refolding a pleat in her apron, while he stared down blindly at the floor.

"So you preferred the slavery of scrubbing floors, did you, Hermione?" he said at last.

"Of course!" she answered without turning or lifting her heavy head.

"And that," said he, his voice as placid, as serenely unhurried as usual, "and that is just why all things are going to be possible to us; yes, even turning my wasted years to profit. Oh, my Hermione, help me to be worthy of you—teach me what a glorious thing life may be——"

Of First and Second Persons

"I?" she said wonderingly, her drooping head still averted, "but I am——"

"Just the one woman I want to be my own for ever and always, more—far more than I have ever wanted anything in my life."

"But," she whispered, "I am only——"

"The best, the noblest I have ever known."

"But a—scrub-woman!"

"With dimples in her elbows, Hermione!" In one stride he was beside her; and she, because of his light tone must turn at last to glance up at him half-fearfully; but those grey eyes were grave and reverent, the hands stretched out to her were strangely unsteady, and when he spoke again his voice was placid no longer.

"Dear," he said, leaning toward her, "from the very first I've been dying to have you in my arms, but now I —I dare not touch you unless you will it so. Ah, don't —don't turn from me, let me have my answer; look up, Hermione!"

Slowly she obeyed, and now, beholding the shy languor of her eyes, the sweet hurry of her breathing, and all the sighing, trembling loveliness of her, he set his arms about her, drawing her close, and she, yielding to those compelling arms, gave herself to the passion of his embrace. And so he kissed her, her warm, soft, quivering mouth, her eyes, her silken hair, until she sighed and struggled in his clasp.

"My hair," she whispered, "see, it's all coming down!"

"Well, let it. I'd love to see it so, Hermione."

"Should you? Why, then, let me go," she pleaded.

Reluctantly he loosed her; and she, standing well beyond his reach, shook her shapely head, and down, down fell the heavy coils, past shoulder and waist and hip, rippling in shining splendour to her knees. Then, while he gazed spellbound by her loveliness, she laughed a little unsteadily, and, flushing beneath his look, turned and fled from him to the door.

The Definite Object

When he would have followed, she stayed him:

"Please," she said, tender-voiced, "I want to be alone; it is all so wonderful, I want to be alone, and —think."

"I may see you again to-night, Hermione? Dear, I must."

"Why, if you must," she said, "how can I—prevent you?"

Then, all at once, her cool, soft arms were about his neck, had drawn him down to meet her kiss, and—he was alone with the pastry-board, the rolling-pin, and the flour-dredger; but he saw them all through a golden glory, and when he somehow found himself out upon the dingy landing the glory was all about him still.

CHAPTER XVII

HOW GEOFFREY RAVENSLEE MADE A DEAL IN REAL ESTATE

THE morning sun blazed down, and Tenth Avenue was full of noise and dust and heat; children screamed and played and fought together, carts rumbled past, distant street-cars clanged their bells, the sidewalks were full of the stir and bustle of Saturday, but Ravenslee went his way heedless of all this, even of the heat, for before his eyes was the vision of a maid's shy loveliness, and he thrilled anew at the memory of two warm lips. Thus he strode unheeding through the jostling throng at a speed very different from his ordinary lounging gait. Very soon he came to a small drug-store weather-beaten and grimy of exterior but very bright within, where everything seemed in a perpetual state of glitter, from the multitudinous array of bottles and glassware upon the shelves to the taps and knobs of the soda-fountain. Yet nowhere was there anything quite so bright as the shrewd, twinkling eyes of the little grey-haired man who greeted Ravenslee with a cheery nod.

" Hot enough ? " he inquired.

" Quite ! " answered Ravenslee.

" Goin' to be hotter."

" Afraid so."

" Rough on th' kiddies, an' ice goin' up. Which reminds me I sent on the mixture you ordered for little Hazel Bowker."

" Good ! " nodded Ravenslee.

" And the pills to Mrs. Sims."

165

The Definite Object

" Good again ! ''

" An' the sleeping-draught for old Martin Finlay.''

" Good once more ! ''

" Won't last long, old Martin, I guess. Never been the same since little Maggie drowned herself, poor child. What d'ye want this morning ? ''

" First, to pay for the medicine," said Ravenslee, laying a five-dollar bill on the counter, " and then the use of your 'phone.''

" Right there," said the chemist, nodding toward a certain shady corner, where, remote from all intruding bustle, was a telephone booth, into which Ravenslee stepped forthwith, and where ensued the following one-sided conversation :

Ravenslee—" Hallo ! ''

Telephone—" Buzz ! ''

Ravenslee—" Hallo, Central, give me thirty-three Wall, please.''

Telephone—" Ting-a-ling—buzz-z ! ''

Ravenslee—" Damn this 'phone—what ? No, I said double-three Wall.''

Telephone—" Buzz ! Ting ! Zut ! ''

Ravenslee—" Sounded different, did it ? Well, I want——''

Telephone—" Buzz ! Zut ! Ting ! ''

Ravenslee—" Thanks. Hallo, that thirty-three Wall ? Dana & Anderson's office ? Good ! I want to speak with Mr. Anderson—say Mr. Ravenslee.''

Telephone—" Zing ! ''

Ravenslee—" Thanks. That you, Anderson ? ''

Telephone—" Pang ! ''

Ravenslee—" Thanks—very well ! What the devil's wrong with this instrument of torment ? Can you hear me ? ''

Telephone—" Crack ! ''

Ravenslee—" Good ! Yes—that's better ! Now listen, I want you to do some business for me. No, I'm buying,

166

A Deal in Real Estate

not selling. I'm going into real estate. What! a bad speculation? Well, anyway, I'm buying tenement property in Tenth Avenue, known as Mulligan's I believe. Oh, you've heard of it, eh? Not in the market? Not for sale? Well, I'll buy it. Oh yes, you can—what d'you suppose is his figure? So much? Phew! Oh, well, double it. No, I'm not mad, Anderson. No, nor drunk—I just happen to want Mulligan's—and I'll have it. When can you put the deal through? Oh, nonsense, make him sell at once—get him on the 'phone. Oh yes, he will if you offer enough—Mulligan would sell his mother —at his own price. You quite understand—at once, mind! All right, good-bye. No, I'm not mad—nor drunk, man, I haven't tasted a cocktail for a month. Eh —go and get one? I will!"

So saying, Ravenslee hung up the receiver and hasted out of the stifling heat of the suffocating booth, mopping perspiring brow.

" You look kinder warm!" nodded the chemist.

" I feel it."

" And it's going to be warmer. Try an ice-cream soda —healthy and invigorating."

" And better than any cocktail on such a day!"

" I guess! Take one?"

" Thank you, yes."

So the bright-eyed chemist mixed the beverage and handed it over the counter:

" Chin-chin!" he nodded.

" Twice," said Ravenslee, lifting the long glass. " To the beautiful City of Perhaps!" and he drank deep.

" Say," said the chemist staring, " that sounds t' me like a touch of the sun. Try a bottle of my summer mixture, good for sunstroke, heat-bumps, colic, spasms, and Hell's Kitchen generally. Try a bottle?"

" Thanks," said Ravenslee, " I will." And grimly pocketing the bottled panacea, he stepped out into the hot and noisy avenue.

CHAPTER XVIII

HOW SPIKE HEARKENED TO POISONOUS SUGGESTION, AND SOAPY BEGAN TO WONDER

SPIKE was on his way from the office, very conscious of his new straw hat and immaculate collar; his erstwhile shabby suit had been cleaned and pressed by Hermione's skilled and loving fingers, hence Spike turned now and then as he passed some shop window to observe the general effect with furtive eye; and, stimulated by his unwontedly smart appearance, he whistled joyously as he betook himself homeward. Moreover, in his breast-pocket was his pay-envelope, not very bulky to be sure, wherein lay his first week's wages, and as often as he turned to glance at the tilt of his straw hat or heed the set of his tie, his hand must needs steal to this envelope to make sure of its safety.

His fingers were so employed when he chanced to espy a certain article exposed for sale in an adjacent shop window; whereupon, envelope in hand, he incontinent entered and addressed the plump Semitic merchant in his usual easy manner.

"Greetin's, Abe! I'll take one o' them hair-combs."

"Hair-gombs?" nodded the merchant. "Vot kind?"

"What kind? Why, the best you got."

"Ve got 'em up to veefty dollars."

"Come off it, Cain, come off! I ain't purchasin' a diamond aigrette to-day, it's a lady's hair-comb I want, good, but not too flossy-lookin'—savvy that? This'll do, I guess—how much? Right there!" said Spike,

Of Poisonous Suggestion

flicking a bill upon the counter. "That's it, stick it in a box—oh, never mind th' wrappin's. S' long, Daniel!"

With his purchase in his pocket, Spike strode out of the shop whistling cheerily, but the merry notes ended very suddenly as he dodged back again, yet not quite quick enough, for a rough voice hailed him, hoarse and jovial.

"Why, hallo, kid, how goes it?" M'Ginnis's heavy hand descended on his shrinking shoulder, and next moment he was out on the sidewalk where Soapy lounged, a smouldering cigarette pendant from his thin, pallid lips as usual. And Soapy's eyes, so bright between their narrowed, puffy lids, so old-seeming in the youthful oval of his pale face, were like his cigarette, in that they smouldered also.

"Holy smoke!" exclaimed M'Ginnis, surveying Spike up and down in mock amazement, "this ain't you, kid—no, this sure ain't you. Looks all t' th' company-promoter, don't he, Soapy?"

"'S' right, kid, 's' right!" nodded the pallid youth, his smouldering eyes always turning toward M'Ginnis.

"Say now, Bud, quit yer kiddin'!" said Spike petulantly.

"But, gee-whiz!" exclaimed M'Ginnis, tightening his grasp, "you sure are some class, kid, in that stiff collar an' sporty tie. How's the stock-market? Are ye a bull or a bear?"

"Ah, cut it out, Bud!" cried the lad, writhing.

"Right-oh, kid, right-oh!" said M'Ginnis, loosing his hold, "You're comin' over t' O'Rourke's to-night, of course?"

"Why no, Bud, I can't."

"Oh, t' hell wid that, I got you all fixed up to go ten rounds wid Young Alf, th' East Side Wonder."

"What!" exclaimed Spike, his eyes bright and eager, "you got me a match wi' Young Alf? Say, Bud, you ain't stringin' me, are ye?"

The Definite Object

"Not much. I told you I'd get ye a real chance."

"Why," cried Spike, "if I was t'lick Young Alf I'd be in line t' meet th' top-notchers!"

"Sure—if you lick him!" nodded M'Ginnis grimly.

"Say," said Spike, his face radiant, "I've just been waitin' an' waitin' for a chance like this—a chance t' show you an' th' bunch I can handle myself, an' now——" He stopped all at once, and, shaking his head gloomily, turned away, "I forgot, I—I can't, Bud."

"Aw, what's bitin' ye?"

"I can't come t'-night."

"Won't come, ye mean!"

"Can't, Bud."

"Why not?"

"I promised Hermy t' quit fightin'."

"Is that all? Hermy don't have t' know nothin' about it. This is a swell chance for ye, kid, the best you'll ever get, so just skin over t'-night an' don't say nothin' t' nobody."

"I—can't, Bud—that's sure."

"Goin' to'give me de throw-down, are ye?"

"I don't mean it that ways, Bud, but I can't break my promise to Hermy."

"She'd never know."

"She'd find out some ways—she always does, and I can't lie t' her."

"So you won't come, hey? We ain't classy enough for ye these days, hey? I guess goin' to an office every day is one thing, an' crackin' a millionaire's crib's another."

"Cheese it, Bud—cheese it!" gasped Spike, pale and trembling.

"Right-oh, kid!" nodded M'Ginnis, "but I've been wantin' t' know how ye made your get-away that night."

"Oh quit—quit talkin' of it!" Spike panted. "I—I want t' forget all about it. I been tryin' t' think it never happened."

Of Poisonous Suggestion

"Ah, but you know it did," said M'Ginnis, "an' I know it, an' Soapy knows it did. Don'tcher, Soapy?"

"'S' right," nodded Soapy, his voice soft, his eyes hard and malevolent.

"So we kinder want t' know," continued M'Ginnis, heedless always of those baleful watching eyes, "we just want t' get on t' how you——"

"Oh, say—give it a rest!" cried Spike desperately, "give it a rest, can't ye?"

"Why then, kid, what about comin' over t' O'Rourke's t'-night?"

Spike wrung his hands. "If Hermy finds out she'll—cry, I guess."

"Hermy!" growled M'Ginnis, black brows fierce and scowling, "a hell of a lot you care for Hermy I—don't think!"

"Say now you Bud, whatcher mean?" demanded Spike, quivering with sudden anger.

"Just this, kid—what kind o' a brother are ye t' go lettin' that noo pal o' yours—that guy you call Geoff—go sneakin' round her mornin', noon, an' night?"

"You cut that out, Bud M'Ginnis, Geoff don't! Geoff ain't that kind."

"He don't, eh? Well, what about all this talk that's goin' on—about him an' her, an' her an' him—eh?"

"What talk?" demanded Spike, suddenly troubled.

"Why, every one's beginnin' t' notice as they're always meetin' on th' stairs—an' him goin' into her flat, an' them talkin' an' laughin' together when you're out o' th' way—ah," growled M'Ginnis between grinding white teeth, "an' likely as not kissin' an' squeezin' in corners."

"That's enough—that's enough!" cried the boy, fronting M'Ginnis fierce-eyed, "Nobody ain't goin' t' speak about Hermy that way."

"Ye can't help it, kid. Here's this guy Geoff, this pal o' yours—been with her—in her flat with her, all th' mornin'. Ain't he Soapy?"

The Definite Object

" 'S' right, kid ! " nodded that pallid individual, the smouldering cigarette a-swing between pale lips ; and, though he addressed Spike, his furtive eyes, watching aslant between narrowed lids, glittered to behold M'Ginnis's scowling brow, also the wolverene mouth curled faintly, so that the pendulous cigarette stirred and quivered.

" Oh, I'm handin' ye the straight goods, kid," M'Ginnis went on, " I'm puttin' ye wise because you're my pal, an' because I've known Hermy an' been kind o' soft about her since we was kids."

" Well then, you know she—she ain't that sort," said Spike, his voice quavering oddly, " so—don't you—say no more—see ? "

" All right, kid, all right—only I don't like t' see this pal o' yours gettin' in his dirty work behind your back. If anything happens—don't blame me."

" What—what you tryin' t' tell me—you, Bud ? " questioned Spike between quivering lips.

" I'm tellin' ye things are gettin' too warm. Oh, Hermy ain't the icicle she tries to make out she is."

" An' I'm tellin' you—you're a liar, Bud M'Ginnis— a dirty liar ! " cried the boy. M'Ginnis's bull neck swelled, between his thick, black brows was a vein that rose and pulsed ; and, viewing this, Soapy's glittering eyes blinked and the pendulous cigarette quivered faintly again.

" Now by—— " began M'Ginnis, lifting menacing fist ; then his arm sank and he shook his big, handsome head. " Oh, pshaw ! " he exclaimed, " I guess you're all worked up, kid, so I ain't takin' no notice. But savvy this, if Hermy ain't goin' t' marry me on th' level, she ain't goin' t' let this guy have her—the other way—not much ! I guess you ain't forgotten little Maggie Finlay ? Well, watch out your pal Geoff don't make Hermy go th' same road."

Uttering a wild, inarticulate cry, the lad sprang—to be

Of Poisonous Suggestion

caught in M'Ginnis's powerful grasp; but, even so, his fist grazed M'Ginnis's full-lipped mouth. For a moment Spike strove desperately to reach Bud's grim, smiling face until, finding all his efforts vain, he ceased all at once, bowed his head upon his arms, and burst into a passion of bitter sobbing; then, with an agile twist, he wrenched himself free, and, turning, sped away, heedless of his jaunty straw hat that had fallen and lay upon the dusty sidewalk. Languidly Soapy stooped and picked it up.

"His noo lid!" said he, "only bought t'-day, I reckon!"

"Gee!" exclaimed M'Ginnis, staring after Spike's fleeing figure already far away, "he sure was some peevish!"

"Some!" nodded Soapy, "if he'd happened t' have a gun handy here's where you'd have cashed in for good, I reckon. Yes, Bud, you'd be deader 'n mutton!" sighed Soapy, turning Spike's hat upon his finger, "you'd be as dead as—little Maggie Finlay you was mentionin'!"

M'Ginnis wheeled so suddenly upon the speaker that he took a long step backwards, but he still spun Spike's hat upon his finger, and the pendulous cigarette quivered quite noticeably.

"Aw, quit it, Bud, quit it!" he sighed, "you know I ain't th' kind o' guy it's healthy to punch around promiscuous."

"You mean if he'd missed there was you, eh?"

"Well, I dunno, Bud, if it had been my sister—maybe——"

"Oh, I know the sort o' dirty tyke you are, Soapy, but I'm awake—an' I've got you, see? If anything was t' happen t' me I've left papers—proofs—'n' it 'ud be the chair for yours—savvy?"

"Anyway, Bud, I—I haven't got a sister," said Soapy, juggling deftly with the hat. "But there's one thing, Bud, th' guy who gets actin' Mr. Freshy with Hermy is sure goin' to ante-up in kingdom come if th' kid's around."

"You're a dirty dog, Soapy, but you've got brains in

173

The Definite Object

your ugly dome. I guess you're right about th' kid, an' that gives me an almighty good idea!" And M'Ginnis walked on awhile deep in thought; and ever as he went, so between those pale and puffy lids two malevolent eyes watched and watched him.

"No," sighed Soapy at last, sliding a long, pale hand into the pocket of his smartly-tailored coat, "no, I ain't got a sister, Bud; but there was little Maggie Finlay— I kind o' used t' think she was all t' th' harps an' haloes —I used t' kind o' hope—but pshaw! she's dead—ain't she, Bud?"

"I guess so!" nodded M'Ginnis, yet deep in thought.

"An' buried—ain't she, Bud?"

"What th' hell!" exclaimed Bud, turning to stare, "What's bitin' ye?"

"I'm wonderin' 'why,' an' I'm likewise wonderin' 'who,' Bud. Maybe I'll find out for sure some day. I'm—waitin', Bud, waitin'. Goin' around t' O' Rourke's, are ye? Oh well, I guess I'll hike along wid ye, Bud."

CHAPTER XIX

IN WHICH THE POISON BEGINS TO WORK

Spike sat glowering at the newspaper, yet very conscious none the less that Hermione often turned to glance at him wistfully as she bustled to and fro ; at last she spoke.

" Arthur dear, why so gloomy ? "

" I ain't—I mean, I'm not."

" You're not sulking about anything ? "

" No."

" Then you're sick."

" I'm all right."

" But you didn't enjoy your dinner a little bit."

" I—I wasn't hungry, I guess," said Spike, frowning down at the paper.

But Hermione was beside him, her cool fingers caressing his curls.

" Boy dear, what is it ? "

" Say Hermy, where'd you get them roses ? " and he nodded to the flowers she had set among her shining hair.

" Oh, Mr. Geoffrey brought them."

" Been here, has he ? "

" Yes, he came in with Ann this morning. Why ? "

" Did he—did he stay long ? "

" N-o, I don't think so. Why ? "

" Comes around here pretty often, don't he ? "

" Why, you see he's your friend, dear, and we are very near neighbours."

" Oh, I know all that, but—folks are beginning to— talk."

The Definite Object

Hermione's smooth brows were wrinkled faintly and her caressing hand had fallen away.

"To talk!" she repeated, "you mean about—me?"

"Yes!" nodded Spike, avoiding her eyes, "about you and—him!"

"Well, let them!" she answered gently, "you and Ann are all I care about, so let them talk."

"But I—I don't like folk t' talk about my sister, an' it's got to stop. You got t' tell him so or else I will. What's he got t' go buying ye flowers for, anyway?"

Hermione's black brows knit in a sudden frown.

"Arthur, don't be silly!"

"Oh, I know you think I'm only a kid, but I ain't—I'm not. If you can't take care of—of yourself, I must and——"

"Arthur, stop!"

"Well, but what's he always crawlin' around here for?"

"He doesn't crawl—he couldn't," she cried in sudden anger; then in gentler tones, "I don't think you'd better say any more, or maybe I shall grow angry. If you have grown to think so—so badly of him, remember I'm your sister."

"But you're a girl, an' he's a man, an'——"

"Stop it!" Hermione stamped her foot, and, meeting her flashing glance, Spike wilted and—stopped it. So, while he glowered at the paper again, Hermione put away the dinner things, making more clatter about it than was usual, and turning now and then to glance at him under her long lashes.

"Where did you meet M'Ginnis as you came home, Arthur?"

"At the corner of—say, who told you I met him?"

"You did."

"I never said a word about meetin' him."

"No, but you've been telling me what he told you. Only M'Ginnis could be vile enough to dare say such

In Which the Poison Begins to Work

things about me. Oh Arthur, for shame—how can you listen to that brute beast—for shame ! "

Now, meeting the virginal purity of those eyes, Spike felt his cheeks burn and he wriggled in his chair.

" Bud only told me Geoff had been—been here," he stammered, "and I guess it was the truth—I—I mean——"

" Oh, boy, for shame ! " and, turning about, she swept from the room, her head carried very high, leaving him crouched in his chair, his nervous fingers twisting and turning a small box in his pocket—the box that held the forgotten hair-comb. He was still sitting miserably thus when he started to hear a knock on the outer door, and a moment later a woman's voice, querulous and high-pitched.

" Oh, Miss Hermy, my Martin's very bad t'-night, an' I got t' go out an' I can't leave him alone. Would ye mind comin' down an' sittin' with him for a bit ? "

" Why, of course I will."

" Ye see, since he had th' stroke he's sorrered for our little Maggie—he was hard on her, ye see, an' since she—she died he's been grievin' for her. Had himself laid in her little room—seemed to comfort him somehow. But to-day, when he heard we had to leave because th' rent was rose it nigh broke his poor heart. An' I got to go out, an' I can't leave him alone, so—if ye wouldn't mind, Miss Hermy——"

" Just a moment—I'll come right now."

As she spoke, Hermione re-entered the kitchen, untying her apron as she came. Spike sat watching, waiting, yearning for a word, but without even a glance Hermione turned and left him. When he was alone he started to his feet, and, tearing the box from his pocket, dashed it fiercely to the floor ; then as suddenly picked it up, and, approaching the open window, drew back his hand to hurl it out, and so stood, staring into the face that had risen to view beyond the window-ledge, a round face with

The Definite Object

two very round eyes, a round button of a nose, and a wide mouth just now up-curving in a grin.

"Hey, you, Larry, what you hangin' around here for?" demanded Spike, slipping the box into his pocket again, "what you doin' on our fire-escape, hey?"

"Brought back yer roof!" replied the lad.

"Well, where is it?"

"Here it is," and, climbing astride the window-sill, Larry handed in the jaunty straw.

"Where'd you find it?"

"Bud give it me. 'N' say——"

"All right," nodded Spike, dusting the straw tenderly with a handkerchief. "Now git, I wanter be alone."

"But, say, kid, Bud says I was ter say as he's sorry for what he said 's mornin', 'n' say, he says you'd better be gettin' over t' O'Rourke's. 'N' say——"

"I ain't comin'!"

"But, say, you're t' fight Young Alf. 'N' say——"

"I ain't comin'!"

"But, say, dere's a lot o' our money on ye—I got two plunks meself; 'n' say, you just gotter fight anyway— Bud says so."

"I can't help what Bud says, I ain't comin'."

"Not comin'!" exclaimed Larry, his eyes rounder than ever.

"No!"

Larry's wide mouth curved in a slow grin, and he nodded his close-cropped head. Said he,

"Say, kiddo, you know Young Alf's a punishin' fighter, I guess—you know as nobody's never stopped him yet, don'tcher, you know as you're givin' him six pounds— say, you ain't—scared, are ye?"

"Scared?" repeated Spike, frowning. "Do I look like I was scared? You know there ain't any guy I'm scared of; but I promised Hermy——"

"Pip-pip!" grinned Larry. "Say, if you don't turn

In Which the Poison Begins to Work

up t'-night d'ye know what de bunch 'll say ? Dey'll say you're a—quitter ! "

" Well, don't you say it, that's all ! " said Spike, laying aside his hat and clenching his fists.

" Not me ! " grinned Larry. " There'll be plenty to do that I guess—dey'd call it after ye in de streets—dey'll give ye th' ha ! ha ! dey'll say Hermy Chesterton's brother's a quitter—a quitter ! "

For a long moment Spike stood with bent head and hands tight-clenched, then crossing to the sideboard he took thence his shabby cap.

" Who's in my corner ? "

" Now you're talkin, kiddo. I know as you——"

" Who's in my corner ? "

" Bud an' Lefty. 'N' say, I guess they can handle you all right, eh ? 'N' say, come on, let's cop a sneak before any one butts in—de fire-escape for ours, eh ? "

" Sure ! " said Spike, climbing through the window. " Oh, there ain't nobody goin' t'call Hermy Chesterton's brother a quitter ! "

" You bet there ain't ! " grinned Larry. " Come on, kid ! "

CHAPTER XX

OF AN EXPEDITION BY NIGHT

" Why, Mr. Geoffrey, what you settin' here in the dark for ? "

" Is it dark, Mrs. Trapes ? "

" My land ! can't you see as it's too dark t' see, an—oh, shucks, Mr. Geoffrey ! "

" Certainly, Mrs. Trapes ! But can't you see that the whole world—my world, anyway—is full of a refulgent glory, a magic light where nothing mean or sordid can possibly be, a light that my eyes never saw till now nor hoped to see, a radiance that may never fail, I hope—a—er——"

" Oh, go on, Mr. Geoffrey, go on ! Only I guess I'll light the gas jest the same, if you don't mind ! " Which Mrs. Trapes did forthwith. " But what was you a-doin' of all alone in the dark ? "

" Glorying in life, Mrs. Trapes, and praising the good God for health and strength to enjoy it and the fullness thereof."

" ' Fullness thereof,' meanin' jest what, Mr. Geoffrey ? "

" The most beautiful thing in a beautiful world, Mrs. Trapes."

" An' that's Hermy, I s'pose. An' all that talk o' glory an' radiance an' magic light means as you've been an' spoke, I guess ? "

" It does."

" An' what did she say ? "

" Nothing."

" Nothin' ? "

Of an Expedition by Night

"Not with her lips, but——"

"Oh, her eyes, was it? Mr. Geoffrey, I'll tell you what—a girl may look ' yes ' with her eyes a whole week an' say ' no ' with her mouth jest once, an' mean ' no '—when it's to a pea-nut man. Lordy-lord! what's that!" And Mrs. Trapes jumped as a hand rapped softly on the door, and stared horrified to see a human head protrude itself into the room, while a voice said:

"Da signorina she out, so me come tell-a you piece-a-da-noos."

"Why, if it ain't that blessed guinney! Go away—what d'ye want?"

Hereupon Tony flashed his white teeth, and, opening the door, bowed with his inimitable grace, grew solemn, tapped his nose, winked knowingly, and laid finger to lip mysteriously.

"My land!" said Mrs. Trapes, staring. "What's the matter with the Eyetalian ij'it now?"

"Spike—he go make-a-da-fight!" whispered Tony hoarsely.

"Eh—Arthur fightin'—where?"

"He go make-a-da-box—he drink-a-da-booze, den he walk-a—so! Den da signorina she-a cry."

"Oh!" exclaimed Mrs. Trapes, "you mean as that b'y's off boxin' again?"

"*Si, si*, he go make-a-da-box-fight."

"Is he over at O'Rourke's, Tony?" inquired Ravenslee, sitting upright.

"I bet-a-my-life, yes."

"Oh, Mr. Geoffrey!" exclaimed Mrs. Trapes, clasping bony hands, "if they bring him home drunk like they did last time!"

"They sha'n't do that, Mrs. Trapes. Don't worry. I'll go and fetch him," said Ravenslee, getting to his feet.

"Fetch him? From O'Rourke's? Are ye crazy? You'd get half-killed, like as not. Oh, they're a bad, ugly lot down there!"

The Definite Object

"I feel rather ugly myself," said Ravenslee, looking around for the shabby hat "anyway, I'm going to see."

"Why, then, if you're goin' t' venture among that lot, you take this with ye, Mr. Geoffrey," and she thrust the poker into his hand, "you'll sure need it—ah, do now!" But Ravenslee laughed and set it aside. "You'd better take it, Mr. Geoffrey, fists is fists, but gimme a poker—every time! A poker ain't t' be sneezed at! What, goin'—an' empty-'anded? Mr. Geoffrey, I'm surprised at you—think of Hermy!"

"That's just what I am doing."

"Well, s'posin' they hurt you, what'll Hermy do?"

"You think she'd mind, then, though I'm—only a pea-nut man?"

"Even a pea-nut man 's a feller-creatur', ain't he—an' Hermy's 'eart is very tender, an'—oh, shucks, Mr. Geoffrey, I guess you know she'd just be crazy if you was hurt bad!"

"Why, then," said Ravenslee smiling and taking up the battered hat, "I'll take great care of myself—trust me!"

"Then good-bye, Mr. Geoffrey, good-bye, an'—the good Lord go with you."

"Thank you, Mrs. Trapes," said Ravenslee, and followed Tony out upon the stair.

Upon one of the many landings the young Italian paused.

"Me put-a-you wise, Geoff, you savvy where-a to find Spike, now me go back t' my lil Pietro, yes. S' long, pal, 'n' good-a luck!"

Ravenslee hastened on downstairs, returning neighbouringly nods and greetings as he went, but staying for none, and so, crossing the court, turned into the avenue.

On the corner he beheld the Spider, hard at work on his eternal chewing-gum, peak-cap drawn low, and hands in pockets, seeing Ravenslee he nodded and lurched forward.

Of an Expedition by Night

" What's doin', Geoff ? " he inquired.

" I'm off to O'Rourke's—coming ? "

" Not much ! An' say, 'tain't worth your trouble—it ain't fightin'. Nawthin' but a lot o' fifth-raters."

" I'm going over to fetch Spike."

" How much ? " exclaimed the Spider, his square jaws immobile from sheer astonishment. " Say, you ain't crazy, are ye—I mean you ain't dippy or cracked in the dome, are ye ? Because de kid's goin' ten rounds with Young Alf de East-side Wonder t' night, see ? "

" Not if I can help it, Spider."

" Aw—come off, bo' ! D'ye think Bud 'll let him go ? "

" I sha'n't ask Bud, or any one else."

" Meanin' as you'll walk right in on Bud's tough bunch an' cop out de kid on yer lonesome—eh ? "

" I shall try."

" Then you sure are crazy, if yer dome ain't cracked yet it's sure goin' t' be. Why, Bud 'n' his crowd 'll soak you good 'n' plenty, 'n' chuck ye out again quicker 'n ye went in—they will sure, bo'—if you go."

" I'm wondering if you'll come along and help ? " said Ravenslee lazily.

" Me ? Not so 's you could notice it. I ain't huntin' that sort o' trouble."

" Oh well, if you think you'd—er—better not, I'll go alone."

" What, yer goin', are ye ? "

" Of course ! You see, Spike is my friend, consequently his trouble is my trouble. Good night, Spider, and whatever else you do, be sure to—er—take good care of yourself ! " And Ravenslee smiled and turned away ; but he had not gone six paces before the Spider was at his elbow.

" Say bo'," said he, " I don't like the way you smile, but you talk so soft an' pretty I guess I'll jest have t'come along t'gather up what they leave of ye."

" Spider," said Ravenslee, " shake ! " The Spider obeyed, somewhat shamefacedly to be sure.

The Definite Object

" It looks like two domes bein' cracked 'stead o' one, an' all along o' that fool kid ! " Having said which he lurched on beside Ravenslee, chewing voraciously. " How you goin' t' work it ? " he inquired suddenly.

" I don't know yet."

" Hully chee ! You've sure gotcher nerve along. There's some o' the toughest guys in little Manhattan Village at O'Rourke's dump t'-night, keepin' th' ring an' fair achin' for trouble."

" We must dodge 'em, Spider."

" S'pose we can't ? "

" Then we must trust our luck, and I've got a hunch we shall get Spike away somehow before Mr. Flowers dopes him or makes him drunk, anyway we'll try. The dressing-rooms are behind the annexe, aren't they ? "

" Know the place, do ye ? "

" I've looked it over. We can get in behind the annexe, can't we ? "

" In ? " repeated the Spider, smiling grimly. " Oh, we'll get in all right—what gets my goat is how we're goin' t' get out again. You sure are a bird for takin' chances, Geoff."

" Life is made up of chances, Spider, and there are two kinds of men, those who take them joyfully, and those who don't."

" Well, say, you can scratch me on the joyful business. I'm the guy as only takes chances he's paid t' take."

" How much are you getting on this job, Spider ? "

" Oh—well—I mean—say, what's th' time, bo' ? "

" Five minutes after eight—why ? "

" I guess de kid's in th' ring, then. There's a full card t'-night, an' he's scheduled for eight sharp, so I reckon he's fightin' now—an' good luck t' him ! "

By this time they had reached that dark and quiet neighbourhood where stood O'Rourke's saloon. But to-night the big annexe glared with light, and the air

184

about it was full of a dull, hoarse, insistent clamour that swelled all at once to a chorus of discordant shrieks and frenzied cries.

"Ah!" quoth the Spider sagely, "hark to 'em howl! that means some guy's gettin' his all right—listen to 'em, they love t' get blood for their entrance money, an' they're sure gettin' it. Some one's bein' knocked out—come on!"

It was a dark night, for there was no moon, and the stars were hidden; thus, as Ravenslee followed the Spider, he found himself stumbling over the uneven ground of a vacant lot, a lonely place beyond which lay the distant river. So they came at last to various outbuildings looming up ugly and ungainly in the dimness.

"Say, bo'," said the Spider, stopping suddenly at a small and narrow door, "you'd best wait here an' lemme go first."

"No, we'll go together."

"Right-oh, only be ready to make a quick get-away!" So saying, the Spider opened the door, and, closely followed by Ravenslee, stepped into a dim-lit passage thick with the blue vapour of cigars and cigarettes. It was a long, narrow corridor, bare and uncarpeted, seeming to run the length of the building; on one hand was a row of dingy windows and on the other were several doors, from behind which came the sound of many voices that talked and sang and swore, together and at the same time, a very babel.

Now at the end of this passage was yet another door which gave upon a small room that contained a rickety sofa, a chair, and a battered desk; a kerosene lamp suspended against the wall burned dimly, and it was into this chamber that the Spider ushered Ravenslee somewhat hastily; the Spider's eyes were very bright and he chewed rather more fiercely than usual.

"Bo'," said he, "this place ain't exactly a bed o' roses for a strange guy like you, ye see, this is Bud's own

185

The Definite Object

stampin'-ground, an' the whole bunch is here t'-night, and most of 'em are heeled. Soapy an' Bud always tote guns, I know. So I guess you'd better mark time here a bit while I chase around an' locate th' kid. If any one asks what you're doin' around here, say as you came in with me. But, bo' ''—and here the Spider laid an impressive hand on Ravenslee's arm—"if you should happen t' see Bud, well, don't stop to look twice, but beat it—let it be th' door or winder for yours—only, beat it!"

" Oh, why ? "

" Well, I know Bud 's got it in fer you ; I heard him say—— Oh, well, if his gun should go off—accidental-like, this place ain't exactly Broadway or Fifth Av'noo, bo'—see ? "

" I see ! " nodded Ravenslee.

" Hold on ! " said Spider, and crossing to the window he unlatched it stealthily and lifted it high, "if I ain't back inside ten minutes, bo', nip out through here an' hike—wait for me at the lamp-post across the lot over there—it 'll be safer. D'ye get me ? "

" I do ! " nodded Ravenslee.

" I guess you'd be less of a fool if you was to get out now an' wait—outside ! " Spider suggested.

Ravenslee shook his head. " I'll wait here," said he ; " there are times when I can be as big a fool as the next, Spider, and this is one of them."

" That's so ! " nodded the Spider, and, chewing viciously, he turned and was gone, to be hailed a few minutes later in uproarious greeting by many discordant voices which died slowly to a droning hum, above which came sounds more distant, shouts and cheers from the auditorium.

Left alone, Ravenslee looked about him, and then espied a newspaper that lay upon the desk, and idly taking it up his gaze was attracted by these words, printed in large block letters :

186

Of an Expedition by Night

NOTORIOUS CRIMINAL RUN TO EARTH
JACOB HEINE THE GUN-MAN ARRESTED IN JERSEY CITY

Below in small type he read this :

" Jacob Heine, believed to be the perpetrator of several mysterious shooting affrays, and member of a dangerous West-side gang, was arrested to-day."

Now, the light being dim, Ravenslee drew closer to the lamp, and, standing thus against the light, his face was in shadow ; also his long figure was silhouetted upon the opposite wall, plain to be seen by any one opening the door. Suddenly, as he stood thus, head bent above the paper, this door opened and M'Ginnis entered ; he also held a paper, and now he spoke without troubling to lift his scowling gaze from the printed column he was scanning :

" That you, Lefty ? Here's a hell of a mix-up— that dog-gone fool Heine 's got himself pinched—and in Jersey City too ! I told him t' stay around here till things was quiet ! It's goin' t' be a hell of a job t' fix things for him over there—'tain't like N' York. But we got t' fix things for him or chance him squealing on th' rest of us, but what beats me is——"

M'Ginnis's teeth clicked together and the paper tore suddenly between his hands as, glancing up at last, he beheld two keen, grey eyes that watched him, and a mouth, grim and close-lipped, that curled in the smile Spider didn't like.

For a long, tense moment they stood motionless, eye to eye, then, reaching behind him, M'Ginnis locked the door, and, drawing out the key, thrust it into his pocket.

" So—I got ye at last—have I ? ' said he slowly.

" And I've got you," said Ravenslee pleasantly ; " we seem to have got each other, don't we ? "

187

The Definite Object

" See here, you," said M'Ginnis, his massive shoulders squared, his big chin viciously out-thrust, " you're goin' t' leave Mulligan's, see? "

" Am I ? " said Ravenslee, lounging upon a corner of the battered desk.

" You sure are," nodded M'Ginnis, " Hell's Kitchen ain't big enough for you an' me, I guess—you're goin' because I say so, an' you're goin' to-night ! "

" You surprise me ! " said Ravenslee sleepily.

" You're goin' t' quit Hell's Kitchen for good, and—you ain't comin' back ! "

" You amaze me ! " and Ravenslee yawned behind his hand.

" An' now you're goin' t' listen why an' wherefore—if you can keep awake a minute ! "

" I'll try, Mr. Flowers, I'll try."

M'Ginnis thrust clenched hands into his pockets and surveyed Ravenslee with scornful eyes—his lounging figure and stooping shoulders, his long white hands, and general listless air.

" God ! " he exclaimed, " that she should trouble t' look twice at such a nancy-boy ! " and he spat loud and contemptuously.

" Almost think you're trying to be rude, Mr. Flowers."

" Aw—I couldn't be to a—thing like you ! An' see here—me name's M'Ginnis ! "

" But then," sighed Ravenslee, " I prefer to call you Flowers—a fair name for a foul thing."

M'Ginnis made a swift step forward, and halted, hard-breathing and menacing.

" How much ? " he demanded.

" A fair name for a foul thing, Mr. Flowers," repeated Ravenslee, glancing up at him under slumberous, drooping lids, " anyway, Flowers you will remain ! " As they stared again eye to eye, M'Ginnis edged nearer and nearer, head thrust forward, until Ravenslee could see the cords that writhed and swelled in his big throat, and he hitched forward a languid shoulder. "Don't come any nearer, Flowers," said he, "and don't stick out your jaw like that; don't do it, I might be tempted to try to—er—hit it!"

"What—you?" said M'Ginnis, and laughed hoarsely, while Ravenslee yawned again.

"An' now, Mr. Butt-in, if you're still awake, listen here. I guess it's about time you stopped foolin' around Hermy Chesterton, an' you're goin' t' quit—see!" Ravenslee's eyes flashed suddenly, then drooped as M'Ginnis continued, "So you're goin' to sit down right here, an' you're goin' t' write a nice little note of fare-well, an' you're goin' t' tell her as you love her, an' leave her because I say so—see? Ah!" he cied, suddenly hoarse and anger-choked, "d'ye think I'll let Hermy look at a thing like you—do ye—do ye?"

Ravenslee sat utterly still, and when at last he spoke his voice sounded even more gentle than before:

"My good Flowers, there is just one thing you shall not do, and that is, speak her name in my hearing—you're not fit to, and, Mr. Flowers, I'll not permit it."

"Is that so?" snarled M'Ginnis. "Well, then, listen some more. I know as you're always hangin' around her flat, an' if Hermy don't care about losing her good name——"

Even as Ravenslee's long arm shot out, M'Ginnis side-stepped the blow, and Ravenslee found himself staring into the muzzle of a revolver.

"Ah, I thought so!" he breathed, and shrank away.

"Kind of alters things, don't it?" inquired M'Ginnis, hoarse and jeering. "Well, if you don't want it to go off, sit down an' write Hermy as pretty a little note as you can. No, shut that window first."

Silent and speechless, Ravenslee crossed to the window and drew down the sash, in doing which he noticed a dark something that crouched beneath the sill.

"An' now," said M'Ginnis, leaning against a corner

The Definite Object

of the desk, " sit down here, nice an' close, an' write that letter—there's a pen an' ink an' paper—an' quick about it, or by——" M'Ginnis sprang up and turned as the glass of the window splintered to fragments—and, almost with the crash, Ravenslee leapt—a fierce twist, a vicious wrench, and the deadly weapon had changed hands.

" Lucky it didn't go off," said Ravenslee, smiling grimly at the revolver he held, " others might have heard, and, Mr. Flowers, I want to be alone with you just a little longer. Of course I might shoot you for the murderous beast you are, or I might walk you over to the nearest police depôt for the crook I think you are, but—oh well, of late I've been yearning to get my hands on you, and so——" Ravenslee turned and pitched the revolver through the broken window. But, almost as the weapon left his hand M'Ginnis was upon him, and, reeling from the blow, Ravenslee staggered blindly across the room till stayed by the wall, and sank there, crouched and groaning, his face hidden in his hands.

With a cry hoarse and fierce, M'Ginnis followed and stooped, eager to make an end—stooped to be met by two fierce hands, sure hands and strong that grasped his silken neckerchief as this crouching figure rose suddenly erect. So for a wild, panting moment they grappled, swaying grimly to and fro, while ever the silken neckerchief was twisted tighter and tighter. Choking now, M'Ginnis felt fingers on his naked throat, iron fingers that clutched cruelly, and in this painful grip was whirled, choking, against the wall, and thence borne down and down. And now M'Ginnis, lying helpless across his opponent's knee, stared up into a face pale but grimly joyous, lips that curled back from gnashing white teeth —eyes that glared merciless. So Ravenslee bent M'Ginnis back across his knee and choked him there a while, then suddenly relaxed his hold and let M'Ginnis sink, choking, to the floor.

Of an Expedition by Night

"A little—rough, Mr. Flowers," he panted, "a trifle —rough with you—I fear—but I want you—to know that you—shall not utter—her name—in my presence. Now the key—I prefer door to window. The key, Mr. Flowers—ah, here it is!" So saying, Ravenslee stood upright, and, wiping blood and sweat from him with his sleeve, turned to the door. "One other thing, Mr. Flowers, have the goodness to take off your neckerchief next time, or I—may strangle you outright."

Half-way down the passage Ravenslee turned to see Murder close on his heels; once he smote, and twice, but nothing might stay that bull-like rush, and, locked in a desperate clinch, he was borne back and back, their trampling lost in the universal din about them, as reeling, staggering, they crashed out through wrecked and splintered door, and, still locked together, were swallowed in the night beyond.

Thus the Spider, crouching in the dark beneath a certain broken window, with Spike beside him, was presently aware of the sickening sounds of furious struggling close at hand, and of a hoarse, panting voice that cursed in fierce triumph—a voice that ended all at once in a ghastly strangling choke; and, recognising this voice, the Spider hunched his great shoulders and bore Spike to a certain remote spot where stood a solitary lamp-post. Here he waited, calm-eyed and chewing placidly, one arm about the fretful Spike.

And presently Ravenslee joined them; the shabby hat was gone, and there was a smear of blood upon his cheek, also he laboured in his breathing, but his eyes were joyous.

"Bo', what about Bud?"

"Oh, he's lying around somewhere."

"Hully chee! d'ye mean——"

"He tried gouging first, but I expected that, then he tried to throttle me, but I throttled a little harder. He's an ugly customer as you said, but "—Ravenslee laughed

The Definite Object

and glanced at his bloody knuckles—" I don't think he'll be keen to rough it with me again just yet."

" Bo', I guess you can be pretty ugly too. Say, when you laugh that way I feel—kind of sorry for Bud."

" Why, what's wrong with Spike ? "

" Dunno. I guess they've been slinging dope into him. And he's copped it pretty bad from Young Alf too. Look at that eye ! "

" Spike ! " said Ravenslee, shaking him, " Spike, what is it ? Buck up, old fellow ! " But Spike only stared dazedly and moaned.

" It's dope all right," nodded the Spider, " or else Bud's mixed th' drinks on him."

" Damn him ! " said Ravenslee softly, " I wish I'd throttled a little harder."

" I guess you give Bud all he needs for the present," said Spider grimly, " anyway, I'm goin' t' see. The kid ain't hurt none. Get him home t' bed an' he'll be all right. S' long, Geoff."

" Good-night, Spider, and—thank you. Oh, by the way, who's Heine ? "

" Heine's a Deutscher, Geoff. Heine's about as clean as dirt an' as straight as a corkscrew. Why, he'd shoot his own mother if ye paid him, like he did—— But say, what d'you know about him anyway ? "

" Well, for one thing I know he's been arrested in Jersey City."

" Heine ! Pinched ? Say, bo', whatcher givin' us— who says so ? "

" Bud, and——"

But the Spider, waiting for no more, had turned about and was running back across the open lot.

CHAPTER XXI

HOW M'GINNIS THREATENED, AND—WENT

"MR. GEOFFREY, prayer is a wonderful prop to a anxious 'eart!" said Mrs. Trapes, leaning over the banisters to greet him as he ascended. "Mr. Geoffrey, my hands has been lifted in prayer for ye this night as so did me behoove, an' here you are safe back with—that b'y. A prayer prayed proper, an' prayed by them as ain't plaguin' the Lord constant about their souls an' other diseases, is always dooly regarded. Yes, sir, a occasional petition is always heard an' worketh wonders, as the—— My land, Mr. Geoffrey, look at yer face!"

"I know, Mrs. Trapes. Has she come in yet?"

"Not yet. An' glad I am. You're all bleedin'— stoop yer head a bit—there!" and very tenderly she stanched the cut below the curly hair with an apron clean and spotless as usual. "An' the b'y—lord, what's come to him?"

"A black eye—two, I'm afraid. Anyhow, I'll look after him and get him into bed before she comes. Can you keep her away till I've done so?"

"I'll try. Poor lad!" she sighed, touching Spike's drooping head with bony fingers, "if she wasn't his sister I'd be sorry for him!"

So Ravenslee took Spike in hand, bathing his bruised and battered features, and setting ice-water to his puffy lips, which the lad gulped thirstily. Thereafter he revived quickly, but grew only the more morose and sulky.

"All right," he muttered, "I'll go t' bed, only—leave me—see?"

The Definite Object

" Can't I help you ? "

" No, you lemme alone. Oh, I know—you think I'm soused, but I ain't, I—I'm not drunk, I tell ye. I wish I was. I ain't no kid, so lemme alone ; an' I ain't drunk. What if me legs is shaky ? So 'u'd yours be if you 'd got—what I got. It was dat last swing t' de jaw as done me ; but I ain't drunk 'n' I ain't a kid t' be undressed—so chase ye'self an' lemme alone ! "

" All right, Spike—only get to bed like a good chap before your sister comes."

" You leave my sister alone, she ain't that kind, an' she ain't for you anyway."

" That will do, Arthur. Get into bed ! I'll give you five minutes ! " So saying, Ravenslee turned away ; but as he closed the door his quick ear detected the clink of glass, and, turning, he saw Spike draw a small flask from his pocket.

" Give me that stuff, old fellow."

" Oh, you can't con me ! I ain't a kid, so you lemme alone ! " and Spike raised the flask to his lips, but, in that instant, it was snatched away. Spike staggered back to the wall and leaned there, passing his hand to and fro across his brow as though dazed, then stumbled out into the room beyond.

" Gimme it ! Geoff, gimme it ! " he panted, " you won't keep it—no, bo'. Bud slipped it to me after I came to. Gimme it, Geoff. I want t' forget—so be a sport an' give it me—you will, won't ye ? "

Ravenslee shook his head, whereat the boy broke out more passionately :

" Oh, don't ye see, Geoff—can't ye understand ? I—I was knocked out t'-night—I took th' count ! I—I'm done for, I had me chance an' I didn't make good ! I —didn't—make good ! " As he spoke the lad hid his bruised face within his hands, while great sobs shook him.

" Why, Spike ! Why, Arthur, old chap, never mind."

How M'Ginnis Threatened, and—Went

"Gimme th' bottle, Geoff! Be a pal an' gimme th' stuff. I want t' forget!"

"This wouldn't help you."

"Give it me, d' ye hear—I want it. I'll have it, anyway—I'll——" Spike's voice failed, and, cowering back, he sank into a chair at sight of her who stood within the doorway so very silent and pale of lip.

"Ah don't, Hermy—don't look at me like that," he whispered, "your eyes hurt me! I ain't drunk—this time!"

"Oh boy!" she sighed, "oh boy—after all your promises!"

Spike rose with hands stretched out appealingly; but, even so, he swayed slightly, and, seeing this, she shivered.

"Is it th' fightin' you mean, Hermy? Why, I did it all for you, Hermy—all for you. I wanted t' be a champion, 'cause all champions are rich. I wanted t' make you a real lady—t' take you away from Mulligan's; but now—I'm only—a 'has-been.' I've lost me chance. Oh, Hermy, I'm done for. I—oh Geoff, I—think I'll go to bed."

So Ravenslee set down the flask, and, clasping an arm about Spike's swaying form, led him from the room, while Hermione stood rigid and watched them go. But when the door had closed behind them she bowed her head upon her hands and sobbed miserably, until, spying the half-emptied flask through her tears, she sprang forward, and, snatching it from the table, dashed it passionately to the floor.

"Oh dear God of Heaven!" she whispered, sinking to her knees, "not that way—oh, save him from that—keep him from treading that path!" With head bowed upon her folded hands she knelt thus awhile until a sound in the passage aroused her, and, rising to her feet, she turned and confronted Bud M'Ginnis.

He stood upon the threshold, and though his glowing, eager eyes dwelt yearningly upon her beauty, he made

The Definite Object

no motion to enter the room. Upon one cheek the skin was torn and grazed from nose to ear, and upon his powerful throat were vivid marks that showed fierce and red, and these seemed to worry him, for even while he stared upon her loveliness his hand stole up to his neck, and he touched these glowing blotches gently with his fingers.

"God, Hermy," said he at last, "you get more beautiful every day!" She was silent, but reading the fierce scorn in her eyes, he laughed softly and leaned nearer. "Some day, Hermy, you'll be all mine! Oh, I can wait, there's others, an' you're worth waitin' for, I guess. But some day you'll come t' me—you shall—you must! Meantime, there's others, but some day it'll be you an' you only—when you're my wife. Ah, marry me, Hermy, I could give you all you want, an' there'd never be any one else for me—then!"

Her eyes still met his unflinchingly, only she drew away from his nearness, shivering a little; seeing which, he frowned and clenched one hand—the other had wandered up to his throat again.

"Won't ye speak t' me!" he demanded savagely, then shrugging his great shoulders, he continued in gentler tones, "I ain't here t' quarrel, Hermy, I only come to see if th' kid got home all right."

Hermione's firm, red lips remained tight-closed
"Did he?"

Hermione slowly inclined her head.

"Say now, Hermy," he went on, and his voice grew almost wheedling, "there was a guy here the other night, a stranger I guess, one o' these tired, sleepy guys, one o' the reg'lar soft-talkin' nancy-boys—who is he?" Hermione only sighed wearily, whereat his voice grew hoarse with passion, and he questioned her fiercely. "Who is he, eh—who is he? What was he doin' around here anyway? Well, can't ye talk? Can't ye speak?"

Hermione only looked at him, and before those calm, fearless eyes he burned in a wild yet impotent rage.

How M'Ginnis Threatened, and—Went

"Won't talk, hey?" he questioned between grinding teeth. "Well now, see here, Hermy, if you let this guy come any love-business with you behind me back it'll be his finish, an' he can blame you for it! An' see here again—watch out for young Arthur. Oh!" he cried, seeing her flinch, "you think you've got that kid tied to ye, you think you've got him I guess; but you ain't! I've got him—right here!" and, holding out his hand, M'Ginnis slowly clenched it into a fist. "I've got th' kid, see—an' he's goin' th' way I want him—he's got to, see?"

"Ah!" she cried, her scorn and fearless pride shattered to trembling pleading at last, "oh, what do you mean— oh, what do you mean?"

"I mean as I want ye, an' I'm goin' to have ye!" he answered. "I mean that instead of 'no' you're goin' t' give me 'yes'—for th' kid's sake!"

"What do you—mean?" she said again between quivering lips, her eyes full of a growing terror.

"Mean?" he continued relentlessly, viewing her trembling loveliness with hungry eyes, "well—that's what I mean!" and he pointed to the broken flask upon the floor, "if you want t' see it in his face more an' more, if you want t' smell it in his breath—say 'no!' If you want t' see his hands begin t' shake, if you want t' hear his foot come stumbling up th' stair—say 'no!' I guess you remember what it's like—you've seen it all before. Well, if ye want Arthur t' grow into what his drunken father was before him, say 'no!'"

"Go away!" she moaned; "go away!"

"Oh, I'll go, but first I'll tell you this——"

"I think not, Mr. Flowers—no, I'm sure you won't!" Ravenslee's voice was soft and pleasant as usual; but before the burning ferocity of his eyes, the merciless line of that grim, implacable mouth, before all the hush and deadly purpose of him, the loud hectoring of M'Ginnis seemed a thing of no account; beholding this pale, set

The Definite Object

face, Hermione, sighing deep, shrank away; even M'Ginnis blenched as, very slowly, Ravenslee approached him, speaking softly the while.

"Get out, Mr. Flowers, get out! Don't say another word—no, not one, if only because of that 'dog-gone fool Heine!' Now go, or, so help me God, this time I'll kill you!"

Hermione leaned her shaking body against the table. And yet, could it be fear that had waked this new glory in her eyes, had brought this glowing colour to her cheek, had made her sweet breath pant and hurry so? Fear?

M'Ginnis stood rigid, watching Ravenslee advance; suddenly he tried to speak, yet uttered no word; he raised a fumbling hand to his bruised and swollen throat, striving again for speech but choked instead, and, uttering a sound hoarse and inarticulate, swung upon his heel and strode blindly away. Then Ravenslee turned, turned to find Hermione sunk down beside the table, her burning face hidden between her arms, her betraying eyes fast shut.

"You are tired," he said gently, "that damned—er—I should say Mr. Flowers—and—er—other unpleasant things have upset you, haven't they?"

Hermione made a motion of assent, and Ravenslee continued, softer than before:

"I wanted you to make up your mind to come away to-night; but—I can't ask you now—can I? It—it wouldn't be—er—the thing, would it?"

Hermione didn't answer or lift her head, and, stooping above her, he saw how she was trembling; but her eyes were still fast shut.

"You—you're not afraid—of me, are you, Hermione?"

"No."

"And you're not—crying, are you?"

"No."

"Then I'd—better go, hadn't I? To Mrs. Trapes,

198

How M'Ginnis Threatened, and—Went

and supper, stewed beef, I think, with—er—carrots and onions."

Her head was still bowed, and his tone was so light, his voice so lazy, how was she to know that his hands were quivering, or see how the passion of his yearning was shaking him, fighting for utterance against his iron will? How was she to know anything of all this until, swiftly, lightly, he stooped and kissed the shining glory of her hair? In a while she raised her head; but then she was alone.

CHAPTER XXII

TELLS OF AN EARLY MORNING VISIT AND A WARNING

RAVENSLEE dreamed that he was in a wood—with Hermione, of course. She came to him, through the leafy twilight, all aglow with youth and love, eager to give herself to his embrace. And from her eyes love looked at him unashamed, love touched him in her soft caressing hands, came to him in the passionate caress of her scarlet mouth, love cradled him in the clasp of her white arms. And the sun, peeping down inquisitively through the leaves, showed all the beauty of her and made a rippling splendour of her hair. But now the woodpecker began tap-tapping soft and insistent somewhere out of sight, a small noise, yet disturbing, that followed them wheresoever they went. Thus they wandered, close entwined, and ever the wood grew darker until they came at last to a mighty tree whose sombre far-flung branches shut out the kindly sun. And, lo! within this gloom the woodpecker was before them—a most persistent bird this, tap-tapping louder than ever —whereat Hermione, seized of sudden terror, struggled in his embrace, and, pointing upward, cried aloud and was gone from him. Then, looking where she had pointed, he beheld no woodpecker, but the hated face of Bud M'Ginnis.

Ravenslee blinked drowsily at the wall where purple roses bloomed, at the fly-blown text in the tarnished frame with its notable legend:

An Early Morning Visit and a Warning

"LOVE ONE ANOTHER,"

and sighed. But in his waking ears was the tap of the woodpecker loud and persistent as ever! Wherefore he started, stared, sat up suddenly, and, glancing towards the window, beheld a large cap and a pair of shoulders he thought he recognised.

"Why, Spider!" he exclaimed, "what the——"

"Sufferin' Mike!" sighed the Spider plaintively, "here I've been knockin' at your all-fired winder—knockin' an' knockin', an' here you've been snorin' an' snorin'."

"No! did I snore, Spider?"

"Bo', you sure are a bird for snorin'."

"Damn it!" said Ravenslee, frowning, "I must break myself of it."

"Thinkin' o' gettin' married, bo'?"

"Married? What the——"

"She'll soon get useter it, I guess—they all do!" said the unabashed Spider. "Anyway, if you didn't snore exactly you sure had a strangle-hold on the snooze-business all right. Here's me crawled out o' me downy little cot t' put ye wise t' Bud's little game, an' here's you diggin' into the feathers t' beat th' band!"

"But the window was open, why didn't you come in right away?"

"Not much, bo', I ain't the kind o' fool as makes a habit o' wakin' your kind out o' their beauty sleep sudden, no more I ain't a guy as takes liberties in strange bed-rooms—see?"

"Well, come in, Spider; sit on the bed, I haven't a chair to offer. By the way, I have to thank you——"

"Whaffor?"

"Breaking that window."

"Oh, I guess it wasn't a bad wheeze."

"It gave me the chance I wanted, Spider."

"Which you sure gripped with both mitts, bo'!"

"Now have a cigar—in that coat pocket."

The Definite Object

"Not me, Geoff! Smoke's bad for the wind, that's why I've took t' gum." Saying which, the Spider proceeded to take out and open a packet of that necessary adjunct, and, having posted it into his mouth piece by piece, fell to grim mastication.

"Bo'," said he suddenly, "you come away without your roof last night."

"Eh?" said Ravenslee, blinking drowsily. "My what?"

"Your lid, bo'."

"You mean my old hat?"

"That's what I'm tryin' t' tell you; an' say, that sure is the hardest bean-cover I ever spotted; made of iron, is it? Where 'd you dig it up?"

"At some dim and distant day it originated in England, I believe."

"Well, that lid would turn a pole-axe, sure, that's why I brought it back, it's out on the fire-escape, now."

"Very kind of you, Spider, but——"

"Bo', you're goin' t' need that hat an' a soot o' tin underwear from now on, unless—well, unless you pack yer trunk an' clear out o' Hell's Kitchen on th' jump."

"Why so?"

"Well, you certainly handed Bud a whole lot more 'n he's ever had before, an' it's a full house to a pair o' dooces he ain't lookin' for no more from you just yet. But then Bud ain't no pet lamb nor yet a peace conference, an' it's four aces to a bum-flush he means t' get back at ye some way—an' get ye good!"

"Oh!" said Ravenslee, yawning.

"And, oh some more!" nodded the Spider. "It's sure comin' t' you. When I got back las' night there's Bud settin' against th' wall lookin' like an exhibit from the Morgue, fightin' for breath t' cuss you with. 'N' say, you sure had done him up some, which I wasn't nowise sad or peeved about—no, sir! Me an' Bud's never been what you might call real kittenish an' playful together.

202

An Early Morning Visit and a Warning

But it seems you ain't only soaked an' throttled him good an' plenty, but he's gone an' let out t' you about that guy Heine, an' consequently you've gotter be kept from openin' yer mouth—see? Consequently, it's you for a sudden an' hasty hike."

" Oh ! " Ravenslee said again.

" Twice," nodded the Spider, " with a F an' a L thrown in—that's what you'll be, Geoff, if you try t' buck Bud an' th' gang. So here I've shinnied up yer fire-escape to put ye wise an' lend a hand to make yer swift get-away."

Ravenslee sighed and settled his head more comfortably on his pillow.

" You think I ought to go, Spider ? "

" I don't think—I know ! Your number's up, Geoff —it's you against th' field, an', bo', they're some field ! "

" You think there's real danger, then ? " inquired Ravenslee, staring up at the fly-blown text with shining eyes.

" As real as—death, bo' ! "

" Not so long ago I regarded Death as my best friend."

" How much ? " demanded the Spider, suspending mastication.

" Nothing, Spider, a mere passing thought."

" Well, I'm tellin' ye they'll get ye sure—it'll be th' water or a forty-four bullet, or a black-jack or a knife ; but you'll get it one way or another."

" Sounds cheering ! "

" An' it ain't over-pleasant t' be sand-bagged."

" No, Spider."

" Nor t' feel a lead-pipe wrapped round th' back o' yer bean ? "

" No, indeed, Spider."

" Nor yet t' feel a stiletta diggin' between yer shoulders or over yer collar-bone ? "

" Worst of all, Spider."

The Definite Object

"Well then, you'd best pack yer little trunk an' fade away, bo'!"

Ravenslee sat up suddenly and looked at the Spider with eyes very bright and wide.

"Not for all the gangs that ever ganged!" said he softly.

"Eh!" exclaimed the Spider staring, "what's yer game?"

"I'm going to try to buck this gang clean out of existence."

"You are, eh?"

"I am."

"Bo'," sighed the Spider, shaking his head, "you ain't a ordinary fool—you're a damned fool!"

"And you're going to help me, Spider!"

"Not me, bo'—not me. I'm only just a ordinary fool!"

"Well, we'll let it go at that," said Ravenslee, and, lying back, he yawned again.

"Don't do that, bo'—don't do that!" exclaimed the Spider. "I'm thinkin' what you'll look like after you've been floatin' around in th' river—a week, say. You'd best get out o' Hell's Kitchen, bo'—don't stop to ask where to, but—go there."

"My Spider," said Ravenslee, shaking his head, "in Hell's Kitchen I should have to leave all that makes life worth while, so—I shall stay, of course, and chance the —er—river and things."

"Well, I guess it's your trouble, not mine."

"But I want it to be yours, too, Spider. You see, I'm counting on you to help me smash this gang."

"Bo', it looks like you're goin' t' do a hell of a lot o' countin'—an' then some more—before you count me in on this fool game. Say"—he paused to stare at Ravenslee, keen-eyed and with jaws clamped rigid— "you ain't a fly-cop—one o' these sleuthy gum-shoe men, are ye?"

An Early Morning Visit and a Warning

" No."

" Well, you ain't one o' those fool amateur guys doin'
the dare-devil detective act like you read about in th
magazines, are ye ? "

" No more than you are one of those dirty gang-loafers
you hear about round O'Rourke's, and that's why you're
going to help me root 'em out."

" Sufferin' Pete ! " sighed the Spider, " here I keep
tellin' you I ain't on in this act, an' here you keep on
ringin' me in frequent all the same."

" Because you are a man, Spider Conolly, and white all
through, and because to smash up this gang is going to
be man's work."

" Well, it sure ain't no job for Sophy the Satin-skinned
Show-girl, nor yet for two nice quiet little fellers like you
an' me."

" We sha'n't be quite alone, Spider."

" That's some comfortin', anyway ! "

" There will be Joe Madden, for one."

" Joe Mad——" The Spider very nearly bolted his
wad of chewing-gum, then he rose and stood staring at
Ravenslee very round of eye. " So you know Joe
Madden, the best all-round champion that ever happened, eh ? "

" I box with him every day."

" Hully chee ! " exclaimed the Spider, and chewed
fervently in silent astonishment. Suddenly he lifted his
head and stood as one that hearkens to distant sounds,
and, crossing stealthily to the window, climbed out.

" What's the matter ? "

" Mother Trapes, bo'—she's just rollin' out o' th'
feathers, an' she's quite enough for me—always has me
fazed to a frazzle. If she caught me here it 'u'd be th'
gimlet-eye for mine—so here's where I fade away."

" Anyway, come and have tea here with me to-night,
Spider, unless you think I am—er—too dangerous to
visit just now on account of M'Ginnis."

The Definite Object

" Dangerous ? " repeated the Spider scowling. " Bo',
when I get a call t' free food with a guy like you, danger
gets lost in th' shuffle an' forgotten. I'll be there.
Now here's your bean-cover—catch ! S' long ! " And
nodding, Spider promptly vanished down the fire-escape.

CHAPTER XXIII

CHIEFLY CONCERNING A LETTER

"SUNDAY!" said Mrs. Trapes sententiously, "Sunday is a holy day to some folks, an' a holiday for other folks, but t' folks like me an' Hermy it sure ain't no day o' rest an' gladness—like the hymn-book says."

"Isn't it?" said Ravenslee, pushing away his coffee-cup, and glancing toward the loud-ticking clock upon the sideboard.

"It sure ain't!" nodded Mrs. Trapes, quick to note the look. "Hermy an' me ain't much given to Sunday observance, Mr. Geoffrey. Ye see, there's always meals t' be cooked an' washin'-up t' be done, an' clo'es t' be mended p'r'aps. I've darned many a heart-felt prayer into a wore-out pair o' stockin's before now, an' offered up many a petition t' the Throne o' Grace with my scrubbin'-brush sloshin' over the floor. Anyway, Hermy 'n' me ain't never had much time for church-goin' or prayer-meetin's or mindin' our souls in our best frocks an' bonnets—no, sir! We jest have t' get on with our work—sewin' an' cookin' an' washin'—mindin' the welfare o' other folks' bodies. So while them as has time an' inclination sing their praises t' the Lord on their knees, Hermy an' me take out our praises in work, an' have t' leave our souls t' God. An', oh well, I guess He'll take care o' 'em all right, don't ye think?"

"I certainly do!" nodded Ravenslee.

"O' course my soul ain't all it should be—a bit stained here an' there, p'r'aps—a bit th' worse for wear, Mr. Geoffrey; but Hermy's—well there, I guess it's jest as

207

sweet as a flower still, an' white—ah, as white as that tablecloth. An' talkin' about her soul, what about her body, Mr. Geoffrey ? "

Ravenslee started. " Her body ? " said he staring. " Well, since you ask, I should say it is like her soul— very sweet and white and——"

" Sure ! " nodded Mrs. Trapes, " but, bein' only flesh an' blood after all—bein' only miserable clay like yours an' mine, Mr. Geoffrey, it'll always need food t' nourish it, clo'es t' keep it warm, an' a roof t' shelter it. Well, if she was t' be s' mad as t' marry a pea-nut man, what about food an' clo'es an' a roof ? "

" I think they could be managed, Mrs. Trapes."

" What ! out o' pea-nuts ? "

" No—er—the fact is, I've given 'em up."

Mrs. Trapes sniffed. " Ye don't say ! " she remarked drily. " Think o' that, now ! "

" The fact is, Mrs. Trapes, I—well, suppose I were to confess to you that I'm not quite so poor as I seem, what should you say ? "

" Why, I should say as I knew that about three weeks ago, Mr. Geoffrey."

" Oh, did you ? " said Ravenslee, staring. " How in the world did you find out ? "

" Why, Mr. Geoffrey, I'll tell ye how. I got eyes an' I got ears, an' sometimes I can see a bit with my eyes an' hear with my ears—that's how ! Oh, I've watched ye, Mr. Geoffrey, I've watched ye careful, because—well, because I sure love Hermy, an' 't would jest break my heart t' see her fallin' in love with a rogue ! "

" So you think—that she is—falling in love, then ? " inquired Ravenslee slowly.

" Well, Hermy's Hermy, an' she's wrote you two letters to my knowin'."

" No, only one, Mrs. Trapes."

" Now, Hermy ain't the kind o' girl t' write twice to a man unless——"

Chiefly Concerning a Letter

"But she has only written me one letter, Mrs. Trapes—the one she left with you last week."

"Oh, well—here's the other!" said Mrs. Trapes, laying before him an envelope addressed in the handwriting he had come to know so well.

"Why didn't you give it to me before?" he inquired.

"Her orders, Mr. Geoffrey."

"Orders?"

"Orders!" nodded Mrs. Trapes. "She come in here last night an' give it me after you was gone t' bed. 'Ann, dear,' she says, 'don't let him have it till half after ten t'-morrer,' she says. An' it's nearly eleven now—so there's yer letter!"

"But," said Ravenslee, "why on earth——"

"P'r'aps th' letter 'll tell you, Mr. Geoffrey. S'pose you read it while I clear away your breakfast things!"

Hereupon Ravenslee opened the letter and read these words:

"MY DEAR,—It would be my joy to trust myself to you utterly, to go with you to the world's end if you would have it so. Only I'm afraid that I am not quite what you would have me. I'm afraid that I might sometimes do things that would remind you that I had been only a scrub-woman. I'm afraid that some day you might regret. Were I to answer you now I should answer you selfishly—so, please, you must give me time to think, for both our sakes. Love has never come near me before, and now I am a little afraid, for love is not little and tender and babyish, but great and strong and very fierce and masterful—that is why I am afraid of it. So I must go away from you, from the sound of your voice, the touch of your hand—to think it all out. My work will take me to Englewood to-morrow, and I want you to wait for your answer until I come back, for then I shall have decided one way or the other. But in Englewood the memory of your words will be with me still Oh, did

209

The Definite Object

you mean all, quite all, you said, and did you say quite all you meant to say, did you—did you? For indeed it has seemed to me that if you really meant all you said you might have said a little more—just a little more. This is a dreadfully long letter, and very badly expressed, I know, but I dare not read it through. But what I have written is written from my heart.

HERMIONE.

"P.S.—I shall be in Englewood three whole days."

"Will strawberry jam an' angel cake an' a bunch or so o' watercress be enough, Mr. Geoffrey?"

Ravenslee sat staring down at the letter, rubbing his square, fresh-shaven chin as one very much at a loss. "'Might have said a little more—just a little more,'" he muttered, his gaze focussed upon a certain line.

"Will watercress an' angel cake an' a pot o' strawberry jam soot, Mr. Geoffrey?"

"Now I wonder what the dickens she can mean?" mused Ravenslee.

"She means jest strawberry jam an' angel cake an' watercress, fer tea—fer your visitors," said Mrs. Trapes with a patient sigh.

"Visitors!" repeated Ravenslee, glancing up, "why, yes, they'll be here about four o'clock."

"An' will watercress an' angel cake an'——"

"Quite enough! Certainly! Admirable!" exclaimed Ravenslee. "But what beats me," he continued, staring down at the letter again, "is what she can mean by writing this."

"Not knowin' what she's wrote I can't say."

"Mrs. Trapes, I know you are Hermione's best and staunchest friend, and lately I have ventured to hope you are mine too. As such I want you to read this letter; see if you can explain it."

So Mrs. Trapes took the letter; and when she had read it through, folded it together with hand very gentle and reverent, and stood awhile staring out into the sunlit court.

"My land!" she said at last, her harsh voice grown almost soft, "love's a wonderful thing, I reckon. No wonder your eyes shine so. Yes, love's a great an' wonderful thing—my land!"

"But can you explain," said Ravenslee as he took back the letter, "can you tell me what she means by——"

"Shucks, Mr. Geoffrey! That sure don't want no explainin'. When you said all you did say to her did ye say anything about 'wife' or 'marriage'?"

"Why, of course I did!"

"Sure?"

"Yes—er—that is—I think so."

"Not sure then?"

"Well, I may have done so—I must have done so, but really I—er—forget."

"Forget!" Mrs. Trapes snorted. "Now look-a-here, Mr. Geoffrey, what d'ye want with Hermy? Is it a wife you're after, or only——"

"Mrs. Trapes!" Ravenslee was upon his feet, and before the sudden glare in his eyes Mrs. Trapes gaped and for once fell silent. "Mrs. Trapes," said he, still frowning a little, "really you—you almost made me angry."

"My land," said she, "I'm kind o' glad I didn't—quite!" and her sniff was eloquent.

"You see," he went on, glancing down at the letter again, "I've learned to love and reverence her so much that your suggestion hurt rather."

"Why then, Mr. Geoffrey, I'm sorry. But if your love is so big an' true as all that—if you want her t' be a wife t' you—why in the 'tarnal didn't ye speak out an' tell her so?"

"I'll go an' tell her so this minute."

"Ye can't. She's gone t' Bronx Park with that b'y, 'n' won't be back all day."

The Definite Object

" Damn ! " exclaimed Ravenslee.

" Sure ! " nodded Mrs. Trapes. " Keep on, it'll do ye good. But anyway, what ye got t' say'll keep I guess— ay, it'll gush out all the stronger fer bein' bottled up a day or two."

" I can write," he suggested.

" You can—but you won't—you'll tell her with your two lips ; a woman likes it better spoke—if spoke proper. I should ! With arms entwined an' eyes lookin' into eyes, an'—oh, shucks ! Will angel cake an' strawberry jam——"

" They'll be ample, and—thank you, dear Mrs. Trapes ! "

CHAPTER XXIV

HOW THE OLD 'UN AND CERTAIN OTHERS HAD TEA

"Old 'un," said Joe, halting his aged companion in the middle of the second flight to wag a portentous finger, "Old 'un, mind this now, if there should 'appen to be cake for tea, don't go makin' a ancient beast of yourself with it, no slippin' lumps of it into your pocket on the sly, mind, because if I ketch you at it——"

"Don't be 'arsh, Joe—don't be 'arsh! Cake comes soft t' me pore old teef."

"An' mind this again, if there should be any jam about, no stickin' yer wicked old fingers into it an' lickin' 'em behind my back."

"You lemme an' the jam alone, Joe, it's a free country, ain't it? Very well, then."

"Free country be blowed! You mind what I say, you venerable old bag of iniquity, you!"

"'Niquity yerself!" snarled the Old 'un, and, snapping bony finger and thumb under Joe's massive chin, turned and went on up the stairs, his smart straw hat cocked at a defiant angle, his brilliant shoes creaking loudly at every step.

"Oh, gorramighty!" he panted, halting suddenly on the fifth landing to get his breath, "these perishin' stairs 'as ketched my wind, Joe. It's worse'n th' treadmill! Is there many more of 'em?"

"Only six flights," nodded Joe grimly.

"Six!" wailed the Old 'un. "Lord, it'll be the death o' me!"

213

The Definite Object

" Well, it's about time you was dead," nodded Joe.

" Dead ye'self ! " snarled the old man. " I'm a better figger of a man than ever you was."

" An' you would come," continued Joe serenely, as he deftly resetted the old fellow's sporty bow-tie, " ye fair plagued me to bring ye along, didn't ye, old packet o' vindictiveness ? "

" Well, an' here I am, Joe, an' here I mean t' stay, no more climbin' fer me, I'm tired, me lad, tired ! " Saying which the Old 'un spread his handkerchief on a convenient stair and proceeded to seat himself thereon with due regard for his immaculately creased trousers.

" Well," growled Joe, " of all the perverse old raspers that ever I did see ! "

" That's enough, Joe—that's enough ! " exclaimed the Old 'un, fanning himself with his rakish hat, " Jest bend down and flick the dust off me shoes with your wipe, like a good lad, will ye ? That's the worst o' these 'ere patent-leathers, they looks well, but they ketches th' dust, Joe, they ketches the dust oncommon bad. So jest give 'em a flick over, me pore old back's too stiff t' let me reach 'em, what wi' me rheumatiz an' a floatin' kidney or so."

" Kidneys ! " snarled Joe, drawing out a large bandanna handkerchief and polishing the old man's natty shoes until they shone resplendent, " what's the matter wi' yer blessed kidneys now ? "

" Don't I tell ye—they floats, Joe—they floats ! "

" Float ! " growled Joe. " Float—where to ? "

" 'Ere, there, an' everywhere, Joe, I can feel 'em. They're always a-gettin' theirselves all mixed up any'ow. Oh, it's a norrible complaint to 'ave kidneys like mine as gets theirselves lost."

" Wish they'd lose you along wi' 'em ! " growled Joe, shaking the dust from his handkerchief.

" Joe," said the old man, putting on his hat and blinking up at him beneath its jaunty brim—" Joe, sometimes I fair despise ye ! "

214

The Old 'un and Others have Tea

"Well, despise away," nodded Joe, "only get up—stand up on them doddering old pins o' yourn."

"Not me," declared the Old 'un, "I ain't goin' to climb no more o' these perishin' stairs—no, not for ye nor nobody. 'Ere I am, me lad, an' 'ere I sits till you give me a piggy-back up to the top—me bein' a pore old cove with rheumatiz—I demands it."

"You'll what?" growled Joe, hard-breathing and indignant.

"Demand it, Joe—a pore old feller wi' kidneys—an' every other ailment as flesh is hair to—a piggy-back, Joe—a piggy-back!"

Without another word Joe stooped, and, lifting the old man beneath one arm, bore him up the stairs regardless of his croaking protestations and fierce invective.

"I said a piggy-back. Oh, you blightin' perisher, I said a piggy-back!" he snarled, his resplendent shoes twinkling in futile kicks. "Oh Joe, there's times when I fair 'ates ye!" Thus, despite virulent curses and feeble kickings, Joe bore him on and up until, as he climbed the last flight, he was arrested by an exclamation from above, and, glancing upwards, beheld a tall, sharp-featured woman who leaned over the rail.

"Oh, land o' my fathers!" exclaimed Mrs. Trapes, "what's the matter—what you got there? Who are ye?"

"The matter, ma'am," answered Joe, for by this time the Old 'un had cursed himself quite breathless, "the matter's contrariness. What I 'ave under my arm, ma'am, is a old reprobate—and I'm Joe Madden, ma'am—come to take tea with my—come, as you might say, a-visiting to Mr. Geoffrey. P'r'aps you'll——"

"Don't 'eed 'im, ma'am, never 'eed 'im!" croaked the Old 'un, who had regained his wind by now, " 'e's a perishin' pork pig, that's wot 'e is—Joe, you blighter, put me down. It's me as the guv expects—it's me as 'as come a-visitin'. Joe, put me down, you perisher—

The Definite Object

Joe's only a hoaf, ma'am, a nass, ma'am. Joe ain't used to perlite serciety, Joe don't know nothin'. Put me down, Joe, like a good lad!"

At this juncture Ravenslee appeared, whereupon Joe, having reached the topmost landing, set the old man upon his natty feet and fell to straightening his smart clothes with hands big but gentle.

"Sir," explained Joe, answering Ravenslee's smiling look, "old Sin an' Sorrer here wouldn't walk up, which forced me to——"

But now the Old 'un, feeling quite himself again, cut in on his own account.

"Ma'am," said he, flourishing off his hat to Mrs. Trapes, "'ere's me an' me lad Joe come to tea—my best respex an' greetin's, ma'am. How do, guv? I do 'ope as you ain't forgot th' cake."

"Oh, we've plenty of cake, Old 'un!" laughed Ravenslee.

"An' watercress an' jam!" nodded Mrs. Trapes.

"Guv," said the old man, gripping Ravenslee's hand, "God bless ye for a true man an' a noble sport. Ma'am, you're a angel! Jam, ma'am, you're a nymp—you're two nymps.

> I oft would cast a rovin' eye
> Ere these white 'airs I grew, ma'am,
> To see a 'andsome nymp go by;
> But none s' fair as you, ma'am.

An' there's me hand on it, ma'am."

"My land!" ejaculated Mrs. Trapes, staring; then all at once she laughed, a strange laugh that came and went again immediately, yet left her features a little less grim than usual, as, reaching out, she grasped the old man's feeble hand. "I guess you're only bein' p'lite," said she, "but jest for that ye're sure goin' t' eat as much cake an' jam as your small insides can hold." So saying, she led the way into her small and very neat domain, and ushered them into the bright little parlour,

216

The Old 'un and Others have Tea

where the Spider sat already enthroned in that armchair whereon sunflowers rioted ; and, like the chair, the Spider was somewhat exotic as to socks and tie, and he seemed a trifle irked by stiff cuffs and collar as he sat there staring at the green-and-yellow tablecloth and doing his best not to tread upon the pink hearthrug.

"Joe," said Ravenslee, "this is Spider Conolly who knocked out Larry M'Kinnon at San Francisco last year in the sixty-ninth—Spider, I want you to shake hands with——"

"Bo'," exclaimed the Spider, rising reverently and taking a step toward Joe's massive figure quite forgetful of the pink hearthrug now, "you don't have t' tell me nothin', I guess I know th' best all-round fightin'-man, the greatest champion as ever swung a mitt, when I see him ! T' shake his hand'll sure be——"

"Young feller, me lad," cried the Old 'un, reaching out nimbly and catching the Spider's extended hand, "you got a sharp eye, a true eye—a eye as can discrimpinate, like—ah, like a flash o' light. You're right, me lad, I was the best fightin'-man, the greatest champeen as ever was—sixty odd years ago. Ho yus, I were the best of 'em all, an' I ain't to be sniffed at now. So shake me 'and, me lad—an' shake—hard ! "

The Spider's grim jaw relaxed and his eyes opened very wide as the Old 'un continued to shake his hand up and down.

"But say," said he faintly at last, "I don't——"

"No more don't I," nodded the Old 'un. "What's the old song say :

> I don't care if it rains or snows,
> Or what the day may be,
> Since 'ere's a truth I plainly knows,
> Love, you'll remember me."

"But say," began the bewildered Spider again, "say, I reckon——"

217

The Definite Object

" So do I," nodded the Old 'un.

" I reckon up my years o' life,
　An' a good long life 'ave I.
Ye see, I never had a wife,
　P'r'aps that's the reason why.

So take it from me, young feller, me cove, don't 'ave nothin' to do with givin' or takin' in marriage."

" Marriage ? "

" Marriage ain't good for a fightin' cove, it spiles him —it shakes 'is nerve—it fair ruinates 'im. When love flies in at the winder champeenships fly up the chimbley —never t' come back no more. So beware o' wives, me lad."

" Wives ! " repeated the Spider, lifting free hand to dazed brow, " I—I ain't never——"

" That's right ! " nodded the Old 'un heartily, shaking the Spider's unresisting hand again, " Marriage ain't love an' love ain't marriage. Wot's the old song say ?

Oh, love is like a bloomin' rose,
　But marriage is a bloomin' thorn.
A 'usband's full o' bloomin' woes,
　An' 'eaves a bloomin' sigh each morn."

" Why, Old 'un," exclaimed Ravenslee, " that's a very remarkable verse ! "

" My land ! " ejaculated Mrs. Trapes, squaring her elbows in the doorway, " I suspects he's a poet—an' him sech a nice little old gentleman ! "

" A poet, ma'am ! " exclaimed the Old 'un indignantly ; " not me, ma'am, not me—should scorn t' be. I'm a 'ighly respected old fightin'-man, I am, as never went on th' cross :

A fightin' man I, ma'am,
An' wish I may die, ma'am,
If ever my backers I crossed.
An' what's better still, ma'am,
Though I fought many a mill, ma'am,
Not one of 'em ever I lost."

The Old 'un and Others have Tea

"My land!" exclaimed Mrs. Trapes again, "what a memory!"

"Memory, ma'am!" growled Joe, "that ain't memory. 'E makes 'em up as 'e goes along."

"Joe," said the Old 'un, glaring, "if the lady weren't here, an' axin' 'er pardon—I'd punch you in the perishin' eye'ole for that!"

"All right, old vindictiveness!" sighed Joe. "An' now, if you'll let go of Spider Conolly's fist I'd like to say 'ow do. Sit down an' give some one else a chance to speak. Sit down, you old bag o' wind."

"Bag o'——" the old man dropped the Spider's nerveless hand to turn to Mrs. Trapes with a gloomy brow. "You 'eard that, ma'am—you 'eard this perishin' porker call me a bag o'—— Joe, I blush for ye!—Ma'am, pore Joe means well, but 'e can't 'elp bein' a perisher, but——" and here the old man raised and shook a feeble old fist—"I've a good mind t' ketch 'im one as would put 'im t' sleep for a fortnight; I've a good mind——"

But Mrs. Trapes caught that tremulous fist, and, drawing the Old 'un's arm through her own, turned to the door.

"You come along wi' me," said she, "you shall help me t' get th' tea, you shall carry in th' cake an'——"

"Cake!" exclaimed the Old 'un. "Oh, j'yful word—ma'am, you're a—a lydy! An' there's jam, ain't there?"

"Strawberry!"

"Straw—oh, music t' me ears, ma'am—you're a nymp—lead me to it!" So saying, the Old 'un followed Mrs. Trapes out into the kitchen, while the Spider stared after him open-mouthed.

"Sufferin' Pete!" he murmured, and, inhaling a long, deep breath turned to grasp Joe's mighty, outstretched hand. Then, drawing their chairs together, they sat down, and Ravenslee, by an adroit question or two, soon had them talking—the Spider quick and eager, and chewing

The Definite Object

voraciously, Joe soft-voiced and deliberate, but speaking with that calm air of finality that comes only of long and varied experience. So, while Ravenslee smoked and listened, they spoke of past battles, of fights and fighters old and new ; they discoursed learnedly on ring-craft, they discussed the merits of the crouch as opposed to the stiff leg and straight left ; they stood up to show tricks of foot and hand—cunning shifts and feints, they ducked and side-stepped and smote the empty air with whirling fists to the imminent peril of the owl that was a parrot, which moth-eaten relic seemed to watch them with his solitary glass eye.

And ever the Spider's respect and admiration for the mild-eyed, quiet-spoken champion waxed and grew.

" Bo' ! " said he, dexterously catching the toppling bird, glass-case and all, for the second time, and addressing Ravenslee with it clasped to his heart, " bo', " he repeated, his eyes shining, " I guess Joe Madden, the greatest battler of 'em all, is—Joe Madden still. I've always wanted t' meet with him, an' say—I wouldn't ha' missed him for a farm."

" Is that so ! " exclaimed Mrs. Trapes, entering the room at this moment with the tea-cloth. " Well, now, you jest put 'im down—you jest put that bird back again, Spider Conolly ! "

" Yes, ma'am, " quoth the Spider, all abashed humility.

" What you doin' with it anyway ? " she demanded, elbows jutted ominously, " It's lost an eye, an' a cat got it once an' sp'iled it some, but I treasure it for reasons o' sentiment, an' if you think you kin steal it——"

" Not 'im, ma'am—not 'im ! " piped the Old 'un from the doorway, " it ain't the pore lad's fault—it's Joe's, blame it all on to Joe. Joe's got a bad 'eart, ma'am, a black, base-'earted perisher is Joe—so no jam for Joe, ma'am, an' only one slice o' cake."

But here Ravenslee hastened to explain, whereupon

The Old 'un and Others have Tea

Mrs. Trapes's grimness abated and her bristling elbows subsided; and now, perceiving how the abashed Spider, meeting her eye, flushed, plucked at his cuffs and shuffled his feet, she reached out to pat his broad and drooping shoulders.

"Mister Conolly," she said, "for harsh words spoke in haste I craves now your pardon, an' I craves it—humble. Am I forgive?"

The Spider, flushing redder than ever, rose to his feet, seized her hand, shook it, and muttered, "Sure!"

And when the table was laid, the Old 'un proposed, and was duly seconded, thirded, and fourthed, that Mrs. Trapes be elected into the chair to pour out the tea, which she proceeded to do forthwith, while the Old 'un, seated at her right hand, kept a wary eye roving between jam-dish and angel cake. And now, by reason of the unwonted graciousness of Mrs. Trapes, of Ravenslee's tact and easy assurance, and the Old 'un's impish hilarity, all diffidence and restraint were banished and good-fellowship reigned supreme, though the Spider was interrupted in the midst of a story by the Old 'un suddenly exclaiming, "Keep your hand out o' the jam, Joe!"

And Joe was, later, rendered speechless, hard-breathing, and indignant by the Old 'un turning to Mrs. Trapes with the shrill warning, 'Ma'am, Joe's 'ad two 'elpin's o' cake an' got 'is 'orrid eye on what remains!"

Nevertheless, the meal was in all ways a success, and Ravenslee was reaching for his pipe when Mrs. Trapes, summoned to the front door by a feverish knocking, presently came back, followed by Tony, whose bright eyes looked wider than usual as he saluted the company.

"Hey, Geoff, me tell-a you piece-a-da-noos!" he cried excitedly, "big-a piece-a-da-noos. Da cops go-a pinch-a Bud-a M'Ginn'!"

"Bud! Bud!" stammered the Spider, "have they pinched Bud? Is this the straight goods, Tony?"

The Definite Object

"Sure—they got-a heem this-a morn in Jersey City. 'N' say, he theenk-a eet a frame-up—he theenk-a Geoff set-a de cops for-a take heem."

"The hell he does!" exclaimed the Spider, starting to his feet.

"So he send-a da word to Soapy," continued Tony, his eyes rolling, "an' now all-a da gang's out layin' for-a Geoff. So when Geoff go-a out on da street—bingo!—dey snuff hees light out."

"Not much they won't!" said the Spider, buttoning up his coat and turning to the door. "I'll mighty soon fix this, I guess."

"Do you think you can, Spider?" inquired Ravenslee. "If you're going to have any trouble don't bother about——"

"Bo'," said the Spider squaring his big jaw, "get onto this—here's where I chip in with ye. From now on we're on this game together, an' I ain't a guy as'll lay down his hand till I'm called—an' called good, see? You said it was goin' to be a man's work, by Jiminy Christmas, it looks like you're right! Anyway I stand in with you, that's sure. Put it there, bo'!"

"But," said Ravenslee as their hands gripped, "I don't want you to take any chances on my account, or run any——"

"Fudge, bo', fudge! I ain't takin' no chances."

"Well, I'm coming along to see you don't!" said Ravenslee, reaching for his hat.

"Not on your life, bo', you'd queer the whole show. Ye see, they're a tough crowd, an' apt t' act a bit hasty now an' then; 'sides, they might think you're heeled, and they know I don't never carry a gun. They all know me."

"Still, I'm coming, Spider."

"Ye can't, bo', Mrs. Trapes ain't goin' t' let ye. Look at her!"

"You never spoke a truer word since you drawed the

222

The Old 'un and Others have Tea

vital air, Spider Conolly!" nodded Mrs. Trapes, hands on hips and elbows at the "engage." " If Mr. Geoffrey stirs out this day he's jest gotter trample over my mangled remains, that's all!"

Now hereupon, heeding the glitter in her eye, and noting the inexorable jut of her elbows, Ravenslee sat down and went on filling his pipe.

"Ye see, bo', I know as it wasn't you as give Bud away, an' the boys'll listen t' my say so—you bet they will. So here's where I ooze away. S' long all!"

But now the Old 'un, having bolted the last handful of cake, got upon his legs and clutched the Spider's coat in talon-like fingers.

"'Old 'ard, young-feller-me-lad!" he cried, "if there's any chance of a scrap comin' off, wot about me?—Gimme me 'at, Joe, an' get yourn; if I don't knock some on 'em stone cold call me a perishin' ass!"

"Why, since you say so, old blood an' bones," said Joe, his mild eye brightening, " we will step along with the Spider a little way if the guv'nor 'll excuse us?"

"Certainly, Joe," nodded Ravenslee, " on condition that you do just as the Spider says."

"You mean, sir?"

"No fighting, Joe—at least not yet."

"Trust me, sir! What ain't to be—yet, is to be sometime, I 'opes," sighed Joe.

"Good-bye, guv, good-bye!" croaked the Old 'un; "if I don't put some o' they perishers in the 'orspitals an' the infirmaries I ain't the man I was.

> Oh, used am I to war's alarms,
> I 'unger for the fray,
> Though beauty clasps me in 'er arms
> The trumpet calls away."

So, having made their adieux, the three took their departure ; though once, despite Joe's objurgations, the Old 'un must needs come back to kiss Mrs. Trapes's toil-worn hand with a flourish, which left her voiceless and

The Definite Object

round of eye until the clatter of their feet had died away. Then she closed the door and fixed Ravenslee with her stoniest stare.

"Mr. Geoffrey," she demanded, "why did they call you ' guv'nor ' and wherefore ' sir ' ? "

Ravenslee, in the act of lighting his pipe, had paused for a suitable answer, when Tony, who had remained mute in a corner, stepped forward and spoke :

"Say, Geoff, I gott-a bit-a—more noos. Old-a Finlay-a want-a spik with-a you."

" Old Finlay—with me ? "

" Sure ! Old-a Finlay-a go die-a very queek, an' he want-a spik with-a you first."

" Dying ! Old Finlay dying ? " questioned Ravenslee, rising.

" Sure ! He go die-a ver' queek."

" I'll come ! "

" An' I guess," said Mrs. Trapes, " yes, I opine as I'll come along wi' ye, Mr. Geoffrey."

Old Martin Finlay lay propped up by pillows, his great, gaunt, useless body seeming almost too large for the narrow bed wherein he lay, staring up great-eyed at Ravenslee—live eyes in a dead face.

" It's dyin' I am, sorr," said he faintly, " an' it's grateful is ould Martin for the docthers an' medicine you've paid for. But it's meself is beyand 'em all— an' it's beyand 'em I'm goin' fast—she's waitin' for me —me little Maggie's houldin' out her little hand to me —she's waitin' for me—beyand, Holy Mary be praised ! An' she's waited long enough, sorr, my little Maggie as I loved so while the harsh words burned upon me tongue —my little Maggie ! I was bitter cruel to my little girl ; but you've been kind to me, an', sorr, I thank ye. But," continued the dying man, slow and feebly, " it aren't to thank yez as I wanted ye, but to give yez something in trust for Miss Hermy. Ye see, sorr, I sha'n't be here when she comes back to-night, I'll be with—little Maggie when the hour strikes—my little Maggie! Norah, wife, give it to him."

Silently Mrs. Finlay opened a drawer, and, turning, placed in Ravenslee's hand a ring, a heavy gold ring curiously wrought into the form of two hands clasping each other.

" It was my Maggie's ! " continued Martin, " an' I guess she valleyed it a whole lot, sorr. I found it hid away with odds an' ends as she treasured. But she don't want it no more—she's dead, ye see, sorr—I killed her—drowned, sorr—I drowned her. Cruel an' hard I was—shut her out onto the streets, I did, an' so—she died. But before the river took—— Oh Blessed Mary—Oh Mother o' God—pity ! Before she went to heaven Miss Hermy was good t' her, Miss Hermy loved her an' tried t' comfort her, but only God could do that, I reckon, so she went t' God. But Miss Hermy was kind when I wasn't, so, sorr, it's give her that ring ye will, plaze, an' say as poor Martin died blessing her. An' now it's go I'll ask ye, sorr, for God's callin' me to wipe away me tears an' sorrers an' bind up me broken heart—so lave me to God an'—my little Maggie."

Very softly Ravenslee followed Mrs. Trapes out of the room ; but they had not reached the front door when they heard a glad cry, and thereafter a woman's sudden, desolate sobbing.

" Go on, Mr. Geoffrey," whispered Mrs. Trapes, " but I guess I'd better stay here a bit."

" You mean ? "

" As poor Martin's sure found his little girl again."

CHAPTER XXV

HOW SPIKE MADE A CHOICE AND A PROMISE

MONDAY morning found Ravenslee knocking at the opposite door, which, opening, disclosed Spike, but a very chastened and humble Spike, who blushed and drooped his head and shuffled with his feet, and finally stammered :

" Hello, Geoff—I—I'm all alone, but you—you can come in if—if you care to."

" I dropped in on my way down just to have a word with you, Spike."

With dragging feet Spike led the way into the sitting-room, where lay his breakfast, scarcely tasted.

" Sit down, Geoff, I—I want to apologise," said the lad, toying nervously with his teaspoon. " I guess you think I'm a mean, low-down sort o' guy, an' you're right, only I—I feel worse'n you think. An' say, Geoff, if I —if I said anything th' other night I want you to— forget it, will you ? "

" Why, of course, Spike."

" Hermy's forgiven me. I—I've promised to work hard an' do what she wants."

" I'm glad of that, Spike."

" She came creepin' into my room this mornin' before she went ; but—me thinkin' she meant to give me a last call down—I pretended t' be asleep, so she just sighed an' went creepin' out again, an' wrote me this," and Spike drew a sheet of crumpled notepaper from his pocket and handed it to Ravenslee, who read these words :

How Spike made a Choice and a Promise

"Boy dear, I love you so much that if you destroyed my love I think you would destroy me too. Now I must leave you to go to my work; but you will go to yours, won't you—for my sake, and for your sake, and because I love you so? Be good and strong and clean, and if you want some one to help you, go to your friend Mr. Geoffrey. Good-bye, dear; and remember your promise."

Ravenslee passed back the pencilled scrawl, and Spike, stooping his head low, read it through again.

"I guess I've just got to be good," he murmured, "for her sake. Oh Geoff," he cried suddenly, "I'd die for her!"

"Better live for her, Spike, and be the honourable, clean man she wishes."

"She sure thinks you're some man, Geoff! I guess she's—kind o'—fond o' you."

"That's what I've come to talk about, Spike."

"Are you—fond of her, Geoff?"

"Fond!" exclaimed Ravenslee forgetting to drawl, "I'm so fond—I love her so much, I honour her so deeply —that I want her for my wife."

"Wife!" exclaimed Spike, starting to his feet, his eyes suddenly radiant, "d'ye mean you'll marry her?"

"If she will honour me so far, Spike."

"Marry her! You'll marry her!" Spike repeated.

"As soon as she'll let me!"

"Geoff—oh Geoff!" exclaimed the boy, and, choking, turned away.

"Won't you congratulate me?"

"I can't yet," gasped Spike, "I can't till I've told ye what a mean guy I've been."

"What about?"

"About you—and Hermy. Bud said you meant t' make her go the way—little Maggie Finlay went, an'— oh Geoff, I—I kind o' believed him."

"Did you, Spike—that foul beast? But you don't

227

believe it any longer, and M'Ginnis is—only M'Ginnis after all."

"But I—I've got to tell you more," said the lad miserably, and, meeting Ravenslee's eye with an effort, he went on feverishly, "the other night after—after Bud slipped me the—the stuff, an' I'd had a—a drink or two, he began askin' all about you. At first I blocked an' side-stepped all his questions, but he kep' on at me, an' at last I—I give you away, Geoff." Here Spike paused breathlessly and cast an apprehensive glance toward his hearer, but, finding him silent and serene as ever, he repeated, " I—gave you away, Geoff ! "

" Did you, Spike ? "

" Yes, I—I told him who you really are ! "

" Did you, Spike ? "

" Yes ! Yes ! Oh Geoff, don't you understand ? "

" I understand."

" Well, why don't ye say something ? Why don't ye tell me what I am ? Say I'm a dirty sneak—call me a yeller cur—anything ! "

" No, you were drunk, that's all, and when the drink is in, honour and all that makes a man, is out—you were only drunk."

" Oh, but I wasn't s' drunk as all that," gasped Spike, cowering in his chair, " but he kep' on comin' at me with his questions, an' at last, when I told him how I met up with you, he kind o' give a jump, an' his face——" Spike clenched his fists, and, slowly raising them, pressed them upon his eyes. " I'll never forget th' look on his face ! So now you know as I've blown th' game on ye —given ye away—you as was my friend ! " With the word Spike sobbed and fell grovelling on his knees. " Curse me, Geoff ! " he cried. " Oh, curse me an' tell me what I am ! "

" You are Hermione's brother ! "

" My God ! " wailed the boy, " if she knew she'd hate me."

How Spike made a Choice and a Promise

" I almost think she would, Spike."

" You won't tell her, Geoff! You won't never let her know ? "

" I don't get drunk, Spike."

" But you won't tell her ? " he pleaded, reaching out desperate hands, " You won't ? "

" Not a word, Spike ! "

" Oh, I know I'm rotten ! " sobbed the lad. " I know you ain't got no use for me any more ; but I'm sorry, Geoff—I'm real sorry. I know a guy can't forgive a guy as gives a guy away if that guy's a guy's friend. I know as you can't forgive me. I know as you'll cut me out for good after this. But I want ye t' know as I'm sorry, Geoff—awful sorry—I—I ain't fit t' be anybody's friend, I guess."

" I think you need a friend more than ever, Spike ! "

" Geoff ! " cried the boy breathlessly, " say—what d' you mean? "

" I mean the time has come for you to choose between M'Ginnis and me ; if I am to be your friend M'Ginnis must be your enemy from now on. Wait ! If you want my friendship, no more secrets ; tell me just how M'Ginnis got you into his power—how he got you to break into my house."

Spike glanced up through his tears, glanced down, choked upon a sob, and burst into breathless narrative :

" There was me an' Bud an' a guy they call Soapy— we'd been to a rube boxin' match up th' river. An' as we come along, Soapy says, ' If I was in th' second-story-lay there's millionaire Ravenslee's wigwam waitin' t' be cracked,' and he pointed out your swell place among th' trees in th' moonlight. Then Bud says, ' You ain't got th' nerve, Soapy. Why, th' kid's got more nerve than you,' he says, pattin' my shoulder. An' Soapy laughs an' says I'm only a kid. An' Geoff, I'd got two or three drinks into me, an' th' end was I agreed t' just show 'em as I had nerve enough t' get in through a winder an' cop

The Definite Object

something—anything I could get. So Bud hands me his 'lectric torch, an' we skin over the fence an' up to the house—an' Soapy has th' winder open in a jiffy, an' me—bein' half-soused an' foolish—hikes inter th' room, an' you cops me on th' jump, an'—an' that's all!"

"And M'Ginnis has threatened to send you up for it now and then, eh?"

"Only for a joke. Bud ain't like me, he'd never split on a pal. Bud wouldn't gimme away."

"Anyway, Spike, it's him or me—which will you have for a friend?"

"Oh Geoff, I—I guess I'd follow you t' Kingdom Come if you'd let me. I do want t' live straight an' clean—honest t' God I do, Geoff, an' if you'll only forgive——"

Spike's outstretched, pleading hands were caught and held, and he was lifted to his feet.

"My Arthur-Spike, art going to the office this morning?"

"Sure I am; my eye ain't—ain't s' bad after all, is it? Anyway, I feel more like what a man should feel like now, an'—gee! look at me doin' the sissy tearspoutin' act! Oh hell—lemme go an' wash me face. 'N' say, if—if any o' them—I mean those dolly office-boys—has anything t' say I'll punch th' sawdust out o' them!"

CHAPTER XXVI

RAVENSLEE, strolling in leisurely fashion along Tenth Avenue, became aware of a slender, pallid youth whose old-young face was familiar, a cigarette dangled from his pale, thin lips, and his slender hands were hidden in the pockets of his smartly-tailored coat. On went Ravenslee, pausing now and then to glance idly into some shop window until, chancing to slip his fingers into a waistcoat pocket, he paused all at once, and, taking thence a ring wrought into the semblance of two clasped hands, drew it upon his finger. Now as he glanced at the ring his eye gleamed, and, smiling as one who has a sudden bright idea, he set off faster than before, striding on light and purposeful feet. But, as he turned a corner, he noticed that the pallid youth was still close behind, wherefore he halted before a shop window where, among other articles of diet, were cans of tomatoes neatly piled into a pyramid. At these he stared, waiting, and thus presently found the pallid youth at his elbow, who also stared upon the tomato pyramid with half-closed eyes and with smouldering cigarette pendant from thin-lipped mouth. And after they had stared awhile in silence, cheek by jowl, Ravenslee spoke in his pleasant, lazy voice :

" Judging by the labels, these tomatoes are everything tomatoes possibly could be."

" 'S' right ! " murmured the pale one, imperturbably.

" Fond of tomatoes ? " inquired Ravenslee.

231

The Definite Object

"Aw!" answered his neighbour, "quit foolin'—talk sense!"

"Certainly! Why do you follow me, Soapy?"

Soapy's eyes grew narrower and the pendant cigarette stirred slightly.

"Know me, hey?" he inquired.

"Heaven forbid! 'Twas a bolt at a venture—a shot in the dark."

"Talkin'—o'—shootin'," said Soapy, grimly deliberate, "pea-nuts ain't a healthy profesh around here—not for your kind it ain't!"

"Oh, I don't know," answered Ravenslee, shaking his head gently at the tomatoes. "I've heard of professions even more unhealthy."

"Aw—well—say what?"

"Well, talking of shooting—yours!"

Soapy's narrow eyes gleamed with an added viciousness, his thin nostrils expanded, but the retort died upon his curling mouth, his puffy eyelids widened and widened as he stared at the ring on Ravenslee's finger, and when he spoke his voice was strangely hoarse and eager.

"Say, sport, where'd you—get that—ring?"

"Why do you ask?"

"'Cause I want to know, I guess."

"Think you've seen it before?"

"Sport, I don't think—I know. I seen it many a time. I'd know it in a million, sure."

"Where did you see it before?"

"On M'Ginnis's mitt. It useter belong t' Bud."

"Ah!" exclaimed Ravenslee, scowling down at the ring, "you make me wish more than ever that I had throttled him a little harder."

"Where'd you get that ring, sport?" Soapy repeated.

"From Maggie Finlay's father."

Soapy turned away to stare at the tomato-cans again.

"Meanin'?" he inquired at last, hoarser than before.

"That once upon a time it belonged to—her."

Which makes further Mention of a Ring

"Sport," said Soapy after an interval, still staring at the pyramid of cans, "I useter know her once, an' I've jest nacherally took a fancy t' that ring. If fifty dollars 'll buy it, they're yours—right now."

"It isn't mine," answered Ravenslee, still scowling at the ring which he had drawn from his finger. "I'm on my way to take it to—its owner. But if that person doesn't want it, and I'm pretty sure—that person—won't, you shall have it, I promise you. And now," said he pocketing the ring and turning, still scowling, on Soapy, "you are one of M'Ginnis's gang I fancy; anyway, if you see him you can tell him from me that if he gives me another chance I'll surely kill him for the foul beast he is."

"Sport," said Soapy, "I guess the Spider's right about you—anyway you ain't my meat. An' as for killin' Bud, you sure ain't goin' t' get th' chance—not while I have the say-so—see? S' long, sport!" and, turning upon his heel, Soapy lounged away.

Reaching Times Square, Ravenslee entered the subway, and, buying his ticket, was jostled by a boy, a freckled boy, round headed and round of nose, who stared at him with a pair of round, impertinent eyes.

Lost in happy speculation, he was duly borne to One Hundred and Thirtieth Street, where he boarded the ferry. Upon the boat he was again conscious of a round head that bobbed here and there amid the throng of passengers, but paid small heed as he leaned watching the broad and noble river and the green New Jersey shore. At Fort Lee, exchanging boat for trolley-car, he was once more vaguely conscious of two round eyes that watched him from a rear seat; but as the powerful car whirled them uphill, plunged them down steep inclines, swung them round sharp curves, through shady woods, past far-flung boughs whose leaves stirred and whispered as the great car fleeted by, he fell again to dreaming of Hermione and the future; and so betimes

233

The Definite Object

he reached Englewood, a small township dreaming in the fierce mid-day sunshine. Here, he inquired of a perspiring butcher in shirt-sleeves the whereabouts of the house he wanted, and, being fully directed and carefully admonished how to get there, set off along the road. And, remembering that her feet must often have traversed this very path, he straightway fell to his dreaming again; thus how should he know anything of the round head that bobbed out from behind bush or tree ere it followed whither he went? So Ravenslee came where the road led between tall trees to smooth green lawns, beyond which was the gleam of water, and so at last to the house he sought.

Now beside this house, separated by a wide stretch of lawn, was a small wood; and, lured by its grateful shade, he turned aside into this wood and began pushing his way through the dense undergrowth, which, presently thinning, formed a small clearing roofed and shut in by leaves and full of a tender green light. Here he paused, and, espying a fallen tree hard by, sat himself down and began to fill his pipe. And now, remembering his shabby person, he felt disinclined to go up to the house and demand to see Miss Chesterton, yet see her he would; but how? He was frowning over this problem when it was resolved for him quite unexpectedly; roused by the sound of a snapping twig, he glanced up, and Hermione was before him. She was coming down a narrow path that wound amid the leaves, and, because she wore no hat, the sunlight filtering through the branches made a glory of her hair as she passed, her head was bowed and she walked very slowly as one in thought; she had brought sewing with her, but for once her busy hands were idle, and as he looked upon her beauty, scarce breathing, he saw again that look of wistful sadness.

As he rose she glanced up and, seeing him, stood utterly still. Thus for a long moment they gazed upon each other; then, even as he hasted to her, she came to him

Which makes further Mention of a Ring

on swift, light feet, and, flushing, tremulous, quick-breathing, gave herself into his arms.

"Oh Hermione, my beloved!" he murmured, his voice tense and eager, "didn't I say enough last time—didn't I? Don't you know I love you—worship you—hunger and yearn for you? I want you with every breath I draw. When will you be my wife? When will you marry me, Hermione?"

For answer she reached up her arms, sudden, passionate arms that clung about him close and strong; and they stood thus, heart beating to heart, thrilling at each other's nearness, yet drawing ever closer until, lifting her head, she gave her lips to his.

"Oh my dear, my dear," she whispered, "is it right to love you so I wonder? I never thought it could be —like this. It frightens me sometimes, because my love is so great and strong, and I so powerless. Is it right I—— Oh!" she broke off breathlessly, "how can I speak if—if you——"

"Kiss you so much?" he ended, "you can't speak, so don't speak, my Hermione!" But now, all at once, he started and glanced up among the leaves above them.

"Dear," she whispered, "what is it?"

"That tapping sound," he answered, still gazing upward.

"It's only the woodpecker."

"Why, of course!" he laughed. "It's strange, but I dreamed a scene like this—yes, the great tree yonder, and you in my arms—though it seemed so impossible then, and——"

But uttering a sudden, low cry of alarm, Hermione broke from his clasp and fled from him along the leafy path, while he stared after her, lost in amazement; then he ran also and caught her upon the edge of the little wood.

"What frightened you, Hermione, who was it?"

"I—I thought I saw some one crouching behind a bush, watching us!"

The Definite Object

"Not M'Ginnis ? " he demanded, fierce-eyed.

"No, no, I'm sure it wasn't ! "

"I'll go and look," said Ravenslee, clenching his fists. But now, as he turned away, two round arms were about him again, soft and compelling, and she was looking up at him all shy-eyed, passionate tenderness; and before the revelation in that look he forgot all else in the world.

"Hermione, when will you marry me ? "

Now, softened by distance, there floated to them the mellow booming of a gong.

"That means I must go," she sighed.

"Hermione, when will you marry me ? "

"Good-bye ! good-bye ! I must run ! "

But his long arms only clasped her the closer. "Hermione, when will you be my wife ? "

"Oh, please, please, let me go—if I'm late——"

"When, Hermione ? "

"When I come home, if—you really—want me. Oh, now my hair's all coming down, I know. Good-bye ! "

Reluctantly he loosed her and stood to watch, until, reaching the veranda of the house, she paused to glance back to where he stood among the leaves ere she vanished between the screen-doors. Then Ravenslee turned, and, remembering her sudden fright, looked sharply about him, even pausing now and then to peer behind bush and thicket; but this time he did not think to glance upward, and thus failed to see the round eyes that watched him from amid the leaves of the great tree. So he came again to the dusty highway and strode along throbbing with life and the lust of life, revelling in the glory of earth and sky, and quite unconscious of the small, furtive figure that flitted after him far behind. And it was not until he sat in the ferry-boat that he remembered he had forgotten to give her the ring after all.

CHAPTER XXVII

MRS. TRAPES UPON THE MILLENNIUM

MULLIGAN'S was in a ferment; bare-armed women talked in every doorway, they talked from open windows, they talked leaning over banisters, they congregated on landings and in passage-ways, but everywhere they talked; while men and youths newly returned from work, lunchcan and basket in hand, listened in wide-eyed wonder, shook incredulous heads, puffed thoughtfully at pipe or at cigarette, and questioned in guttural wonderment. But Ravenslee, lost in his own happy thoughts, sped up the stairs all unheeding, abstractedly returning such neighbourly salutes as he happened to notice. Reaching his lofty habitation in due course, he let himself in, and, seated in his armchair, was in the act of filling his pipe when Mrs. Trapes appeared. In one hand she grasped a meat-skewer and in the other an open Testament, and it was to be noted that her bright eyes, usually so keen and steady, roved here and there, from pink rug to green-and yellow table-cloth, thence to the parrot-owl, and so at last to her lodger; finally she spoke.

" Mr. Geoffrey, are ye saved ? " she demanded in awe-struck tones.

" Why, really, Mrs. Trapes, I——"

" Because, Mr. Geoffrey, this day it behooveth us all t' think of our souls an' th' hereafter, I reckon."

" Souls ? " said Ravenslee, staring in his turn.

" Fire," she continued, shaking portentous head, " fire

The Definite Object

I'm prepared for, a earthquake I could endoor, battle, murder, and sudden death I could abide; poverty is me lot, Mr. Geoffrey, an' hardship is me portion, an' for all sich am I dooly prepared, sich things bein' nacheral; but for this—well, there! "

" What is the matter, Mrs. Trapes? "

" Matter, Mr. Geoffrey? Well, the millennyum's at hand, that's all—the lion is about t' lay down with th' lamb, tigers has lost their taste for blood, an' snakes an' serpents has shed their vennymous fangs! Mr. Geoffrey —the day is at hand—beware! "

" What in the world—— " began Ravenslee, but Mrs. Trapes stayed him with uplifted skewer, and, laying it down, drew from the mysterious recesses of her apron a folded circular, which she proceeded to spread open, and from which she read in a hollow voice as follows:

" NOTICE

1st August 1910.

" On and after the above date all tenants soever residing within the tenement house known as Mulligan's are warned that all rents will be reduced 50 per cent.

BY ORDER."

" Now what," said Mrs. Trapes, refolding the circular very reverently, and shutting it into the Testament, " jest what d'ye think o' that? "

" Quite a—er—remarkable document, Mrs. Trapes! "

" Remarkable! " snorted Mrs. Trapes.

" Yes," said Ravenslee, beginning to fill his pipe, " extraordinary, most extraordinary—er—very much so."

" Extraordinary? Mr. Geoffrey, is that all you got t' say about it? " And Mrs. Trapes sniffed loudly.

" Well, what more should I say? "

" Why, ain't it th' wonder o' th' whole round world? Ain't it th' merrycle of all time? "

" Certainly! Not a doubt of it! " he agreed. " By

the way, what do you happen to have for supper? You see, I've been——"

"Supper?"

"I'm quite hungry—I'm always hungry lately, and——"

"Hungry!" ejaculated Mrs. Trapes, rolling her eyes. "Here I tell him of wonders an' omens beyond pore huming understandin', an'—he's hungry! Lord, ain't that jest like a man! A man's soul, if a man has a soul, lays in his stummick. Hungry! But you shall be fed—prompt, Mr. Geoffrey. How 'll b'iled salmon an' peas soot?"

"Splendidly! And I think——"

"'On and after,'" said Mrs. Trapes slow and dreamily, "'on and after the above date all tenants soever residin''—I've learned it by heart, Mr. Geoffrey. Then it goes on to say, 'within the tennyment house known as Mulligan's are warned'—h'm! I wonder why 'warned?' —'are warned that all rents will be re-dooced 50 per cent.!' Fifty per cent.!" she repeated in a dreamy rapture, "which is jest half, ye see. An', Mr. Geoffrey, that's jest what's got me plumb scared—it's all so unnacheral. I've heard o' rents bein' rose—constant, but who ever heard of 'em bein' took down before? Well, well! My land! Well, well!" With which remark Mrs. Trapes went about her household duties, leaving Ravenslee to lounge and smoke and dream blissfully of Hermione.

"Ye see," said Mrs. Trapes, wandering in with a plate, "it'll make things s' much easier for all of us, we shall begin t' feel almost rich—some of us. 'Are warned that all rents will be re-dooced 50 per cent.' Well, well!" and she wandered out again.

But presently she was back once more, this time with the tablecloth, which she proceeded to spread, though still lost in dreamy abstraction.

"At first I couldn't an' I wouldn't believe it, Mr.

The Definite Object

Geoffrey—no, sir!" she continued in the same rapt voice.
" But every one's got a notice same as mine, so I guess
it must be true, don't ye think ? "

" Not a doubt of it !" answered Ravenslee.

" But the burnin' question as I asks myself is—who ?
It's signed ' By Order,' ye see. Well—whose ? One
sure thing it ain't Mulligan."

" But he owns the place, doesn't he ? "

" He did, Mr. Geoffrey, an' that's what worries me—
continual. What I demands is—who now ? "

" Echo, Mrs. Trapes, methinks doth answer, ' Who ? '
By the way, it was—er—salmon and green peas I think
you——"

" My land, that bit o' salmon'll bile itself t' rags !"
and incontinent she vanished.

However, in due time Ravenslee sat down to as tasty
a supper as might be, and did ample justice to it, while
Mrs. Trapes once more read aloud for his edification from
the wondrous circular, and was again propounding the
vexed and burning question of " who," when she was
interrupted by a knocking without, and going to the door
presently returned with little Mrs. Bowker, in whose tired
eyes shone an unusual light, and whose faded voice held
a strange note of gladness.

" Good-evenin', Mr. Geoffrey," said she, bobbing him
a curtsey as he rose to greet her. " My Hazel sends you
her love an' a kiss for them last candies ; an' thank ye
for all th' medicine. But, oh, Mr. Geoffrey, an' you Ann
Trapes, you'll never guess what's brought me. I've
come t' wish ye good-bye, we're—oh, Ann—we're goin'
at last !"

" Goin' !" exclaimed Mrs. Trapes, clutching at her
elbows, " ye never mean as you're leavin' Mulligan's
now the rent's been took down—re-dooced 50 per cent.
—by order ? "

" That's just what I'm tellin' ye. Oh Ann, ain't it
just—heavenly ? "

Mrs. Trapes Upon the Millennium

"Heavenly!" repeated Mrs. Trapes, and sank into a chair.

"Yes, heavenly, t' see th' trees an' flowers again—t' live among them, Ann!"

"Samanthy Bowker, what do you mean?"

"Why, Ann, my Tom's had a gardener's job offered him at a gentleman's mansion in the country. Tom went after it t'-day—an' got it. Fifteen dollars a week an' a cottage—free, Ann! Hazel's just crazy with joy —an' so'm I!"

Mrs. Trapes fanned herself feebly with her apron.

"All I can say is," said she faintly, "if the world don't come to an end soon, I shall. A gardener's job! A cottage in th' country! Why, that's what you've been hungerin' for, you an' Bowker, ever since I've know ye. And to-day it's come! An' to-day the rent's re-dooced itself 50 per cent. by order. Oh dear land o' my fathers! When d'ye go?"

"T'-morrow mornin', Ann. Hazel 'll sure grow a strong, well girl in th' country, doctor said so last week. You heard him, Mr. Geoffrey, didn't you?"

"I did, Mrs. Bowker."

"And my Tom's that excited he couldn't eat no supper! Oh, an' have ye seen in t'-night's paper, Ann, about Mulligan's?"

"No, what now?" inquired Mrs. Trapes feebly.

"Well, read that—right there!" and unfolding an evening paper, Mrs. Bowker pointed to a paragraph tucked away into a corner; and, drawing a deep breath, Mrs. Trapes read aloud as follows:

"'It is understood that Geoffrey Ravenslee, the well-known sportsman and millionaire, winner of last year's International Automobile Race and holder of the world's long-distance speed record, has lately paid a record price in a real estate deal. A certain tenement building off Tenth Avenue has been purchased by him, the cost of which, it is rumoured, was fabulous.'"

241

The Definite Object

"Fab'lous!" repeated Mrs. Trapes, and sniffed. "Well, I never had no use for millionaires anyway—they're generally fools or rogues—this one's a fool sure. Any one is as would give much for a place like Mulligan's—an' yet, come t' think of it again—' are warned as all rents will be re-dooced 50 per cent., by order '—yes, come t' think of it again, what I say is—God bless this millionaire, an' whoever he is, Ann Angelina Trapes is sure goin' t' mention him before th' Throne this night."

CHAPTER XXVIII

WHICH SHOULD HAVE RELATED DETAILS OF A WEDDING

" It's all very, very wonderful, Ann dear ! But then—
everything is so wonderful—just lately ! "

" Meanin' what, Hermy ? "

Hermione was darning one of Spike's much-mended
socks, while Mrs. Trapes sat drinking tea. " Meanin'
jest what is wonderful, my dear, and—since when ? " she
persisted.

" Oh—everything, Ann ! "

" Yes, you said 'everything' before. S'pose you tell
me jest the one thing as you find so wonderful ? An'—
why an' wherefore that blush ? "

" Oh, Ann—Ann dear ! " Down went sock and needle,
and, falling on her knees, Hermione clasped her arms
about Mrs. Trapes and hid her glowing face in her lap.
" Ann dear, I'm so happy ! " she sighed—her speech a
little muffled by reason of the voluminous folds of Mrs.
Trapes's snowy apron.

" Happy ? " said Mrs. Trapes, setting down her teacup
to fondle and stroke that shapely head. " Sich happiness
ain't all because of the rent bein' re-dooced, by order, I
reckon. Is it ? "

" Dear Ann," said Hermione, her face still hidden,
" can't you guèss ? "

" No, my dear," answered Mrs. Trapes, her harsh tones
wonderfully soft, " I don't have to—I guessed days ago.
D'ye love him, Hermy ? "

243

The Definite Object

"Love him!" repeated Hermione, and said no more, nor did she lift her bowed head; but, feeling the quick, strong pressure of those soft embracing arms, the quiver of that girlish body, Mrs. Trapes smiled, and, stooping, kissed Hermione's shining hair.

"When did he speak, my dear?"

"Last Monday, Ann."

"Did he say—much?"

"He asked me to—marry him."

"Spoke of marriage, eh? Did he happen t' mention th' word—wife?"

"Oh, many times, Ann."

"Good f'r him! An' when's it t' be?"

"Oh, Ann, dear, I—I'm afraid it's—to-night!"

"T'-night! My land, he's sure some hasty!"

"And so—so masterful, Ann!"

"Well, ye sure need a master. But t'-night—land sakes!"

"He wrote and told me he would fix things so he could marry me to-night, Ann!"

"Then he's sure out fixin' 'em right now. Lord, Hermy, why d'ye tremble, girl—ye sure love him, don't ye?"

"So much, Ann, so very much—and yet——"

"You ain't scared of him, are ye?"

"No—and yet, I—I think I am—a little."

"But you'll marry him, all the same?"

"Yes."

"An' t'-night?"

"Yes. But, Ann dear, when he comes in I want you to keep him with you as long as you can—will you?"

"Why, sure I'll keep him, jest as long as—he'll let me! Lord, t' think as my little Hermy'll be a married woman this night!"

"And—oh, Ann, I haven't any—trousseau."

"Shucks! You don't need none. You're best as you are. You won't need no fluffs an' frills, I reckon."

"But, Ann dear," said Hermione, lifting her head and

shaking it ruefully, " I have—nothing ! And my best dress—I made it in such a hurry, you remember—it needs pressing, and——"

" He ain't marryin' you for your clo'es, Hermy—no, sir ! It's you he wants an'—oh, shucks ! what do clo'es matter t' you anyway ? You was meant to be one o' them nymphs an' goddesses as went about clad—well, airy. You'd ha' done fine with them soft arms an' shoulders an'——"

" But I'm not a goddess, Ann, I'm only poor Hermy Chesterton—with a hole in one stocking and the lace on her petticoat torn, and her other things—well, look here ! "—and up whirled gown and petticoat—" see what a state they're in—look, Ann ! "

" My dear, I am," nodded Mrs. Trapes over her teacup, " an' what I say is, it don't matter a row o' pins if a stockin' 's got a bit of a hole in it if that stockin' 's on sich a leg as that ! An' as for——"

" But," sighed Hermione, " don't you understand ? "

" My dear, I do. I was a married woman once, mind. An' I tell you ' beauty doth lie in the eye o' the beholder,' my dear, an' the two eyes as is a-goin' t' behold you this night is goin' t' behold so much beauty as they won't behold nothin' else."

" But—he loves dainty things, I'm sure."

" Well, ain't he gettin' a dainty thing ? Ain't he gettin' the daintiest, sweetest, loveliest——" Here Mrs. Trapes set down her cup again to clasp Hermione in her arms.

" Do you think he'll—understand, Ann ? "

" He'll be a fool if he doesn't ! "

" And make allowances ? He knows how poor we are and how busy I have to be."

" He does so, my dear. But, if it's goin' t' comfort you any, there's that corset-cover you made me last Christmas. I ain't never wore it, I ain't dared to with all them trimmin's an' lace insertion, an' me s' bony here an' there. You can have it an' willin', my dear, an' then there's them——"

"Ann, you dear thing, as if I would ! "

"Why not ? That corset-cover's a dream ! An' then there's them——"

"Dear, I couldn't—I wouldn't ! No, I'll go to him just as I am, he shall marry me just like I am."

"An' that's a goddess ! " nodded Mrs. Trapes, " yes, a young goddess—only, with more clo'es on, o' course. I'm glad as he's quit pea-nuts. Pea-nut men don't kind o' jibe in with goddesses."

"Ann," said Hermione, sitting back on her heels, " I think of him a great deal, of course, and, just lately, I've begun to wonder——"

"My dear," said Mrs. Trapes, blowing her tea, " so do I. I been wonderin' ever since he walked into my flat, cool as I don't know what ; an', my dear, when I sets me mind t' wonderment, conclusions arrive—constant ! I'll tell ye what I think. First, he ain't s' poor as he seems—he wears silk socks, my dear. Second, he's been nurtured tender—he cleans them white teeth night an' morn. Third, he ain't done no toil-an'-spinnin' act —take heed t' his hands, my dear. He's soft-spoke, but he's masterful. He's young, but he's seen a lot. He ain't easy t' rile, but when he is—my land ! He don't say a lot, an' he don't seem t' do much, an' yet—he don't seem t' starve none. Result—he may be anything ! "

"Anything ! Ann, dear."

"Anything ! " repeated Mrs. Trapes. " An' havin' studied him good an heeded him careful, I now conclood he's jest the thing you need, my dear."

"Then you like him, Ann—you trust him ? "

" I sure do."

"Oh you dear—dear—dear thing ! " And once again Mrs. Trapes was clasped in these vigorous young arms and kissed with every " dear."

"Though, mind you," said Mrs. Trapes, pushing cup

and saucer out of harm's way, "though, mind you, he's
a mystery I ain't found out—yet. D'ye s'pose he made
any money out o' them blessed pea-nuts? Not him!
Mrs. Smalley, as lives down along 'Leventh, she told me
as she's seen him givin' 'em away by the bagful t' all
the children down her way—repeated."

"How sweet of him!" said Hermione, her red mouth
all tender curves.

"Yes, but how did he live? How does he? How
will he?"

"I don't know, dear; I only know I would trust him
always—always!" And, sitting back chin in hand,
Hermione fell again to happy thought.

"When he give up the nuts," pursued Mrs. Trapes,
draining the teapot and sighing, "he tells me some fool
tale of makin' a deal in real estate, an' I—ha, real estate!"
Mrs. Trapes put down the teapot with a jerk. "A deal
in real estate!" she repeated, and thereafter fell to such
unintelligible muttering as "'Record price! Fab'lous!'
No, it couldn't be! An' yet—silk socks! 'On an' after
above date all tenants soever residin'—will be re-dooced
50 per cent!'" Suddenly Mrs. Trapes sat bolt upright.
"My land!" she ejaculated, "oh, dear land o' my
fathers, if sech could be!"

"Why, Ann," exclaimed Hermione, roused from her
reverie, "whatever is the matter?"

"My dear," said Mrs. Trapes, laying gentle hand on
Hermione's blooming cheek, "nothin—nothin' 't all.
I'm jest goin' over in my mind sich small matters as silk
socks an' tooth-brushes, that's all."

"But you do mean something—you always do."

"Well, if I do this time, my dear, I'm crazy—but the
Bowkers have gone, mind that! An' him so fond o'
little Hazel!" Here Mrs. Trapes nodded almost
triumphantly.

"The Bowkers! why, yes—I've been wondering——"

"I guess you know he went t' O'Rourke's an' give

that M'Ginnis the thrashin' of his dirty life ? " said Mrs. Trapes rather hastily. " Nigh killed the loafer, Spider Conolly told me."

" He's so strong," said Hermione softly, her eyes shining. " But, Ann, what did you mean about—about tooth-brushes and socks ? "

" Mean ? Why, socks and tooth-brushes o' course ! An', my land ! here's me guzzlin' tea, an' over in my kitchen th' finest shin o' beef you ever saw a-b'ilin f'r his supper. But now the question as burns is, if a married man this night will he be here t' eat ? An' if him—then you ? An' if man an' wife suppin' in my parlour—where will ye sleep ? "

" I—oh Ann—I don't know. His letter just said that when I come home it would be our—wedding night."

" Why, then, it sure will be. An' f'r a weddin' supper ye couldn't have nothin' better 'n shin o' beef. I'll go an' watch over that stoo with care unfailin', my dear ; believe me, that stoo's goin' t' be a stoo as is a stoo ! What, half after five ? Land-sakes, how time flies ! "

CHAPTER XXIX

IN WHICH HERMIONE MAKES A FATEFUL DECISION

WHEN Mrs. Trapes was gone, Hermione stood a long time to look at herself in her little mirror, viewing and examining each feature of her lovely, intent face more earnestly than she had ever done before ; and sometimes she smiled and sometimes she frowned, and all her thought was, ' Shall I make him happy, I wonder ? Can I be all he wants—all he thinks I am ? '

So, after some while, she combed and brushed out her glorious hair, shyly glad because of its length and splendour, and, having crowned her shapely head with it, viewed the effect with cold, hypercritical eyes.

' Can I, oh, can I, ever be all he wants—all he thinks I am ? '

And now she proceeded to dress, the holey stockings were replaced by others that had seen less service, the worn frills and laces were changed for others less threadbare ; which done, Hermione, with many supple twists, wriggled dexterously into her best dress, pausing now and then to sigh mournfully and grieve over its many deficiencies and shortcomings, defects which only feminine eyes, so coldly critical, might hope to behold.

Scarcely was all this accomplished when she heard a soft knock at the outer door, and at the sound her heart leapt, she flushed and paled and stood a while striving to stay the quick, heavy throbbing within her bosom ; then breathlessly she hastened along the passage, and, opening the door with trembling hands, beheld Bud M'Ginnis.

The Definite Object

While she yet stared dumb and amazed, he entered, and, closing the door, leaned his broad back against it.

"Goin' away, Hermy?" he inquired softly, looking her over with his slow gaze.

"Yes."

"Goin' far, Hermy?"

"I don't know."

"Goin'—alone, Hermy?"

"Why are you here? What do you want?"

"T' save ye from—hell!" he answered, his voice rising loud and harsh on the last word. "Oh, I know," he went on fiercely, "I know why you're all dolled up in your best. I know as you mean t' go away to-night with—him. But you ain't goin', girl—you ain't."

"To-night," she said gently, "is my wedding night."

M'Ginnis lifted a hand and wrenched at the silken neckerchief he wore as though it choked him.

"No!" he cried, "you ain't a-goin' t' get no weddin', Hermy. He don't mean t' give ye a square deal. He's foolin' ye—foolin' ye, girl! Oh," said he through shut teeth, "ye thought I was safe out o' the way, I guess. You ought t' known better; th' p'lice couldn't hold me, they never will. Anyway, I've kept tabs on ye—I know as you've been meetin' him—in a wood. I know"— here M'Ginnis seemed to choke again—"I know of you an' him—kissin' an' cuddlin'—oh, I've kept tabs on ye."

"Yes," she said gently, "I saw your spy at work."

"But ye can't deny it. Ye don't deny it! Say, what kind o' girl are you?"

"The kind that doesn't fear men like you."

"But ye can't deny meetin' him," he repeated, his hoarse voice quivering, "you don't deny—kissin' him —in a wood! Only deny it, Hermy, only say you didn't, an' I'll choke th' life out of any guy as says you did—only deny it, Hermy."

"But I don't want to deny it. If your spy had ears he can tell you that we are going to be married. Now go."

250

Hermione makes a Fateful Decision

Once more M'Ginnis reached up to his throat and wrenched off the neckerchief altogether.

"Married!" he cried, "an' t' him? He's foolin' ye, Hermy, by God, he is! Girl, I'm tellin' ye straight and true, he'll never marry ye. His kind don't marry Tenth Av'ner girls—Newport an' Fifth Av'ner's a good ways from Hell's Kitchen an' Tenth Av'ner, an' they can't ever come t'gether, I reckon."

"Ah!" sighed she, falling back a step, "what do you mean?"

"Why, I mean," said M'Ginnis, twisting the neckerchief in his powerful hands much as if it had been the neck of some enemy, "I mean as this guy as comes here bluffing about bein' down an' out, this guy as plays at selling pea-nuts is—Geoffrey Ravenslee the millionaire."

"But—he is—Arthur's friend!"

"Friend—nothin'," said he, wringing and wrenching at the neckerchief, "I guess you ain't found out how th' kid an' him came t' meet, eh? Well, I'll tell ye—listen! Your brother broke into this millionaire's swell house, through the winder, an' this millionaire guy caught him."

"Oh," said she, smiling in bitter scorn, "what a clumsy liar you are, Bud M'Ginnis!"

"No," he cried eagerly, "no, I ain't tellin' ye no lies —it's God's own truth I'm givin' ye."

"No, you're just a liar, Bud M'Ginnis!" and she would have turned from him, but his savage grip stayed her.

"A liar, am I?" he cried, "why then, you're sister to a crook, see! Your brother's a thief—a crook! You ain't got much t' be s' proud over."

"Let me go!"

"Listen! Your brother got into this guy's house t' steal, an' this millionaire guy caught him—in the act! An' havin' nothin' better t' do, he makes young Spike bring him down here—just t' see th' kind o' folks as lives in Hell's Kitchen—see? Then he meets you—you look kind o' good t' him, so he says t' th' kid, 'Look here' he says, ' you help me game along with yer sister, and we'll call it quits.' "

Breaking from his hold, Hermione entered the little parlour, and, sinking down beside the table, leaned there, hiding her face, while M'Ginnis, standing in the doorway, watched her, his strong hands twisting and wrenching at the neckerchief.

" Ah, leave me now," she pleaded, " you've done enough, so—go now—go ! "

" Oh, I'll go. I come here t' put ye wise—an' I have ! You're on to it all now, I guess. Newport and Fifth Av'ner's a good way from Hell's Kitchen and Tenth Av'ner, an' they can't never come together, I guess ; there's sure some difference between this swell guy with all his millions an' a Tenth Av'ner girl as is a—thief's sister."

Slowly Hermione lifted her head and looked up at him, and M'Ginnis saw that in her face which struck him mute, the neckerchief fell from his nerveless fingers and lay there all unheeded.

" Hermione," he muttered, " I—girl, are ye—sick ? "

" Go," she whispered, " go ! "

And, turning about, M'Ginnis stumbled out of the place and left her alone. For a long time she sat there motionless and crouched above the table, staring blindly before her, and in her eyes an agony beyond tears, heedless of the flight of time, conscious only of a pain sharper than flesh can know.

Suddenly a key was thrust in the lock of the outer door, footsteps sounded along the passage, accompanied by a merry whistling, and Spike appeared.

" Hello, Hermy, ain't tea ready yet ? " he inquired, tossing aside his straw hat and opening a newspaper he carried. " Say, the Giants are sure playin' great ball this season. What, are ye asleep ? "

" No, dear ! "

" Why, Hermy," he exclaimed, dropping the paper

and clasping an arm about her, " oh, Hermy—what is it ? "

" Oh boy—dear, dear boy—you didn't, did you ? " she cried feverishly. " You are a little wild—sometimes, dear, just a little—but you are good—and honourable, aren't you ? "

" Why, yes, Hermy, I—I try t' be," he answered uneasily, " but I don't know what you mean."

" You're not a thief, are you ? You're not a burglar ? You never broke into anyone's house ? I know you didn't, but tell me you didn't—tell me you didn't ! "

" No—no, 'course not," stammered Spike, and, averting his head, tried to draw away, but she clung to him all the closer.

" Boy—boy dear," she whispered breathlessly, " oh boy, look at me ! "

But seeing he kept his face still turned from her, she set a hand to his cheek and very gently forced him to meet her look. For a long moment she gazed thus—saw how his eyes quailed, saw how his cheek blanched, and, as he cowered away she rose slowly to her feet, and into her look came a growing horror ; beholding which Spike covered his face and shrank away from her.

" Oh boy," her voice had sunk to a whisper now, " oh, boy—say you didn't ! "

" Hermy—I—can't ! "

" Can't ? "

" It's—it's all—true. Yes, I did ! Oh Hermy, for-give me."

" Tell me ! "

" Oh, forgive me, Hermy ! forgive me ! " he cried, reaching out and trying to catch her hand. " Yes, I'll tell ye. I—I got in—through th' winder, an' Geoff caught me. But he let me go again—he said he'd never tell nobody if—— Ah, don't look at me like that ! "

" If what ? "

" If I'd—bring him back here with me. Hermy,

don't! Your eyes hurt me—don't look at me that way."

" So it—is—all—true ! "

" Oh, forgive me ! forgive me ! " he pleaded, throwing himself on his knees before her, and writhing in the anguish of remorse. " They doped me, Hermy. I didn't know what I was doin', they didn't give me no time t' think. Oh, forgive me, Hermy, Geoff forgave me, an' you must—oh, God, you must, Hermy!" Again he sought to reach her hand, but now it was she who shrank away.

" I loved you so ! I—loved you so ! " she said dully.

" Hermy," he cried, catching hold of her dress, " forgive me—just this once, for God's sake ! I ain't got nobody in the world but you. Forgive me ! " And now his pleading was broken by fierce sobs, and he sought to hide his tear-stained face in the folds of her dress, but she drew it from him, shrinking away almost as if she feared him.

" A thief ! " she whispered. " Oh God—my brother a thief ! I don't seem—able to—think. Go away—go away, I—must be—alone ! "

" Hermy dear, I swear—oh, I swear I'll——"

" Go away ! "

" Oh Hermy, I didn't think you'd ever—turn away—from me ! "

" Go away ! "

" Oh Hermy—won't you listen ? "

" I can't ! Not now. Go away."

Sobbing, the boy got to his feet, and, taking his hat, crossed slow-footed to the door—there he paused to look back at her, but her staring eyes gazed through him, and, turning hopelessly away, he brushed his sleeve across his cheek, and treading slow and heavily along the passage, was gone.

Dry-eyed, she stood awhile, then sank again beside the table and crouched there with face bowed between outstretched arms, and hands tight clenched.

Hermione makes a Fateful Decision

Evening began to fall, but still she sat huddled there, motionless, and uttering no sound, and still her eyes were tearless. At last she stirred, conscious of a quick, firm step near by, and, thrilling to that sound, rose and stood with her back to the fading light as Ravenslee entered.

"Dear," said he, tender and eager, "I found the door open, did you leave it for me? Why, Hermione—oh, my love, what is it?" and he would have caught her to him, but she held him away, and questioned him, quick-breathing.

"You are—Geoffrey Ravenslee—the millionaire—aren't you?"

"Why—er—I—I'm afraid I am," he stammered. "I'm sorry you found it out so soon, dearest, I wanted to tell you after we——"

"Oh, why didn't you tell me before—why didn't you? No, please wait! You—you caught my—brother, didn't you?" she went on breathlessly. "He had broken in—was burgling your house, wasn't he—wasn't he?"

"How in the world——" began Ravenslee, flinching, "who told——"

"He broke into your house to—steal, didn't he—didn't he?"

"But, good heavens—that was all forgotten and done with long ago! They'd made the poor chap drunk, he didn't know what he was doing, it's all forgotten long ago! Dear heart, why are you so pale. God, Hermione, nothing can alter our love?"

"No, nothing can alter our love," she repeated in the same dull tones, "oh, no, nothing can ever alter that, even though you deceived me I shall always love you, I can't help it. And just because I do love you so, and because I am a thief's sister, I—oh, I can never be your wife—I couldn't, could I?"

"By God, Hermione, but you shall!" As he spoke he caught her in his arms, passionate arms that drew and held her close. Very still and unresisting she lay in his

I   255

The Definite Object

embrace, uttering no word ; and, stooping, he kissed her fiercely—her lips, her eyes, her white throat, her hair, and, silent still, she yielded herself to his caresses.

" You are mine, Hermione, mine always and for ever ! You are the one woman I long for—the wife nature intended for me ! You are mine, Hermione ! "

Very softly she answered, her eyes closed :

" I felt at the first there was a gulf dividing us—and now—this gulf is wider—so wide it can never be crossed by either of us. Your world is not my world after all ; you are Geoffrey Ravenslee, and I am only—what I am. Newport and Fifth Avenue are a long way from Hell's Kitchen and Tenth Avenue, and they can never—never come together. And I—am a thief's sister, so please, please loose me ! Oh have mercy, and let me go ! "

His arms fell from her, and, shivering, she sank beside the table, and the pale agony of her face smote him.

" But you love me, Hermione ? " he pleaded.

" If I had only known," she sighed, " I might not have learned to love you—quite so much ! If I had only known ! " Her voice was soft and low, her blue eyes wide and tearless, and, because of this, he trembled.

" Hermione," said he gently, " all this week I have been planning for you and Arthur—I have been dreaming of our life together, yours and mine, a life so big, so wonderful, so full of happiness that I trembled sometimes, dreading it was only a dream. Dear, the gates of our paradise are open, will you shut me out ? Must I go back to my loneliness ? "

" I shall be lonely too," she murmured brokenly, " but better—oh, far better—loneliness than that some day——" She paused, her lips quivering.

" Some day, Hermione ? "

" You should find that you had married not only a scrub-woman, but—the sister of a—thief ! " Suddenly she sprang to her feet, her clinging arms held him to her bosom, and, drawing down his head, she pressed her

Hermione makes a Fateful Decision

mouth to his ; and, holding him thus, she spoke, her voice low and quick and passionate. "Oh my love, my love ! I do love you with every thought, with every part of me —so much, so very much that my heart is breaking, I think. But, dearest, my love is such that I would be everything fair and beautiful for you, everything proud and good and noble for you if I could. But I am only Hermy Chesterton, a Tenth Avenue girl, and—my brother—— So I'm going to send you away back to your own world, back to your own kind, because—because I do love you so ! Ah, God, never doubt my love, but—you must go."

"Never, Hermione—never ! "

"You must ! You will, I know, because your love is a big, generous love, because you are chivalrous and strong and gentle, because I beg and implore you if you have any pity for me—go ! "

"But why ? Why ? "

"Oh, must I tell you that—can't you understand ? "

"Why must I go, Hermione ? "

"Because," she murmured, her yearning arms close about him, her face close hidden against his breast, "because I'll never—marry you—now ; but I love you —love you so much that I'm afraid—ah ! not of you. So I must be alone—quite alone to fight my battle. And now—now that I've shown you all my heart, told you all my weakness, you'll go for my sake—just for my sake —won't you ? "

"Yes—I'll—go ! " he answered slowly.

"Away from here—to-night ? "

"Yes," he answered hoarsely, " yes ! "

Then Hermione fell suddenly before him on her knees, and, before he could stay her, had caught his hands, kissing them, wetting them with her tears, and pressing them passionately to her bosom.

"I knew," she cried, "I knew that you were strong and gentle and—good. Good-bye—oh, my love, good-bye ! "

The Definite Object

"Hermione," said he, kissing her bowed head, "oh, my Hermione, I love you with a love that will die only when I do. I want you, and I'll never lose hope of winning you—some day, never give up my determination to marry you—never, so help me, God!" Then swiftly he turned away; but, reaching the door, stooped and picked up M'Ginnis's neckerchief, and, recognising it, crumpled it in fierce hand. So, with it clenched in griping fingers, he hurried away and left her there upon her knees.

CHAPTER XXX

HOW GEOFFREY RAVENSLEE DEPARTED FROM HELL'S KITCHEN

"WHAT, back again already, Mr. Geoffrey?" exclaimed Mrs. Trapes, poking her head round the kitchen door as Ravenslee entered the flat, "back so soon?"

"Only for a minute, Mrs. Trapes."

"Supper 'll be ready soon—your wedding supper—eh, Mr. Geoffrey? You'll have it here with me, you an' Hermy, o' course. Smells kind o' good, don't it?"

"Delicious, Mrs. Trapes!"

"Delicious is the word, Mr. Geoffrey—stooed beef with carrots——"

"And onions, Mrs. Trapes—onions, I'm sure?"

"Well, I'll not deny a onion here an' there, Mr. Geoffrey —a stoo needs 'em."

"Ah, I knew it!" sighed Ravenslee. "I grieve that I sha'n't be able to eat it."

"Not eat—what, you? Say, ye ain't sick, are ye?"

"Not in body, Mrs. Trapes."

"Then why no stoo?"

"Because I sha'n't be here. I'm going, Mrs. Trapes— I'm leaving Mulligan's now—for good."

"Leavin'—ye mean with Hermy?"

"No, alone. Good-bye, Mrs. Trapes!"

"My land!" gasped Mrs. Trapes, "what you tellin' me?"

"Good-bye, Mrs. Trapes!"

"But why? Oh, dear Lord, what is it? Who——"

The Definite Object

" I want to thank you, for all your kindness. Good-bye ! "

As one in a dream, Mrs. Trapes extended a limp hand and stood wide of eye and pale of cheek to watch him go ; and as he descended the stairs her look of helpless, pained surprise went with him. Swiftly he strode across that familiar court, shoulders squared, chin out-thrust and eyes that glowed ominously in his pale face beneath fierce scowling brows. As he turned into Tenth Avenue there met him the Spider.

" What you chasin' this time, bo' ? " he inquired.

" M'Ginnis."

" Then you're sure chasin' trouble."

" That's what I want. D'you know where he is ? "

" Sure I do, but——"

The Spider paused, drawing in his breath slowly, as with experienced gaze he viewed Ravenslee's pale, set face—the delicate nostrils wide and quivering, the relentless mouth and burning eyes and all the repressed ferocity of him ; and, drawing back a step, the Spider shook his head.

" Bo'," said he, " that's jest what I ain't goin' t' tell ye."

" Very well, I must find him."

" Don't ! " said the Spider, walking on beside him, " if I didn't think a whole lot o' ye I'd lead ye to him."

" Oh, I shall find him, if it takes me all night."

" An' if ye do it'll be murder I'm dead sure."

" Murder ! " said Ravenslee with a flash of white teeth, " well, I shall certainly kill him—this time ! "

" Is it th' kid again ? "

" No—oh no, it's just for my own satisfaction—and pleasure."

" You ain't heeled, are ye ? There ain't goin' t' be no gun-play—eh ? "

" No, I haven't a gun, but I've brought his—necker-chief."

Ravenslee leaves Hell's Kitchen

"Sufferin' Pete !" murmured the Spider in a strangely awed voice, and walked on in silence, chewing viciously.

"Bo'," said he at last, " I'm thinkin' th' kindest thing I could do would be t' slip one over t' your point while you wasn't lookin', an' puttin' you t' sleep a bit—you want soothin' ! Bud'll be too big for you or any other guy t' tackle now, ye see, his stock's rose since th' Noo Jersey p'lice wasn't strong enough t' hold him."

"That's where I'm different—I can ! " said Ravenslee, opening and shutting his right hand convulsively. " Yes, I'll hold him till his last kick—and after ! "

"My God ! " exclaimed the Spider softly, and, beholding that clutching right hand, he edged away.

"Where you goin' t' look for him ? " he inquired after a while.

"O'Rourke's ! "

"Why not try Raynor's first ? " and he nodded to a saloon on the adjacent corner.

"Because I'm not a fool."

"Bo', I ain't s' sure o' that ! O'Rourke's 'll be full o' tough guys t'-night, all th' bunch 'll be there, an' if Bud tips 'em the say-so they'll snuff your light out quicker 'n winkin'."

"That wouldn't be such a hardship."

"Oh, so that's it, hey ? You got a kiss-me-an'-let-me-die sort o' feelin', hey ? Some nice bit o' stuff been turnin' ye down, bo' ? "

"That 'll be about enough ! " said Ravenslee, quick and fierce, and, meeting the flash of his eye, the Spider edged away again.

"Sufferin' Mike ! " said he, " you sure ain't doin' the affable chat stunt t'-night ! "

But Ravenslee strode along in silence, and the Spider, heeding the pale, set ferocity of his expression, grew troubled.

"Say," said he at last, " this don't happen t' be th' night as you've fixed up t' smash th' gang, does it ? "

261

The Definite Object

" No—only M'Ginnis."

" S'posin he ain't at O'Rourke's ? "

" He'll be somewhere else."

" Bo', if I was your ma I should be prayin' you don't find Bud, yes, sir ! An' I should pray—damn hard ! "

By this time they had reached Eleventh Avenue and were close upon the saloon, when Ravenslee halted suddenly, for beneath a lamp on the opposite sidewalk he saw M'Ginnis in talk with two other men.

Drawing the neckerchief from his pocket, Ravenslee crossed over and tapped M'Ginnis on the arm, who, turning about, stared into a pallid face within a foot of his own.

" What th' hell——" he began.

But Ravenslee cut him short.

" You left this behind you," said he, thrusting forward the neckerchief, " so I've brought it to twist round that foul throat of yours. Now, M'Ginnis—fight ! "

Thrusting the neckerchief into his pocket, Ravenslee clenched his fists, and, saying no word, they closed and fought—not as men, but rather as brute beasts eager to maim and rend. M'Ginnis's companions, dumbfounded by the sudden ferocity of it all, stayed a while inactive, staring at these two forms that lurched and swayed, that strove and panted grimly speechless. Then, closing in, they waited an opportunity to smite down M'Ginnis's foe from behind. But the Spider was watching, and, before either of them could kick or strike, his fists thudded home twice—hard blows aimed with scientific precision ; after which, having dragged the fallen away from those fierce trampling feet, he stood, quivering and tense, to watch that desperate encounter.

Cnce Ravenslee staggered back from a vicious flush-hit, and once M'Ginnis spun round, to fall upon hands and knees ; then they clinched, and, coming to the ground together, fought there, rolling to and fro hideously twisted together. But slowly Ravenslee's clean living

Ravenslee leaves Hell's Kitchen

began to tell, and M'Ginnis, wriggling beneath a merciless grip, uttered inarticulate cries and groaned aloud. And now the deadly neckerchief was about his gasping throat, and in his ears his conqueror's fierce laugh—lost all at once in a roar of voices, a rush of trampling feet.

Wrenched at by fierce hands, smitten by unseen fists, Ravenslee was beaten down—was dimly aware of the Spider's long legs bestriding him, and, staggering up through a tempest of blows, hurled himself among his crowding assailants, felled one with his right, stopped another with his left, and, as the press broke to the mad fury of his onslaught, felt his hand wrenched from a man's windpipe, and heard a frantic voice that panted:

"Leg it, bo'—leg it. Holy gee! ain't ye had enough?" So, mechanically, he set off at a run with his arm still gripped by the Spider. "Leg it, bo'—leg it good, or here's where we snuff it sure! This way—round th' corner, only keep goin', bo'—keep goin'."

Very fleetly they ran, with their pursuers close on their heels, across open lots, over fences, along tortuous alleys, until the rush and patter of the many feet died away, and the Spider, pulling up at the corner of a dismal, narrow street hard by the river, stood a while to listen.

"Jiminy Christmas! but you're some hot stuff at the swattin' business, you're a glutton, you are, bo'. I been in one or two scraps meself, but I never seen a guy so hungry for——"

"Where are we?"

"Thirteenth an' Twentieth."

"Are we safe?"

"F' th' time, I reckon. But all Hell's Kitchen 'll be out after us t'-night, sure. So I guess it's us for th' immediate hike."

"Us? Will they be after you too?"

"Well," said the Spider, smiling down grimly at his damaged knuckles, "I guess yes! Hell's Kitchen an' Tenth Av'ner's got t' get along without me from now on,

The Definite Object

I reckon. They ain't losin' much, an' I ain't leavin' much, but——"

"What the devil had you got to follow me to-night for?" demanded Ravenslee, scowling.

"Bo'," said the Spider, as they went on again, "there's times when my likin' f'r you gets a pain, there's times when yer talk gives me th' earache, an' yer lovin' looks the willies. I ain't lookin' f'r no gratitood, nor yet a gold dinner-set an' 'loominated address, but, not ownin' a hide like a sole-leather Saratoga, I'll jest get on me way. S' long!"

"Where are you goin'?"

"I dunno, but—I'm goin' there, right now."

But as the Spider turned away, his hand was caught and gripped, and Ravenslee was smiling, his features looked somewhat battered, but his smile was as pleasant as ever.

"Forgive my cursed temper, Spider. I owe you my life again, and—I ought to be grateful, I suppose. Forgive me, I'm—not quite myself to-night."

"Sure thing!" said the Spider, returning his grasp, "but bo', I'm kind o' wonderin' in me little mind what Bud's feelin' like! You sure swatted him good an' heavy. I never seen cleaner foot-work, an' them left jabs o' yours,—gee!"

"The question is, how do you feel, Spider, and what are you going to do?"

The pugilist scratched his big chin.

"Well, that's what gets my goat, I dunno quite, bo'. Ye see, I sha'n't be able t' get no more fights here in the East now, not wi' Bud 'n' his old man against me, ye see, Bud's old man's about the biggest——"

"I wonder if you'd care to come with me?"

"Whaffor?"

"Well, for one thing, I need another chauffeur, and——"

"A—what?" The Spider halted under a lamp-post

264

to stare at Ravenslee a little anxiously. " Say now, take a holt of ye'self, an' jest put that one over th' plate again. You need a—what ? "

" Another chauffeur."

" Another shuvver—another ? Bo', ye didn't happen t' get a soak on th' bean just now, did ye ? "

" No."

" Well then, I guess you're some shook up, what you want's food, right now ! "

" Why, yes, now you mention it, I'm devilish hungry."

" Leave it t' me, bo'—I know a chewin'-joint close by —soup, joint, sweets and coffee, an' only a quarter a throw —some feed, bo' ! Skin right along, I'll——"

" No, you shall come home and dine with me."

" Home ? " repeated the Spider, halting to stare again ; " you're sure talkin' ramblin'."

" We can discuss the chauffeur's job then."

" Shuvver ? " said the Spider uneasily, " but what's a guy like you want with a shuvver ? "

" Well, to drive my car—and——"

" Car ? " said the Spider, his uneasiness growing, " got a car now, have ye, bo' ? "

" I rather think I've got six."

" Sufferin' Sam ! " The Spider scratched his big chin while his keen eyes roved over Ravenslee's exterior apprehensively. " Say, bo', you quite sure none o' th' bunch booted you on th' dome—eh ? "

" Quite sure."

" An' yet you got six autormobiles. I say—you *think* so."

" Now I think again, they're seven with the newest racer."

" Say now, jest holt still a minute ! Now, swaller twice, think damn hard, an' tell me again ! You got how many ? "

" Seven ! "

" Got anythin' else ? "

The Definite Object

" Oh yes, a few things."

" Tell me jest one."

" Well, a yacht."

" Oh, a yacht ? "

" A yacht."

" 'S'nuff, bo', 's' nuff! But go on—go on, get it all off if you'll feel better after. Anythin' more ? "

" Why, yes, about twenty or thirty houses and castles and palaces and things."

" That settles it sure ! " sighed the Spider. " You're comin' t' see a doctor, that's what ! Your dome's sure got bent in with a boot or somethin'."

" No, Spider, I just happen to be born the son of a millionaire, that's all."

" Think o' that, now ! " nodded the Spider, " a millionaire now—how nice ! An' what do they call ye at home ? "

" Geoffrey Ravenslee."

" How much ? " exclaimed the Spider, falling back a step, " the guy as went ten rounds with Dick Dunoon at th' ' National ? ' The guy as won th' autormobile race ? Th' guy as bought up Mulligan's—you ? "

" Why, yes. By the way, I sat in the front row and watched you lick Larry M'Kinnon at 'Frisco, I was afraid you were going to recognise me, once or twice."

" Then you—you have got a yacht, th' big one as lays off Twenty-third Street ? "

" Also seven cars, that's why I want you for a chauffeur."

" Ho-ly gee ! " murmured the dazed Spider. " Well, say, you sure have got me goin' ! A millionaire ! A pea-nut cart ! A yacht ! Well, say, I—I guess it's time I got on me way. S' long ! "

" No you don't, my Spider, you're coming home with me."

" What—me ? Not much I ain't—no, sir ! I ain't no giddy gink t' go dinin' with millionaires in open-faced clo'es—not me ! "

"But you're coming to have dinner with that same pea-nut man who learned to respect you because you were a real white man, Spider Conolly. And that's another reason why I want you for my chauffeur."

"But—say, I—I can't shuv."

"Joe shall teach you."

"Joe? Ye mean Joe Madden?"

"He'll be chauffeur No. 1—and there's a cross-town car! Come on, Spider! Now, in with you!"

CHAPTER XXXI

IN WHICH SOAPY TAKES A HAND

O'ROURKE'S was full; its long bar, shaped something like the letter J, supported many lounging arms and elbows, its burnished foot-rail was scraped by boots of many shapes and sizes, its heavy air, thick with cigarette-smoke, hummed with many voices. In one corner, a corner remote where very few ventured to penetrate, Soapy leaned, as pallid and non-committal as ever, while Spike poured out to him the story of his woes.

" She drove me out, Soapy ! She drove me away from her ! " he repeated for the hundredth time. The boy was unnaturally flushed and bright of eye, and his voice was as shaky as the hand which fidgeted with his whisky-glass ; and the sense of his wrongs was great and growing greater with every sip.

" She told me t' leave her ! She drove me away from her."

" So you come here—eh, kid ? " drawled Soapy, pendant cigarette smouldering, " you skinned over here t' Bud f' comfort, an' you'll sure get it, kid—in a glass ! "

" Bud's always good t' me."

" 'S' right, kid, 's' right, Bud's a angel sure, though he ain't got no wings yet. Oh, Bud 'll comfort ye—frequent; an' by-an'-by he'll take ye back t' Hermy good an' soused, you can get your own back that ways—eh, kid ? It 'll sure make her sit up an' take notice when she sees ye come in reelin' an' staggerin'—eh, kid ? An' to-morrow

268

In which Soapy takes a Hand

you'll be sick mebbe, an' she'll have ter nurse ye—eh?
Oh, Bud 'll fix things for ye, I guess."

Spike glowered and pushed his half-emptied glass
farther way.

" I ain't goin' home soused ! " he muttered.

" No ? " said Soapy, faintly surprised. " Bud 'll feel
kind o' hurt, won't he ? "

" I ain't goin' home soused—not for Bud nor nobody
else ! "

" Why then, if I was you, kid, I should beat it before
Bud comes in."

" I guess I will," said Spike, rising.

But now was sudden uproar of voices in the street hard
by, a running and trampling of feet, and, the swing
doors opening, a group of men appeared, bearing among
them a heavy burden, and coming to the quiet corner
they laid M'Ginnis there. Battered, bloody, and torn
he lay, his handsome features swollen and disfigured, his
clothes dusty and dishevelled, while above him and
around him men stooped and peered and whispered.

" Why it's—it's—Bud ! " stammered Spike, shrinking
away from that inanimate form, " My God ! it's Bud ! "

" 'S' right, kid ! " nodded Soapy imperturbably, hands
in pockets, and, though his voice sounded listless as
ever, his eyes gleamed evilly, and the dangling cigarette
quivered and stirred.

" Ain't—dead, is he ? " some one questioned.

" Dead—not much ! " answered Soapy, " guess it's
goin' to take more 'n that t' make Bud a stiff 'un. Besides, Bud ain't goin' t' die that way, no, not that way,
I reckon. Dead ? Watch this ! " So saying, he reached
Spike's half-emptied glass from the bar, and, not troubling
to stoop, poured the raw spirit down upon M'Ginnis's
pale, blood-smirched face.

" Dead ! " said Soapy, " well, I guess not—look at
him ! " And, sure enough, M'Ginnis stirred, groaned,
opened swollen eyelids, and, aided by some ready arm,

269

The Definite Object

sat up feebly. Then he glanced up at the ring of peering faces and down upon his rent and dusty person, and fell to a sudden fierce torrent of curses; and, cursing thus, his strength seemed to return all at once, for he sprang to his feet, and with clenched fists drove through the crowd, and, lifting a flap in the bar, opened a door beyond and was gone.

"No," said Soapy, shaking his head, "I guess Bud ain't dead—yet, fellers. I wonder who gave him that eye, kid? An' his mouth too! Did ye pipe them split lips? Kind o' painful, I guess. An' a couple o' teeth knocked out too? Some punchin', kid! An' Bud kind o' fancied them nice white teeth of his a whole heap!"

Here the bar-tender glanced toward the corner where they stood, and, lifting an eyebrow, jerked his thumb at the door behind him with the words:

"Kid, I reckon Bud wants ye."

For a moment Spike hesitated; then, lifting the mahogany flap, crossed the bar with familiar foot, and opened the door.

"Guess I'll come along, kid," and, hands in pockets, Soapy followed.

They found M'Ginnis sprawling at a table and scowling at the broken knuckles of his bruised right hand, while at his elbow were a bottle and two glasses. He had washed the blood and dirt from him, had brushed and straightened his dusty garments, but he couldn't hide the cuts and bruises that disfigured his face nor his scratched and swollen throat.

"What you here for?" he demanded, as Soapy closed the door, "didn't send for you, did I?"

"No, that's why I come, Bud."

"But, say, Bud, what—what's been th' matter?" stammered Spike, his gaze upon M'Ginnis's battered face. "Who's been——"

"Matter? Nothin'! I had a bit of a rough-house as I come along."

In which Soapy takes a Hand

" 'S' right," nodded Soapy, " you sure look it! Never seen a fatter eye."

" Well, what you get t' beef about ? "

" Nothin', Bud, only——"

" Only what ? "

" It's kind o' tough you losin' them couple o' teeth—or is it three ? "

M'Ginnis turned on him with a snarl.

" A-r-r, you! Some day I'm goin' to kick the insides out o' ye ! "

" Some day, Bud, sure. I'll be waitin'! Meantime, why not get some doctor-guy t' put yer face back in shape. Gee, I hate t' see ye—ye look like a butcher's shop ! An' them split lips pains some, I guess ! "

Here, while M'Ginnis choked in impotent rage, Soapy lit a fresh cigarette from the butt of the last and held out the packet.

" Try a coffin-nail, Bud ? No ? Well, I guess ye couldn't smoke good with a mouth on ye like that."

" Who did it, Bud ? " questioned Spike eagerly. " Who was it ? "

" Hush up, kid, hush up! " said Soapy, viewing M'Ginnis's cuts and bruises with glistening eyes, " I guess that guy's layin' around somewheres waitin' f'r th' coroner. Bud wouldn't let him make such a holy mess of his face an' get away with it—not much ! Bud's a killer, I know that—don't I, Bud ? "

" You close up that dog's head o' yours, Soapy, or by——"

" 'S' all right, Bud—'s' all right. Don't get peeved. I'll close up tighter 'n a clam, only—it's kinder tough about them teeth."

" Are ye goin' t' cut it out, or shall——"

" Aw, calm down, Bud—calm down! Take a drink, it 'll do ye good." And, filling a glass with rye whisky, Soapy set it before M'Ginnis, who cursed him, took it up, and turned to Spike :

271

The Definite Object

" Fill it up, kid," he commanded.

" Not me, Bud, I—I ain't here for that," said Spike.
" I come t' tell ye as some dirty guy's been an' blown the
game on me t' Hermy. She—she knows everything, an'
to-night she drove me away from her."

" Did she, kid, eh—did she ? " said M'Ginnis, a new
note of eagerness in his voice, " Drove ye out on to the
streets, kid ? That's damn hard on you ! "

" Yes, Bud, I—guess she—don't want me around."

" Kind o' looks that way ! " nodded M'Ginnis and,
filling Spike's glass, he put it into the boy's unwilling
fingers. " Take a drink, kid, ye sure need it ! " said he.

" 'S' right," murmured Soapy, " told ye Bud 'u'd
comfort ye, didn't I, kid ? "

" So Hermy's drove ye away ? " said M'Ginnis ;
" throwed ye out—eh ? "

" She sure has, Bud, an' I—oh, I'm miserable as hell ! "

" Why then, get some o' Bud's comfort into ye, kid,"
murmured Soapy, " lap it up good, kid, there's plenty
more—in th' bottle ! "

" Let him alone," growled M'Ginnis ; " he don't want
you buttin' in ! "

" 'S' right too, Bud ! " nodded Soapy, " he's got you,
ain't he ? An' you—got him, ain't you ? "

" I didn't think Hermy 'u'd ever treat me—like this ! "
said Spike tearfully.

" You mean—throwin' ye out on to th' streets, kid ?
Why, I been expectin' it ! "

" Expectin' it ! " repeated Spike, setting down his
glass and staring. " Why ? "

" Well, she's a girl, ain't she, an' they're all th' same,
I reckon."

" An' Bud knows all about girls, kid ! " murmured
Soapy, " Bud's wise t' all their tricks. Ain't you,
Bud ? "

" But whatcher mean ? " cried Spike. " What ye
mean about expectin' it ? "

In which Soapy takes a Hand

" Well, she don't want ye no more, does she ? " answered M'Ginnis, his bruised hands fierce-clenched, his voice hoarse and thick with passion, " she's got some one else now—ain't she ? She's—in love—ain't she ? She's all worked up an' palpitatin' for—for that damn——"
He choked, and set one hand to his scratched throat.

" What d'ye mean, Bud ? "

" Ah ! " said Soapy, softer than before, " I'm on, Bud, you put me wise ! He means, kid, as Hermy's in love with th' guy as has just been punchin' hell out of him— he means your pal Geoff."

With a hoarse strangling cry M'Ginnis leapt up, his hand flashed behind him, and—he stood suddenly very still, staring into the muzzle of the weapon Soapy had levelled from his hip.

" Aw, quit it, Bud, quit it," he sighed, " it ain't come t' that, yet. Besides, the kid's here, so loose ye gun, Bud— no, give it t' me, you're a bit on edge t'-night, I guess, an' it might go off an' break a glass or somethin'. So gimme ye gun, Bud ; that's it ! Now we can sit an' talk real sociable, can't we ? Now listen, Bud. What ye want is t' get your own back on this guy Geoff, an' what the kid wants is t' show his sister as he ain't a kid, an' what I want is t' give ye both a helpin' hand."

But while M'Ginnis stood scowling at the imperturbable speaker, Spike rose, a little unsteadily, and turned to the door.

" I'll be gettin' on me way, Bud," said he.

" Where to ? "

" Home."

" What ! Back t' Hermy ? After she turned ye out ? "

" But I—I got t' go somewheres."

" Well, you stay right here with me, kid. I'll fix ye up all right."

" 'S' right, kid ! " nodded Soapy. " Bud 'll fix ye up all right, we'll have in another bottle when that's empty ! "

" What about your sister, kid ? " demanded M'Ginnis

273

The Definite Object

fiercely, "what about Hermy an' this swell guy? Are ye goin' t' sit around an' do nothin'?"

"But Geoff's goin' t' marry her."

"Marry her! What, him? A millionaire marry your sister? You think so, an' she thinks so, but I know different!"

"But Hermy ain't that sort, Hermy's—good."

"Sure, but this guy's got her fazed, she thinks he's square all right—she'll trust him, an' then, s'posin' he ain't?"

"I—I ain't s'posin' nothin' like that!" said Spike, gulping his whisky.

"Well, s'posin' he's been meetin' her—in a wood—on the sly—eh? S'posin' they been huggin' an' kissin'——"

"Say now—you cut that out," stammered Spike, his voice thick. "I tell ye—she ain't—that kind."

"S'posin," continued Bud, refilling the lad's glass, "s'posin' I could show 'em to ye in a wood—eh? Ah! What's she want t' meet him in a wood for, anyway—nice an' quiet, eh?"

"Say now, Bud, I—I ain't goin' t' listen t' no more!" said Spike rising and clutching at the table. "I—I'm goin' home!" and, swaying on unsteady feet, he turned to the door.

But M'Ginnis gripped his shoulders.

"Wait a bit, kid."

"N-o, I'm—goin' home—see!" said Spike, setting his jaw obstinately. "I'm goin'—right now!"

"That's just what you ain't!" snarled M'Ginnis. "Sit down! Hermy's only a work-girl, don't forget that, kid, an' this guy's a millionaire. I guess he thinks Hermy 'll do—till he gets tired of her, an'—then what?"

"He—told me he's goin' t' marry her!" said Spike slowly, speaking with an effort, "an' I guess Geoff ain't a liar. An' I wanter—go home."

"Home—after she throwed ye out? Ain't ye got no pride?"

In which Soapy takes a Hand

" Aw, say, Bud," sighed Soapy, " I guess d' kid ain't soused enough for pride yet ; sling another glass int' him—that 'll fix him good, I reckon."

" I ain't g-goin' t' drink no more," said Spike, resting heavy head between his hands. " I guess I'll b-beat it home, f'lers."

" Bud," suggested Soapy, " ain't it about time you rang in little Maggie on him ? "

M'Ginnis whirled upon the speaker, snarling ; but Soapy, having lighted another cigarette, nudged Spike with a sharp elbow.

" Kid," said he, " Bud's goin' t' remind ye of little Maggie Finlay—you remember little Maggie as drowned herself ? "

Spike lifted a pale face and stared from the placid Soapy to scowling Bud, and shrank away.

" Yes," he whispered hoarsely, " yes—I'll never forget how she looked—pale, so pale an' still, an' th' water runnin' out of her brown curls. I—I'll never forget."

" Well," growled M'Ginnis, " watch out Hermy don't end th' same way."

" No ! " cried Spike, " Oh my God—no ! "

" What's she meetin' this millionaire in a wood for— on the sly ? "

" She don't ! Hermy ain't like that."

" I tell ye she does ! " cried M'Ginnis, " an' him kissin' an' squeezin' her, an'—nobody by."

" It's a lie, Bud, she—she wouldn't ! "

" S'posin' I could show ye ? S'pose you see him there waitin' for her ? "

" If—if he means any harm t' Hermy I—I'll kill him ! "

" Aw—you wouldn't have the nerve, kid ! "

" I'd shoot him dead—by God I would ! "

" You ain't man enough, kid."

" You g-give me a gun an' see. I'd shoot any one t' save my sister from—th' river. Oh my God—I—I'd die for her, an' she don't love me no more ! " And, leaning his head upon his arm, Spike burst into a passion of tears.

M'Ginnis watched him a while, then, filling the boy's glass, clapped him on the shoulder, and held it to his lips.

"Neck this, kid," said he, "neck it all—so, that's good, ain't it! T'-morrow evenin' I'll take ye where they meet, maybe you'll ketch him waitin' for her, but instead of Hermy and kisses there'll be you an' me—hey? Will ye come?"

"S-sure I will if—you'll gimme—your gun."

"Pshaw, kid, what's a kid like you want with a gun?"

"T' shoot him."

"Eh? What d'ye mean?"

"If he's after my sister I'll—kill him. I will, by God I will!"

"'S' right," nodded Soapy, staring into the boy's drawn face. "'S' right, Bud, if ever I see a killer, th' kid's sure it!" Slowly the glare died out of Spike's eyes, his body drooped, and, sighing, he pillowed his heavy head upon the table and fell into a drunken slumber. For a while the two men sat there hearkening to his stertorous breathing, then Soapy laughed soft and mirthlessly. "You sure got th' kid all worked up an' mad enough t'—kill— eh, Bud? If he does get up against this guy Geoff, this guy Geoff's sure goin' t' cash in—sudden. Consequently I guess you'll be wantin' paper an' pencil—both here!" said Soapy, producing the articles in question.

"What th' hell——" began M'Ginnis.

"Telegram, Bud. You're goin' t' frame up a nice little telegram t' this guy Geoff—eh, you sure are th' fly gazebo'! A nice little message, 'Meet me t'-morrow in the wood at sunset. Hermy.' Somethin' nice 'n' romantic like that'll bring him on th' run—eh, Bud? Then, 'stead of Hermy comes you an' th' kid—eh, Bud? An' 'stead of kisses this guy Geoff gets a lead pill—eh, Bud? Th' kid can't miss if you get him close enough. It sure is some scheme, Bud. I couldn't have thought

In which Soapy takes a Hand

it out better myself. Paper 'n' pencil, Bud—get busy, an' I'll sashay over an' send it off for ye—t'-night."

During Soapy's unusually long speech, M'Ginnis sat staring at him under frowning brows, but now he turned and scowled down at the sheet of paper, picked up the pencil, laid it by again, and sat opening and shutting his big hands, while Soapy, lighting another cigarette, watched him furtive-eyed ; when at last he spoke his voice was thick, and he didn't lift his scowling gaze.

"Send that kid Larry t' me—an' say—you don't have t' come back."

"All right, Bud—all right, only, you'd best send two telegrams t' make sure—one t' Fift' Av., 'n' one t' his place up th' river. S' long, Buddy ! "

Some fifteen minutes later, the boy Larry, stepping out of O'Rourke's, was swung to the wall in Soapy's grip.

"Aw—say, cheese it now ! Is that you, Soapy ? "

" 'S' right, my bucko. Fork out that telegram—quick ! "

"Aw, say, whatcher mean. 'N' say, Bud told me to hustle ; 'n' say——"

"Dig it out—quick ! " said Soapy, the dangling cigarette glowing fiercely. " I want it—see ? "

"But say," whimpered Larry, " what 'll Bud say ? "

"Nothin' ! Bud ain't goin' t' know. You take this instead ; take it ! " And Soapy thrust another folded paper into the boy's limp hand, who took it whimpering.

" Bud tol' me t' bring it back."

" Well, you tell him you lost it."

" Not much. I'll skin right back an' tell him you pinched it."

" You won't, my sport—you won't ! " said Soapy, and, speaking, moved suddenly ; and the boy, uttering a gasp of terror shrank, cowering, with the muzzle of Soapy's revolver against the pit of his stomach. " You ain't goin' t' say a word t' Bud nor nobody else, are ye, Larry boy—are ye ? "

The Definite Object

" No, no ! "

" Because, if ye ever did, old sport, I should give it ye there—right there in the tum-tum—see? Now, chase off, an' see ye get them addresses right. S' long, Larry boy, be good now ! "

When the boy had scudded away, Soapy opened the paper and scanned the words of M'Ginnis's telegram; and, being alone, smiled as he glanced through it.

" You got th' kid, Bud," he murmured, " you got th' kid ; but if th' kid gets the guy Geoff, why—I've sure got you, Bud, got ye sure as hell ! "

CHAPTER XXXII

OF HARMONY AND DISCORD

MR. BRIMBERLY, comfortably ensconced in Young R.'s favourite armchair, nodded ponderously and beat time to the twang of Mr. Jenkins's banjo, whereto Mr. Stevens sang in a high-pitched and rather shaky tenor the latest musical success yclept "Sammy." Thus, Mr. Jenkins strummed, Mr. Stevens trilled, and Mr. Brimberly alternately beat the *tempo* with a plump, white finger and sipped his master's champagne, until, having emptied his glass, he turned to the bottle on the table beside him, found that empty also, crossed to the two bottles on the mantel, found them likewise void, and had tried the two upon the piano with no better success, when, the song being ended, Mr. Jenkins struck in with:

"All dead men, Brim! Six of 'em between us—not bad goin'—what?"

"And very good fizz too, on the whole!" added Mr. Stevens. "I always sing better on champagne. But come, Brim, my boy, I've obliged with everything I know, an' Jink 'e's played everything 'e knows, an' I must say, with great delicacy an' feelin', now it's your turn—sing somethin'."

"Well," answered Mr. Brimberly, squinting at an empty bottle, "I used to know a very good song once, called, 'Let's drownd all our sorrers an' cares.' But, good 'eavens! we can't drownd 'em in empty bottles, can we?"

"Oh, very good!" chuckled Mr. Jenkins, "oh, very

279

The Definite Object

prime! If I might suggest, there's nothin' like port—port's excellent tipple for drowndin' sorrer an' downin' care—what?"

"Port, sir!" repeated Mr. Brimberly, "we 'ave enough port in our cellars to drownd every sorrer an' care in Noo York City. I'm proud of our port, sir, an' I'm reckoned a bit of a connyscor."

"Ah, it takes a eddicated palate to appreciate good port!" nodded Mr. Jenkins loftily, "a eddicated palate —what?"

"Cert'nly!" added Mr. Stevens, "an' here's two palates waitin', waitin' an' ready to appreciate till daylight doth appear."

"There's nothin' like port!" sighed Mr. Brimberly, setting aside the empty champagne bottle, "nothin' like port, an' there's Young Har 'ardly can tell it from sherry —oh the Goth! the Vandyle! All this good stuff would be layin' idle if it wasn't for me! Young Har ain't got no right to be a millionaire, 'is money's wasted on 'im— 'e neglects 'is opportoonities shameful—oh shameful! What I say is—what's the use o' bein' a millionaire if you don't air your millions?"

Hereupon Mr. Jenkins rocked himself to and fro over his banjo in a polite ecstasy of mirth.

"Oh, by Jove!" he gasped, "if that ain't infernal clever I'll be shot! Oh, doocid clever I call it—what?"

"Er—by the way, Brim," said Mr. Stevens, his glance roving towards the open window, "where does he happen to be to-night?"

"Where?" repeated Mr. Brimberly, fingering a slightly agitated whisker, "where is Young Har, sir! Lord, Mr. Stevens, if you ask me that I throws up my 'ands an' I answers you—'eavens knows! Young Har is a unknown quantity, sir——a will o' the wisp, or as you might say, a ignus-fattus. At this pre-cise moment 'e may be in Jerusalem or Jericho, or—a-sittin' outside on the lawn —which Gawd forbid! But there! don't let's talk of it.

280

Of Harmony and Discord

Come on down into the cellars an' we'll bring up enough port to drownd sorrer an' care all night."

" With all my heart ! " said Mr. Jenkins, laying aside his banjo.

" Ditto, indeed ! " nodded Mr. Stevens, slipping a hand in his host's arm, and thus linked together they made their way out of the room.

Scarcely had their hilarious voices died away when a muscular brown hand parted the hangings of a certain window, and Geoffrey Ravenslee climbed into the room. His rough clothes and shabby hat were powdered with dust, and he looked very much out of place amid his luxurious surroundings as he paused to glance swiftly from the bottles that decorated the carved mantel to those on table and piano. Then, light treading, he crossed the room, and, as the hilarious three were heard approaching, vanished in his turn.

" 'Ere we are, Jubilee port ! " exclaimed Mr. Brimberly, setting down two cobwebbed bottles with elaborate care, " Obleege me with the cork-screw, somebody."

" Won't forget as you promised us a song, Brim ! " said Mr. Jenkins, passing the necessary implement.

" Oh, I won't disappoint ye," answered Mr. Brimberly, drawing the cork with a practised hand, " my father were a regular songster, a fair carollin' bird 'e were, sir."

" 'Ow about ' Knocked 'Em in the Old Kent Road ' ? " Mr. Stevens suggested.

" Sir ! " exclaimed Mr. Brimberly, pausing in the act of filling the glasses, " that's rather a—a low song, ain't it ? What do you think, Mr. Jenkins ? "

" Low ? " answered Mr. Jenkins, " it's as low as—as mud, sir. I might say it's infernal vulgar—what ? "

" Why, I don't care for it myself," Mr. Stevens admitted rather humbly, " it was merely a suggestion."

" With your good favour," said Mr. Brimberly, after a tentative sip at his glass, " I'll sing you a old song as was a rare favourite of my father's."

The Definite Object

"Why then," said Mr. Jenkins, taking up his banjo, "oblige us with the key."

"The key, sir?" answered Mr. Brimberly, pulling down his waistcoat, "what key might you mean?"

"The key of the note dominant, Brim."

Mr. Brimberly stared and felt for his whisker. "Note dominant," he murmured. "I don't think my song has anything of that sort, sir."

"Oh well, just whistle a couple o' bars."

"Bars," said Mr. Brimberly, shaking his head, "bars, sir, is things wherewith I do not 'old; bars are the 'aunt of the 'umble 'erd, sir."

"No, no, Brim," explained Mr. Stevens, "Jenk merely means you to 'um the air."

"Ah, to be sure, now I appre'end! I'll 'um you the hair with pleasure."

Having said which, Mr. Brimberly cleared his throat vigorously, and thereafter emitted certain rumbling noises, whereat Mr. Jenkins cocked a knowing head.

"B sharp, I think?" he announced.

"Not much, Jenk!" said Mr. Stevens decidedly, "it was C flat—as flat a C as ever I heard!"

"It was B!" Mr. Jenkins maintained. "I appeal to Brim."

"Well," said Mr. Brimberly ponderously, "I'm reether inclined to think I made it a D—if it wasn't D it was F nat'ral. But if it's all the same to you I'll accompany myself at the piano-forty."

"What," exclaimed Mr. Stevens, emptying and refilling his glass, seeing which Mr. Jenkins did the same, "what—do you play, Brim?"

"By hear, sir—only by hear," said Mr. Brimberly modestly, as, having placed bottle and glass upon the piano within convenient reach, he seated himself upon the stool, struck three or four stumbling chords, and then, vamping an accompaniment a trifle monotonous as to bass, burst forth into song:

Of Harmony and Discord

"It was a rich merchant that in London did dwell,
  He had but one daughter, a beautiful gell,
  Which her name it was Dinah, scarce sixteen years old,
  She'd a very large fortune in silver and gold.
      Chorus—Ri tooral, ri tooral, ri tooral i-day,
                Ri tooral, ri tooral, ri tooral i-day."

It was now that Mr. Ravenslee, his rough clothes replaced by immaculate attire, entered unostentatiously, and, wholly unobserved by the company, seated himself and lounged there while Mr. Brimberly sang blithely on:

"As Dinah was a-walking in her garden one day,
  Her father came to her and thus he did say:
  ' Come wed yourself, Dinah, to your nearest of kin,
  Or you sha'n't have the benefit of one single pin!'
      Ri tooral, ri too——"

Here Mr. Jenkins, chancing to catch sight of that unobtrusive figure, let fall his banjo with a clatter, whereupon Mr. Brimberly, glancing round, stopped short in the middle of a note and sat open-mouthed, staring at his master.

"Enjoying a musical evening, Brimberly?"

Mr. Brimberly blundered to his feet, choked, gasped, groped for his whiskers, and finally spoke.

"Why sir, I—I'm afraid I—we are."

"I didn't know you were such an accomplished musician, Brimberly."

"Mu-sician, sir?" Brimberly stammered, his eyes goggling, "'ardly that, sir—oh, 'ardly that. I—I venture to—to tinkle a bit now an' then, sir. No offence I 'ope, sir?"

"Friends musical too, it seems?"

"Y-es, sir, music do affect 'em, sir, uncommonly, sir."

"Yes, makes them thirsty, doesn't it?"

"Why, Mr. Ravenslee, sir, I—that is, we did so far venture to—er—I mean—oh Lord!" and mopping perspiring brow, Mr. Brimberly groaned, and goggled helplessly from Mr. Jenkins, who stood fumbling with his banjo, to Mr. Stevens, who gaped fish-like.

283

The Definite Object

" And now," said Young R., having viewed them each in turn, " if these—er—very thirsty musicians have had enough of—er—my wine to—er—drink, perhaps you'll be so obliging as to see them—off the premises ? "

" I—I beg parding, sir ? "

" Please escort your friends off the premises."

" Certingly, sir—at once, sir."

" Unless you think you ought to give them each a handful of my cigars."

But Mr. Brimberly had already bundled his dazed guests to the door, out of the door, and out of the house with very little ceremony. It was a very deferential and officiously eager Brimberly who presently knocked, and, bowing very frequently, begged to know how he might be of further service.

" Might I get you a little supper, sir ? We 'ave 'am, sir, we 'ave beef, cold, salmon and cucumber likewise cold, a ditto chicken——"

" Sounds rather a quaint bird," said Ravenslee.

" Yes, sir, very good, sir, chicken an' a nice slice of 'am sir, say and——"

" Thank you, Brimberly, I dined late in New York."

" Why, then, sir, a sandwich or so, pray permit me, sir, cut nice an' thin, sir."

" Thank you—no."

" Dear, dear ! Why then, sir, whisky, brandy, a lickyour ? "

" Nothing."

" A cigar, sir ? "

" H'm ! Have we any of the Garcias left ? "

" Y-es, sir. Ho, certingly, sir. Shall I——"

" Don't bother, I prefer my pipe, only let me know when we get short, Brimberly, and we'll order more ; or perhaps you have a favourite brand ? "

" Brand, sir," murmured Brimberly, " a—er—certainly, sir."

" Good-night, Brimberly."

Of Harmony and Discord

" Good-night, sir ; but first can't I do—hanything ? "

" Oh yes, you do me, of course. You do me so con-
sistently and well that I really ought to raise your wages.
I'll think about it."

Mr. Brimberly stared, coughed, and fumbled for his
whisker, whence his hand wandered to his brow and
hovered there.

" I—I bid you good-night, sir ! " he murmured.

" Oh, by the way, bring me the letters."

" Certainly, sir ! " and, crossing the room, Mr. Brimberly returned bearing a salver piled high with letters,
which he set at his master's elbow ; this done, he bowed
and went from the room, one hand still at his dazed brow.

Left alone, Ravenslee took up the letters one by one.
Some he threw aside, some few he opened and glanced
at carelessly ; among these last was a telegram, and the
words he saw were these :

" Meet me to-morrow, sunset, in wood. All shall be
explained. HERMY."

For a while he sat staring at this, then, laying it by,
drew out a letter-case from which he took another telegram, bearing precisely the same message. Having
compared them, he thrust them into his pocket, and,
filling his pipe, sat a while smoking and lost in thought.
At last, his pipe being out, he rose, stretched, and turned
toward the door ; but, in the act of leaving the room,
paused to take out and compare the telegrams again,
and so stood with puckered brows.

" Hermy ! " he said softly. " Hermione is so much
prettier. ' All shall be explained.' A little trite perhaps ! Oh, well——" So saying, he folded up the
telegrams, switched off the lights, and went to bed.

CHAPTER XXXIII

OF TRAGEDY

It was close on the hour of sunset when Ravenslee stopped his car before a quiet hotel in Englewood and sprang out.

"Will you be long, sir?" inquired Joe, seating himself at the wheel and preparing to turn into the garage.

"Probably an hour, Joe."

"Very good, sir."

But, as the big car turned, Ravenslee spoke over his shoulder:

"By the way, if I shouldn't be back in an hour, come and meet me." Then, having given Joe full and particular directions as to the little wood, he turned and went upon his way.

It had been a stifling day, and even now, though a soft air was abroad tempering the humid heat, when this light wind languished there was over all things a brooding stillness foreboding storm. But Ravenslee strode on, unheeding dust and heat, hasting on to that which awaited him, full of strength and life and the zest of life, gladhearted and with pulses that throbbed in expectation. Thus, as the sun sank in fiery splendour, he reached the little wood.

Evening was falling, and already, among the trees, shadows were deepening to twilight, but in the west was a flaming glory; and upon the edge of the wood he turned to glance back at this radiance, splashes of gold and pink flushing to an ominous red. For a long moment he stood thus, to stare round about the soli-

286

Of Tragedy

tary countryside, joying in life and the glory of it. Then he turned, and with a smile on his lips stepped into the gloom of the wood. On he went, forcing his way through the underbrush until, reaching the clearing, he halted suddenly and faced about, fancying he had heard a rustle in the leaves hard by; and Spike, cowering behind a bush, with M'Ginnis's fingers gripping his arm, shivered and sweated and held his breath until Ravenslee moved on again, and, coming to a fallen tree, seated himself there and sat chin on fist, expectation in every tense line of him.

"Now!" whispered M'Ginnis hoarsely. "Get him now—before Hermy comes t' him!"

Shuddering, Spike levelled the weapon he held, but at that moment Ravenslee was filling his pipe, and something in this homely action checked the lad, paralysed finger on trigger, and, shrinking, he cowered down upon the grass despite the fierce hand that gripped him.

"Get him now, kid—get him now! Aim f'r his chest, ye can't miss at this distance."

"I—I can't, Bud!" gasped the boy, writhing. "I can't do it—I can't!" Dropping the revolver, he hid his face in sweating hands, and shivered.

From somewhere near by a woodpecker was tapping busily, but save for this no sound broke the pervading stillness, for the gentle wind had died away. Suddenly the quiet was rent and shivered, and Spike, deafened by the report, glanced up to see Ravenslee rise to his feet, stagger forward blindly, then, with arms out-flung, pitch forward upon his face and lie there.

"By God, you—you've shot him, Bud!" he whimpered. "You—you've killed dear old Geoff. Oh, my God!"

"Aw, quit—quit all that!" whispered M'Ginnis breathlessly. "That's what we came for, ain't it? What you lookin' at?"

"It lays so—still; so awful still!" Spike gasped.

The Definite Object

" Well, what ye got t' go starin' at it that ways for? Come on—let's beat it, it's us for th' quick get-away, in case any one heard. Come on, kid ! "

" But you've killed Geoff ! "

" I guess he don't need no more. 'N' say, kid, you're in on this job, too, don't forget ! Come on, it's little old N' York for ours ! "

But though M'Ginnis dragged at him, Spike huddled limply on his knees, his glaring eyes always staring in the one direction ; whereupon M'Ginnis cursed and left him.

And now, all at once, finding himself alone, to horror came fear, and, stumbling to his feet, Spike began to draw away from that awful thing that held his gaze ; slowly he retreated, always going backwards, and, though he stumbled often against tree and sapling, yet so long as it was in sight needs must he walk backwards. When at last a kindly bush hid it from his sight he turned and ran—ran until, panting and wild-eyed, he burst from the wood and was out upon the open road. Even then he paused to stare back into that leafy gloom, but saw and heard nothing. Then, uttering a moan, he turned and ran sobbing along the darkening road.

But within that place of shadows, from amid the leaves of a certain great tree, dropped one who, coming beside that motionless form, knelt there a while. When at last he rose a ring lay upon his open palm—a ring in the shape of two hands clasping each other ; then, with this clenched in a pallid fist, he also turned and left that still and awful thing with its face hidden in last year's dead and rotting leaves.

CHAPTER XXXIV

OF REMORSE

FOR three miserable days Spike had remained indoors, eating little, sleeping less, venturing abroad only at dusk to hurry back with the latest paper, and locked within his bedroom to scan every scare-head and column with eyes dilating in dreadful expectation of beholding the awful word ' MURDER.'

For three interminable days Hermione, going about her many duties slow of foot and listless, had scarcely heeded him, conscious only of her own pain, the agony of longing, the yearning ache that filled her, throbbing in every heart-beat—an ache that would not be satisfied. Thus, lost in her own new sorrow, she spoke seldom, sighed often, and sang not at all ; often sitting at her sewing-machine with hands strangely idle and gaze abstracted. And often Spike, watching furtively, had seen her eyes brim over with great, slow-falling tears ; more than once he had heard her bitter weeping in the dawn. At such times he had yearned to comfort her, but between them was memory dividing them like a wall—the memory of a still form with arms wide-tossed and face hidden among dead leaves. And at such times Spike writhed in the grip of horror, and groaned under the gnawing fangs of remorse ; and sometimes he prayed wild, passionate prayers, and sometimes he wetted his pillow with unavailing tears while in his ears like a small voice soft and insistent, repeated over and over again, was the dread word ' MURDER.' By day it haunted him also ; it stared up at him from

The Definite Object

the white cloth of the breakfast table, forbidding him to
eat, he read it on floor and walls and ceiling, he saw it
in bloody characters that straggled across the very sky,
wherever he turned his haggard gaze there he needs must
read it.

And then there were the footsteps. All day long they
tramped up and down the stairs outside, everyday sounds
that he had never heeded before, but now they were
warnings to hearken to and shudder at, and he would
sit pretending to read, but with ears straining for the
sound of feet upon the landing or on the stair. Now
they were feet that crept—the stealthy steps of one that
lurked to catch him unaware ; or, again, they were the
loud tramp of those who came with authority to drag him
to doom ; and, staring wide-eyed, he would watch the
door, waiting for the thundering knock he expected, yet
which never came. All day long they haunted him,
and at night, locked within his bedroom, he must needs
lift heavy head from the pillow to hearken with ears
straining even yet, until, haggard and worn, he had
shivered and groaned and wept himself to sleep, only
to awake and start up in sweating terror thinking he
heard a fierce hand knocking, knocking upon the outer
door.

Thus, for three long days, Spike had lived in torment,
and to-night, as he leaned throbbing head between clutching hands, his haggard eyes sought vainly for that fell
word which he could read everywhere except in the newspaper before him ; his sufferings had grown almost
beyond his strength, for to his old torments was added
harrowing suspense.

Why ? Why ? Why was the word that stared at him
from ceiling and walls and blue expanse of heaven, why
was it there and not in the news-sheets ? Could it be
that it was lying there yet, that awful still thing, lying
as he remembered it, as he could see it now, its ghastly
features hidden among the leaves that rotted, its long

arms out-flung, and strong hands that gripped among the grass with clutching fingers. Could it be?

"Arthur—boy—what's the matter?"

Spike started and looked up to find Hermione beside him, and instinctively he shrank away.

"Arthur—oh, what is it? Are you sick?"

"N-o; why?"

"You were moaning."

"Oh, well, I—I'm all right, I guess. Got a headache, that's all."

"Why have you avoided me lately, Arthur? I'm not angry any more, I'm only disappointed"

"Ye mean because I lost me job? They don't want my kind, I—oh, I'm too mean—too rotten, I guess."

"I heard you cry out in the night, Arthur. What was it?"

"Nothin'—I didn't cry out las' night, I tell ye."

"I heard you!"

"Oh, well, I—I was only dreamin', I guess."

"Why have you acted so strangely lately? You don't eat, you don't go out, you sit around staring big-eyed, and seem to be listening—almost as if you were afraid."

"I ain't—I ain't afraid. Who says I'm afraid? An' I don't want you to go worryin' yourself sick over me. I ain't a kid no more."

"No, I'm afraid you're not," and, sighing, she turned away.

But now, as she crossed the room, her step slow and listless, he spoke, his head down-bent and face hidden between clenched hands, voicing, almost despite himself, the questions that had tortured him so long:

"Say, Hermy, where's Geoff? How is he? I mean you—you ain't heard anything, have you?"

"No," she answered softly without turning, "what should I hear? I only know he's—gone. How should I hope to hear anything any more?"

The Definite Object

" I—I thought he was—goin' t' marry you."

" So he was, but I—couldn't let him—marry—a thief's sister," she said in the same low, even voice.

" Ah ! " cried Spike, writhing. " Why did he go an' tell ye about me, after he told me he never would ! Why did he tell ye ? "

" He didn't tell me ! " cried Hermione with curling lip.

" Didn't he ? Oh, didn't he ? " said Spike, his voice high and quivering, " didn't Geoff tell ye ? Then, say, Hermy, who—who did ? "

" It was Bud M'Ginnis, and for once it seems he told the truth ! "

" Bud ! " cried Spike, stumbling to his feet. " Oh my God ! "

At sound of his voice she turned, and, seeing his face, cried out in sudden fear :

" Arthur—oh Arthur ! what is it ? "

" Bud told ye ? " he gasped. " Wasn't it Geoff—oh, wasn't it Geoff ? "

" No."

Spike was down on his knees. " Oh God ! Oh Geoff —dear old Geoff, forgive me "

Spike was huddled upon the floor, his face pressed to the worn rug, his clenched fingers buried in his curls, while from his lips issued gasping sobs harshly dry and awful to hear. " Forgive me, Geoff—forgive me ! I thought you told her ! I thought you meant t' steal her from me ! Oh, forgive me, Geoff ; I wish I was dead like you."

" Arthur ! " She was down beside him on her knees, shaking him with desperate hands. " Arthur ! Oh Arthur —what—what are you saying ? "

" Nothin'—nothin' ! " he stammered, staring up into her face, suddenly afraid of her. " Nothin'. I—I was only—thinkin'. I——"

" What did you mean ? " she cried, her grasp tightening. " Tell me what you meant—tell me, tell me ? "

Of Remorse

"Nothin'," he mumbled, trying to break her hold. "Lemme go, I—I didn't mean anything."

"Tell me what you meant—tell me, tell me?"

"No, I can't—I——"

His voice failed suddenly, his whole frame grew tense and rigid, and, lifting a stiff arm, he pointed a trembling finger towards the open doorway.

"Hush! hush!" he panted, "Oh, for God's sake, hush! There's—don't you hear—there's some one outside on th' landing—footsteps—hark! They're coming to our door! They're stoppin' outside. Oh my God, it's come at——"

The word ended in a scream, drowned all at once in a thunderous knocking on the outer door; and Spike, crouching upon his knees, clutched at her as she rose.

"Don't—don't open—the door!" he gasped, while Hermione gazed at him, terrified by his terror, as again the thunderous summons was heard. Then, despite the boy's passionate prayers and desperate, clutching hands, she broke from him, and, hasting into the little passage, opened the door.

Upon the threshold stood a little old man, very smartly dressed, who saluted her with a gallant flourish of his dapper straw hat, and bowed with his two small and glittering patent-leather shoes posed at position No. 1 in waltzing.

"Ma'am," said he, "miss, respectful greetin's. Your name's Hermione, ain't it?"

"Yes," she answered, wondering.

"Knowed it was. An' a partic'ler fine gal too! Though not 'oldin' wi' marridge, I don't blame the guv— 'e always 'ad a quick eye for beauty—like me."

"But who are you? What do you want?"

"Miss, I want you—leastways, 'e does. Been callin' for you the last three days 'e 'as, ever since 'e ketched one as fair doubled 'im up."

"I—I don't understand. Who are you?"

The Definite Object

"A admirer of the guv, ma'am. A trusted friend of 'is, miss, come t' take ye to 'is poor yearnin' arms, lady."

"But who—oh, what do you mean?"

"Mr. Ravenslee, ma'am."

"Mr. Ravenslee!" she echoed, her colour changing.

"Yes. Ye see, he's dyin', miss!"

Hermione gasped and leaned against the wall as if suddenly faint and sick; perceiving which, the Old 'un promptly set his arm about her waist and led her unresisting into the parlour. There, having aided her tenderly into a chair and nodded to pale-faced Spike, he sighed, shook his ancient head, and continued:

"Ho, lor lumme, lady, it fair wrung my old 'eart to 'ave to tell ye. But, 'aving to tell ye (Joe couldn't), I told ye almighty quick to get it over—sharp an' quick's my motter. Fate's crool 'ard when Fate takes the gloves off, miss, an' I know as Fate's been an' took ye one in the wind wot's fair doubled ye up; but take time, ma'am, take time—throw back your pretty head, breathe deep an' reg'lar, an' you'll soon be strong enough to go another round. If I'd got a towel handy I'd fan ye a bit, not 'avin' none, no matter. Fate's 'ard on you, so fair an' young, miss, but Fate's been 'arder on the guv—ketched the poor young guv a fair spiflicator."

"Oh please—please," cried Hermione, reaching out appealing hands, "oh, tell me, is he hurt—sick—dying? Oh quick, quick, tell me!"

"Lady, ma'am—my pretty dear," said the Old 'un, taking those pleading hands to pat them tenderly, "that's what I'm tryin' to do. The guv ain't dead yet—no, not yet."

"You mean he's—dying?"

"My dear," said the old man, blinking at her through sudden tears, "that's what the doctors say." Here he loosed one hand to rub at each bright eye with a bony knuckle, "An' 'im so young, so game an' strong, three days ago."

Of Remorse

"How—did it—happen?" she questioned, her voice low and steady.

"It was Fate!" said the old man, taking her hand again, "Three days ago, Fate (the ‿ perisher) sends 'im a telegram—two on 'em—tellin' 'im to meet you in a wood, an' signed with—with your name, both on 'em."

At this she cried out and would have risen, but his kindly clasp checked her.

"I sent no telegram!" she whispered.

"Me an' Joe an' the Spider know that now, miss. But, anyway, to this 'ere wood the guv do 'aste away, an' in this wood Fate's a-layin' for 'im wi' a gun, an' down goes the poor guv wi' a perishin' bullet in 'is gizzard. An' there Joe finds 'im, an' 'ome Joe brings 'im in the car, an' Joe an' me an' the Spider 'ushes things up. An' now in bed lays the guv with nurses an' doctors 'anging over 'im, a-callin' for you—I mean the guv, d'ye see? So now for you I've come. I've brought Joe an' the car for you. Joe's across wi' Mrs. Trapes, an' the car's below —both waitin'. So you'll come t' th' pore young guv, ma'am, won't ye, lady?"

"Have you—any idea—who—did it?" she questioned, speaking as if with an effort.

"We got our suspicions, ho yus!" the Old 'un nodded. "Joe's got a wonnerful gift o' suspicion—oh a rare 'ead 'as my lad Joe. Joe an' th' Spider's on th' track, an' they're goin' to track Fate to doom, ma'am—to perishin' doom! Ye see,"—here the old man leaned suddenly nearer—" ye see, Joe's found a cloo!"

"A clue! Yes, yes!" she whispered breathlessly, moistening lips suddenly dry, and conscious that Spike's lax form had stiffened to painful alertness.

"Well, ma'am, Joe an' th' Spider's been a-seekin' an' a-searchin' of that there wood, an' they found," here the Old 'un leaned nearer yet and whispered harshly, "they found—a coat-button! Lorgorramighty!" he exclaimed

The Definite Object

suddenly, pointing a trembling, bony finger, "What's took th' lad—look!"

Spike had risen, and now stood breathing loud, one hand clenched upon his breast; turning swiftly he took a stumbling pace toward the open window, tripped and fell prone upon his face.

"Oh poor lad! poor lad!" cried the Old 'un, rising hastily. "Fate's been an' ketched 'im one too—a fair knock-out! Leave 'im to me, ma'am, I'll bring 'im round; bitin' 'is ears is good, or vinegar on a sponge. Leave 'im to a old fightin' man."

"No!" cried Hermione passionately, "No, I say. Leave him to me!"

Quelled by something in her tone and manner, the old man sank back in his chair, while she, kneeling beside Spike, lifted him in her strong young arms so that he was hidden from the Old 'un's bright, piercing eyes. Holding him thus, she loosed Spike's rigid fingers and drew away that clutching hand; then, seeing what that hand had striven to hide, she blenched suddenly away letting the boy's inanimate form slip from her clasp, and, as she knelt there above him, her shapely body was seized with fierce tremors. So she knelt for a long moment until Spike sighed, shivered, sat up, but, beholding the look in her wide eyes, uttered a hoarse sound that was like a cry of fear, and, starting from her nearness, crouched down, huddled upon his knees.

Then Hermione rose, and, turning to the old man, smiled with pallid lips.

"You see—he's all right—now!" she said. "If you'll please go and tell Mrs. Trapes I'm leaving, I'll get ready."

Obediently the Old 'un rose.

"Mrs. Trapes is a-gettin' into her bonnet to come along wi' us!" said he, and putting on his hat with a flourish, took his departure. When he was gone, Hermione turned and looked down at Spike, who, meeting her eyes, flinched

Of Remorse

as from a blow, and made no effort to rise from his knees.
So she packed her grip and dressed for the journey, while
he watched her with eyes of mute appeal ; twice he would
have spoken, but her look smote him to silence. At last,
as she took up her suit-case and turned to go, he implored
her in a hoarse whisper, reaching out his arms to her :

" Hermy ! "

But she shrank from his contact, and, hastening from
the room and along the little passage, closed the door
and left him to his hopeless misery.

As one in a dream she followed the old man down the
stairs, was aware of his ushering her through the crowd
of women and children who thronged about the big car ;
as one in a dream she found herself seated beside Mrs.
Trapes, whose motherly solicitude she heeded no more
than the bustle and traffic of the streets through which
the swift car whirled her, on and on until, turning, it
swung in between massive gates and pulled up before a
great, gloomy house ; as one in a dream she ascended
the broad steps, crossed a stately hall, was ushered up a
noble stairway and along thick-carpeted corridors until,
at last, she found herself in a dim-lighted chamber, where,
his dark head conspicuous upon the white pillow, he lay.
A nurse rose from beside the bed as Hermione entered
and softly withdrew. Left alone, she stood for a long
moment utterly still, her hands tight-clasped, her breath
in check, gazing at that dark head upon the pillow, at
that outstretched form lying so silent and so very
still.

" Hermione ! "

A feeble whisper, a sigh faintly breathed ; but at the
sound she had crossed the wide chamber on feet swift
and noiseless, had sunk upon her knees beside the low
bed to lean above him all murmurous love and sighing
tenderness, while she stole a timid hand to touch the hair
that curled upon his pallid brow ; then, for all his helplessness, she flushed beneath his look.

The Definite Object

"How beautiful—you are!" he said faintly, "and I—weak as—confounded rat! Hermione—love, they tell me I—must die. But first I want you for—my very own, if only for a little while!"

"Oh, my dear," she whispered, soft mouth against his pale cheek, "I always was yours—yours from the very first, I always shall be."

"Then you'll—marry me?"

"Yes, dear."

"Now?"

"Yes, dear."

"I—hoped you would, so—I arranged—minister's waiting now. Will you—ring?" And he motioned feebly towards an electric bell-push that stood upon a small table beside the bed. And now once again, as one in a dream, she obeyed, and was presently aware of soft-treading figures about her in the dim chamber—among them the Old 'un, whose shoes for once creaked not at all; as one in a dream she made the responses, felt the feeble clasp of that hand whose strength and masterful power had thrilled her once, heard the faint echo of that loved voice that had wooed her so passionately, yet wooed in vain, while now——

She was alone again, alone with him who lay so very still and pale and with eyes closed wearily; from him she glanced to that which gleamed so bright and new upon her finger, and, bending her head, she pressed the wedding-ring to her lips.

"Wife!" he whispered; the weary eyes were open and his look drew her. So she knelt beside the bed again, stooping above him low and lower until her head lay beside his upon the pillow. Slowly, slowly his feeble hand crept up to her glowing cheek, to the soft waves of her hair, and to the little curl that wantoned above her eyebrow. "Hermione—wife—kiss me!"

Tenderly her arms enfolded him, and with a soft little cry that was half a sob she kissed him—his brow, his

298

Of Remorse

hair, his lips—kissed him even while she wetted him
with her falling tears.

"Beloved," he murmured, "my glorious—scrub-woman
—if I must—leave you—those dear hands need never—
never slave again. Never—any—more, my Hermione."

Long after he had fallen asleep she knelt there, cradling
his weakness in her arms, looking down on him with
eyes bright with love.

After this, were days and nights when the soul of him
wandered in dark places filled with chaotic dreams and
wild fancies; but there was ever one beside him whose
gentle voice reached him in the darkness, and whose
tender hands hushed his delirium and soothed his woes
and troubles.

CHAPTER XXXV

SHE was knitting; and, opening sleepy eyes, he watched drowsily and wondered what it might be, and was minded to inquire, but sighed instead and fell asleep again.

She was knitting; knitting something in red wool, and, opening sleepy eyes, he lay watching awhile and pondered dreamily as to what it could be she wrought at so busily, for the wool was so very red and so extremely woolly.

Her chin was set at an angle somewhat grim, she was sitting very upright in her chair, and, though scrupulously hidden from sight, her elbows—truly how portentous were the undisguisable points of those elbows! And she was knitting fiercely in wool that was so remarkably red and woolly.

" Pray, what is it, Mrs. Trapes ? "

A feeble whisper; but at the sound, faint though it was, Mrs. Trapes started, half rose from her chair, sank down again heavily, and letting fall her knitting, stared at the invalid.

" Land sakes alive ! " she gasped.

" Now you've dropped it ! " said Ravenslee, his voice a little stronger.

" Oh, dear beloved land o' my fathers—it's come ! " she exclaimed clasping her hands, " the Lord be praised for evermore, it's come ! "

" What has ? "

" The turn ! An' you've took it ! Dr. Dennison says

300

last night as you'd take it soon, one way or t'other. But
all night long, while they waited an' watched, here you've
laid so pale an' still as a corp'. An' now, while I'm a
settin' here, you go an' take th' turn so sudden as fair
takes my breath away. Lord be praised! I mean—I
mean—oh, I guess I'll go wake the doctor."

" But you haven't told me what it is," said Ravenslee
drowsily.

" What what is ? "

" That very peculiar—woolly thing."

" This ? " said Mrs. Trapes, picking up the object in
question, " this is my knittin'. Doctor said t' call him
th' moment th' turn came." Her voice seemed to sink
to a slumberous murmur as, having smoothed his pillow
she crossed the room and very softly closed the door behind her, wherefore Ravenslee blinked sleepily at the
door until its panels seemed slowly to become confused
and merge one into another, changing gradually to a
cloud, soft, billowy, and ever growing until it had engulfed
him altogether, and he sank down and down into unknown
deeps of forgetfulness and blessed quietude.

. . . . .

She was knitting ; knitting a shapeless something in
red wool, and Ravenslee thought he had never known
her elbows more threatening of aspect nor seen wool
quite so red and woolly, wherefore he presently spoke,
and his voice was no longer a feeble croak.

" Pray, what is it, Mrs. Trapes ? "

Mrs. Trapes jumped.

" Well, for th' love o' heaven ! " she exclaimed, and
down fell her knitting.

" Now you've dropped it ! " said Ravenslee a little
petulantly.

" Your very—identical words ! " said Mrs. Trapes in
awed tones. " Nacher sure 'moves in a mysterious way
her wonders to perform ' ! "

" What do you mean ? "

The Definite Object

" I mean as them was the identical words as you addressed to me when you took th' turn two days ago ! "

" Two days ! " exclaimed Ravenslee, staring.

" Ever since you did take the turn two days ago you've laid there so quiet an' peaceful—no more dreams an' ravin'—you've jest laid there ' wrapped in infant slumbers pure an' light,' Mr. Geoffrey—Ravenslee, I mean."

" Why, then, it's about time I got up. If you'll kindly —er—retire and send Patterson I'll get dressed."

" Dressed ? " echoed Mrs. Trapes, hollow-voiced and grim. " Get up ? Lord, Mr. Geoffrey ! "

" Certainly. Why not ? "

" What you—you as is only jest out o' the valley o' th' shadder ! You as we've all give up for dead over an' over ! You get up ! Lord, Mr. Geoffrey—I mean Ravenslee ! "

" Oh ! " said Ravenslee, knitting his dark brows thoughtfully, " have I been sick long ? "

" Four weeks."

" Weeks ! " he exclaimed, staring incredulously.

" Four weeks an' a bit ! For four weary, woeful weeks you've been layin' here with death hoverin' over you, Mr. Geoffrey. For four long weeks we've been waitin' for ye t' draw your las' breath, Mr. Ravenslee. For four heartrendin' weeks your servants has been carryin' on below stairs an' robbin' you somethin' shameful."

" My servants ? Oh yes, they generally do. But tell me——"

" The amount o' food as they consoom constant ! The waste ! The extravagance ! The beer an' wine an' sperrits they swaller ! Them is sure the thirstiest menials ever I heard tell of ! An' the butler—such airs, such a appetite, an' sherry an' bitters t' make it worse ! Lord, Mr. Geoffrey, your servants sure is a ravenin' horde ! "

" Don't be too hard on 'em, Mrs. Trapes," he answered gravely. " I'm afraid I've neglected them quite a good deal. But it's a woman's hand they need over them."

How Ravenslee came out of the Dark

" It's a pleeceman's club they need—on 'em—frequent! I'd learn 'em different, I guess."

" So you shall, Mrs. Trapes, if you will. You are precisely the kind of housekeeper I need."

" What, me ? "

" You, Mrs. Trapes. A lonely bachelor needs some one to—er—take care of his servants for him, to see they don't over-eat themselves too often, or—er—strain themselves spring-cleaning out of season, or——"

" But you got a wife t' do all that for you. I guess Hermy 'll know how to manage."

" Hermione ! " said Ravenslee, starting, " Wife? Am I really—married ? "

" Sure ! Didn't she go an' let you wed 'er when we all thought you was dyin' ? "

" Oh, did she ? " said he very gently. " Why then it —it—wasn't all a dream ? "

" Mr. Geoffrey, Hermy's been Mrs. Ravenslee, your lawful wedded wife, just exactly four weeks."

Ravenslee stared up at the ceiling dreamy-eyed.

" Good heavens ! " he murmured, " I thought I'd only dreamed it."

" Hermy's watched over you night an' day almost— like th' guardian angel she is—prayin' f'r you, workin' f'r you, fightin' death away from you. Oh I guess it's her fault as you're alive this day ! Anyway, her an' you's man an' wife till death do you part."

" But death—hasn't, you see."

" An' death sure ain't goin' to—yet."

" No, I'm—I'm very much alive still, it seems."

" You sure are, glory be t' th' Lord of Hosts to who I have also petitioned frequent on your behoof. An' now I'll call th' doctor."

" No, no—not Dennison, let me see her first. Can't I speak to Hermione first, Mrs. Trapes ? "

" She was up with you all las' night, sweet lamb ! It 'd be a shame to wake 'er. '

The Definite Object

"So it would. Don't disturb her."

'But I guess she'd never forgive me if I didn't wake her. So if you'll promise t' be good——"

"I will."

"An' not go gettin' all worked up an' excited ?"

"I will not."

"Why, then, perhaps ten minutes wouldn't hurt."

"God bless you, Mrs. Trapes ! "

Left alone, he tried to sit up, and finding this strangely difficult, examined his hands and arms, scowling to find himself so weak. Then he clapped hand to bony jaw, and was shocked to feel thereon a growth of ragged beard, and then she was before him. Fresh from her slumbers she came, wrapped in a scanty kimono whose thin, clinging folds revealed more of her shapely beauty than he had ever seen, as she hurried across the wide chamber.

"Hermione ! " he said, and reached out his hands to her. And his voice was no longer the feeble echo it had been, the hand that clasped hers, though still thin and weak, thrilled her anew with its masterful touch ; and, because of all this, her words of tender greeting remained unspoken and the arms which had been eager to cradle his helplessness crossed themselves on her bosom. She became aware of naked ankles and of bare feet thrust into bedroom slippers, and needs must hide them and, the better to do so, sank upon the bed, feet tucked under her. So she sat just beyond his reach, and, conscious of scanty draperies, shook her shining hair about her, veiling herself in its glory.

"Hermione," he said unsteadily, " I—I never knew quite how beautiful you were—and we—we are married, it seems ! "

"Yes," she said softly.

"And now I'm—I'm afraid I'm going to—live ! "

"Afraid ? "

"It—it almost seems as though I had married you

under false pretences, doesn't it ? But the doctors and everybody were so certain I was to die that I thought so too. And now—we're married and I'm going to live, it seems."

She was silent, and slowly his hand went out to her again, and slowly hers went to meet it ; but though her fingers clasped and twined, thrilling in mute passion to his touch, she came no nearer, and watched him from the shadow of her hair with great, troubled eyes.

" Dear," he said, very humbly, " you do—love me still, don't you ? "

" More than ever."

" Then you're not—sorry to be my wife ? "

" No—ah, no, no ! " she whispered, " never that ! "

" Then, dear, won't you—will you kiss me ? " Seeing she hesitated, he sank back on his pillow and laughed a little ruefully. " I forgot those confounded whiskers," he sighed, " I must look an unholy object. Patterson shall shave me, and then perhaps——" But sudden and warm and soft her arms were about him, and her eyes, troubled no longer, gazed into his, brimful of yearning tenderness.

" Oh my dear, my dear," she murmured, quick and passionate, " as if I should ever care how you looked as long as you were—just you. My dear, my dear, you have come back to me from the very gates of death because I—I——"

" Because you nursed me so tenderly ! "

" Ah, no ! there were others to do that. No, God gave you back to me because He is merciful, and because I love you—want you—need you so much ! "

" Oh my Hermione—kiss me ! "

A knock at the door, and, quick-breathing, she drew from him as the voice of Mrs. Trapes reached them.

"Ten minutes is up ! " she announced as she entered, " and, Hermy, if you don't want th' doctor t' see you in your night-dress an' that——"

The Definite Object

"Ann!" gasped Hermione, drawing the folds of her kimono about her.

"Anyway, he's comin'."

Up sprang Hermione, in doing which she lost a slipper.

"Give it me!" she pleaded, for Ravenslee had caught it up.

"Dear, you have one—be content," he answered. "And surely I may kiss my wife's slipper without you having to blush so—so deliciously, Hermione?"

"It's so—old and shabby!" said she faintly.

"That's why I kiss it."

"An' here comes th' doctor!" said Mrs. Trapes. Whereat Hermione incontinent fled away, white foot agleam. Then Ravenslee, having kissed the little slipper quite brazenly under Mrs. Trapes's staring eyes, tucked it beneath his pillow.

"Why, Mr. Geoffrey!" said Mrs. Trapes

CHAPTER XXXVI

CONCERNING A CLUE

"MRS. TRAPES," said Ravenslee, laying aside the book he had been reading and letting his glance wander across smooth lawns and clipped yew hedges, "Mrs. Trapes, what about that stewed shin of beef with carrots and onions you prepared for—our wedding supper?"

"Which," said Mrs. Trapes, glancing up from her everlasting knitting, "which you never stopped to eat."

"Which omission I will now haste to rectify. Mrs. Trapes, pray go and get it ready. I'm ravenous!"

"Good f'r you!" said Mrs. Trapes, "in about half-an-hour you shall have a nice cup of beef-tea to raven at."

"Confounded slops!" growled Ravenslee.

"Doctor's orders!" nodded Mrs. Trapes, clicking her knitting-needles.

"Can't I have something to chew at?"

"Sure. How'll a cracker soaked in milk soot?"

"Cracker!" snarled Ravenslee.

"Doctor's orders!"

Ravenslee muttered and took up his book.

"Helen who, did you say?" inquired Mrs. Trapes, glancing up. "Mr. Geoffrey—I mean Ravenslee—I'm surprised at you, swearin' ain't good for a invalid, your temperature 'll be rose if you swear."

"But, my dear Mrs. Trapes, I'm hungry—very hungry—darned hungry!"

"Which is a sign as you're improvin' rapid. Beef-tea 'll be 'ere soon."

"I won't drink the stuff!"

The Definite Object

" Oh but you will, when Hermy brings it."

" Hermione ! " said Ravenslee, his voice grown gentle, and laying down his book again. " Mrs. Trapes, have you noticed any change in her lately ? "

" A bit handsomer, p'r'aps."

" Yes, but I don't mean that, it's something that puzzles me. She seems to have grown more—more reserved and shy."

" Well, she was married to you before she knew it kind of, almost."

" Do you suppose that's it ? "

" Sure. What you got t' do, Mr. Geoffrey, is—woo her ! Woo her all you know how. The best woman can't be wooed too hard nor too frequent—so you start in an' woo."

" But sometimes it has almost seemed that she— avoided me."

" Well, don't let her."

" Do you suppose she's grieving for Spike ? "

" Well, he aint exactly a j'y t' her. There 'e is goin' straight to the devil along o' that Bud M'Ginnis ! "

" I must go and fetch him as soon as I can get about again."

" If he'll come."

" Oh, he'll come," said Ravenslee grimly. " I've decided to send him to college."

" If he'll go."

" Oh, he'll go ; there's quite a lot of good in him, Mrs. Trapes."

" Only it's mighty hard to find, Mr. Geoffrey. If that b'y wants t' go t' th' devil, to the devil he'll go. What you got t' do is t' make her forget him—if you can. Oh, drat him, anyway ! " and, squaring her elbows, Mrs. Trapes knitted so angrily that her knitting-needles clashed like weapons fiercely opposed.

" Yes, but suppose she is grieving for him, Mrs. Trapes ? "

Concerning a Clue

"Why then," said Mrs. Trapes, "why then—— Oh shucks! I guess I'll go an' see after that beef-tea."

When she had gone, Ravenslee sat plunged in gloomy thought until roused by the sound of approaching feet with a creak of shoes, a loud, arrogant creak there was no mistaking, and the Old 'un appeared, followed by Joe and the Spider, the latter looking very smart in his new livery.

"Guv," said the Old 'un, "best respex! 'Ere we be, come to say 'ow glad we are t' see ye come up smilin' an' ready for more after Fate ketchin' ye a perishin' wallop as we all thought 'ad doubled ye up till the day o' doom. 'Ere ye are, on your pins again, an' 'ere's us come t' give ye greetin's doo an' j'y o' your marriage. Shut up, Joe!"

"Why, I wasn't speakin'!" growled Joe.

"No, but you meant to—you're always meanin' to, you are. Guv," continued the Old 'un, "folks is allus a-givin' an' takin' in marriage in this 'ere world, such bein' their natur'—they can't 'elp it! But never in this world nor no other was there ever sich a weddin' as yourn. There was 'er so young an' fair an' full o' life, an' there was you so pale an' nigh to death—one leg in the grave —an' there was me s' full o' years an' wisdom an' sorrer for ye both—oh, my pore old bowels was fair yearnin' over ye."

"Lord, Old 'un," expostulated Joe, "you keep them bowels o' yours out o' it."

"Shut up, Joe, in your ignorance; bowels is in the Bible, an' bowels I abide by now an' for ever, amen! Well, there we all were, guv, bendin' o'er your couch o' care very silent an' solemn. 'Not a drum was 'eard, not a funereal note,' an' there was you s' pale an' nigh t' death."

"You said all that afore, Old 'un!" growled Joe.

"You leave me alone, Joe," said the Old 'un, scowling and flourishing a trembling fist, "you lemme be, or you'll be pale an' nigh t' death next! Well, there was you,

The Definite Object

guv, an' all s' pale an' still, when, ''oo giveth this woman?' says the parson-cove very solemn. 'That's me!' says I, quick an' ready. An' so, me 'avin' 'elped t' marry ye, I've brought Joe an' Spider t' wish ye 'ealth an' 'appiness an' a j'y continual. Now Joe, it's your round—speak up!"

"Sir," said Joe, heavily, "I—we—I mean—Lord, sir, I am that glad—ah, glad as—as never was."

"That'll do for you, Joe!" snapped the Old 'un. "Spider's round."

Hereupon the Spider lurched forward, hunched his wide shoulders, took off his smart cap, and stared at it very hard.

"Bo'," said he, chewing vigorously. "I mean boss —er—no, that ain't right either—this is sure a bum start I'm makin'."

"'Bo' will do, Spider," said Ravenslee, "let it go at that."

"Why then, bo', I ain't one as is ever goin' t' win any gold-mounted testimonials at any talk-fest or heart-throbbin' spiel-act, but what I wanter tell you is this —an' I guess you know I ain't only breathin' out puffs o' hot air—I wancher t' know as I feel about you like —like Joe an' the Old 'un does—an' then some more. Ye see, bo', though I ain't never held a straight flush agin four aces 'n' don't expect to, though I sha'n't ever be a world's champion like Joe here, I guess I know to-day what it feels like, because you ain't goin' t' snuff it after all; and now I guess you're on." Saying which, the Spider dexterously shifted his wad to the other cheek and chewed faster than ever.

"I am, Spider, and I want you to know I'm grateful to you all three. Also, I want to thank you all for keeping this affair out of the papers, though how you managed it beats me."

"Guv," cried the Old 'un, tremulous and eager, " oh guv, we're fair sleuth-hounds, we are—'specially me!

310

Concerning a Clue

There ain't a 'tective nor secret-service cove nor bloomin'
bobby fit to black our shoes—'specially mine! Ye see,
guv, I know who done it, Joe thinks he knows, an'
Spider don't think at all!"

"Oh!" said Ravenslee, and looking round, caught
the Spider watching him wide-eyed, his jaws grimly tense
and immobile; but, meeting his glance, the Spider
lowered his eyes, shifted his smartly-gaitered legs, and
chewed viciously.

"So, guv," piped the Old 'un cheerily, "we're out for
the criminal's gore—'specially me. We're goin' to track
the perisher to 'is 'orrible doom.

> Where'er 'e be
> To th' gallers tree,
> Oh guv, we mean t' bring 'im;
> An' laugh with j'y
> When, nice an' 'igh,
> The blinkin' bobbies swing 'im."

"And you think you know who it was?"

"I do, guv—I do!" nodded the Old 'un. "I knows
as 'twas a enemy as done it. Joe thinks it was one o'
them gang fellers, an' Spider don't say who 'e thinks done
it."

Once again Ravenslee caught the Spider's eye watching
him furtively, and once again he noticed that the Spider's
jaws were clamped hard, while he was twisting his natty
chauffeur's cap in fingers strangely agitated.

"Sir," said Joe, "me an' the Spider searched that
wood an' we found a coat——"

"Shut up, Joe," snarled the Old 'un, "you're tellin'
it all wrong! Guv, Joe an' the Spider went a-seekin' an'
a-searchin' that wood, an' they found a—cloo."

"Oh!" said Ravenslee.

"A cloo as is a-goin t' hang somebody yet—a cloo,
guv, as ain't t' be ekalled for blood-guilt an' mystery!
Joe," said the Old 'un, sinking his voice to a hoarse
whisper, "the hour is come—perjooce the cloo!"

The Definite Object

Hereupon Joe produced a pocket-book and took thence a highly ornate coat-button, whereto a shred of cloth was attached.

"I found this, sir," said he, "close by where you was a-lyin'."

So Ravenslee took the button upon his palm, and, as he eyed it, the Spider saw his black brows twitch suddenly together.

"And you found this in the wood, Joe?" he inquired sleepily.

"I did, sir. With that to 'elp 'em the perlice would 'ave the murderin' cove in no time, an' more than once I've been goin' to 'and it over to 'em. But then I thought I'd better wait a bit; if you died was time enough, an' if you didn't I'd keep it for you; so, sir, there it is."

"You did quite right, Joe. Yes, you did very right indeed!" For a long moment Ravenslee sat languidly twisting the button in thin, white fingers, then flicked it far out over the balustrade down among the dense evergreens in the garden below. The Old 'un gasped, Joe gaped, and the Spider sighed audibly.

"Lorgorramighty! Oh, guv, guv," quavered the old man, "you've throwed away our cloo—our blood-cloo—th' p'lice—you've lost our evidence!"

"Old 'un, of course I have! You see, I don't like clues, or blood, or the police. You have all been clever enough, wise enough to keep this confounded business quiet, and so will I."

"But oh, guv, arter somebody tryin' t' kill ye like a dog, ain't there goin' t' be no vengeance, no gallers-tree, no 'lectric chair, nor nothin'?"

"Nothing!" answered Ravenslee gently. "Somebody tried to kill me, but somebody didn't kill me; here I am, getting stronger every day, so we'll let it go at that."

"Why then, I'm done!" said the Old 'un, rising. "Guv, you're crool an' stony-'earted! 'Ere's me, a pore old cove as 'as been dreamin' an' dreamin' o' gallers-trees an' 'lectric chairs, an' 'ere's you been an' took 'em off me! Guv, I'm disapp'inted wi' ye. Oh ingratitood, thou art the guv!" So saying, the Old 'un clapped on his hat and creaked indignantly away.

"Crumbs!" exclaimed Joe, "what a blood-thirsty old cove 'e is, with 'is gallers-trees! This means jam, this does."

"Jam!" repeated Ravenslee, wonderingly.

"Sir, whenever the Old 'un's put out 'e flies to jam same as some chaps do to drink, makes a fair old beast of hisself, 'e do. If you'll excuse us, sir, Spider an' me'll just keep a eye on 'im to see as 'e don't go upsettin' 'is old innards again."

Ravenslee nodded and, smiling, watched them hurry after the old man; but gradually his amusement waned, and he became lost in frowning thought. So deeply abstracted was he that he started to find Mrs. Trapes regarding him with her sharp, bright eyes.

"Mr. Geoffrey, here's a cup o' beef-tea as I've prepared with my own hand."

"But where's——"

"She's gone t' bed. Here's a cup o' beef-tea as is stiff with nourishment, so get it into your system good an' quick."

"Gone to bed!"

"She says it's headache, o' course—drink it down while it's hot—but I reckon it's more 'n a headache—yes, sir. A while back I says t' you, 'woo her,' I says, Mr. Geoffrey. I now says—let her alone awhile. The pore child's all wore out—it's nerves as is the matter wi' her, I reckon. So, Mr. Ravenslee, be patient, this ain't no wooin' time, it's rest she needs, an' change of air."

"Why then, Mrs. Trapes, she shall have them!"

CHAPTER XXXVII

THE WOES OF MR. BRIMBERLY

MR. BRIMBERLY, having dined well, as was his custom, lay at his ease in a luxurious lounge chair in the shade of the piazza ; the day was hot, wherefore, on a table at his elbow was a syphon, a bottle, and a long glass in which ice tinkled alluringly ; between his plump fingers was a large cigar, and across his plump knees was an open paper, over which he yawned and puffed and sipped in turn. Nevertheless, Mr. Brimberly was bored ; and, dropping the paper languidly, cherished a languorous whisker, staring dull-eyed across stately terraces and wide, neat lawns to where, beyond yew-walks and noble trees, the distant river flowed.

Presently as he sat he was aware of a small girl in a white pinafore approaching along one of these walks— a small being who hopped along by means of a little crutch, and sang to herself in a soft, happy voice.

Mr. Brimberly blinked.

Heedless of the eyes that watched her, the child turned into the rose-garden, pausing now and then to inhale the scent of some great bloom that filled the air with its sweetness.

Mr. Brimberly sat up, for he permitted few to enter the rose-garden.

All at once the child, singing still, reached up and broke off a great scarlet rose.

Mr. Brimberly arose.

Little girl!" he called, in voice round and sonorous, "Little girl, come you 'ere, an' come immediate!"

The Woes of Mr. Brimberly

The child started, turned, and after a moment's hesitation hobbled forward, her little face as white as her pinafore. At the foot of the broad steps leading up to the piazza she paused, looking up at him with great, pleading eyes.

Mr. Brimberly beckoned with portentous finger.

"Little girl, come 'ere!" he repeated. "Come up 'ere, an' come immediate!"

The small crutch tapped laboriously up the steps, and she stood before Mr. Brimberly's imposing figure—mute, breathless, and trembling a little.

"Little girl," he demanded, threatening of whisker, "'oo are you, an'—what?"

"Please, I'm Hazel."

"Oh indeed," nodded Mr. Brimberly, pulling at his waistcoat. "'Azel 'oo, 'Azel what—an' say 'sir' next time, if *you* please."

"Hazel Bowker, sir," and she dropped him a little curtsy, spoiled somewhat by agitation and her crutch.

"Bowker—Bowker!" mused Mr. Brimberly. "I've 'eard the name—I don't like the name, but I've 'eard it."

"My daddy works here, sir," said Hazel timidly.

"Bowker—Bowker!" repeated Mr. Brimberly. "Ah, to be sure—one of the hunder-gardeners as I put on three or four weeks ago."

"Yes, please, sir."

"Little girl, what was you a-doin' in that garden! Why are you wanderin' in the vi-cinity of this mansion?"

"Please, I'm looking for Hermy."

"'Ermy?" repeated Mr. Brimberly. "'Ermy? Wot kind of creater may that be? Is it a dog? Is it a cat? Wot is it?"

"It's only my Princess Nobody, sir!"

"Oh, a friend of yours—ha! Persons of that class do not pervade these regions! And wot do I be'old grasped in your 'and?"

The Definite Object

Hazel looked down at the rose she held, and trembled anew.

" Little girl—wot is it ? " demanded the inexorable voice.

" A rose, sir."

" Was it—your rose ? "

" N-no, sir."

" Don't you know as it's a wicked hact to take what ain't yours ? Don't you know as it's thievin' an' robbery, an' that thievin' an' robbery leads to prison-bars an' shackle-chains ? "

" Oh, sir, I—I didn't mean——" The little voice was choked with sobs.

" Well, let this be a warnin' to you to thieve no more, or next time I shall 'ave to become angry. Now—go 'ence ! "

Dropping the rose, the child turned and hobbled away as fast as her crutch would allow, and Mr. Brimberly, having watched her out of sight, emptied his glass and took up his cigar but, finding it had gone out, flung it away. Then he sighed, and, sinking back among his cushions, closed his eyes, and was soon snoring blissfully.

But by-and-by Mr. Brimberly began to dream, a very evil dream, wherein it seemed that for many desperate deeds and crimes abominable he was chained and shackled in a dock, and the judge, donning the black cap, sentenced him to be shorn of those adornments, his whiskers In his dream it seemed that there and then the executioner advanced to his fell work—a bony hand grasped his right whisker, the deadly razor flashed, and Mr. Brimberly awoke gurgling—awoke to catch a glimpse of a hand so hastily withdrawn that it seemed to vanish into thin air.

" 'Eavens an' earth ! " he gasped, and clapping hand to cheek was relieved to find his whisker yet intact ; but for a long moment sat clutching that handful of soft and fleecy hair, staring before him in puzzled wonder, for the hand had seemed so very real he could almost feel

The Woes of Mr. Brimberly

it there yet. Presently, bethinking him to glance over
his shoulder, Mr. Brimberly gasped and goggled, for
leaning over the back of his chair was a little old man,
very slender, very upright, and very smart as to attire,
who fanned himself with a jaunty straw hat banded in
vivid crimson ; an old man whose bright, youthful eyes
looked out from a face wizened with age, while up from
his bald crown rose a few wisps of white and straggling
hair.

" 'Oly 'eavens ! " murmured Mr. Brimberly faintly.

The visitor, settling his bony elbows more comfortably, fanned himself until his sparse locks waved gently
to and fro, and, nodding, spoke these words :

> " Oh wake thee, oh wake thee, my bonny bird !
> Oh wake and sleep no more !
> Thy pretty pipe I 'aven't 'eard,
> But, lumme, how you snore ! "

Mr. Brimberly stared ; Mr. Brimberly's mouth opened,
and eventually Mr. Brimberly rose and surveyed the
intruder slowly up from glittering shoes to the dome of
his head and down again ; and Mr. Brimberly's ample
bosom surged, his eyes kindled and his whiskers bristled.

" Cheer-oh ! " nodded the Old 'un.

Mr. Brimberly blinked and pulled down his waistcoat.

" Me good man," said he, " you'll find the tradesmen's
entrance round the corner. Go away, if you please, and
go immediate—I'm prehoccupied."

" No you ain't, you're the butler, you are, I lay my
oath—

> Spoons an' forks
> An' drawin' corks.

That's your job, ain't it, chum ? "

" Chum ! " said Mr. Brimberly, in tones of horror.
" Chum ! " he repeated, grasping a handful of indignant
whisker. " Oh, outrageous ! Oh, very hobscene ! 'Ow
dare you, sir ? 'Oo are you, sir. Answer me, an'
answer—prompt ! "

The Definite Object

"Leave them cobwebs alone an' I'll tell you, matey."

"Matey!" groaned Mr. Brimberly, turning up his eyes.

"I'm the guv's familiar friend and personal pal, I am. I'm 'is adviser—confeedential, matreemonial, circumstantial, an' architect'ral. I'm 'is trainer, advance-agent, manager, an' sparrin'-partner—that's who I am. An' now, mate, 'avin' 'elped to marry 'im I've jest took a run down 'ere to see as all things is fit an' proper for 'is 'oneymoon!"

"My word, this is a mad feller, this is!" murmured Mr. Brimberly, "or else 'e's drunk!"

"Drunk!" exclaimed the Old 'un, clapping on his hat very much over one eye and glaring. "Wot—me?"

"I repeat," said Mr. Brimberly, addressing the universe in general, "I repeat as 'e is a narsty, drunken little person!"

"Person?" cried the Old 'un scowling. "Why, you perishin'——"

"'Old!" said Mr. Brimberly—"'Old, I beg! Enough 'as been said—go 'ence! 'Oo you are I do not know, wot you are I do not care, but in these regions you do not remain—your langwidge forbids an'——"

"Langwidge!" snorted the Old 'un, "why I ain't begun yet, you blinkin', fat-faced, owl-eyed piece o' sooet——"

"Your speech, sir," continued Mr. Brimberly, with calm austerity and making the most of whiskers and waistcoat, "your speech is re-dolent of slums and back-halleys. I don't know you. I don't want to know you! You are a feller! Go away, feller!"

"Feller?" snarled the Old 'un. "Why you——"

"I repeat," said Mr. Brimberly, with dignified deliberation, "I repeat as you are a very low, vulgar little feller!"

The Old 'un clenched his fists. "Right-oh!" he nodded cheerily, "that's done it! F' that I'm a-goin' t' punch ye in the perishin' eye-'ole!" and he advanced upon the

318

The Woes of Mr. Brimberly

points of his toes, shoulders hunched, and head viciously
out-thrust.

"My word!" exclaimed Mr. Brimberly, retreating
rather precipitately, "this is very discomposing, this is!
I shall have to call the perlice."

"Perlice!" snarled the Old 'un, fiercer than ever,
"you won't have nothing t' call with when I've done wi'
ye. I'm goin' t' jab ye on th' beak t' begin with, then
I'll 'ook my left t' your kidneys an' swing my right to
your p'int, an' crumple ye up with a jolt on your perishin'
solar plexus as'll stiffen you till th' day o' doom!"

"'Oly angels!" murmured Mr. Brimberly, glancing
hastily about.

"Then while you lay bathed in 'orrible gore I'm goin'
t' twist them whiskers into a 'angman's knot!"

"This is most distressing!" sighed Mr. Brimberly.

"Then," continued the Old 'un, grinding his remaining
teeth, "I'm a-goin' t' tread your face in an' dance on yer
blighted stummick. Arter that——"

"Oh, dear me!" exclaimed Mr. Brimberly, retreating
before the oncoming peril and mopping perspiring brow.
But suddenly his wandering eye was arrested by velvet
and gold braid, and lifting up his voice he called:

"William! James! Come 'ere—and come sharp!"

Two vast and splendid shapes loomed upon the scene,
supermen whose silken calves quivered with unaccus-
tomed haste; at a sign from Mr. Brimberly they seized
upon the Old 'un, and, despite ghoulish threats, solemnly
bore him off.

Down the broad sweep of drive they went, the Old 'un
pouring forth fluent curses at every step, until they came
where stood a powerful automobile, from beneath which
a pair of neatly gaitered legs protruded.

"Joe!" cried the Old 'un, apostrophising these legs,
"Joe, stop bein' a crawlin' worm—come out an' bash
these perishers for me, like a good lad!"

But even while he spoke, the footmen hauled him

The Definite Object

along, so that when Joe eventually wriggled from under the car the three were close against the great gates. The Old 'un was earnestly explaining to his captors exactly what he thought of them, of their fathers and mothers, their kith and kin, and the supermen were heeding him not the least, when a thunderbolt seemed to smite them asunder, and Joe was glancing, mild-eyed, from one splendid, supine form to the other.

"Hallo, Old 'un!" said he, "what's the matter now, you old book o' bad language, you?"

But Mr. Brimberly, somewhat shaken with his late interview, and, feeling the need of a stimulant, had just refilled the long glass when, hearing a rustle behind him, he turned and beheld a tall woman, elderly and angular, especially as to chin and elbows, which last obtruded themselves quite unpleasantly, at least, as he eyed them there was manifest disapprobation in every hair of his whiskers.

"Now I wonder," he sighed plaintively, "I wonder what under the blue expandment of 'oly 'eaven you might be, because if you 'appen to be the washing——"

"I—am—not!"

"Or the cannybal missions——"

"No—sech—thing!"

"Oh!" said Mr. Brimberly, and his gaze wandered to the elbows. "Why, then, let me hinform you——"

"Ann Angelina Trapes is me name."

"Why, then, mam, you've took the wrong turning. 'Owbeit an' notwithstanding, 'ooever you are and nevertheless, you will find the tradespeople's entrance——"

"You're the gentleman as is so obligin' as to be Mr. Ravenslee's butler, ain't you?"

"Sich is my profession," Mr. Brimberly admitted.

"I am in sole charge of these pre-mises, and so being, will ask you to withdraw 'ence immediate. I will ask——"

"An' I'll ask you, very p'inted, what you reckon you're doin' in that chair?"

320

The Woes of Mr. Brimberly

" Doin' ? "

" I'll ask you, very p'inted, why you're loafin' around wastin' your master's time ? "

" Loafing ! " cried Mr. Brimberly, very red in the face. " Loaf——"

" I also ask you, very p'inted, wherefore an' why you loaf, guzzlin' and swillin' your master's good liquor ? "

" Guzzling ! " gasped Mr. Brimberly. " Oh 'eavens, this is a houtrage, this is ! I'll——"

" It sure is ! An' so are you, wine-bibber ! "

" Wine-bib——" Mr. Brimberly choked, his round face grew purple, and he flourished pudgy fists, while Mrs. Trapes folded her cotton-gloved hands and watched him.

" Wine-bibber ! " she nodded. " An' the wine you now bib is your master's, consequently it was stole, an' bein' stole, you're a thief, an' bein' a thief——"

" Thief ! " gurgled Mr. Brimberly. " Ha, thief's a hepithet, thief is, and a hepithet's hactionable ! I'll have you indented for perjoorious expressions."

" Wine-bibber ! " she sighed. " Snake an' plunderer ! "

" Never," cried Mr. Brimberly, " never in all my days did I ever 'earken to such contoomacious contoomacity ! 'Oo are you, an' wot——"

" Hand over that bottle and what you've left o' them cigars ! "

" Woman, begone ! " he cried hoarsely. " Woman, if you don't go 'ence this very moment I'll have you persecuted with the hutmost vigour o' the law for a incorrigible female ! "

" Female ! " repeated Mrs. Trapes, and clasping herself in her long, bony arms she shuddered and smiled, though her eyes glared more stonily and her elbows suggested rapier-points, daggers, and other deadly weapons of offence.

" Female it were, I think ? " she inquired, with another grim and smiling shudder. " Now, sir, to you, I sez,

The Definite Object

debased creecher, I sez, vulgar an' dishonest loafer,
I sez, sly an' subtle serpent, I sez—return to the back
scullery wherefrom you sprang lest I seize you by the
hair of your cheeks an' bounce your silly head against the
wall—frequent, I sez!" and very slowly Mrs. Trapes
moved towards him.

Mr. Brimberly hesitated, but before those deadly
elbows he blenched, his whiskers wilted all at once, and
he retreated backwards; across the spacious drawing-
room, along the hall and down the stairs he went, his
pace ever accelerating, until, in full flight, he reached the
sanctuary of his pantry, where, having locked himself
securely in, he sank, panting, into a chair to mop his
beaded brow.

"My word!" gasped Mr. Brimberly.

CHAPTER XXXVIII

IN WHICH SOAPY TAKES UPON HIMSELF A NEW RÔLE

SOAPY was alone, which in itself was no new thing, for Soapy was a solitary soul at all times ; but just now he sat close against the rotting fence which skirted that desolation behind O'Rourke's Saloon. Moreover, it was night, and solitude profound was his. He sat on a battered and disused pail that chanced to be handy, a smouldering cigarette dangled from his thin-lipped mouth, his long hands pendulous between his knees, his pallid eyelids sleepily a-droop ; but his eyes, quick and watchful, scanned the deeper gloom of fence and dismal outbuilding, and he sat there very patient and very still. At last he stirred slightly, the cigarette quivered and was motionless again ; for, amid the shadows, he had seen a dim shape that flitted swiftly towards him. On it came, creeping swift and silent beside the fence, nearer and nearer until it resolved itself into a slender form. Then Soapy spoke :

" Hello, kid ! "

Ensued a moment of tense silence, then Spike answered, his voice unnaturally thin and high-pitched :

" That—that you, Soapy ? "

" 'S' right, kid ! "

" What you—doin' around—here ? "

" Who, me ? Y' see, I'm kind o' yearnin' for that gun you got there."

" Gun ? I—I ain't got—no gun."

" Well, kid, I know Heine's all kinds of a liar, but he tells me he's loaned you one of his, an' so——" Soapy's

323

The Definite Object

long arm shot out in the gloom, and seizing Spike's right hand he drew it near. " Why, kid," said he, " it kind o' looks like Heine told the truth for once by accident, don't it ? "

" You leggo my wrist ! "

" Right-oh, kid, right-oh ! Don't get peeved."

" Well, leggo, then ! "

" Sure ! Only this artillery ain't goin' t' be no good t' you t'-night. Ye see, Bud—ain't here. 'S' rough on ye, kid—'s' rough, but he ain't ! "

" W-what—d'ye mean ? " stammered the boy.

" I mean as you're comin' here t' plug holes in Bud's carcass it's kind o' rough on ye as there ain't goin' t' be no carcass here t' plug. Ye see, Bud's took his carcass up-town with him t'-night."

" You're a liar, Soapy—a liar ! Bud's inside, I know he is. Leggo my arm, you can't con me ! "

" 'S' right, kid, I ain't tryin'. Only I'm tellin' ye Bud's left me an Lefty t' run things here t'-night. Bud's up-town at his old man's place. I know, because—I sent him. See ? "

" You sent him—you ? Ah, come off ! You couldn't ! "

" 'S' right, kid. I got him away by a fake telegram."

The boy vented a long, quivering sigh, his whole frame relaxed, and in that instant Soapy wrenched the weapon from his loosened hold and rose. Choking with passion Spike sprang at him, but Soapy fended him off with a long arm.

" Gimme that gun ! "

" Behave, kid, behave, else I'll have t' dot ye one ! Be good an' chase off home, this ain't no place for you t'-night—nor no other time."

" Gimme that gun ! "

" No ! "

Spike ceased the useless struggle, and leaned against the fence, panting, while Soapy reseated himself upon the battered pail.

Soapy takes upon Himself a New Rôle

"What you got t' come buttin' in for?" demanded the boy. "This ain't your show, an' I guess you ain't so mighty fond o' Bud either."

"'S' right too," nodded Soapy, "no, I ain't exactly fond of him, kid—leastways I don't run t' help him if he falls, nor kiss th' place t' make it well—no, kid! But I kind o' feel that Bud's too good t' snuff it this way, or snuff it—yet!"

"Good?" said the lad bitterly, "Good—hell! He's ruined me, Soapy; he's done me in! He's come between me an'—an' Hermy. He tried t' make me think dirt of her, an' now—now I—I'm all alone; I ain't got nobody left—oh my God," and huddling to the fence, Spike broke out into a fierce and anguished sobbing, while Soapy, spinning the revolver dexterously on his finger, watched him under drooping lids.

"She was mighty good t' ye, Hermy was!" said he thoughtfully.

"Don't—ah, don't!" gasped Spike.

"An' when he spoke dirt of her, you—believed him. kid!"

"I didn't."

"You did, else you'd have been with her now. She was always good t' you, Hermy was, but you—well, you preferred Bud."

"I didn't, Soapy—God knows I didn't—only—I thought Bud would make me a champion."

"By gettin' ye soused, kid."

"Oh, I know—I know now he's only been stringin' me all along! I know now it's too late—that's why I'm goin' t' kill him."

"Kill him!" mused Soapy. "Kid, there's good killin's an' bad killin's, an' I reckon this 'ud be a good killin', maybe. But this ain't your job."

"Why—why ain't it?"

"Well, you got a sister, f'r one thing; an' besides, you ain't a killer."

The Definite Object

" You gimme that gun an' see ! " cried the lad, reaching out a hand tremulous and eager.

" When the time came, kid, 'stead o' shootin' you'd drop your gun, like that time in th' wood."

" Th' wood ! " Spike's voice dropped to a strangled whisper, and he shrank back against the fence. " You—my God !—you—saw——"

" 'S' right, kid, I was there ! An' I'm kind o' glad ye couldn't do it, glad for your sister's sake. But what I'm thinkin' is that maybe she thinks it was you—eh, kid ? "

Spike writhed and groaned.

" Eh, kid ? "

" Yes ! "

" Why, then, if I was you I'd skin off right now an' put her wise ; it may mean a whole lot t' her. Ye know where she is—go an' tell her, kid."

" I can't ! I can't—she don't want me no more, she's done wi' me, I guess I'm—oh, I'm too low-down an' rotten ! "

" Sure ! " nodded Soapy. " But she's good, an' she's a woman, an' good women are only made t' forgive, I reckon."

" But there's Geoff. I couldn't face Geoff again."

" That's because you think a heap too much about a low-down, rotten guy called Spike. I guess it's about time you began t' think about your sister f'r a change. Well, s' long, kid. I guess I'll be movin', this pail comes a bit sharp after an hour of it." So saying, Soapy rose, nodded, and strolled away, still twirling the revolver upon that long and dexterous finger. For a moment Spike stood looking after him, then, chin on breast, turned and went his solitary way across the desolate waste. But now it was Soapy who, pausing, turned to watch him safe out of sight. Scarcely had the sound of Spike's departure died away than a door opened and closed hard by, and heavy steps approached, halted suddenly, and a hoarse voice demanded, " Who's there ? "

Soapy takes upon Himself a New Rôle

" Why, this is me, Bud."

" What th' hell are ye hangin' around out here for ? " questioned M'Ginnis suspiciously.

" Countin' the stars, Bud, an' doin' th' Providence act —' midst of life we are in death ' gag."

" Aw, cut out that slush an' hike along t' Raynor's wi' me.   I got a job for you an' Heine."

Side by side they crossed the gloomy, open lot until they were come beneath a lamp at a certain bleak street corner.   Here Soapy paused and held out his hand, open to the light :

" This don't happen t' be your ring, Bud ? " he inquired, lazily.

M'Ginnis glanced at the ring upon that narrow palm, a ring wrought into the semblance of two hands that clasped each other, looked closer, drew in his breath suddenly, then straightened his shoulders and threw back his head.

" No ! " he answered, frowning into Soapy's imperturbable face, " What th' hell made you think it was ? "

" Why, ye see, Bud, it happens t' have your name scratched inside it, that's all.   But if it ain't yours, it ain't ! "   And speaking, Soapy tossed the ring back over his shoulder far out into the open lot.

For a long moment M'Ginnis stood motionless, staring back at that desolate plot of ground.   When at last he glanced towards his companion, Soapy was lighting a fresh cigarette.

CHAPTER XXXIX

THE OLD 'UN ADVISES, AND RAVENSLEE ACTS

In the rose-garden was an arbour smothered in riotous bloom and in the arbour was a divan, wide and low and voluptuously soft, meet for the repose of an invalid on a languorous afternoon, or indeed any other time. But just now the invalid reposed not at all, but sat, elbow on knee and square chin on fist, very lonely and therefore very grim.

All about him roses bloomed, filling the air with their sweetness, but he had no eyes for their beauty ; upon the table within reach of his hand were books and magazines, but he was in no mood for reading; clasped between strong, white teeth he held his favourite pipe, unlighted and cold, for tobacco had for him no savour. So he sat and scowled at the universe in general, and in particular at a robin that had boldly ventured near and was regarding him with a very round, bright eye.

"She's avoiding me!" said Ravenslee bitterly, teeth clenched upon his pipe-stem, "there's no doubt about it—damn it, she's avoiding me! And she's not happy here either!"

The robin turned his head to regard the speaker with his other eye, then fluttered his wings and flew away as the lazy quiet of the afternoon was broken by the squeak of shoe-leather, and glancing up, Ravenslee beheld the Old 'un.

"What cheer, guv," said he, "greetin's doo and how's the invalid ? "

The Old 'un Advises, and Ravenslee Acts

"Invalid!" repeated Ravenslee, scowling again. "I'm no invalid."

"Spoke like a true-bred game-cock, s' help me!"

"I'm as right as rain, physically, Old 'un, but——"

"Talkin' o' physic, guv," said the old man, seating himself and nodding brightly, "talkin' o' physic, the physic as set you on your pins again was love, guv—love!"

"But it so happens——"

"Wait a bit, I ain't done, guv! 'Ere's me, a old cove as 'as lived 'ears an' 'ears an' 'ears an' 'ears longer 'n you, so nacherally I'm a powerful lot fuller o' th' wisdom o' life than you, 'specially in matters o' th' 'eart, guv. Now me, 'avin' 'elped you into th' matrimonial ring, as you might say, 'ave took your 'appiness under my wing, an' guv, I don't like the way you're shapin'——"

"But you see——"

"'Old 'ard, guv, let a pore old cove get a word in for a change. Now there's you an' 'er, your fair young spouse, both up to each other's weight, sound in wind an' limb an' meant for j'y—what I want is t' see you come to a clinch! This ain't no time for sparrin' an' out-fightin'—yet 'ere you are a feintin' at each other from opposite corners——"

"But——"

"'Arf a mo', guv, 'arf a mo'—gimme a chance for a occasional word! An' don't frown, guv, don't frown at a pore old cove. Ye see, there's jest three blokes in this 'ard world as my old 'eart warms to, an' one on 'em's Joe, an' t'other un's you, an' t'other un's 'er—which ain't a bloke. Lord, guv, what a soft armful o' beauty! 'Ow warm an' cuddlesome! Oh, guv, what a waist! What lips! What——"

"Old 'un, for heaven's sake shut up! D' you think I'm blind? D' you think——"

"Guv, I dunno wot t' think! 'Ere's you with your 'ead in your 'ands, an' there's 'er sighin' an' sighin'——"

The Definite Object

" Sighing ? Where ? When ? Why——"

" Sighin' an' sighin', guv, so soft an' pretty—I 'eard 'er ! Also she wep'—I seen 'er——"

" Where ? "

" An' 'er tears, guv, them pearly tears went t' my 'eart, an' nobody t' put an arm round that waist, nor kiss them sweet lips, nor soothe them tears away :

> Oh, alone she sat sighin' by a green willer tree,
> With 'er 'and on 'er bosom, 'er 'ead on 'er knee,
> Weepin' willer, willer, willer, my garlan' shall be.

So, guv, I ax you, man to man, why, oh why, are ye neglectin' your fair young spouse ? An', guv, I only ax because your 'appiness an' 'ers is mine—s' help me ! "

" How if it's the other way about, Old 'un ? Suppose she avoids me ? "

" Why, lumme, guv ! 'Tis a sure sign she needs persoot. Remember this :

> 'Im as would lovely woman woo
> 'E lovely woman must persoo,
> For if 'e don't, 'tis plain as plain
> That feller 'e will woo in vain.

An', guv, I've only took th' liberty o' sayin' this because my pore old bowels yearns to ye—both on ye. Persoot's the word, guv—per-soot ! "

The Old 'un nodded, rose and creaked away ; and Ravenslee, looking after him, scowled no longer, but rising, sauntered across the trim garden to where there was a lily-pool, and leaning over the marble rim, stared down into the placid water.

Now as the Old 'un went his way, there met him a little girl, very neat and tidy, who sang to herself in a small, happy voice, and tapped along on a crutch, but, beholding the Old 'un, his dazzling shoes, his rakish hat, she stood silent all at once, glancing up wistfully into that fierce, battered old face.

" Lumme—crutches ! " he exclaimed.

330

The Old 'un Advises, and Ravenslee Acts

"No, please—only one, sir!" she answered, dropping him a little, old-fashioned curtsy.

"Crikey!" said he, staring, "so young, so tender, an'—a game leg! A little angel wi' a broke wing—lumme!"

So Age and Youth stared at each other, and she, being a child, was quick to heed that the eyes so bright beneath their hoary brows were kindly eyes, and the smile upon the grim old mouth was very reassuring, wherefore she smiled also.

"Only one crutch, sir," she repeated. "An' the doctor says as I won't want it much longer, sir." Here, dropping another curtsy, she held up for his acceptance a bunch of wild flowers.

"What—f' me, little maid?" he inquired.

"Yes, please, sir."

"Why, bless—bless your lovin' little 'eart!" quavered the old man, and stooped to touch her rosy cheek with a hand gnarled and scarred with much hard punching, yet a very gentle hand indeed. "God bless that little game leg, but pretty flowers 'ud be wasted on a old bloke like me. You take 'em to th' guv, see—over there—that tall chap leanin' over th' pool. But first gimme a—a kiss instead, will ye, little lass?"

"I'd like to, sir."

And when the Old 'un had kissed and been kissed right heartily, he pointed to Ravenslee's distant, lounging figure, winked, nodded, and squeaked away.

Thus it was that Ravenslee, absorbed in thought, was presently roused by the quick, light tapping of the little crutch, and glanced up.

"Oh!" she cried softly. The flowers fell, and lay neglected as, clasping her hands, she stared up at him in radiant-eyed wonder.

"Welcome, Highness!" said he, and bowed.

"Oh, it's the Prince—my dear Prince! Oh, goody!" and she hastened towards him, then stopped all at once, puzzled and abashed because of his elegant attire. Per-

ceiving which he reached out and drew her down by him
on the marble seat beside the pool.

" Why this sudden change of demeanour, Princess ? "
he inquired. " What's the matter ? "

" You're—you're so different, sir—so different an'
grand in all them cute clo'es, sir."

" Am I, dear ? But I'm just the same inside, you
know. And, for heaven's sake, Princess, do not call
me ' sir.' "

" But the big gentleman that belongs here an' has all
these lovely flowers an' everything—he says as I must
always say ' sir.' "

" Big gentleman ? "

" Yes, the big, soft gentleman with the cute little curls
on his cheeks."

" Oh—him ! " said Ravenslee, laughing suddenly.
" Indeed a very just description, Princess. But you
don't have to worry about him any more, he's gone."

" Gone ? For good ? "

" For very good indeed ! "

" Doesn't all this beautiful, beautiful place belong t'
him any more ? "

" Never any more."

" Have you come here 'stead of him ? Come t' stay ? "

" Yes."

" An' can I pick a rose t' kiss sometimes ? "

" As many as you like."

" Oh," sighed the child rapturously, nestling within
his arm, " isn't that just—fine ! I guess this sure is
the Beautiful City of Perhaps, after all ! "

" I wonder ? "

" Oh, but I'm sure it is—now th' gentleman's gone I
just know it is ! "

" What makes you so sure ? "

" Everything ! 'Cause, you see, Prince, my daddy
don't have t' be away all day any more. An' mumsey
don't have t' sew late, nights, any more. An' when we

332

came into the cute little house where we live—there was the doll that says 'mamma' jest waitin' f' me. An' there was a big box o' candies, an' a doll-carriage with real rubber on th' wheels—jest like we used to talk about. So, you see, this must be Perhaps at last, an' I'm so— so happy—only——" Hazel sighed.

" Only what ? "

" I do wish Hermy could find her way here too ; she used t' be so tired sometimes."

" You mean that you would like to find Princess Nobody, I guess."

" Oh, but I can't ! I used to look an' look for her every day till th' gentleman said she wasn't here, an' told me never t' come near th' big house any more."

" But he's gone, and you never had me to help you."

" Oh, will you—will you help me right now ? " she pleaded.

" Surest thing you know ! " he nodded, " your hand, Princess."

So, hand in hand, he led her, suiting his long legs to hers, along shady walks, up terrace steps, across smooth lawns and so to the great house. Here Hazel paused to question him further concerning " the gentleman," but Ravenslee laughed, and seating her upon his shoulder bore her into the house.

And here, in her housekeeper's room, surrounded by many dusty bill-files and stacks of account-books, they presently found Mrs. Trapes, whose hawk-eye viewed bills and tradesmen's books while she frowned and muttered such comments as : " Rogues ! " " Thieves ! " "Scand'lous ! " " Wicked ! " Until, glancing up, her sharp features softened, and she smiled up into the child's happy face.

" So Hazel's found ye, has she, Mr. Geoffrey ? An' talkin' o' her, you've sure made the Bowkers a happy fam'ly. But, my land, Mr. Ravenslee, the scand'lous prices as th' tradespeople has been allowed t' charge you these last six months! Here's th' butcher—listen t' this——"

"Heaven forbid, Mrs. Trapes! Rather let that butcher listen to you—miserable wretch!"

"An' there's the milkman—that milkman's cows ought t' blush at th' sound o' your name! Here's his accounts for the last six months, an' I've found——"

"Have you, Mrs. Trapes? We're trying to find Hermione. Where is she?"

"Oh, she's in her room—laying down, I guess."

"Not," inquired Ravenslee—"not—er—in bed, is she?"

"Mr. Geoffrey, I don't know, I'm busy. Go an' see for yourself. She's your wife, ain't she?"

"Why, since you ask, I—er—hardly know," he answered a little ruefully. "Anyway, found she shall be."

With the child perched upon his shoulder, he strode upstairs and along wide corridors, whose deep carpets gave forth no sound, and so reached a certain door. Here he hesitated a moment, then knocked with imperious hand.

"Come!" called that voice whose soft inflection had always thrilled him, but never as it did now, as, turning the handle, he entered his wife's chamber.

Hermione was standing before a long mirror, and she neither turned nor looked from the radiant vision it reflected, her eyes, her attention, all the feminine soul of her being just then fixed and centred upon the tea-gown she was trying on. Such a garment as she had gloated over in the store-windows, yearned for, but never thought to possess.

"Ann," she sighed, "oh Ann, isn't it exquisite! Isn't it a perfect dream! Of course it needs a wee bit of alteration here and there, but I can do that. Isn't it good of him to have bought it without saying a word! And there are heaps of dresses and robes and—and every-

thing! A complete trousseau, Ann dear—think of it!
I wonder how he knew my size——"

"Oh, I just guessed it, my dear," answered Ravenslee
in the voice of a much-experienced husband.

Hermione gasped, and turning, stared at him wide-
eyed, seeing only him, conscious only of him; and he,
lifting Hazel to the floor, seated himself upon her bed,
and, crossing his legs, eyed her flushed loveliness with a
matter-of-fact air.

"Really," he continued, "I don't see that it needs
any alteration; perhaps the sleeves might be a trifle
shorter—show a little more arm. But those flounces
and things are perfect! I hope all the other things fit
as well?"

Hermione flushed deeper still and caught her breath.

"Oh Hermy," said a soft, pleading little voice, "won't
you see me, please?"

Hermione started, her long lashes drooped suddenly,
and then—then, forgetful of costly lace, of dainty ruffles
and ribbons, she was on her knees and had the child close
in her arms. And beholding the clasp of those round,
white arms, the lovely, down-bent head, and all the tender,
craving, inborn motherhood of her, Ravenslee held his
breath, and into his eyes came a light of reverent adora-
tion.

Presently he rose and left them together, but as he
went, the light was in his eyes still.

CHAPTER XL

CONCERNING A HANDFUL OF PEBBLES

" AND so," said Hermione, as she waved good-bye to Hazel, who stood in the cottage doorway with Mrs. Bowker—a Mrs. Bowker no longer faded—" you didn't forget even the doll that says ' mamma ? ' "

" It was such a little thing ! " he answered.

" What a—man you are ! " she said softly.

" Just that, Hermione," he answered, " and—frightfully human ! " She was silent. " Do you know what I mean ? " he demanded, glancing at her averted face.

" Yes ! " she answered without looking round. So they walked for a while in silence.

Suddenly he seized her hand and drew it through his arm.

" Hermione," he said gently, " I want my wife."

She still kept her head averted, but he could feel how she was trembling.

" And you think——" she began softly.

" That I have been patient long enough. I have waited and hoped because——"

" Because you are so generous, so kind—such a man ! " she said softly and with head still averted.

" And yet since I have been well again you have kept me at arm's length. Dear, you—love me still, don't you ? "

" Love you ? " she repeated. " Love you ? " For a moment she turned and looked up at him, then drew her arm from his and walked on with head averted once more.

336

Concerning a Handful of Pebbles

So they entered the rose-garden, and coming to the lily-pool leaned there side by side.

" Hermione," said he, staring down into the water, " if you really love me, why do you hate to kiss me ? Why do you hardly suffer me to touch you ? And you've never even called me by my name that I remember ! "

" Geoffrey ! " she breathed, " and I—love you to touch me ! And I don't hate to kiss you, Geoffrey dear."

" Then why do you keep me at arm's length ? "

" Do I ? " she questioned softly, gazing down at the lily-pads.

" You know you do. Why ? "

" Well—because."

" Because what ? "

" Oh well, just—because."

" Hermione—tell me."

" Well, everything is so strange—so unreal ! This great house, the servants, all the beautiful clothes you bought me ! To have so much of everything after having to do with so very little—it's all so wonderful and—dreadful ! "

" Dreadful ? "

" You are so—dreadfully rich ! "

" Is that the reason you keep me at such a distance ? Is that why you avoid me——"

" Avoid you ? "

" Yes, dear. You've done it very sweetly and delicately, but you have avoided me lately. Why ? "

Hermione didn't answer.

" And you haven't touched any of the monthly allowance I make you," he went on, frowning a little, " not one cent. Why, Hermione ? "

Hermione was silent.

" Tell me ! "

Still she was silent, only she bent lower above the pool, and drew farther from him, whereat his pale cheek flushed and his frown grew blacker.

The Definite Object

And presently as he scowled down into the water, she stole a look at him, and when she spoke, though the words were light, the quiver in her voice belied them.

"Invalid dear, if you want to be angry with me, wait—till you're a little stronger."

Ravenslee stooped and picked up a handful of small pebbles that chanced to lie loose.

"Wife dear," said he, "I'm as well and strong as ever I was. But I've asked you several questions which I mean you to answer, so I am going to give you until I have pitched all these pebbles into the water, and then——"

Hermione glanced up swiftly.

"Then?" she questioned.

"Why, then, if you haven't answered I shall—take matters into my own hands. One!" and a pebble splashed into the pool.

"What do you want to know?"

"Two! Why haven't you condescended to take your allowance?"

"Dear, I—I didn't need it, and even if I had I—oh, I couldn't take it—yet!"

"Three! Why not?"

"Because you have given me so much already, and I—have given you—nothing."

"Four! Why—haven't you?"

"Oh—well—because!"

"Five! What does 'because' mean, this time?"

"It means—just—because!"

"Six! Seven! Eight! Why have you avoided me lately?"

Hermione was silent, watching him with troubled eyes while he slowly pitched the pebbles into the pool, counting as they fell.

"Nine! Ten! Eleven! Twelve! Why do you keep me at arm's length?"

"I don't—I—I—you won't let me——" she said, a

338

Concerning a Handful of Pebbles

little breathlessly, while one by one he let the pebbles fall into the pool, counting inexorably as they fell.

" Thirteen ! Fourteen ! Fifteen—and that's the last ! " As he spoke he turned towards her, and she, reading something of his purpose in his eyes, turned to flee, felt his long arms about her, felt herself swung up and up, and so lay crushed and submissive in his fierce embrace as he turned and began to bear her across the garden.

Then, being helpless, she began to plead with him. " Ah, don't, don't—dear ! Geoffrey ! Put me down ! Where are you taking me ? If any one sees us——"

" Let them," he muttered grimly, " you're my wife ! "

So he bore her across the garden into the arbour, and laying her upon the divan, sank beside it on his knees, panting a little.

" A little weak—still ! " said he, " but not so bad—you're no scraggy sylph, thank heaven ! Hermione—look at me ! " But she turned and hid her face against him, for his clasp was close about her still. So he stooped and kissed her hair, her glowing cheek, her soft, white neck, and, in that instant—wonder of wonders—her arms were round him, strong, passionate arms that clung and drew him close—then strove wildly to hold him away.

" Loose me ! " she cried, " let me go ! Geoffrey—husband, be generous and let me go ! " But he lifted her head—back and back across his arm, until beneath her long lashes her eyes looked into his.

" Hermione, when will you—be my wife ? "

Against him he could feel the sweet hurry of her breathing, and stooping he spoke again, lip to lip.

" Hermione, when will you be my wife ? "

But, even while he kissed her, between those quivering, parted lips came a murmur of passionate prayer and pleading :

" Oh my love, wait—wait ! Let me tell you—ah, loose me and let me tell you."

339

The Definite Object

Slowly his hold relaxed, and, twisting in his arms, she slipped upon her knees beside him, and, crouching close, hid her face against him.

"Beloved," she whispered quickly, breathlessly, "oh, dear man that I love so—there is something between us, a shadow of shame and horror that is with me day and night and always must be While you lay sick it was there, torturing me with every moan and sigh you uttered. It is with me wherever I go—it is between us now—yes, now, even while I strain you in my arms like this. I have watched you grow strong and well again, I've seen the love in your eyes and I've yearned to be to you— all you would have me, but because of this shadow I— dare not. Ah, God! how can I be wife to you when—let this answer for me." And she placed in Ravenslee's hand a coat-button whereto a piece of cloth had adhered. "Dear love, I saw you throw it away," she explained, "and I searched and searched until I found it."

"Why ? "

"Because I knew you would soon ask me—this question, and I have kept it for my answer. Ah, God ! how can I be wife to you when my brother would have killed you—murdered you ! "

Ravenslee hurled the button far away, then lifting Hermione's bowed head, spoke very tenderly.

"How does all this affect our love, Hermione, except to show me you are even sweeter and nobler than I had thought ? And as for the shadow, it is—only a shadow, after all."

"But it is my shame ! " she answered, "You might have had for wife the sister of a thief, but not—oh God ! —not the sister of a would-be murderer. If—if I came to you now I should come in shame—ah, Geoffrey, don't shame me ! "

"God forbid ! " he murmured.

Close, close she clasped him, hiding her face against him, kissing and kissing the rough cloth of his coat.

340

Concerning a Handful of Pebbles

" Oh Geoffrey," she murmured, " how we do love each other ! "

" So much, Hermione, that I will never—claim you until you are ready to come to me of your own will. But, dear, I am only a man—how long must I wait ? "

" Give me time," she pleaded, " with time the horror may grow less. Let me go away for a while—a little while. Let me find Arthur——"

" No," he answered, frowning, " you sha'n't do that, there will be no need—to-morrow I go to fetch him."

" To bring him—here ? "

" Why, of course. You see, I intend him to go to college——"

Hermione rose and, coming to the entrance of the arbour, leaned there.

" Why, Hermione—dear love—you're crying ! What is it ? "

" Nothing," she answered, bowing her face upon her arm, " only—I think—if you ask me again—I can't—keep you—waiting—very long ! "

CHAPTER XLI

OF A PACKET OF LETTERS

M'GINNIS jerked aside the roll-top desk, and falling on his knees before a small but massive safe built into the wall behind, set the combination and swung open the heavy door, talking to his companion as he did so, and quite unconscious of the pale face that watched him through the dingy window.

"That dam' Soapy's gettin' ugly," he was saying, "an' it don't do t' get ugly with me, Heine boy! Soapy thinks he's smart Alec all right, but I guess I'm some smarter. Why, I got evidence enough in here t' 'lectrocute a dozen Soapys."

"So?" said Heine, chewing on his cigar and peering into the safe. "Say, what's all them tied up in sassy blue ribbon, Bud?"

"These?" said M'Ginnis, and he took out a bundle of letters, turning them over in his big hands.

"Skirt—hey, Bud?"

"Sure thing!" he nodded, and as he stared down at this packet, how should he guess how tense and rigid had become the lounging form in the darkness beyond the window, of the wide glare of watchful eyes or of the sudden quiver of a smouldering cigarette?

"Yes, a girl's letters, Heine! An' a hell of a lot of 'em. I dunno why I keep 'em, but—oh, hell!" So saying, he tossed the letters back again and turned to his companion. "Hand over that dope!" he commanded, and Heine passed over a bundle of papers, which M'Ginnis carefully slipped into a certain compartment.

342

Of a Packet of Letters

As he did so, Heine spun round upon his heel. " Gee-whiz ! " he exclaimed, " you shook me that time, Soapy ! Where 've you been blown in from ? "

" An' what th' hell are you nosin' around here for, anyway ? " snarled M'Ginnis, shutting the heavy safe with a fierce slam. " Since you've come in you can get out again—right now ! "

Soapy seated himself upon a corner of the desk, and placidly breathed out two spirals of cigarette smoke.

" Heard about Hermy being married, Bud ? " he inquired.

" Married ? You're a liar ! Hermy married ! "

" 'S' right ! " nodded Soapy, " she's married th' million-aire-guy as got shot—you know—got shot in that wood. You'll remember, Bud ? "

M'Ginnis sank into a chair, and fell to biting his nails, staring blindly before him.

" Is — this — straight goods ? " he inquired thickly, without altering his gaze.

" Sure ! Ye see she nursed him through his sickness, Bud—kind of did the piller-smoothin' an' brow-strokin' act. Oh, I guess she comforted him quite some."

M'Ginnis stared before him, worrying his nails with sharp, white teeth.

" Ravenslee's a well man again, I hear, an' they're honeymoonin' at his place on the Hudson—devotion ain't the word, Bud ! 'S' funny," said Soapy, " but the bullet as downed this guy drove Hermy into his arms. 'S' funny, ain't it, Bud ? "

With a hoarse, inarticulate cry that was scarcely human M'Ginnis sprang from his chair, his quivering fists up-flung. For a moment he stood thus, striving vainly for utterance, then wrenched loose his neckerchief, while Soapy methodically lighted a new cigarette from the butt of its predecessor.

" Easy, Bud, easy ! " he remonstrated gently when M'Ginnis's torrent of frenzied threats and curses had

343

The Definite Object

died down somewhat, "If you go on that way, you'll go off—in a fit or somethin', an' I shouldn't like t' see ye die—that way!"

"Up th' river, is he?" panted M'Ginnis.

"'S' right, Bud, up th' river in his big house—with her. I——"

"Is he, by——"

"A dandy place f' honeymoonin', Bud!"

"Loan me your gun, Soapy. I'll get him, by God if I have t' shoot him in her arms! Loan me y'r gun!"

"I guess not, Bud, no, I guess not. I'd feel kind o' lonesome without th' feel of it. Ask Heine, he'll loan you his, it's gettin' t' be quite a habit with him. Ain't it, Heine?"

M'Ginnis sat awhile glaring down at his clutching right hand, then he rose, and opening his desk took thence a heavy revolver and slipped it inside his coat. "You're comin' with me, Heine," said he, "I'll want you."

"Sure thing, Bud," nodded Heine, chewing his cigar, "but what about lettin' Soapy tag along too."

"Soapy," said M'Ginnis, striding to the door—"Soapy can go t' hell right now."

"Why then, Bud," drawled Soapy, "I'll sure meet you —later. S' long."

Left alone, Soapy's languor gave place to swift action In two strides, it seemed, he was in the saloon, had beckoned the quick-eyed bar-tender aside, and put the question :

"Where's the kid, Jake?"

The bar-tender lifted an eyebrow and jerked a thumb upwards. "Shut-eye," he nodded, and turned back to his multifarious duties.

Up a narrow stair sped Soapy, and opening one of the numerous doors, crossed to a truckle-bed, wherefrom a tousled head upreared itself.

"Who th'——"

"Say, kid, are ye drunk, or only asleep?"

344

Of a Packet of Letters

"Whatcher want, Soapy? You lemme be. Whatcher want?" began Spike drowsily.

"Nothin' much, kid, only Bud an' Heine's gone to shoot up y'r sister's husband."

"Husband!" cried Spike, drowsy no longer. "Husband—say, d'ye mean Geoff?"

"That's who, kid. You was crackin' on t' me about wantin' t' make good—well, here's y'r chance. Bud aims t' get there 'bout midnight—up th' river, you know—so you got two hours. You'll have t' go some t' get in first, but I guess you can do it."

"I will if it kills me!" cried Spike, springing towards the door.

"Hold on, kid! you'll need some mazuma, maybe. Here's a ten-spot. It'll be more useful t' you than me after t'-night, I reckon. So get your hooks onto it; an' now—beat it!"

Without more words Spike snatched the money, crammed it into his pocket, and running down the stairs, was gone.

Then, after having lighted another cigarette, Soapy descended to M'Ginnis's dingy office, where, having dragged away the desk, he brought a chair and sat with his ear against the safe, turning the combination lock with long, delicate fingers. To and fro he turned it, very patiently, hearkening to the soft clicks the mechanism gave forth, while the cigarette smouldered between his pallid lips. Soapy, among other accomplishments, was a yegg-man renowned in the profession, and very soon the heavy door swung softly back, and Soapy became lost in study. Money there was and valuables of many kinds; these he didn't trouble with, but to the papers he gave a scrupulous attention. Sometimes as he read, his white eyelids fluttered somewhat, and sometimes the dangling cigarette quivered. Presently he arose, and bore these many papers to the sheet-iron upon which stood the rusty stove. Here he piled them and set them

345

alight, and stood watching until they were reduced to a heap of charred ash. Then, returning to the safe, he took out a bundle of letters tied up in a faded blue ribbon, and seating himself at M'Ginnis's desk he slipped off the ribbon and, very methodically, began to read these letters one after the other.

But as he read the humble entreaties, the passionate pleading of those written words, blotted and smeared with the bitter tears of a woman's poignant shame and anguish, Soapy's pendant cigarette fell to the floor, and lay there smouldering and forgotten, and his lips were drawn back from sharp, white teeth—pallid lips contorted in a grin the more awful because of the two great drops that welled from the fierce, half-closed eyes. Every letter he read, and every word ; then, very methodically, set them back within the faded blue ribbon, and sat staring down at them with eyes wider open than usual—eyes that saw back into the past. And as he sat thus, staring at what had been, he repeated a sentence to himself over and over again at regular intervals, speaking with a soft inflection none had ever heard from him before:

" Poor little Maggie—poor little kid ! "

CHAPTER XLII

" Past eleven o'clock, dear ! " said Hermione.

" Still so early ? " sighed Ravenslee.

They were sitting alone in the fire-glow, so near that by moving his hand he could touch her where she sat curled up in the great arm-chair ; but he did not reach out his hand, because they were alone and in the fire-glow, and Hermione had never seemed quite so alluring.

" How cosy a fire is—and how unnecessary ! " she sighed contentedly.

" I'm English enough to love a fire, especially when it is unnecessary," he answered.

" English, dear ? "

" My mother was English, that's why I was educated in England."

" Your mother ! How she must have loved you."

" I suppose she d'd, but, you see, she died when I was a baby."

" Poor lonely mite ! " Here her hand came out impulsively to caress his coat-sleeve, and to be prisoned there by two other hands, to be lifted and pressed to burning lips ; whereat she grew all rosy in the fire-glow.

" I suppose," said he, the words coming a little unevenly, " it would be too much to ask my wife to—come a little—nearer ? "

" Nearer ? Why, Geoffrey dear, our chairs are touching now."

" Our chairs ? Why, yes—so they are ! I suppose,"

347

The Definite Object

sighed he—" I suppose it would be breaking my word to my wife if I happened to kiss my wife ? "

" Why, Geoffrey—of course it would ! "

" Yes, I feared so ! " he nodded, and kissed her hand instead, and there fell a silence.

" How heavenly it is ! " she whispered softly, leaning a little nearer to him.

" Heavenly ! " he answered, leaning a little nearer to her and watching the droop of her lashes.

" So—so quiet and—peaceful ! " she added, drawing away again, conscious of his look.

" Horribly ! " he sighed.

" Geoffrey ! "

" Quiet and peace," he explained, " may hold such an infinitude of possibilities impossible of realisation to a husband who is bound by promises, that it is apt to be a little—trying."

Hermione did not speak, but drew his hand to be caressed by the soft oval of a cheek and touched by the velvet of shy lips.

" And yet," he went on, staring resolutely at the fire, " I wouldn't change this for anything else the world could offer me ! "

" Bear with me—a little longer, dear ! " she murmured.

" As long as you will, Hermione, providing——"

" Well, my Geoffrey dear ? "

" That it is only—a little longer."

" You don't think I'm very silly, do you, dear ? " she inquired, staring into the fire.

" No, not very ! "

" Oh ! " she said softly, glancing at him reproachfully. " You don't think me cruel ? "

" Not very," he answered, kissing her hand again.

" Dear Geoffrey, you don't think I'm very selfish, do you ? " she questioned wistfully.

" No—never that ! " he answered, keeping his gaze averted.

348

How Ravenslee broke his Word, and Why

" Because if——"

" If ? " said he.

" If it is hard for you——"   The soft voice faltered.

" Yes, Hermione ? "

" If you really think I'm—cruel and—silly, you—needn't wait—any longer—if you wish——"

His arms were about her, drawing her near, clasping her ever closer, and she held him away no more ; but beholding her wistful eyes, the plaintive droop of her vivid mouth and all the voiceless pleading of her, he loosed her and turned away.

" I love you so much, Hermione—so much, that your will shall be my will."

She rose, and leaning against the carved mantel stared down into the fire.   When at last she spoke there was a note in her voice he had never heard before.

" Geoffrey dear, this world is a very bad world for a lonely girl, and sometimes a very hateful world, and I have been lonely nearly all my life—and I didn't think there were such men as you ; I didn't think any man could love so unselfishly.   All my life I shall treasure the recollection of this hour—yes, always ! always ! "

Then she turned, and, ere he knew, was on her knees before him, had twined soft arms about his neck, and was looking up at him through shining tears.

" Yes, I'm crying a little !   I don't do it often, dear —tears don't easily come with me.   But now I'm crying because—oh, because I'm so proud—so proud to have won such a wonderful love.   Good-night—good-night ! Oh, break your word for once—kiss me, my husband ! "

So while she knelt to him thus, he kissed her until she sighed and stirred in his embrace.   Then she rose, and hand in hand they crossed the room, and he opened the door.   For a blissful moment they stood there, silent in the shadows ; but when he would have kissed her again, she laughed at him through her tears and fled from him up the wide stairway.

349

CHAPTER XLIII

HOW SPIKE GOT EVEN

A CLOCK in the hall without struck midnight; but Ravenslee sat on long after the silvery chime had died away, his chin sunk on broad chest, his eyes staring blindly at the fading embers, lost in profound but joyful meditation. Once he turned to look where she had stood beside the mantel, and once he reached out to touch the thrice-blessed chair that had held her.

The curtains stirred and rustled at the open window behind him; but he sat looking into the flickering fire, seeing there pictures of the future, and the future was full of a happiness beyond words, for in every picture Hermione moved.

All at once he started, and glanced swiftly round, his lounging attitude changing to one of watchful alertness, for he had heard a sound that drew rapidly nearer—the hiss and pant of breath drawn in quick gasps. Silently he arose, and turned to see the curtains swing apart, and a shapeless Something stagger forward and fall heavily. Then he reached out to the switch beside the hearth, and the room was flooded with brilliant light; the figure kneeling just inside the swaying curtains uttered a strangled cry, and threw up a hand before his face, a hand dark with spattering blood.

"Oh Geoff—oh Geoff!" panted Spike, "I ain't come thievin' this time—honest t' God, I ain't!"

"Why, you're hurt! What's the matter?"

"They see me down th' road as I came, an' shot me;

350

but this ain't nothin'. Out th' lights, Geoff! Out 'em
—quick!"

But Ravenslee had crossed the room, had seized the
lad's arm, and was examining the ugly graze that bled
so freely.

"That ain't nothin'. Douse th' lights, Geoff! Out
'em quick; Bud's coming here close behind—Bud and
Heine, they mean t' plug you. Oh, put out th' lights!"

Instinctively Ravenslee turned, but even as he did so
Spike uttered a hoarse cry. "No ye don't, Bud—not
this time, by God!" and sprang upon the form that
towered between the curtains. Came the sound of fierce
scuffling, a deafening report, and running forward Ravenslee caught Spike as he staggered back; heard a rush and
trample of feet along the terrace, the sound of blows and
fierce curses behind the swaying curtains; heard the
Spider's fierce shout and Joe's deep roar, two more
shots in rapid succession, and the swift patter of feet in
flight and pursuit.

"How is it, Spike? Are you hurt, old chap?"

But Spike just then was beyond words, so Ravenslee
bore the swooning boy to a settee, and laying him there,
began to search hastily for the wound.

But now the door was flung wide, and Hermione was
beside him.

"Geoffrey—oh, my love! Have they hurt you?"

"No, dear—thanks to Spike here!"

"Arthur! Oh, thank God! Did he——"

"Took the bullet meant for me, Hermione. I owe
your brother my life!"

She was down on her knees, and very soon her skilful
fingers had laid bare the ugly wound in the lad's white
arm. But now came Mrs. Trapes, looking taller and
bonier than ever in a long, very woolly garment, and
while she aided Hermione to bandage the wound, Ravenslee brought water and brandy, and very soon Spike sighed
and opened his eyes.

The Definite Object

"Hello, Hermy!" he said faintly. "Don't worry, I'm all O.K. Bud shot me, an' I'm glad, because now I can ask you t' forgive me. Y' see, he'd have got old Geoff sure if it hadn't been for me, so you—you will forgive me, won't you?"

For answer, Hermione bent and kissed his pallid cheek.

"I'll go and 'phone for the doctor," said Ravenslee.

"Which," said Mrs. Trapes, "I done ten minutes ago, Mr. Geoffrey. Doctor'll be right along."

Ravenslee turned to Spike. "How are you now, old fellow?"

"Only a bit sick-like. But say, Geoff—I know I played it low down on you, but—will you—shake an' try t' forget it?"

Ravenslee took and held the boy's outstretched hand.

"I think we're going to be better friends than ever, Spike!" he answered.

"Good!" said Spike, smiling wearily. "But say, Geoff—dear old Geoff—if I got t' die, I don't mind—because I guess this makes us quits at last—don't it, Geoff?"

CHAPTER XLIV

RETRIBUTION

HALF-STUNNED by a blow from Joe's mighty fist, M'Ginnis saw Heine felled by Spider, who, having promptly and scientifically kicked him unconscious, snatched the revolver from his lax fingers and turned to pursue. As he came, M'Ginnis fired rapidly but, dazed by the blow, his aim was wild. So he turned and ran, with the Spider in hot pursuit. The moon was down and it was very dark, and soon M'Ginnis found himself in the denser gloom of trees. On he ran, twisting and doubling, on and on, until spent and breathless, he paused to hearken. Far away, voices shouted to each other—voices that gradually grew more distant; so, in a while, having caught his breath, M'Ginnis went on again. But the wood was full of noises—strange rustlings and sudden, soft night-sounds, and at every sound the fugitive paused to listen, finger on trigger. And ever as he went the wild blood throbbed and pulsed within his brain, sounding now like the pad-pad of pursuing feet that would not be shaken off, and again like a voice that mumbled and muttered querulous words in the air about him, and at such times he glanced round upon the dark, but the words would not be stilled.

" She's married—married—married ! You drove her into his arms—you did—you did—you did ! And he's alive still and with her, alive—alive—alive ! "

And sometimes, as he stumbled along through that place of gloom, he cursed bitterly beneath his breath, and sometimes he ground sweating jaws since needs must he hearken to that taunting devil-voice.

353

The Definite Object

" Alive and with his wife beside him—alive! And yours the fault—yours—yours! Your shot at Spike so near the house lost you the game—lost—lost! Your shot at Spike was a call for help—saved the life of the man you came to kill! Your shot at Spike lost you the game—lost—lost! "

So, followed by the pad-pad of running feet, haunted by the querulous demon-voice, M'Ginnis stumbled out upon the road—a lonely road at most times, but quite desolate at this hour. The fugitive hastened along, dogged by sounds that none but he might hear. Yet to him these sounds were dreadfully real, so real that once, goaded to a paroxysm of blind fury, he whirled about and fired wildly—a shot that seemed to split asunder the deep night-silence filling it with a thousand echoes. Once more he turned and ran, ran until his breath laboured painfully and the sweat ran from him, but ever the sounds were close about him. At last he beheld lights that moved, and reaching a wayside halt clambered aboard a late trolley, and crouched as far from the light as possible. But even so, his disordered dress, his pallor, and the wild glare of his eyes drew the idle glances of the scanty passengers.

" Looks like you'd been through th' mill, bo' ! " said one, a great, rough fellow, but meeting M'Ginnis's answering glare, he quailed and shrank away.

Dawn was at hand when at last he reached O'Rourke's saloon, and letting himself in, strode into the bar. The place was deserted at this hour, but from a room hard by came the sound of voices, hoarse laughter, and the rattle of chips that told a poker-game was still in progress.

Scowling, M'Ginnis stood awhile to listen. Then lifting the flap of the bar, passed through the narrow door beyond, along the passage and so to that dingy office, from the open door of which a light streamed.

Scowling still, M'Ginnis strode in, then stood suddenly still, lifted his right hand toward his breast, and paused

354

Retribution

as Soapy, turning about in the swing-chair, took a heavy, ivory-handled revolver from where it had lain on the desk beside a packet of letters tied up in a faded blue ribbon.

"Lock th' door, Bud—lock th' door!" said he softly. "So!" he nodded, as M'Ginnis obeyed. "'N' say, Bud, take that hand away from y'r gun, an' keep it away. See?" And the lamplight glittered on the long barrel that rested on Soapy's knee.

"So—this is th' game—hey?" demanded M'Ginnis hoarsely, his bloodshot eye fixed on Soapy unwinkingly.

"'S' right, Bud. Y'see, I been takin' a peek int' that little tin safe o' yours. Say, it looks like you'd had a bit of a rough house, Bud!"

Soapy's cigarette quivered, and was still again; while M'Ginnis watched him, breathing thickly, but speaking no word. Soapy went on again: "I been takin' a peek into that little tin safe o' yours, an' I found some papers you'd been kind o' treasurin' up about me, so I burnt 'em, Bud—not as they mattered very much, there ain't nobody t' worry when I snuff it—but I found as you'd got other papers about other guys as would matter some t' them, I guess—so I burnt 'em too, Bud."

"Burnt 'em!" cried M'Ginnis in a strangled voice— "burnt 'em—you——"

"It ain't no use t' get riled, Bud—I burnt 'em. There's the ashes!"

M'Ginnis glanced at the heap of ash by the stove, and burst into a frenzy of curses and fierce invective, while Soapy, lounging back in the chair, watched him unmoved until he had done. Then he spoke again:

"Also I found—letters, Bud, a packet tied up in blue ribbon—an', Bud, they matter a whole lot. Here they are—look at 'em!"

For a moment Soapy's baleful eye turned aside to the desk as he reached for the letters, and in that moment M'Ginnis's pistol spoke, and Soapy, lurching sideways,

The Definite Object

sagged to his knees, his back against the desk. Again
and again M'Ginnis's weapon clicked, but no report
followed, and Soapy slowly dragged himself to his feet.
His cigarette fell, and lay smouldering for a moment.
He stared at it ; then he laughed softly, and glanced at
M'Ginnis.

" You fool, Bud—you dog-gone fool ! Forgot t' load
up y'r gun, eh ? But I guess you got me all right, anyway. You're shootin' better t'-night than you did in
the wood that time—eh, Bud ? Now I want t' tell
you——" He was choked suddenly with a ghastly coughing, and when he spoke again his voice was fainter, and
he held a smartly bordered handkerchief to his mouth.

" They say God made this world, Bud. If He did, I
guess He was asleep when you was made, Bud. Anyway,
remembering little Maggie, you ain't no right to breathe
any longer—so that's for me ; an' that's for her ! "

Lounging still, he fired twice from the hip, and M'Ginnis,
twisting upon his heels, fell and lay with his face at his
slayer's feet. Then, spying the packet of letters that
lay upon the grimy floor, Soapy stooped painfully and
fired rapidly four times ; when the smoke cleared, of
those tear-blotted pages with their secret of a woman's
anguish there remained nothing but a charred piece of
ribbon and a few smouldering fragments of paper. And
now Soapy was seized with another fit of coughing, above
which he heard hoarse shouts, and hands that thundered
at the door. Lazily he stood upon his feet, turned to
glance from that scorched ribbon to the still form upon
the floor, and lifting a lazy foot, ground his heel into that
still face. and crossing unsteadily to the door, opened
it, Beyond was a crowd—very silent now—who drew
back to give him way; but Soapy paused in the doorway
and leaned there.

" What's doin' ? " cried a voice.

" Say, run f'r a doctor somebody—quick—Soapy's
hurt bad, I reckon——"

Retribution

" Hurt ? " said Soapy, in soft, lazy tones. " 'S' right !
But—say fellers, there's a son of a dog in there—waitin'
f'r a spade—t' bury him ! " Then Soapy laughed, choked,
and groping before him blindly, staggered forward, and
pitching sideways, fell with his head beneath a table, and
died there.

CHAPTER XLV

OF THE OLD 'UN AND FATE

SPIKE leaned back among his cushions, and glancing away across close-cropped lawns and shady walks, sighed luxuriously.

" Say, Ann," he remarked, " gee whiz, Trapesy, there sure ain't no flies on this place of old Geoff's ! "

" Flies ! " said Mrs. Trapes, glancing up from her household accounts, " you go into the kitchen an' look around."

" I mean it's aces up."

" Up where ? " queried Mrs. Trapes.

" Well, it's a regular Jim-dandy cracker-jack—some swell dump, eh ? "

" Arthur, that low, tough talk don't go with me," said Mrs. Trapes, and resumed her intricate calculations again.

" Say, when'll Geoff an' Hermy be back ? "

" Well, considerin' she's gone to N' York t' buy more clo'es as she don't need, an' considerin' Mr. Ravenslee's gone with her, I don't know."

" An' what you do know don't cut no ice. Anyway, I'm gettin' lonesome."

" What ! Ain't I here ? " demanded Mrs. Trapes sharply.

" Sure. I can't lose you ! "

" Oh ! Now I'll tell you what it is, my good boy——"

" Cheese it, Trapes, you make me tired—that's what."

" If you sass me I'll box your young ears—an' that's what ! "

" I don't think ! " added Spike. " Nobody ain't goin'

Of the Old 'un and Fate

t' box me. I'm a sure enough invalid, an' don't you forget it."

"My land!" exclaimed Mrs. Trapes, "a bit of a hole
in his arm—that's all."

"Well, I wish you got it, 'stead o' me—it smarts like
sixty!"

"Shows it's healin'. Doctor said as it'll be well in a
week."

"Doctor!" sniffed Spike, "he don't know what I
suffer. I may be dyin' for all he knows."

"You are!" sighed Mrs. Trapes, with a gloomy nod.

"Eh—what?" exclaimed Spike, sitting up.

"So am I—we all are—by the minute. Every night
we're 'a day's march nearer home'! So now jest set right
there an' go on dyin', my b'y!"

"Say now, cut it out," said Spike, wriggling, "that
ain't no kind o' way t' cheer an invalid."

"It's th' truth."

"Well it don't cheer me none, so let's have a lie for a
change."

Mrs. Trapes snorted, and fell to adding and subtracting
busily.

"Say, Ann," said he after a while, "if you got any
more o' that pumpkin-pie I could do some right now."

"It ain't eatin'-time yet."

"But—gee! ain't I a invalid?"

"Sure! Consequently you must be fed slow an'
cautious."

"Oh, fudge! What's the good of a guy bein' a invalid
if a guy can't feed when he wants to!"

"What's a hundred an' ninety-one from twenty-
three?" inquired Mrs. Trapes.

"Skidoo!" murmured Spike sulkily. But after Mrs.
Trapes had subtracted and added busily a while, he
spoke again. "You ain't such a bad old gink—sometimes," he conceded.

"Gink!" said Mrs. Trapes, glaring.

The Definite Object

" I mean you can be a real daisy when you want
to."

" Can I ? "

" Sure ! Sometimes you can be so kind an' nice I like
you a whole lot ! "

" Is that so ? "

" You bet it is—honest Injun."

" Arthur, if it's that pie you want——"

" It ain't ! "

" Well, what is it ? "

" How d'ye know I want anything ? "

" Oh, I just guess, maybe."

" Well, say—if you could cop me one o' Geoff's cigarettes—one o' them with gold letterin' onto 'em."

" You mean—thieve you one ! "

" Why, no—a cigarette ain't thievin'. Say now, dear
old Trapesy, I'm jest dyin' for a gasper ! "

" Well, you go on dyin', an' I'll set right here an' watch
how you do it."

" If I was t' die you'd be sorry for this, I reckon."

" Anyway, I'd plant some flowers on you, my lad, an'
keep your lonely grave nice."

" Huh ! " sniffed Spike, "A lot o' good that 'ud do me
when I was busy pushin' up th' daisies. It's what I
want now that matters."

" An' what you want now, Arthur, is a rod of iron, good
an' heavy. Discipline's your cryin' need, an' you're sure
goin' t' get it."

" Oh ! Where ? "

" At college. My land, think of you at Yale or Harvard
or C'lumbia ! "

" Sure you can think—thinkin' can't cut no ice."

" Anyway, you're goin' soon as you're fit, Mr. Geoffrey
says so."

" Oh, Geoff's batty—he's talkin' in his sleep. I ain't
goin' t' no college—Geoff's got sappy in th' bean."

" Well, you tell him so."

Of the Old 'un and Fate

"Sure thing, you watch me!"

"No, I'll get you somethin' t' eat—some milk an'——"

"Say, what about that pumpkin-pie?"

"You sit right there an' wait."

"Chin-chin!" nodded Spike, and watched her into the house.

No sooner was he alone than he was out of his chair, and, descending the steps into the garden, sped gleefully away across lawns and along winding paths, following a haphazard course. But as he wandered thus, he came to the stables, and so to a large building beyond, where were many automobiles of various patterns and make. And here, very busy with brushes, sponge, and water, washing a certain car and making a prodigious splashing, was a figure there was no mistaking, and one whom Spike hailed in joyous surprise. "Well, well, if it ain't th' old Spider! Gee, but I'm glad t' see ye! Say, old sport, I'm a invalid—pipe my bandages, will ye?"

"Huh!" grunted the Spider, without glancing up from the wheel he was washing.

"Say, old lad," continued Spike, "I guess they told you how I put it all over Bud, eh?"

"Mph!" said the Spider, slopping the water about.

"Heard how I saved old Geoff from gettin' snuffed out, didn'tcher?"

"Huh-umph!" growled the Spider.

"That's sure some car, eh? Gee, but it's good t' see ye again, anyway. How'd ye come here, Spider?"

"U-huh!" said the Spider.

"Say!" exclaimed Spike, "quit makin' them noises an' say somethin', can'tcher? If you can't talk to a pal, I'm goin'."

"Right-oh, kid!" said the Spider, "only see as you don't go sheddin' no more buttons around."

"B-buttons!" stammered Spike, "Whatcher mean? What buttons?"

The Old 'un, who happened to have been dozing in the

361

The Definite Object

limousine that stood in a shady corner, sat up suddenly and blinked.

" Why, I mean," answered the Spider, wringing water from the sponge he held and speaking very deliberately, " I mean the button as you—left behind you—in th' wood ! "

Spike gasped, and sat down weakly upon the running-board of a car, and the Old 'un stole a furtive peep at him.

" So you—know ? "

" Sure I know—more 'n I want t' know about you; so—chase yourself out o' here—beat it ! "

Spike stared in mute amazement, then flushed painfully.

" You mean—you an' me—ain't goin' t' be pals no longer ? " he asked wistfully.

" That's what ! " nodded the Spider, without lifting his scowling gaze from the sponge. " Kid, I ain't no gold-medal Sunday-school scholar, nor I ain't never won no prizes at any Purity-League conference, but there's some guys too rotten even for me ! "

" But I—I—saved his life, didn't I ? "

" That ain't nothin' t' blow about after what you did in that wood. Oh, wake up an' see just how dirty an' rotten you are ! "

Spike rose, and stood, his hands tight-clenched, and though he tried to frown, he couldn't hide the pitiful twitching of his lips nor the quaver in his voice.

" I guess you mean you're goin' t' give me the throw-down ? "

" Well," answered the Spider, scowling at the sponge in his hand, " there's jest two or three things as I ain't got no use for, an' one of 'em's—murder ! "

Hereupon Spike shrank away, an' the Old 'un, reaching out stealthily, opened the door of the limousine, while the Spider fell to work again, splashing more than ever. Thus as Spike crept away with head a-droop, the Old 'un,

362

Of the Old 'un and Fate

all unnoticed, stole after him, his old eyes very bright
and bird-like, and as he followed, keeping in the shade
of hedge and tree as much as possible, he whispered a
word to himself over and over again:

"Lorgorramighty!"

But Spike went on with dragging feet, ignorant that
any followed, lost in a sudden sense of shame such as he
had never known before—a shame that was an agony;
for though his bodily eyes were blinded with bitter tears,
the eyes of his mind were opened wide at last, and he
saw himself foul and dirty, even as the Spider had said.
So on stumbling feet Spike reached a shady, grassy corner
remote from all chance of observation, and throwing
himself down there, he lay with his face hidden, wetting
the grass with the tears of his abasement.

When at last he raised his head he beheld a little old
man leaning patiently against a tree near-by and watching him with a pair of baleful eyes.

"Hello!" said Spike wearily, "who are you?"

"I'm Fate, I am!" nodded the Old 'un. "Persooin'
Fate—that's me."

"Whatcher here for, anyway?" inquired the lad,
humble in his abasement.

"I'm here to persoo!"

"Say now, what's your game? Whatcher want?"

"I want you, me lad."

"Well, say—beat it, please—I want t' be alone."

"Not much, me lad. I'm Fate, I am, an' when Fate
comes up agin' murder, Fate ain't t' be shook off."

"Murder!" gasped Spike. "Oh, my God! I—I—
ain't——"

The lad sprang to his feet and was running on the
instant, but turning to glance back, tripped over some
obstacle and fell. Swaying, he rose and stumbled on,
but slower now by reason of the pain in his wounded arm.
Thus, when at last he came out upon the road, the Old
'un was still close behind him.

363

CHAPTER XLVI

IN WHICH GEOFFREY RAVENSLEE ATTAINS HIS OBJECT

MRS. TRAPES glanced sadly round her cosy housekeeper's room, and sighed regretfully. She was alone, and upon the table ready to hand lay her neat bonnet, her umbrella, and a pair of white cotton gloves, beholding which articles her lips set more resolutely, her bony arms folded themselves more tightly, and she nodded in grim determination.

" 'The labourer is worthy of his hire,' " she sighed, apparently addressing the bonnet, " but, if so be the labourer ain't worthy—why, then, the sooner he quits——"

A sound of quick, light feet upon the stair, and a voice that laughed gaily, a laugh so full of happiness that even Mrs. Trapes's iron features relaxed and her grim mouth curved in her rare smile. At that moment the door opened and Hermione appeared, a radiant Hermione, who clasped Mrs. Trapes in her arms and tangled her up in her long motor veil, and laughed again.

" Oh, Ann, such a day ! " she exclaimed, laying aside her dust-coat. " New York is a paradise—when you're rich ! No more bargain-days and clawing-matches over the remnant counter, Ann ! Oh, it's wonderful to be able to buy anything I want—anything ! Think of it, Ann ! isn't it just a dream of joy ? And I've shopped and shopped, and he was so dear and patient ! I bought Arthur a complete outfit——"

" Arthur ! " said Mrs. Trapes, and groaned.

" And you, Ann, you dear thing, I bought you—guess what ? But you never could ! I bought you a gold watch, the very best I could find, and *he* bought you a chain for it, a long one to go round your dear neck, set

364

with diamonds and rubies. I mean the chain is—it's the cutest thing, Ann! You remember you used to dream of a gold chain set with real diamonds, some day? Well, ' some day's' to-day, Ann."

"But—oh, Hermy, I—I——"

"He wants to give it to you himself, because he says you're the best friend he ever had, and—oh, here he is! —You did say so, didn't you, Geoffrey? "

"And I surely mean it," answered Ravenslee, tossing his driving gauntlets into a chair, " though you certainly threw cold water upon my pea-nut barrow, didn't you, Mrs. Trapes? "

"Oh, Geoffrey dear, do give her that precious package. I'm dying to see her open it! "

So Ravenslee drew the jeweller's neat parcel from his pocket, and put it into Mrs. Trapes's toil-worn hand. For a moment her bony fingers clutched it, then she sighed tremulously and, placing it on the table, rose and stood staring down at it.

When at last she spoke her voice was harsher than usual. "Hermy dear—I mean Mrs. Ravenslee, mam— I can't—take 'em! "

"But, dear—why not? "

"Because they're coals of fire."

"But you must take them, dear, we bought them for you."

"Which jools, mam, I can in no wise accept."

"Why, Ann dear, whatever——"

"Which jools, mam, having been a dream must for me so remain, me not bein' faithful in my dooties to you an' Mr. Geoffrey. Consequently, I begs to tender now my resignation, yieldin' up my post in your service to one better worthy, and returnin' t' th' place wherefrom I come."

Here Mrs. Trapes put on her bonnet, setting it a little askew in her agitation.

" ' Th' labourer is worthy of his hire,' but if he ain't— so be it! "

The Definite Object

Here Mrs. Trapes tied her bonnet-strings so tightly and with such resolute hands that she choked.

"Why, Ann dear," cried Hermione, "whatever do you mean? As if I could bear to part with you!" Here she untied the bonnet strings. "As if I could ever let you go back to Mulligan's!" Here she took off the bonnet. "As if I could ever forget all your tender love and care for me in the days when things were so hard and so very dark!" Here she tossed the bonnet into a corner.

"My land!" sighed Mrs. Trapes, "me best bonnet——"

"I know, Ann. I made it for you over a year ago, and it's time you had another, anyway! Now open that parcel—this minute!"

But instead of doing so, Mrs. Trapes sank down in the chair beside the table, and bowed her head in her hands.

"Hermy," said she, "oh, my lamb, he's gone! You left Arthur in my care, an'—he's gone, an' it's my fault. Went away at five o'clock, an' here it is nigh on to ten—an' him sick! God knows, I've searched for him—tramped to th' ferry an' back, an' th' footmen they've looked for him an' so have th' maids—but Arthur's gone —an' it's my fault! So, Hermy—my dear—blame me an' let me go."

The harsh voice broke, and bowing her head she sat silent, touching the unopened packet of jewellery with one long, bony finger.

"Why, Ann—dear Ann—you're crying!" Hermione was down on her knees, had clasped that long, bony figure in her arms. "You mustn't, Ann—you mustn't. I'm sure it wasn't your fault, so don't grieve, dear—there!" and she had drawn the disconsolate grey head down upon her shoulder and pillowed it there.

"But—oh, Hermy, he's gone! An' you told me to —look after him."

"Ann, if Arthur meant to go, I'm sure you couldn't have prevented him, he isn't a child any longer, dear. There, be comforted—we'll hunt for him in the car. Won't we, Geoffrey?"

366

Geoffrey Ravenslee Attains His Object

"Of course," nodded Ravenslee. " I'll 'phone the garage right away."

But as he opened the door he came face to face with Joe, who touched an eyebrow and jerked a thumb over his shoulder.

" 'Scuse me, sir," said he, " but it's that Old 'un, covered wi' dust 'e is, sir, an' wants a word wi' you. And, sir, 'e's that mysterious as never was. Shall I let him come in, sir ? "

" You try an' keep me out, lad, that's all ! " panted the Old 'un, ducking under Joe's great arm. " I'm a better man nor ever you'll be ! "

So saying, the Old 'un hobbled forward, and, sinking into the nearest armchair, fanned himself with his hat, which, like the rest of his garments, bore the dust of travel.

" Greetin's, guv ! " said he when he had caught his breath. " 'Ere I be—a old man as 'as done more for ye than all th' young 'uns put t'gether. Mrs. Ravenslee, mam, best respex ! "

" And what have you been doing now ? " inquired Ravenslee, smiling.

"Well, guv, I been an' got th' murderer for ye, that's all!"

Hermione caught her breath suddenly, and gazed at the fierce, dusty old man with eyes full of growing terror, beholding which Ravenslee frowned, then laughed lightly, and, seating himself on a corner of the table, swung his leg to and fro.

" So you've found him out, have you, Old 'un ? "

" Ah, that I have ! "

" Are you sure ? "

" Ah, quite sure, guv ! "

" Well, where is he ? Trot him out."

" 'E's comin' along—th' Spider's bringin' un. Ye see, he's a bit wore out, same as I am, we been trampin' all th' arternoon. Look at me shoes, that's th' worst o' patent-leather, they shows th' dust. Joe, my lad, jest give 'em a flick over with yer wipe."

The Definite Object

But at this moment steps were heard slowly approaching, and Hermione uttered an inarticulate cry, then spoke in an agonised whisper:

" Arthur ! "

Pallid of cheek and drooping of head, Spike stood in the doorway, his shabby, threadbare clothes dusty and travel-stained, his slender shape encircled by the Spider's long arm. At Hermione's cry he lifted his head and looked up yearningly, his sensitive mouth quivered, his long-lashed eyes swam in sudden tears, he strove to speak, but choked instead.

Then Ravenslee's calm, pleasant voice broke the painful silence. " Old 'un," said he, rising, " I understand you are fond of jam—well, from now on you shall bathe in it if you wish."

" Spoke like a true sport, guv ! "

" Why, you see, you have surely done me a very great service——"

" Meanin' because I found ye th' murderer——"

" Murderer ? " exclaimed Ravenslee, staring.

" Why, yes—there 'e is ! " and the old man pointed a long finger at the shrinking Spike.

" Old 'un," said Ravenslee, shaking his head, " don't joke with me."

" I—I ain't jokin', guv," cried the Old 'un, rising. " Why—oh, Lorgorramighty ! you don't mean t' say as this ain't 'im ! Why, 'e's confessed, guv, I 'eard 'im ! "

Ravenslee smiled gently, and shook his head again.

" But he has been sick, Old 'un ; he was hurt, you know, when he saved my life."

" But lord, guv, if 'e confessed——"

" He has been sick, Old 'un, and when we are sick the wisest of us are apt to say silly things. Even I did, so they tell me."

" What ! " quavered the old man, " Ain't I—ain't I found no murderer for ye arter all, guv ? "

" You've done something much, very much better, Old 'un—you've found me my brother ! "

368

Geoffrey Ravenslee Attains His Object

"Brother!" echoed Spike. "Brother? Oh Geoff——" he sighed deeply, and as Ravenslee crossed towards him, he smiled wanly and sank swooning into the supporting arms of the Spider, who, at a word from Hermione, bore the boy upstairs. But scarcely was he laid upon his bed than he opened his heavy eyes. "Say, Spider," said he wearily, " old Geoff, sure, does play square—even to a worm like me—well, I guess! No, don't go yet; I wantcher to hear me try to explain the kind o' dirty dog I been—I guess he won't want t' call me 'brother' after that. No, siree, he'll cut me out same as you have, an' serve me right too." Then turning towards where Ravenslee and Hermione stood, he continued, "Geoff—Hermy dear—ah, no, don't touch me, I ain't worth it, I'm too dirty—Spider says so, an' I guess he's right. Listen. I meant t' go away t'-day an' leave you, because I felt so mean, but th' old man followed me, an' I couldn't run because my arm pained some—ye see, I fell on it. So I let him bring me back, because I guess it's up t' me t' let you know as I ain't fit t' be your brother, Geoff—or Hermy's." For a moment Spike paused, then, with an effort, he continued, but kept his face averted, "Geoff, it was me—in the wood that time! Yes, it was me, an' I had a gun. I—I meant—t' do you in, Geoff——"

Spike's voice failed, and he was silent again, plucking nervously at the sheet, while Hermione's proud head drooped, and her hands clasped and wrung each other in an agony of shame, but to these painfully rigid hands came another hand, big and strong yet very gentle, at whose soothing touch those agonised fingers grew lax and soft, then clung to that strong hand in sudden, eager passion.

"Poor old Spike!" said Ravenslee, and his tone was as gentle as his touch.

"But—but, Geoff," stammered the boy, "I—oh, don't you see, I meant to—kill you?"

369

The Definite Object

" Yes, I understand; you thought I deserved it.
Why ? "

" Oh, I was crazy, I guess ! Bud told me lies—an' I
believed him—lies about you an' Hermy. He said—
you'd make Hermy go—the same road—little Maggie
Finlay went ; so I came t' kill you."

" Spike, if you believed that, if you really believed
that, I don't blame you for trying a shot."

" But I didn't—I couldn't ! When I saw you sittin'
there, so unsuspectin', I just couldn't do it. I tried to,
but I couldn't. An', somehow, I dropped th' gun, an'
then I heard a shot ; an' when I looked up I saw you
throw out your arms an' fall. My God, I'll never forget
that ! Then I saw Bud starin' down at you, an' th' pistol
smokin' in his hand. I meant t' do it, but I couldn't ;
so Bud did it himself. I'm as bad as him, I reckon, but
it was Bud shot you. Soapy saw him, an' knows it was
Bud. Ask Soapy. An' now I've told you all, I guess I
ain't fit t' stay here any longer."

Spike's voice choked upon a sob. He buried his face
in the pillow, and so there fell a silence—a strange, tense
hush, a pause so unexpected that he looked up and saw
that Hermione's head was bowed no longer, but she
stood, very proud and tall, gazing upon her husband, and
in her eyes was a great and wondrous light, and as she
looked on him, so he gazed on her. They had no thought,
no eyes for Spike just then, wherefore he hid his face again.

" I guess this about puts the kybosh on th' brother
business ! " he sighed miserably, " an' I sure ain't fit
t' be th' Spider's pal, I reckon ! "

But now the Spider spoke, rather quick and jerkily :

" Say, kid—get on to this ! I'm takin' back—everything I says t' you t'-day. See ? Because, oh well—I
guess you've sure woke up at last ! So, kid—give us
your mitt ! "

Eagerly Spike grasped the Spider's big fist and they
shook gravely and very deliberately, looking into each

other's eyes the while. Thereafter, still quick and jerkily, the Spider turned and hurried out of the room.

Then Spike turned to Ravenslee.

"Geoff," he sighed, "I'm not goin' to ask you to forgive me yet, I can't. I'm goin' t' wait an' show you——"

But as he paused, Ravenslee's hand was upon the lad's drooping shoulder.

"Arthur," said he, "from now on—from to-night you are going to be my brother more than ever—a brother we shall both be proud of. What do you say?"

But Spike's eyes were wet, his mouth quivered, and instead of answering he buried his face in the pillow again.

"Say, Hermy," he mumbled, "take him away before I do th' tear-gushin' act! Take him downstairs—give him a drink—light him a cigarette—kiss him! Only take him away before I get mushy. But, say—when I'm in bed you'll—you'll come an'—say good-night like—like you used to, Hermy dear?"

Swiftly she stooped and kissed that curly head.

"I'll come—oh, I'll come, boy dear!" she murmured, and left him with Mrs. Trapes.

Downstairs the fire glowed, filling the room with shadows, and side by side they stood looking down into the heart of the fire, and were silent awhile, and though she was so near he didn't touch her.

"So it wasn't Arthur, after all!" he said at last.

"No," she answered softly, "it wasn't Arthur—thank God!"

"Amen!" said he, so fervently that she glanced up at him swiftly, then looked into the fire again, and seeing how the colour deepened in her cheek, he came a little nearer; but still he didn't touch her. Instead, he took out tobacco-pouch and pipe and began to fill it with strangely clumsy fingers, and Hermione saw that his hands were trembling.

"Let me!" she said gently. So he surrendered pipe

and pouch, and, watching, saw that her hands trembled also. When at last she had filled the pipe, he took it and laid it on the table.

" Aren't you going to smoke, dear ? "

" No, not now. You'll remember that Arthur also suggested you should——"

" Give you something to drink ! " she added, a little breathlessly, and crossed to the tantalus in the corner. " Will you have brandy-and-soda ? "

" Thanks—yes—that will do," he answered absently ; and when she dutifully brought the filled glass, he took it and set it down untasted beside the pipe.

" Why, Geoffrey ! " she said in murmurous surprise, " aren't you thirsty ? "

" No, not now. You will probably remember that Arthur also suggested you should——"

" I know ! " she breathed, " But, oh Geoffrey dear— wait—just a little longer."

" Why ? " he demanded hoarsely.

" Because ! " she answered, staring down at her clasped hands.

" Why ? "

" Because, my Geoffrey, if—if I let myself—kiss you now, I—shall never be able to—tear myself away, and I must say good-night to Arthur and——"

She paused as a knock sounded on the door, and Mrs. Trapes appeared.

" Why, dear land o' my fathers ! " she exclaimed, " ain't you had time t' take off your bonnet yet, Hermy ? "

" Goodness me," exclaimed Hermione, " I forgot it ! " So saying, off it came, and there was the curl above her eyebrow more wantonly alluring than ever.

" An' there's that blessed b'y," continued Mrs. Trapes, " a-layin' upstairs yearnin' for you, Hermy, an' him s' pale an' gentle—God bless him ! An' it now bein' exackly twenty-two an' a half minutes past 'leven by my beautiful

Geoffrey Ravenslee Attains His Object

new watch as ticks most musical! Time as you was in bed —both of you! An' that reminds me, Hermy, I sent your maid t' bed like you told me, an' with my own hands I laid out one o' them lovely noo night-dresses— the one with the short sleeves an' lace as you showed me last night an'—— Land sakes, she's gone! Think o' that now—my, my! Mrs. Ravenslee's wonderful quick an' light on her feet, Mr. Geoffrey!"

Here Mrs. Trapes raised the watch to her ear, and hearkened to its tick again, smiling at Ravenslee's broad back as he turned to reach his glass.

"Them night-dresses," she sighed, "as is all fluffs an' frills an' openwork, may be all right when you're young, but for true comfort give me flannel, every time."

Here Ravenslee, in the act of sipping his brandy-and-soda, choked. When at last he glanced round, Mrs. Trapes was gone.

Then he drew a chair to the fire, and sitting down took up his pipe and tried to light it, but Hermione's nervous white fingers had packed it too tightly for mortal suction, whereat he sighed and, yielding to the impossible, sat with it in his hand, lost in happy thought and waiting for the swift, light footsteps he yearned to hear.

The clock in the hall without struck midnight, and long after the mellow chime had died away he sat there waiting. But the great house lay there very still about him, and no sound broke the pervading quiet. Wherefore at last he grew restless, frowned at the dying fire, and his strong fingers clenched themselves fiercely about the pipe they held.

All at once he started, rose to his feet, and turned towards the door, eager-eyed, as a hand knocked softly. Before he could speak it opened, and Mrs. Trapes reappeared. She was clad in a long flannel dressing-gown, and as she stood in the shadows by the door he could vaguely define that she still held the precious watch to her ear.

The Definite Object

" It do tick that musical," she said, " an' I can't sleep this night till I've tried t' thank ye both for—for all your goodness to a lonely woman. Ah, Mr. Geoffrey, I guess th' day as you came seekin' lodgin's at my little flat was a good day for Ann Angelina Trapes—— Why, my land, Mr. Geoffrey—ain't Hermy here ? "

" No," answered Ravenslee, a little bitterly—" oh no, I'm quite alone—as usual, Mrs. Trapes."

" Why now, that's queer ! "

" How queer ? "

" Because I've jest been into her bedroom, an' there's her things—except that night-dress ; but she ain't ! "

" Not there ? She must be ! Did you look in—her bed ? "

" Lord, Mr. Geoffrey, her bed ain't been tetched ! "

" Then where in the world is she ? "

" Well," said Mrs. Trapes consulting her watch again, " it is now exactly fifteen and three-quarter minutes after midnight, so I guess she's in bed somewhere. But this is a big house, an' there's lots of bedrooms ; so if I was you, I'd go an' look—till I found her."

Ravenslee was at the door so swiftly that Mrs. Trapes started, and she saw that his eyes were very bright, and the hands he laid on her bony shoulders were quivering.

" Mrs. Trapes," said he, " I will ! "

Then he stooped, very suddenly, and kissed the thin, grey hair above her grim eyebrow, and so was gone.

" Find her ? " mused Mrs. Trapes glancing after him up the wide stairs—" why yes, I guess he will sure find her—where she should have been weeks ago. Lord, what a silly, beautiful, lovely thing love is ! " and she stood awhile smiling down into the fire, and her smile was very tender.

Then she sighed, switched off the lights, and went softly away.

374

JEFFERY FARNOL

Wizard of Romance

BY

HAROLD ARMITAGE

Author of "Chantry Land,"
etc.

IN the year 1910, Jeffery Farnol seemed to achieve popularity at one stride with *The Broad Highway;* and fourteen years later we had an assurance that his fame in 1924, with *Sir John Dering*, had not only been maintained, but extended; for in a quiet street of a small, remote town we were talking to the owner of a little suburban circulating library, and she said that almost all her subscribers were asking for *Sir John Dering*, at that time his latest book, and were having their names put down to borrow the work as soon as it should be available, though the charge per day was as high as the charge per week for the other books. She had stocked three times as many copies of *Sir John Dering* as she had of other novels, and yet there was a long waiting list of readers; and, since 1924 it has become more and more clear that a name unknown in 1909 is familiar now even in the most sequestered places.

As *The Broad Highway*, Mr. Farnol's first book took the world by storm in the year 1910, readers may harbour the notion that the author had nothing to do but sit at his ease writing the romance, and then to send it to the first publisher whose name occurred to him. It is easy to be wise after the event, so that readers will find it hard to believe that a number of publishers in the United States refused to issue it, and that *The Broad Highway* falls into that long list of rejected masterpieces.

The romance of *The Broad Highway* was written when Mr. Farnol was enduring hard times in New York; and when he offered the manuscript to three leading publishers in America, they showed no hesitation in rejecting it, one of them remarking that the book was "too long and too English."

An actor acquaintance of the author offered to take the manuscript to Boston, to show it to a publisher there; but though actors usually have good memories, this one forgot his errand, and at the end of a year returned the parcel to the author unopened. It occurred then to Jeffery Farnol to put the manuscript in the fire; but he remembered in time that if no one else cared to have it, his mother might like to read it, so he posted it off to her in England. She enjoyed the tale, but wondering how far this love of the book was caused by her love for the author, she passed it on to her friend Mr. Shirley Byron Jevons, at that time

2

editor of the *Sportsman*. He read it, recognised its merits, and having faith, moreover, that it would be popular, he sallied out to see the publishing firm of Messrs. Sampson Low, Marston & Co., Ltd., and infected them with enthusiasm for the romance. One of the directors smelt the bacon in the story, and popularity in the book. To him it made a double appeal, to the romantic man and to the business man. His long familiarity with the book trade had taught him that here was a possible "best seller." The literary adviser for the firm at that time recommended publication, but in more guarded terms.

Other opinions were taken, including the views of Mr. Clement K. Shorter, who, recalling the incident in later years, wrote, "I read *The Broad Highway* with avidity, and recognised at once—as who would not have done?—that here was a striking addition to picaresque romances, that the author had not read *Don Quixote*, *Gil Blas*, and the best stories by Defoe and Fielding for nothing, nor had he walked along the broad highways of England without observation and profit any more than had the creator of *Lavengro* and *Romany Rye*. For the vast multitude of readers of each epoch the dictum of Emerson stands: 'Every age must write its own books.' It is of no use for the pedantic critic to affirm, with pontifical fervour, that Cervantes and Le Sage and Defoe are masters of literature and that our contemporaries are but pigmies in comparison. The great reading public of any age will not be bullied into reading the authors who have reached the dignity of classics. The writer who can catch some element of the spirit of the 'masters' and modernise it, is destined to win the favour of the crowd. And thus Mr. Jeffery Farnol has entered into his kingdom."

The success of *The Broad Highway* was not immediate, but when the sales hung fire the firm applied themselves to the task of making the book known, bringing to bear the fruits of their long experience, and urging the booksellers to do their part, until in a short time the run upon the story commenced, and Mr. Jeffery Farnol woke up one morning, like Byron, and found himself famous.

The period of which this masterpiece treats is the early nineteenth century. The scene is laid in Kent, within a radius of thirty miles from London. The story treats of that broad highway which is life, and of its unexpected windings and turnings which yet lead ever to an ultimate goal, which some call Death, and some, the Fullness of Life. The action is rapid—the incidents abundant and absorbing and the book is full of cleverness and freshness, passionate love and fierce hate, and all the elements of moving life.

There are two creations in the story that did much to carry it into fame. One is an old man, designated by the author "the Ancient"; the other is a golden-haired black-smith, known as "Black George." Both these characters have become great favourites with the reading public. The fresh, crisp style of the author, too, is most pleasing; it reminds one of all that is best in George Borrow.

Soon afterwards came that charming story, *The Money Moon*, and here we had Jeffery Farnol "with a difference," as Ophelia might have said. Instead of dealing with the rollicking Georgian times, like *The Amateur Gentleman*, and *The Broad Highway*, it is a modern story. One critic described this book as "the sweetest story ever told."

Readers were delighted when *The Amateur Gentleman* appeared, especially as it reminded them of their first love, *The Broad Highway*. As the *Pall Mall Gazette* said, "Some of the exploits are magnificent, and the style in which they are related rings with the true metal of manliness and heroism."

Mr. Farnol is a careful, conscientious worker who will not be hurried; and yet by close application he managed to maintain a steady procession of books for the delight of his numerous following. A cordial welcome was given to *The Honourable Mr. Tawnish*. In this charming story Mr. Farnol tells how Sir John Chester's daughter Penelope and a fine London gentleman fell head over heels in love with each other, thus arousing Sir John's ire—for he despised the Honourable Horatio Tawnish for an effeminate dandy and a writer of sentimental verses. "The Lady Penelope Chester," said Sir John, hitting himself on the chest, "must marry a man—not a clothes-horse or a dancing master." So to try his worth young Mr. Tawnish was set three difficult tasks by Sir John and his two friends, Mr. Bentley and Sir Richard Eden. How he accomplished them, proved

4

himself a brave man and a gentleman, and won pretty Penelope to wife, is told in a story possessing just the qualities to which *The Amateur Gentleman* and *The Broad Highway* owe their extraordinary popularity.

Remembering the iron worker in *The Broad Highway*, readers gave an eager reception to *Beltane the Smith*, and were charmed with *The Chronicles of the Imp* (*My Lady Caprice*). Also in this stream of romance came *The Definite Object, Our Admirable Betty, Black Bartlemy's Treasure, Martin Conisby's Vengeance, Peregrine's Progress* and other romances.

Of *The Chronicles of the Imp, The Tatler* said, ". . . This is the plot of Mr. Jeffery Farnol's charming story, *The Chronicles of the Imp*. It is a fairy tale with every fairy but one grown up. For Lisbeth is no less a fairy because her hair is up, nor is Dick any the less a fairy prince because he is in trousers, nor the Imp any less Puck because he is in the disguise of the dearest, naughtiest, most lovable little boy in the world. These, then, are the fairies. The 'humans,' of course, do the deeds usually left for humans to do. They try to separate young lovers, marry charming girls against their will, and possess no sense of humour. Happily, they do not count—at least, not at the end. All who matter are the lovers and the little boy, and these make the happiest, pleasantest, most adorable little trio of romantics with whom to pass a few hours of an April day. There is about *The Chronicles of the Imp* that indescribable quality called 'charm.' What matter if you can easily guess the end the moment you have grasped the beginning? The story is not important. It is the way Mr. Farnol tells it that will place *The Chronicles of the Imp* among those few books with which every reader falls immediately in love."

In *Peregrine's Progress*, the author returns to the scenes and times of *The Broad Highway*. He tells, as only Farnol can tell, of quickly moving scenes, of lovely summer mornings when the birds are singing and the brooks are rippling; of great adventure, and—of love itself. He tells of Diana, a gipsy maid, feared by all and tamed by none, in whose company Peregrine travels whilst learning the tinker's trade and the meaning of the "brotherhood of the roadside."

Following *Peregrine's Progress* came *Sir John Dering*, and here Farnol is at his best. The action takes place in his favourite period in Paris, London, and Sussex; and duels, smugglers, maidens in distress, and ladies in disguise pass across the scene with a delightful rapidity that rivets our attention and carries us triumphantly through to a satisfactory conclusion. Soon after they had read *Sir John Dering*, admirers of Jeffery Farnol received *The Loring Mystery*, a tale of the stirring days of Waterloo and Trafalgar, a romance of rural England, with a murder puzzle, of which the secret is well kept to the end; and in 1926 came another similar story, *The High Adventure*.

In writing all these books, how much has Mr. Farnol drawn upon his own experiences? Although he has written much of the Georgian period, our author has put more of his own life into his books than would be expected, for we know that Mr. Farnol did not live during that age; and yet we are apt to forget that in England we have many survivals from past periods; and that in spite of railways, and even of motor cars, we have an England that belongs still to the era of the water wheel and the wind mill; so that with even a little imagination it is possible for a man, especially if he reads, to transport himself into any age.

To the last, Dickens deplored the neglect which, during his childhood, committed him to poverty and hardship, to mean streets and warehouses; but we, who look at his life as a whole, know that his bitter experiences yielded a rich harvest.

In a similar way, although Jeffery Farnol was spared the fate of having negligent parents, it happens that he, too, passed through periods of hardship and anxiety, and lived a life full of variety before he began to write. He knew romance and encountered adventures before he wrote of them.

Mr. Farnol was born in the Six Ways region of Birmingham, on February 10, 1878, and he enjoyed a happy childhood, with kind parents, and indulgent friends. When he was ten years of age, his parents moved to London; and he spent some years at Lee, in Kent, where he began to reveal those traits that have caused him to be compared with George Borrow, for he became both a rural wanderer, and a reader of romance; but a time came all too soon when he was sent back to Birmingham, to learn the prosaic craft of engineering.

Like other good-tempered people whom we have known, Jeffery Farnol had yet a very pugnacious side, a part of his delight in many forms of sport. This zest for fisticuffs, developed at school, came out strongly in the rough crude world of the engineering shops, and the future author of *The Broad Highway* was soon engaged in a most dogged series of fights. On one day he fought a man three times; and though he was badly beaten and battered during the two first struggles, in the end he conquered. It was this fighting that brought his career as an engineer to a close. A foreman called him a liar, whereupon Jeffery knocked him down; and as the foreman's head struck a piece of iron, he became unconscious. A serious view of the incident was taken, so that Jeffery was dismissed, and he returned to his parents in London.

As Jeffery Farnol had shown some talent for sketching, it was thought that perhaps he might succeed as an artist. Not far away was the Westminster Art School. To this institution Jeffery Farnol was sent. There is an illustrated account of Mouat Loudan's work in the volume of *The Artist* for the year 1899, from which it is clear that Jeffery Farnol studied under a good master; but he felt that though he enjoyed the work, he could not hope to aspire to front rank, and so, abandoning his brushes for a pen, he achieved a few small successes with short stories.

With that disdain for prudential considerations which is so characteristic of the romantic temperament, Mr. Farnol married at twenty years of age. Mrs. Farnol was an American, and she and her husband went to New York, where Jeffery began to work hard to make a living. Here his art training helped him, for he eked out the scantiness of the income that he derived from the writing of short stories by painting the scenery at the Astor Theatre. It was during this period that he often saw O. Henry, who afterwards became a famous author. He admired his shy, retiring, gentle ways, and regrets now that he never spoke to him.

Still harder times banished Jeffery Farnol to a sojourn amongst the poorest of the New York population, with residence in the notorious "Hell's Kitchen" for a spell; and though this experience was bitter and depressing, it had its uses when Mr. Farnol made the writing of romances his chief occupation.

7

Romances by Jeffery Farnol

THE BROAD HIGHWAY. 4s. net.
A romance of Kent

THE AMATEUR GENTLEMAN. 4s. net.
A romance of the Regency

THE MONEY MOON. 4s. net.
A romance of to-day

CHRONICLES OF THE IMP. 4s. net.
My Lady Caprice.

BELTANE THE SMITH. 4s. net.
A mediæval romance

THE HONOURABLE MR. TAWNISH. 4s. net.
The rollicking days of the eighteenth century

THE DEFINITE OBJECT. 4s. net.
A romance of New York

OUR ADMIRABLE BETTY. 4s. net.
An early Georgian story

BLACK BARTLEMY'S TREASURE. 4s. net.
A stirring pirate story

MARTIN CONISBY'S VENGEANCE. 4s. net.
Continues Black Bartlemy's adventures

PEREGRINE'S PROGRESS. 4s. net.
In the author's original vein

SIR JOHN DERING. 4s. net.
A romantic comedy

THE LORING MYSTERY. 4s. net.
A mystery story of " Merrie England "

THE HIGH ADVENTURE. 7s. 6d. net.
Another intriguing mystery story

OBTAINABLE FROM ANY BOOKSELLER

SAMPSON LOW, MARSTON & CO., LTD., PUBLISHERS
100 SOUTHWARK STREET, LONDON, S.E.1

CPSIA information can be obtained
at www.ICGtesting.com
Printed in the USA
BVHW072155280619
552220BV00010B/254/P